Families of Nations

Families of Nations

Patterns of Public Policy in Western Democracies

Edited by
FRANCIS G. CASTLES

Dartmouth

Aldershot • Brookfield USA • Hong Kong • Singapore • Sydney

Published by
Dartmouth Publishing Company Limited
Gower House
Croft Road
Aldershot
Hants GU11 3HR
England

Dartmouth Publishing Company
Old Post Road
Brookfield
Vermont 05036
USA

A CIP catalogue record for this book is available from the British Library

Library of Congress Cataloguing-in-Publication Data
Families of nations : patterns of public policy in Western democracies
/ edited by Francis G. Castles.
p. cm.
Includes bibliographical references and index.
ISBN 1-85521-345-1 : $67.95 (U.S. : est.)
1. Policy sciences. I. Castles, Francis Geoffrey.
H97.F36 1993
320'.6–dc20 93-20004
CIP

ISBN 1 85521 345 1

Printed and bound in Great Britain by
Hartnolls Limited, Bodmin, Cornwall

Contents

List of Tables and Figures

Tables

Figures

Acknowledgments

This volume represents a far more genuinely collaborative endeavour than is common in most edited books, and were it not for the fact that the named editor is the only native English-speaker amongst the major contributors, it might well have been more appropriate for all of them to have appeared as co-authors. The findings reported here are the culmination of many years of collaboration in comparative public policy research by these scholars, in Castles' and Schmidt's case dating back more than a decade and a half, with Therborn joining the endeavour in the mid-1980s. Moreover, insofar as the ideas presented here are novel and of value in comprehending the nature of public policy outcomes in Western democratic states, any credit is due to these three contributors equally. The families of nations concept and its working out in diverse policy areas have been developed over no less than four years of meetings between the three, including a period of joint research and discussion in the same institution for several months at the beginning of 1991.

International collaboration as intensive as this is rare, not least because it is extremely expensive to fund. We were extraordinarily fortunate in this respect and must acknowledge the authors of our good fortune. Professor Rudolf Wildenmann and his Research Unit for Societal Development at the University of Mannheim provided the intellectual and material support for four meetings held in Mannheim between 1988 and 1991. This is now the third volume of collaborative research on comparative policy organized by Castles and Schmidt that Professor Wildenmann has helped to bring to fruition and our gratitude increases each time. Our gratitude is also extended to the Research School of Social Sciences of the Australian National University, which made it possible for the three senior authors to spend nearly three months working together by offering professors Schmidt and Therborn Visiting Fellowships half the world away from their normal teaching commitments. Only a few institutions in the world offer such valuable assistance to collaborative work and Professor Castles, much of whose research on public policy in recent years has been carried out whilst a Senior Research

Fellow in the Research School, acknowledges the vital contribution made by the School's generosity. Finally, the research of Professor Schmidt's two younger colleagues – Busch and von Rhein-Kress – was made possible by a grant from the Deutsche Forschungs Gesellschaft (DFG), the German Research Foundation.

Given the length of gestation of this project, a number of pieces have found their way into print, albeit in a much abbreviated form and with an emphasis on substantive policy areas rather than on the families of nations concept which is the central focus here. This applies to Chapter 1 which, in a much shorter form, appeared in the *European Journal of Political Research* in 1990 (Vol. 18, 491–513); to Chapter 3, some (but by no means all) of the ideas of which appeared in *Governance* early in 1992; and to Chapter 7 which, stripped of its historical discussion of the development of legal families of nations, appeared in *Acta Sociologica*, No. 4, 1991.

The editor wishes to record his gratitude to Susan Lindsay who kindly provided a final check on the prose presentation of the majority of chapters. For someone whose interest is in literary rather than academic prose, that is service well beyond the call of duty.

Introduction

The Families of Nations Concept

This is a book which seeks to explore the potential utility of a particular concept as a guide to the understanding of observed patterns of policy outcomes in Western democracies. The concept derives from the notion that it may be possible to identify distinct *families of nations*, defined in terms of shared geographical, linguistic, cultural and/or historical attributes and leading to distinctive patterns of public policy outcomes. The term 'families of nations' apart, this notion is anything but new. Academically, it harks back to the guiding paradigm of comparative research commonly employed in the study of government and law in the late 19th century and early decades of the 20th century, when it was commonplace to locate the contemporary character of governmental forms and outputs in a matrix constituted by the evolution of ideas and institutions through imperial ties and shared historical roots. At a more popular level and as a descriptive category, it is a notion which has never lost its currency. Often the adjectives 'Anglo-American' or 'English-speaking', 'Scandinavian', 'Germanic' or 'German-speaking' and 'Latin' are used to describe and organize our knowledge of groupings of nations, with the assumption, implicit or explicit, that they convey something of those nations' common experience and common outcomes.

But if the notion that groups of countries have shared national attributes has a long intellectual pedigree and is still extensively used in contemporary commentary, it has not found much favour in the post-war flowering of research in comparative politics and comparative public policy. Indeed, comparative public policy analysis was a child of what Almond (1968) called the 'comparative politics movement', a movement distinguished by a shift away from the traditional focus of political studies on the institutional and legal attributes of government towards an emphasis on political functions and their socio-economic context. But whereas institutional and legal analysis necessarily highlighted national affinities derived from such factors as geography, a common history, the diffusion of ideas through channels etched by shared possession of a common language and traditions and the continuity of legal tradition, the new approach located similarities in function, masked by diverse institutional and legal forms, and differences in socio-economic context, despite shared institutional and legal forms. Moreover, in this, the comparative politics movement was only reflecting a broader dimension of the post-war intellectual trend away from earlier attributions in terms of national character – or indeed, more generally, away from intrinsic, and hence relatively unchanging, attributions of any kind – which were perceived as leading to a situation in which morally aberrant or unwanted behaviour ceased to be an object of analysis and became one of blame and, perhaps ultimately, of punitive sanction.

In the new perspective, the focus of investigation moved away from individual nations and their historical and cultural evolution or progress and became directed to the underlying macro-structural determinants that shaped politics and policy, irrespective of national context. As Przeworski (1987, 38–9) so elegantly puts it, the causal programme of comparative analysis is to 'reduc[e] proper names to explanatory variables'. The proper names in question are the names of nations. The job of the comparativist, seen in these terms, is not merely to compare and contrast the behaviour of nations, much less to attribute differences and similarities to factors intrinsic to their national experience, but rather to uncover the configuration of economic, political and social variables which would make any nation behave in such ways under like circumstances.

The contributors to this volume have no quarrel with the view that the search for explanatory variables in this sense is a crucial component of all comparative analysis that aspires to scientific status, but question the *a priori* assumption that all that is particularistic to individual nations or groupings must be set aside, or rather disaggregated into more generalized components, in the search for an understanding of why politics and policies are shaped in the way they are. Recent research in the comparative history tradition and, in particular, the researches that comprised an earlier volume in this series, *The Comparative History of Public Policy* (Castles, 1989), demonstrate conclusively that historical events and their assimilation into an individual nation's accumulative policy experience can decisively shape policy outcomes for many decades thereafter; also that a failure to contextualize policy decisions in the particularity of their historical context renders them substantially incomprehensible to contemporary observers. To offer some examples from that earlier work, we must understand Germany's experiences of hyper-inflation in the 1920s and 1940s in order to explain that country's consistently anti-inflationary policy settings throughout the post-war era; we must be aware of Sweden's 19th century development of radical 'popular movements' in order to comprehend the subsequent development of that country's welfare state; moreover, in order to understand Japan's contemporary policy stance of 'creative conservatism', we must locate its origins in a response to the dramatic intrusion of Western influence in Japan in the mid-19th century.

In a practical sense, the message of *The Comparative History of Public Policy* represented only a marginal challenge to the dominant paradigm of post-war comparative research, since the prevailing compartmentalization of contemporary scholarship has always permitted the coexistence of generalized comparative explanations of the determinants of policy outcomes with particularist and historical accounts of the origins of policy in individual nations. In effect, all that the volume did was to suggest that comprehensive explanation actually required a complementarity of these divergent scholarly approaches. The families of nations concept, however, implicitly involves a greater challenge. If taken seriously and empirically demonstrated, it suggests that some of the more important policy similarities between groups of nations and their differences from other groups may be attributable as much to history and culture and their transmission and diffusion amongst nations as to the immediate impact of the economic, political and social variables that figure almost exclusively in the contemporary public policy literature.

This new research project does take the notion of families of nations very seriously indeed, but makes no prior assumptions as to its ultimate policy relevance. It starts from two observations that are not easily contestable. First, that there are groupings of nations that to varying degrees share common historical and cultural experiences. Second, that families of nations defined in this sense do, in some areas, appear to manifest rather similar policy outcomes. One has merely to think of the forests of trees sacrificed to the discussion of the Scandinavian welfare state and the Anglo-American phenomenon of New Right economic policy. The question each author addresses is whether an apparent policy commonly owes anything to an origin in shared historical and cultural experience and, to the extent that it does, what are the mechanisms for the transmission of that experience.

In deference to the prevailing methodology, but with the intention of exploring its outer limits, we start out our investigations in terms of the conventional paradigm. Is it wholly possible, we ask, to dissolve the apparent policy similarities of nations grouped in terms of shared historical and cultural attributes by reducing proper names to explanatory variables? For a families of nations approach to (re)assert its role as being a proper part of the comparative endeavour, it must be shown that it illuminates what cannot be illuminated otherwise. Therefore, what each chapter seeks to establish is the extent to which apparent family similarities may be understood in terms of economic, political and social antecedents, leaving to the end discussion of the extent to which those antecedents are themselves conditioned by shared historical and cultural experience.

Perhaps a few words need saying about what would satisfy us that a families of nations approach was vindicated by the researches contained in this volume. An important point to emphasize is that we do not proceed from any clearly articulated theory of how history and culture impact on public policy outcomes, but only with the conviction that a whole class of potential explanations has been substantially neglected both because such explanations do not dovetail neatly with the prevailing intellectual paradigm and because they are difficult to come to grips with in terms of our present methodology of comparison. We highlight the potential importance of history and culture because together they capture the essence of that class of explanations in stressing the importance of the transmission from the past of constraints on present-day behaviour. History leaves a legacy of ideas, customs and institutions – in sum, a culture – that influences the present behaviour of those who shape the policies of the state and those who make demands of the state. That history may itself be perfectly explicable in terms of economic, political and social forces which impinged on individuals of another era, but its influence on present behaviour is not readily accessible to a methodology, the operational code of which is exclusively to locate explanations of policy outcomes in the contemporary variation of socio-economic and political phenomena.

Thus, we would consider our approach vindicated if the commonalities of policy outcomes that characterize groupings of nations could be explained, in whole or in part, by common ideas, common customs and common institutions transmitted from the past. Having said that, it is clear that there are stronger and weaker senses in which it may be claimed that we have located families of nations. The weakest sense, and perhaps disputable as the manifestation of a distinctive phenomenon, is where a group of nations with some common historical and cultural affinities arrives at distinctive outcomes, but via different routes of historical causation. Commonalities exist here, both historical and contemporary, but there is no shared causal mechanism. The existence of families of nations is far less open to question when the historical route to common outcomes is a shared one. Most definitive of all, it seems to us that there is an unanswerable case for the explanatory importance of the families of nations concept where a common route from the past is simultaneously reinforced by commonalities of culture, identity and a shared sense of belongingness to a wider communality of nations in the present.

The potential variety of explanations that might facilitate an understanding of common routes from the past or the cultural reinforcement of commonality in the present is enormous. A shared culture and language may facilitate the transmission of policy ideas amongst the political elite and policy demands amongst the political masses within a particular group of nations, but impede their transmission beyond those cultural and linguistic boundaries. A shared core of historical experience may make some policy issues particularly salient and downgrade the importance of others. The logic of institutional structures common to a group of nations may facilitate certain types of policy solutions and make others inconceivable. A common legal tradition may shape the subsequent trajectory of the permissible bounds of both public and private behaviour. Imperial ties long since severed and patterns of imperial settlement may shape the institutional legacy and influence the sequence of economic, social and political development of countries spread far across the globe. In the mainstream of comparative public policy analysis, explanations such as these are rarely encountered. That could be because they are relatively unimportant compared to the massive impact of the factors that over several centuries have transformed the socio-economic and political structures of modern Western societies. Alternatively, it could be because their possible impact is not a topic for investigation within the bounds of the prevailing intellectual paradigm. It is this latter possibility which provides the impetus for the current research endeavour.

The Scope of the Research

The families of nations project has been a genuine research endeavour in the sense of having no predetermined conclusion. It started from the hypothesis that the shared experience of families of nations might be significant as a factor shaping contemporary public policy outcomes and set out to discover whether this was so. The research strategy was to locate a series of policy areas in which particular families of nations – the English-speaking, German-speaking and Scandinavian families from which the authors come – appeared to be characterized by distinctive policy outcomes and to investigate the determinants of those outcomes. However, the choice of relevant policy areas was far from arbitrary, and an attempt was made to select topics relating to certain key aspects of the state's public policy role: (1) its intervention in the macro-economy and its part in social protection, (2) its function as a regulator of labour supply, and (3) its legal controls over the sphere of domestic and family relations. These topics provide the organizing basis for this volume's division into three parts. The economic and

Table 0.1: Commonalities and questions

	English-speaking nations	German-speaking nations	Scandinavian nations
Economic Policy & Social Protection	*Chapter 1* Commonality: 1980s shift to anti-statism. Question: What are the dynamics of economic policy change?	*Chapter 2* Commonality: Success in maintaining price stability. Question: What are the determinants of low inflation rates and restrictive monetary policies?	
	Chapter 3 Commonality: Low social welfare transfers. Question: Does low social expenditure necessarily lead to inequality?		
The Politics of Labour Supply		*Chapter 4* Commonality: strong downward flexibility of labour supply in face of potential unemployment. Question: What factors make possible the rapid adjustment of labour supply to decreasing demands for labour?	

		Chapter 5 Commonality: Relatively high levels of labour market gender inequality. Question: What are the institutional determinants of the supply and demand for female labour?	
Families and Families of Nations	*Chapter 7* Commonality: Rapid increase in post-war divorce rates. Question: To what extent are divorce rates a function of the continuity of legal families of nations?		*Chapter 6* Commonality: Earlier and more extensive children's' rights Question: What are the determinants of the rights of children?
Conclusion	*Chapter 8* Discussion of the nature and value of the families of nations concept in comparative public policy analysis.		

social interventions of the state, which are the subject of Part I, are essentially the domain of recent comparative public policy research which falls within the conventional 'reducing proper names' paradigm; whether it is possible to demonstrate the utility of the families of nations concept in this area constitutes a fair test of whether this new approach can add to what we already know from research utilizing that paradigm. On the other hand, unemployment apart, issues concerning labour supply, which are the subject of Part II, and family policy, covered in Part III, have received rather little systematic attention in the comparative literature (amongst the few exceptions being the work of Norris, 1987). We believe that situation to be far from coincidental insofar as these realms of policy centrally involve cultural factors with which, it is our contention, the prevailing paradigm has inherent problems in dealing, and to which our own conceptual approach may well be much better suited.

The exploration of themes relating to each of these aspects of the state's role led to the analysis contained in the seven substantive chapters of this volume, each proceeding from an observed commonality of policy outcomes to a broader questioning of the determinants of public policy in Western democracies in general. These commonalities and questions are summarized in Table 0.1.

The topics and questions summarized in Table 0.1 and explored in subsequent chapters are extremely wide-ranging and diverse, with much of the analysis venturing into areas of policy hitherto almost untouched by systematic comparative analysis. However, we do not wish to be misunderstood. We are not making an *a priori* claim that all these policy areas can best be understood in terms of a families of nations approach. What we are saying is that, in all of them, we can identify similarities of policy outcomes in nations that happen to share historical and cultural attributes. We have selected broadly only in order to subject our hypothesis to testing across the widest possible range of policy contexts. If the project starts from any assumption, it is that policy arenas are likely to differ widely in the extent to which historical and cultural factors matter – assuming, that is, that they matter at all. In some areas, apparent similarities between nations with a common historical experience may simply mask the presence of common economic, political or social attributes conducive to a particular set of policy outcomes. In other areas, such similarities may be irreducible to such attributes and may only be explained by reference to the transmission of ideas or the impact of institutional structures common to different nations because of their shared historical experience. Without investigation in depth, and unless armed with an inventory of hypotheses allowing for the possible relevance of both types of factors, we have no way of establishing which areas are which. Thus, we range widely not in order to make a case for the families of nations approach, but rather to map the policy terrain with the objective of discovering whether such a case can be made.

In characterizing the scope of this study, something also needs to be said about the countries included and those excluded. Three points are in order. First, although it might appear from Table 0.1 that the Scandinavian grouping of nations features less centrally in this study than the English and German-speaking nations, that is more apparent than real. Certainly, our method is to proceed from a commonality exhibited by a putative family of nations and then to broaden the focus to the variation manifested by Western democratic nations in general; in this, only one of the commonalities listed in Table 0.1 (earlier and more extensive children's rights) is of Scandinavian provenance. On the other hand, broadening the focus often brings into purview new and contrasting commonalities shared by other groups of nations. Indeed, to the extent that the families of nations concept is important in illuminating public policy variation, what we might expect to discover is a repeated pattern of diverse families behaving in distinctive ways in diverse policy arenas. Here we simply note that it is the Scandinavian group of nations which features most conspicuously as a distinctive group across the whole range of policies analysed in this study. Although only one chapter proceeds from an explicitly Scandinavian commonality, virtually all identify a Scandinavian family of nations in the course of their various classifications of policy outcomes in different areas. Indeed, in this sense, it is arguable that the Scandinavian policy scene provides many of the clearest examples of the kind of phenomena that this volume is concerned to explore.

Second, we do not pretend to anything like an exhaustive coverage of the potential subject-matter in focusing on only three families of nations. Clearly, there is room for an investigation of the commonalities of the French-speaking nations or, making the obvious point that nations can simultaneously belong to more than one family, those of the Benelux countries. Still more obviously, once we turn our eyes away from the Western democracies, there would seem to be strong *a priori* indications of the existence of a Latin family, comprising Italy from within our sample plus Spain and Portugal within Europe and all of Latin America outside it. In what is an exploratory research endeavour, we do not feel that we need apologise for these omissions. Nor do we claim that any findings reached in respect of the three groupings of nations examined here can be readily extrapolated to other potential families. That, of course, would require further research which, to the extent that the family of nations concept is vindicated in this study, we hope may be the more readily forthcoming.

But whilst we do not claim a comprehensive focus, we most certainly do claim that the approach adopted in this volume involves a fully comprehensive analysis of the families of nations hypothesis in comparative perspective. The research design of each chapter starts from an observed policy commonality of a family of nations and then proceeds to test the validity of the linkages between outcomes and familial characteristics in the context of a comparative analysis of 18 Western democracies. In this sense, we make far more strenuous explanatory demands of our analysis than would be the case if we adopted an exclusively historical, institutional or cultural approach. For us, it is not enough that we can show that members of our supposed families of nations are marked by many similarities, but that, in addition, those similarities mark them off from other nations.

Third, it is also quite apparent from the outset that certain countries within the groupings of nations on which we do focus have a lesser shared inheritance of historical, cultural and linguistic factors than the other nations constituting that particular grouping. Is Canada really an English-speaking country when such a significant proportion of its population is French-speaking and shares a cultural inheritance with other French-speaking nations? Our answer is pragmatic. We treat it as English-speaking when we deal with the socio-economic policy outcomes which we assume to be a function of an historical and institutional inheritance shared with the other nations of the British Empire, but are ready to treat Québec separately in policy arenas, such as divorce and other aspects of family law, where cultural considerations are self-evidently more important. A similar strategy is appropriate in the case of Ireland, but here not even an historical and institutional affinity can be assumed. The settler colonies of North America and the Antipodes can be seen in terms of the English transplanted overseas; Ireland has a colonial inheritance of another sort, in which a subject-people were ruled not to produce mutual benefit for colonized and colonizers, but rather to enhance political and military control and to exploit economic resources. Finally, is Switzerland a German-speaking country when ethnically and linguistically divided into four segments? Here our treatment is rather different. We consider Switzerland as a German-speaking country throughout because we can offer empirical justification that the German-speaking population group within Switzerland is the largest and most economically and politically dominant. Nevertheless, we concede that Switzerland (like, say, Belgium) may well share the characteristics of more than one family of nations. That, in turn, might well imply that we expect the German-speaking group to manifest family of nations characteristics to a weaker degree than the other families examined here. The justifications for these inclusions and exclusions from the families of nations treated here can only ultimately be assessed in light of the findings contained in the various chapters below.

In this Introduction, we have not, for the most part, sought to preview our findings. More than is commonly the case, the families of nations project was genuinely an exploration in setting out into the unknown. What has been said here represents the departure point of each author as he or she embarked on the various comparative analyses of public policy outcomes presented in this volume. We did not know whether a family of nations perspective would prove appropriate in some or even any of the areas to be investigated. Nor, to the extent that it did prove appropriate, did we know what aspects of nations' historical and cultural experiences would be relevant in particular policy areas. Such conclusions had to await an evaluation of the sum of our investigations once completed. We believe that our readers will be best equipped to draw their own conclusions as to the utility of the families of nations concept by making the same voyage of discovery: that is, by moving directly to the substantive policy areas which are our test-bed of whether families of nations do or do not matter, without any substantial prior discussion of the findings. In our concluding chapter, we do seek to offer a broad overview of the character and significance of the families of nations concept, at a point at which the reader should be in a position to inform his/her final judgement by a critical evaluation of the conclusions drawn in the volume as a whole.

References

Almond, G. A. (1968), 'Comparative Politics' in *International Encyclopedia of the Social Sciences*, Vol. 13, New York: Macmillan, 331–6.

Castles, F.G. (ed.) (1989), *The Comparative History of Public Policy*, Cambridge: Polity.

Norris, P. (1987), *Politics and Sexual Equality. The Comparative Position of Women in Western Democracies,* Boulder: Rienner.

Przeworski, A. (1987), 'Methods of Cross-National Research, 1970–83: An Overview' in M. Dierkes, H.N. Weiler, and A.B. Antal (eds), *Comparative Policy Research*, Aldershot: Gower.

PART I
ECONOMIC POLICY AND SOCIAL PROTECTION

1 Changing Course in Economic Policy: The English-Speaking Nations in the 1980s

Francis G. Castles

Introduction

In attempting to answer the question of whether groupings of nations with a common historical and cultural heritage manifest similar and distinctive public policy patterns, we start by asking whether the families of nations concept is pertinent to understanding the dramatic politico-economic events of the past two decades. From the early 1970s onwards, all the capitalist democracies were faced with a major alteration in the economic premises on which public policy was grounded and, to varying degrees, were forced to address the issue of the extent to which existing policy responses remained appropriate in what was a changed and more threatening economic environment. What we seek to discover is whether this reassessment of what amounts to the ground-rules of the national political economy had diverse outcomes in groupings of countries with distinct and shared national attributes and, to the extent that was so, whether the explanation is to be found in systemic structural characteristics or in historical and cultural factors?

In this chapter, the focus of attention is less on the specifics of particular aspects of macroeconomic policy outcomes and more on the broad and enduring patterns which give an overall coherence to the thrust of public intervention in a given society. Quite often public policy is seen exclusively as an arena of partisan controversy and conflict; however, for long periods of time and across a broad range of areas, it is also a sphere of tacit, and sometimes quite explicit, consensus. Whilst controversy and conflict are the stuff of both short-term political disagreements between parties and groups and long-term political cleavage lines along which those disagreements usually flare up, consensus is the substance of those long-term, coherent strategies of public intervention which define 'an overall understanding, among those who exercise effective power, of a set of decision premises integrating world views, goals and means' (Scharpf, 1983, 260–61). Controversy and conflict – which is to say politics – comprise the mechanism of policy change, but long-term strategy is the ingredient without which policy decisions 'are unlikely to achieve the minimal degree of coherence and consistency which is essential to their overall success' (Scharpf, ibid.). The overall pattern by which we locate the distinctiveness of a nation's or an epoch's policy interventions is one largely given by the particular nature of its policy consensus rather by than its policy conflicts.

But consensus is not immutable, and policy strategies, long taken as aspects of the conventional wisdom, may be challenged and ultimately transformed. It is when established policy strategies are questioned and become the object of an explicit political challenge that we may meaningfully discern a watershed in public policy development. The period from the mid-1930s to the late 1940s was an era in which such a transformation – from the principles of sound finance to those of the Keynesian welfare state – was a general phenomenon in all advanced capitalist states. The period of the 1980s has also been one of major transformation, but one in which the national scope of change has been more partial. Certainly, all Western nations experienced some degree of challenge to the policy orthodoxies elaborated during the 'long boom'. However, in some that challenge was contained, whereas in others there were major attempts to change established policy directions.

What is of particular interest, given the theme of this book, is that all of these latter countries attempting change belonged to the English-speaking family of nations. In somewhat different ways, governments in Australia, Canada, New Zealand, the UK and the US sought to effect major alterations in the relationship between the state and the economy in their respective nations. In what follows, we seek to explore why it was this family of English-speaking nations which experienced the greatest pressure for public policy transformation, as well as to uncover the mechanisms facilitating policy transformation in these countries. The method is comparative: to examine the experience of policy development and change in the English-speaking nations and to contrast it with experience elsewhere. The analysis is deliberately exploratory and tentative, the objective being to locate and assess plausible hypotheses on a topic which has been given surprisingly little attention by scholars in comparative politics and comparative public policy.

In this chapter, Ireland is not counted as a part of the English-speaking family of nations. As pointed out in the Introduction, whether or not it should be included in such a designation involves a variety of problems. On the one hand, it enjoyed or endured a long period of British rule; on the other, it is self-evidently substantially different from the other five nations in terms of economic development, culture and social structure. Most pertinent in terms of the topic to be discussed here, Ireland did not (in the period under review) contemplate the sort of major departure from accustomed patterns of state intervention that was experienced in the other English-speaking nations. One might argue that this *a priori* made it a critical case, already demonstrating that family of nations' characteristics could not be the explanation of a changed policy dynamic in the 1980s. In some ultimate sense that might be so, although it does depend on precisely what it might be about the English-speaking countries that defined their consanguinity. Our view here is that to include Ireland would distract the analysis from its main objective, which is to establish what it was about the other five English-speaking nations which made them seek to refashion the relationship between state and economy to a degree unparalleled elsewhere in the world of advanced capitalism.

Transforming the Role of the State: The Experience of the 1980s

For most Western democratic nations, the economic crises of the 1970s and the continuation of slow economic growth into the 1980s were a stimulus to reassess, rather than retreat from, existing public policy strategies. This is clearly reflected in the tone of the post-crisis welfare state debate, where the initial flood of crisis predictions (see OECD, 1981; Mishra, 1984) quite rapidly gave way to formulations of the 'irreversibility' of the welfare state (Offe, 1984; Therborn and Roebroek, 1986). Obviously, economic crisis occasioned a search for means of containing the rising trajectory of aggregate social expenditure experienced almost universally in the 1960s, but in the majority of nations this involved no fundamental retreat from the principles of the socially protective state; rather a process of rationalization and reformulation was embarked upon that would have become inevitable in any case as the welfare state emerged as 'a mature social institution' (Klein and O'Higgins, 1988).

What was true of social policy was also largely true of economic and industrial policy arenas. Although there was a general disaffection with Keynesian principles and some flirtation with monetarist nostrums, economic crisis in many cases reinforced a renewed reliance on state-directed strategies for coping with economic vulnerability. This was manifestly the case in the smaller democratic corporatist nations of Western Europe, which saw negotiated tripartite agreements between the government and both sides of industry as the vital key to containing real wages and avoiding the worst excesses of stagflation (see Katzenstein, 1985). Larger countries, like Germany and Japan, also intensified their efforts in doing what they were already good at: in Germany's case, directing the full force of policy intervention to minimizing inflation (Schmidt, 1989) and, in Japan's, fostering rapid industrial transformation through a 'creative' partnership between government and private business (Pempel, 1989).

Only in Australia, Canada, New Zealand, the UK and the US did economic crisis occasion a major reappraisal of the role of the state and an attempt, either in the arena of the welfare state and/or economic regulation, to diminish the degree of public intervention that had become customary in the post-war period. Although at some level of generality, it is possible to identify common themes in attacks on the state in these countries (expenditure and taxation were seen as being too high, the state's direct role in production and regulation was seen as too extensive, and market forces were seen as a means of enhanced efficiency), the immediate focus of challenge to existing policy strategies varied appreciably.

Unlike the countries of democratic corporatism, the policy strategies of Britain and the US were not premised either on detailed and negotiated agreement between major societal interests or on microeconomic policy intervention, but rather rested on the management and manipulation of broad macroeconomic policy parameters (Heidenheimer, Heclo and Adams, 1990, 155–6). That being so, the natural focus for policy challenge was on the general character of the outcomes of such management, the obvious solutions to present themselves involving changes in the preferred instruments of macroeconomic policy-making.[1] In these countries, the central theme of a challenge to the established policy orthodoxy was a New Right disavowal of the 'over-mighty' state, manifested in an attack on the Keynesian welfare state as a subversive force undermining the values of individual initiative on which an efficient market system rests. To Thatcherites, what was required was a reversal of post-war developments, which had simultaneously encouraged reliance on the state as provider and lessened incentive for the individual to provide for himself and his family. A monetarist macroeconomic strategy was necessary to undercut not just inflation, but also the temptation to respond irresponsibly to demands for ever greater social protection, demands which were seen as the root cause of inflation. The trade unions had to be weakened because they were the chief agency of such demands, and the economy was to be privatized, not merely because a large nationalized sector was an important manifestation of the degree to which market principles had been superseded, but also because state industries were seen as the breeding ground for high union density and militancy. Of all the strands which together made up Thatcherism, that with the greatest impact on the prior pattern of public policy was the constant pressure to replace public ownership of nationalized industries with private enterprise. Arguably, this emphasis on the need for privatizing the economy may be seen as a response to the unusual salience of state-owned industry and public service provision through collective consumption in the UK (see Dunleavy, 1989).

For the architects of the Reagan revolution, to be carried out in a nation with a welfare state smaller than Britain's, with weak and declining trade unionism and a far smaller public sector, the diagnosis for required change was somewhat different. Unleashing individual initiative as a precursor of economic growth was to be a consequence of a radical attack on 'confiscatory' taxation which diminished incentives to greater effort. In the short-run at least, that was more important, not to mention more politically feasible, than the sort of financial rectitude inherent in monetarist or 'balanced budget' strategies (Stockman, 1986). Both Thatcherites and Reaganites saw the size of the state as inimical to economic efficiency but, whereas the solutions of the former were directed at the demand mechanisms which made the state grow, those of the latter were primarily on supply-side mechanisms that prevented the individual from maximizing his own advantage and, supposedly in the process, the welfare of the community as a whole.

In Australia and New Zealand, the central theme in challenging the existing role of the state was not so much its size, measured in terms of expenditure or extractive capacity, but rather its regulative activities and the way in which these impeded economic competition. Just as the exceptional emphasis on privatization in Thatcher's Britain can be seen as a reaction to the particular historical manifestation of statism in that country, the Antipodean thrust to 'deregulate the economy' was equally grounded in distinctive aspects of those nations' political economies. From as early as the first decade of this century, the Antipodean nations had consolidated a set of coherent and consistent policies clearly distinguishable from those of other democratic capitalist nations (see Butlin, Barnard and Pincus, 1982). Elsewhere I have labelled this policy stance as the strategy of 'domestic defence' (Castles, 1988, 91).

'Domestic defence' had three major components, each involving strong regulative intervention in the economy, but rather little in the way of state ownership on the British model (Castles, 1988, 91–108). First, tariff policy and/or import controls were used to protect domestic manufacturing from overseas competition. Second, quasi-judicial powers of compulsory conciliation and arbitration of industrial disputes were used to regulate the labour market with the aims of simultaneously achieving a social policy minimum (a 'fair' wage sufficient to support a breadwinner and family) and of adjusting wage levels to take account of fluctuations caused by dependence on highly unstable primary commodity markets. Third, migrant intake was regulated in order to adjust labour supply in the hope of minimizing unemployment and protecting the wage levels decided on through the arbitration system. The 'domestic defence' strategy may be characterized in terms of its 'conservative social welfare function', by which any decline in real income was minimized, the government provided insurance against income loss, and social peace was protected by ensuring that 'no significant income shall fall if that of others is rising' (Corden, 1974, 108).

In this policy mix, the social security aspects of welfare provision assumed less salience than in most European nations, since the social policy objective of protecting minimum living standards was assigned to labour market and industrial mechanisms (see Castles, 1985 and 1988). On the other hand, the strategy involved far more detailed government intervention in the economy than was common in either the US or Britain. It also differed markedly from the policy stance of democratic corporatism insofar as it rested on direction from above by government departments and/or quasi-judicial organs of the state rather than on consensus achieved through routine negotiation by strongly organized political interests. By the mid-1980s, this distinctively Antipodean strategy was identified by newly elected Labour governments as the primary cause of weak competitiveness in world markets and of persistently poor economic growth.

In 1983 Labour was elected in Australia and in 1984 in New Zealand. In each case, it was a return from the political wilderness, Labour having lost the three previous national elections in both countries. Moreover, whilst in both nations Labour had played a vital role in the initial formulation of the 'domestic defence' strategy, that policy orthodoxy had been largely presided over by its Conservative rivals in the post-war period. Between 1949 and the early 1980s, the Australian Labor Party (ALP) spent only three years in office and the New Zealand Labour Party (NZLP) only six years.

Quite significantly, and reflecting the economic and industrial policy focus of the Antipodean policy challenge, new policy directions were identified more with the holders of the main economics ministry in each country than with the head of the executive branch. Both Paul Keating, the Australian Federal Treasurer, and Roger Douglas, New Zealand's Finance Minister, saw their primary role as removing the regulatory shackles which impeded economic progress by shielding the manufacturing and financial sectors and the labour market from overseas competition. Tariffs had to go, import restrictions had to be lifted, foreign banks should be free to compete, interest rates should be free from regulation, currencies should float, and real wages should be more responsive to market forces and comparable in level to those in competing nations.

At least ostensibly and in line with a Labour ideology, the challenge to the accustomed role of the state was not immediately directed at its socially protective activities, but was presented in terms of the need for a greater 'wealth production' in which all could share. The size of the state – whether measured in terms of expenditure, employment, taxation or the underwriting of wage levels – was problematic in this conception too, but the challenge was not the overtly ideological one of Thatcher or Reagan. Rather, the issues were seen as ones of sound economic management. It was argued that competitive efficiency had been undermined and economic restructuring was necessitated by balance-of-payments problems and the crowding-out of investment, resulting from a state larger than the nation's current economic means to support it and from wage levels higher than warranted by productivity. In Keating's words – but they might just as well have been those of Douglas about New Zealand – without 'internal economic adjustment' to the 'international hole Australia is in … we will just end up being a third-rate economy … a banana republic' (Statement, 14 May 1986).

No more than in the countries in which the main thrust of the challenge was to the size of the state were the Australian and New Zealand policy routes to economic restructuring identical. To a far greater degree than in New Zealand, the Australian Labor party rested on trade union support, and Australian labour market policy on a more strongly institutionalized system of state conciliation and arbitration. Both of these factors impelled Labor policy-makers to favour a hybrid and uneasy combination of economic rationalist solutions for freeing up markets and corporatist negotiation to buy-off trade dissent (Sandlant, 1989). In fact, the Hawke Labor government had come to office in 1983 on the basis of an 'Accord' between the trade unions and government which promised government by consensus in place of the confrontational style of the previous Conservative coalition. In subsequent years, the trade unions continuously pressed for policy transformation to take on a character more akin to the Swedish corporatist than to the British economic rationalist model. Given this Australian policy context, real wages might be restrained in the cause of national economic survival, but they could not be frontally attacked by undermining the trade unions and traditional wage-fixing mechanisms.

In New Zealand, without these inherited constraints, the economic policies of 'Rogernomics' veered quite close to monetarist principles and with much the same consequences in terms of a rapidly increasing level of unemployment. Taxation was another issue where New Zealand moved much further away from traditional Antipodean policy solutions. In both countries aggregate taxation was low, but was substantially based on a rather steeply progressive income tax, regarded by leftist elements in the Labour party as an important contribution to their egalitarian objectives. To Douglas, progressivity stifled incentive and he succeeded in instituting a proportional goods and services tax designed to shift the balance of the taxation system away from incomes. In contrast, Keating, who shared much the same view, failed to persuade the Australian trade unions of the wisdom of a similar move. However, in 1988, Douglas failed in his attempt to impose a 'flat tax' proposal which 'undermined the work of the government's own Royal Commission on Social Policy' (Davidson, 1989, 321) and, thereafter, lost much of his influence in the economic policy sphere.

The Canadian case is somewhat less clear-cut than that of the other English-speaking nations. There is some disagreement as to the implications of the advent of the Mulroney Conservative government for welfare state policy. In rhetoric, the government came to office with many of the same monetarist and supply-side doctrines as Thatcherism and Reagonomics; indeed, one early commentator on its proposed policy programme described its philosophy as sharing their appeal to selfishness and disregard for the helpless (Laxer, 1984). However, despite an early challenge to the principle of welfare state universalism, the new government failed miserably in its attempt to gain acceptance for a more targeted system of benefits (see Myles, 1988, 78).

An American commentator, explicitly contrasting the American, British and Canadian experiences of conservatism in the 1980s, suggests that 'the Mulroney government to date does not provide convincing evidence that the Canadian policy agenda has been revolutionized or even profoundly altered' (Thomas, 1988, 129). Whilst that may well be a fair assessment in respect of the role of the welfare state and in terms of the virulence of anti-statist rhetoric in these countries, the Mulroney government did echo the New Right in its emphasis on privatization and deregulation, with this latter theme featuring at least as strongly as in Australia and New Zealand. Still more significant, by signing a free trade agreement with the US, the government did make a very decisive and highly controversial break with the past by moving away from Canada's traditional economic nationalism – a protective stance quite akin to the politics of 'domestic defence' in terms of economic rationale, but also strongly overlaid by the objective of maintaining economic and policy autonomy from its giant neighbour. Judged in terms of purely economic criteria, this departure may not have been revolutionary, but it nevertheless represented a complete reorientation of traditional understandings of the goals and means of Canadian public policy. The Canadian Conservatives' justification for free trade was akin to that impelling change in the Antipodes: the protective regulation of the state, however much it had once been associated with goals of national development and equity, had to be abandoned in the search for greater economic efficiency. The policy strategies of the past had to be transformed under the pressure of new economic circumstances.

In broad terms, the policy transformations embarked on by these English-speaking countries can thus be divided into two types: a retreat from the socially protectionist welfare state and a shift away from economic nationalism or 'domestic defence' towards internal economic deregulation and/or freeing up trade barriers. In each case, the general thrust of policy change and its particular manifestation may be interpreted, at least, in part, as a response or reaction to the peculiar character of existing policy strategies. Nonetheless, what is of particular interest is the overall contrast between these countries and the other advanced Western nations in which a redefinition of the role of the state did not surface on the political agenda as a serious issue on anything like the same scale. In subsequent sections we shall ask whether this latter contrast is a function of the particular character of the development of the state in the English-speaking nations, or whether the pressure for policy transformation in these countries reflected the emergence of a new balance of economic and/or political forces.

The Role of the State in the English-Speaking Nations

Given that a reduction of the size of the state is either an ultimate goal of or an instrumental means to the policy transformations envisaged in the English-speaking countries, one might suspect that this common policy response could well be a consequence of the unusual extent of development or growth of state expenditures or state personnel in these countries. This hypothesis is tested by the data which appear in Tables 1.1, 1.2, 1.3 and 1.4, showing the level, absolute and proportional change in aggregate social security transfers, the ratio of transfers to need, civilian public consumption expenditure and government employment in each of the English-speaking nations. They also contrast this group of countries' performance in respect of each of these measures with the average of some 12 or 13 other OECD nations[2] over a span of nearly a quarter of a century preceding the early 1980s.

Social Security Transfers

Table 1.1 looks at social security transfers, the component of public expenditure most frequently identified with the welfare state and that which addresses the major social problem of contemporary societies – the poverty remaining after the initial distribution of incomes through the market mechanism.

The table makes it quite apparent that, far from being large welfare states, the English-speaking nations as a group have lagged well behind most other OECD nations throughout the post-war era. Nor can the impetus to challenge the Keynesian welfare consensus in the English-speaking nations be readily attributed to unusual efforts by these countries to match the performance of other advanced states. In terms of absolute change, all five English-speaking nations fell markedly below the mean of the other OECD nations; in respect of proportional change, only the UK matched the OECD average. In fact, in the period 1960–83, the already wide gap between the welfare spending levels of English-speaking and other OECD nations increased quite markedly. The paradox of Thatcher's and Reagan's ideological onslaughts against the welfare state is that they occurred in nations which were quite manifestly welfare state laggards, at least in terms of aggregate expenditure.

Table 1.1: Social welfare transfers as a percentage of GDP

	1960	1983	Absolute change	Proportional change (per cent)
Australia	4.7	9.1	4.4	94
Canada	5.9	10.3	4.4	75
New Zealand	6.9	10.9	4.0	58
UK	5.4	11.3	5.9	109
US	5.2	9.6	4.4	85
Mean English-speaking	5.6	10.2	4.6	84
Mean other OECD	7.6	15.9	8.3	109

Source: Rita Varley, *The Government Household Transfer Data Base 1960-84*, Paris: OECD, 1986.

The Needs Ratio

The data in Table 1.1 provide a picture of the welfare state relativities seen from the top down which is particularly appropriate for comparing the budgetary burden of social provision in different nations. That is the picture as it is usually portrayed by anti-statist critics of Keynesian policy orthodoxy. But, as Richard Rose has been at pains to point out in his recent writings on public policy, there are other perspectives possible, in particular an 'underall' perspective from the viewpoint of the 'ordinary people' on whom policy impacts (Rose, 1989). From this latter perspective, it is as important to look at what the different categories of individuals in need and generally in receipt of state benefits actually receive from the government, as it is to measure the aggregates that governments disburse. In comparative terms, we should be asking whether clients of the welfare state do better in some countries than in others and whether their situation is improving over time.

Table 1.2 provides a measure which attempts to capture this needs dimension by taking the transfer expenditure of Table 1.1 and dividing it by

Table 1.2: The ratio of welfare transfers to need

	1960	1983	Absolute change	Proportional change (per cent)
Australia	.47	.44	–.03	–6
Canada	.42	.47	.05	12
New Zealand	.76	.62	–.14	–18
UK	.41	.44	.03	7
US	.36	.45	.09	25
Mean English-speaking	.48	.48	0	0
Mean other OECD	.58	.72	.14	24

Sources: Calculated from Rita Varley *The Government Household Transfer Data Base 1960–84*, Paris: OECD, 1986; OECD, *Historical Statistics 1960–86*, 1988; UN, *Demographic Yearbook*, various years.

the number of the aged and unemployed, much the two most significant categories of welfare beneficiaries in all the OECD countries.

The resulting ratio indicator offers a rough approximation of cross-national and cross-time relativities in welfare state generosity. On this measure, the picture of English-speaking laggardliness is strongly reinforced. Not only does this grouping of nations start out behind the rest of the OECD, but also there is no improvement in its average level of generosity, whilst the rest of the OECD is forging ahead. Only in the case of the US is there a proportional increase in generosity matching the OECD norm, but that is as the consequence of an all out 'war on poverty', whose only result was to match the levels of welfare provision of the laggards two decades earlier.

The data in both Tables 1.1 and 1.2 relate essentially to aggregate levels of expenditure. Their implications for more fundamental welfare outcomes, such as the distribution of incomes and the extent of poverty in different nations, are debatable. These are matters discussed in detail in Chapter 3 below. Nevertheless, the failure of the English-speaking nations to provide or improve welfare generosity implied by these expenditure figures can hardly be regarded as a determinant of a challenge to the state premised on the need to reduce state expenditures. To argue that would be to set out the very opposite of the case made by those who have sought to curtail the reach of the state: that we should cut back state expenditure because it was too low!

Public Consumption

Table 1.3 focuses on civilian public consumption expenditure, that part of state expenditure which covers the goods and services purchased by the state as well as the wages and salaries of those employed by the state. Although less exclusively related to welfare, this dimension of expenditure is frequently singled out as particularly reprehensible in contemporary anti-statist ideology since, far more than transfers, it is a measure of the intrusion of the state to the detriment of the market.

With respect to this dimension of state size, the English-speaking countries are on average much more like their other OECD counterparts: slightly lower than the OECD average in respect of 1960 and 1983 levels and absolute change, but very marginally higher in respect of proportional change. The only one of our family of nations for which a case might be made for exceptional development is Canada, where very high rates of absolute and proportional growth since 1960 have given that country, after Sweden and Denmark, the third biggest domain of public consumption in the OECD (O'Connor, 1989, 133). It is not apparent, however, that the

Table 1.3: Civilian public consumption expenditure as a percentage of GDP

	1960	1983	Absolute change	Proportional change (per cent)
Australia	8.7	16.2	7.5	86
Canada	9.1	18.9	9.8	108
New Zealand	8.4	15.0	6.6	79
UK	10.0	16.7	6.7	67
US	7.7	11.9	4.2	55
Mean English-speaking	8.8	15.7	6.9	79
Mean other OECD	9.4	16.6	7.2	75

Source: OECD, *Historical Statistics 1960–86*, Paris, 1988.

health and education spending, which make up by far the largest part of Canadian expenditures under this head, have been a particular target for rationalizers. Certainly, in respect of the other English-speaking nations, there is nothing in Table 1.3 to suggest any reasons for a policy reaction to public consumption expenditure development of an order of magnitude different from that in other OECD nations.

Public Employment

Table 1.4 examines the post-war development of civilian public employment, a frequent focus of New Right rhetoric against the 'over-mighty' state.

These data, which are derived from OECD sources, must be treated with some caution in the context of our discussion, since they do not include those employed in state business enterprises; as we have already noted, in Britain at least it was these nationalized industries which were amongst the main targets of the Thatcherite policy challenge. However, the high degree of public ownership in Britain is not, and has never been, a feature of the economies of the other English-speaking nations and hence cannot be seen

Table 1.4: Civilian public employment as a percentage of the working-age population

	1960	1983	Absolute change	Proportional change (per cent)
Australia	13.9	15.7	1.8	13
Canada	8.9	12.4	3.5	40
New Zealand	11.3	11.1	–.2	–2
UK	10.1	13.4	3.3	32
US	8.4	10.2	1.8	21
Mean English-speaking	10.5	12.5	2.0	21
Mean Other OECD	6.0	12.3	6.3	105

Source: T.R. Cusack, T. Notermans and M. Rein (1989), 'Political-economic aspects of public employment', *European Journal of Political Research*, **17** (4).

as a general determinant of the policy transformation experienced by those countries in the 1980s, even if its prevalence in Britain helped to shape the particular form of the policy challenge in that country.

In Table 1.4, at last, we do encounter an aspect of the performance of the English-speaking nations which may be regarded as distinctively statist. In 1960, the level of public employment in each of these five nations was higher than in any other OECD country. It is, however, very difficult to attribute the anti-statist policy challenge of the 1980s to this cause, since a quarter of a century of rapid public employment growth elsewhere in the OECD region together with very sluggish growth in the English-speaking nations had led to almost complete convergence between the groupings by the early 1980s. Rather than seeing public employment levels as a reason why the English-speaking nations might have taken a different view of policy strategy from other nations in the 1980s, these figures could well be taken to suggest that the sorts of problems imputed by the Right as stemming from this cause had already been adequately resolved without requiring any fundamental change in policy direction.

Summing up the Data

This very simple comparative analysis offers no support for the view that the impetus for the anti-statist policy challenge of the 1980s was grounded in a real predicament concerning the size of the state or its rate of growth (for a fuller discussion, see Castles, 1989). Other countries – most conspicuously Denmark, the Netherlands, Norway and Sweden – experienced public expenditure and/or public employment growth far greater than in the English-speaking nations, entering the 1980s with expenditure and/or employment levels which were far higher than in most of this latter group. Yet with the exception of Denmark (of which much more will be said below), these European big-spenders and big-employers are countries in which anti-statist ideas have had very little impact. Moreover, there is nothing in the above tables which enables us to understand the differences in the particular focus of the policy challenges experienced in the English-speaking nations. By 1983, New Zealand was the English-speaking nation in which social security was greatest in proportion to need, Canada recorded the greatest expenditure on public consumption and Australia had the highest level of public employment, yet the challenge to the size of the state was most virulent in Britain and the US. All this is not to say that the size of the state was irrelevant in shaping the thrust of controversy concerning established policy strategies in the English-speaking nations. But if relevance there was, it can hardly have resulted from an automatic response to the deleterious consequences for economic efficiency of state size above a certain level, as postulated by the New Right. Rather it must have been a matter either of facets of state development specific to particular countries (as in the case of the unusual salience of public enterprise in Britain) or of the way in which state size and growth were differentially *perceived* in different nations. Why such perceptions may have differed in the English-speaking world is the subject of the next section.

The State of the Economy

National willingness to increase public expenditure as a percentage of GDP must be presumed to be dependent in some degree on expectations of future growth in the economy from which such increases may be funded. All other things being equal, one would expect a nation with better growth prospects to expand the state more willingly than a nation with a lower rate of growth. A perception that growth was too slow to sustain the existing trajectory of expenditure development might rationally lead to policy reappraisal directed at either a slowing or reversing of expenditure trends or a revamping of economic policy instruments to foster greater economic growth.

Since these were precisely the policy transformations envisaged in the English-speaking nations in the 1980s, the notion that weak economic growth was at the root of the policy challenge experienced in these countries is worthy of examination. Table 1.5 presents data on these nations' per capita economic growth rates for the periods 1950/52–60, 1960–73 and 1973–80 and also provides a comparison with the average growth rate of other OECD nations.

Table 1.5: GDP per capita growth rates

	1950/52–60	1960–73	1973–80
Australia	2.1	3.0	1.5
Canada	1.0	3.9	1.5
New Zealand	1.9	2.4	0.7
UK	2.3	2.6	1.1
US	1.0	2.8	1.3
Mean English-speaking	1.7	2.9	1.2
Mean other OECD	4.0	4.3	1.8

Source: S. Dowrick and D.T. Nguyen (1989), 'Australia's post war economic growth: measurement and international comparison', *American Economic Review*, **79** (5), 1010–30.

It is immediately apparent from these data that the economic growth hypothesis does have quite a strong *a priori* plausibility. Throughout the post-war period, the average GDP growth rate was appreciably lower in the English-speaking nations than in the remainder of the OECD. That a policy challenge should have occurred in these nations when it did is also understandable from this data. The boom in growth experienced by these nations between 1960–73, albeit at a level well below that of other advanced industrial nations, could have been seen as sufficient to finance their relatively modest expansion of transfers, but with the disruption to growth consequent on the oil crises of the 1970s, such a perception might well have become much more precarious.

But why, if this interpretation is correct, did the other OECD countries not experience a policy challenge of at least comparable magnitude? Their absolute decline in GDP growth rate in the 1970s was greater than that of the English-speaking nations, while their rate of expansion of transfers and government employment was appreciably higher. One possible clue from the data is that, whereas the other OECD nations could have interpreted the oil shock decline in growth as a temporary aberration from a previously sustained high rate of post-war growth, the English-speaking nations had more reason to see the 1970s as a return to the 'normal' pattern of low growth experienced in the 1950s.

The general tendency to low growth in these nations is only one aspect of a broader trend towards convergence in the growth trajectories of advanced capitalist countries in the post-war period as demonstrated by recent cross-national research (see Dowrick and Nguyen, 1989). The richer a nation was in 1950 – and all the English-speaking nations were then in the top half of the distribution – the slower its growth thereafter. Moreover, the convergence hypothesis is strongly confirmed by analysis going back to the pre-war period, demonstrating that the low growth rates of the English-speaking nations after the war were very substantially attributable to the fact that these five nations, together with Denmark, were the world's richest in the late 1930s (see Castles, 1991). Nor was slow economic growth merely a post-war phenomenon. Comparative research on pre-war economic performance shows that, even between 1910 and 1937, Australia, Britain and Canada were all well below the average per capita growth rate for the period. These countries, at least, had several generations of low economic growth as their normal expectation of economic policy performance. Indeed, it seems more than probable that a major academic growth industry of recent times – explaining in particularistic country-specific terms the origins of the 'British disease' of low economic growth (see Wiener, 1981; Gamble, 1981; Marquand, 1988) – has been based on the mistaken premise that the British experience is fundamentally different from that of all other Western nations, when the evidence seems to suggest that the phenomenon of slow growth is one common to the majority of rich Western nations this century.

Having been rich for at least half a century, thereafter experiencing slow growth and, hence, slowly sinking down the league-table of affluent nations – an experience shared by Australia, New Zealand and the UK – is a very potent reason why policy-makers might see the luxury of additional state services as being beyond a nation's means. Once when these nations were rich, they could afford a big state and, as we have seen, all of them had such a state, at least as measured in public employment terms circa 1960. At one time some of these nations (in fact, those whose position on the national wealth league-table declined most dramatically in the post-war era) could afford to be welfare state pioneers. As will be shown in Chapter 3 below, Australia, New Zealand and the UK were amongst the world's leading welfare states. Now it could seem that such public generosity was no longer economically practicable, or even that past generosity was amongst the causes of present discontents.

Policy Effectiveness

Although slow economic growth could be part of the answer to the question of why some countries experienced policy challenge and transformation in the 1980s, it is not the whole answer. Some countries like Denmark, Sweden and Switzerland had rates of post-war growth almost as low, and the first two of these countries experienced post-war welfare growth far in excess of anything in the English-speaking nations. Denmark, in the early 1970s, did have a period of political instability caused by the emergence of the anti-tax and anti-welfare Progress Party; given that it was also one of the richer nations in the pre-war era, Denmark may be considered as a case confirming the logic of the argument offered in the previous section. However, neither Sweden nor Switzerland manifested any serious challenge to prevailing policy strategies.

Low economic growth therefore appears not to be a sufficient condition of policy challenge, although it may be a necessary one. Policy ineffectiveness in respect of growth may well have to be conjoint with perceived failings in other policy areas if a serious push for transformation is to occur. The argument is that longish periods of slow growth can be sustained without any dramatic loss of regime legitimacy, unless there is some catalyst for popular dissatisfaction with outcomes of a kind that provide additional grounds for belief that economic policy management is inadequate. The very experience of several of the English-speaking nations during the first 75 years of this century is testament to how long such a period may be.

Table 1.6 provides data on unemployment and inflation levels, together with figures for the so-called 'misery index', which is merely the sum of unemployment and inflation. Data are averaged across the years 1978–83, a time during which the British and American policy transformations had already begun and when the themes of the policy challenges in Australia, Canada and New Zealand were being elaborated by the major parties in opposition.

Table 1.6: Unemployment, inflation and misery index 1978–83

	Unemployment	Inflation	Misery index
Australia	6.8	9.7	16.5
Canada	8.9	9.6	18.5
New Zealand	3.1	13.6	16.7
UK	7.7	10.8	18.5
US	7.6	8.7	16.3
Mean English-speaking	6.8	10.5	17.3
Mean other OECD	5.4	8.5	13.9

Source: OECD, *Historical Statistics 1960–86*, Paris, 1988.

The table shows that average unemployment and inflation levels and, consequently the overall misery index, were on average higher in English-speaking than in other OECD nations. All five countries fall in the bottom half of the distribution together with Ireland, Italy, Denmark and France.[3] A misery index figure for Switzerland of 4.4 per cent shows why policy-makers and people in that country might have been far less concerned about the overall effectiveness of existing policy strategy. Although the misery index in Sweden was appreciably higher, an unemployment level of 2.6 per cent demonstrated that the government was in sufficient control of the economy to keep faith with the chief tenet of what had been Sweden's Social Democratic policy orthodoxy ever since 1932. Even if these countries' growth was slow, the existing policy strategy – whether statist or otherwise – appeared to offer better than average protection against those scourges of the capitalist economy which transform economic disruption into personal disaster.

Sweden and Switzerland are, of course, exemplars of the kind of democratic corporatist policy strategy with which policy-making in the English-speaking countries was earlier contrasted. In general, studies of economic performance in corporatist nations have shown that they were better able to cope with problems of unemployment and inflation in the 1970s and early

1980s than most other nations (see Bruno and Sachs, 1985; Crouch, 1985). This is also true of countries like Germany and Japan, which various authors have suggested share at least some features in common with the corporatist model (see Schmidt, 1982, 135; Lehner, 1987, 70–71). On the other hand, it is not true of countries like Ireland and Italy, whose performance in respect of unemployment and inflation was very markedly worse than the group of nations on which this study focuses. Indeed, the true gap between the economic performance of the English-speaking nations and the majority of the OECD nations may be assessed by excluding the Irish and Italian cases, a calculation which suggests that policy effectiveness in the English-speaking world was almost 50 per cent below the norm for the more highly advanced OECD nations. What distinguishes the policy configurations of Ireland and Italy from the English-speaking family of nations as defined here is that neither had ever been rich and that their rates of growth were higher, if not (in Ireland's case) a great deal higher. They may have been both poor and 'miserable' by international comparison, but they did not suffer from invidious comparisons with a grandeur that was now in decline.

It would, therefore, seem to follow that the occasion for policy challenge and subsequent transformation of policy strategy in the 1980s was a combination of sustained low economic growth in nations which had once been rich, together with poor policy effectiveness in arenas affecting popular support for the existing policy regime. This was a combination of circumstances which characterized all five English-speaking countries during the 1970s. In the period of the greatest economic crisis of the Western world since the 1930s, it was in these nations (together with Denmark) that the populace had the strongest reasons for feeling that existing policy orthodoxy had outlived any utility it might once have possessed.

Denmark is in many ways the critical case for our analysis. Its post-war political economy is in many respects a paradigm of all the developments that constitute the basis of the critique concerning the 'over-mighty' state. In the 1960s, Denmark rapidly became one of the OECD leaders in respect of social security transfers, public consumption expenditure and public employment. In the years immediately preceding the irruption of the Progress Party onto the political scene, it experienced a massive rise in the level of taxation – most specifically personal and highly progressive taxation on incomes (see Wilensky, 1976). Clearly, if the English-speaking nations had experienced state development comparable to Denmark's, an explanation of the impetus to policy challenge in terms of the size of the state would be highly persuasive. But, in fact, the real similarity between Denmark and the English-speaking nations is one of economic performance rather than state development, this was already apparent in the early 1970s when the Danish tax revolt took place. In the period 1960–73, the Danish per capita growth rate was below the OECD mean, while its inflation rate was almost the highest in the OECD. Overall, despite an unemployment performance better than the OECD average, it is possible to characterize the Danish economy as one of the worst performers of the period: on the basis of an estimate combining growth, inflation and unemployment, only Ireland, the UK and the US score lower (see Castles, 1988, Table 2.2). It is this, far more than any dimension of state development, which Denmark in both the 1960s and 1970s has in common with the English-speaking nations. That, of course, leaves the question of why the early policy challenge in Denmark did not lead to a major transformation of the prevailing policy strategy as in the English-speaking world. This is a matter on which we speculate below.

The Politics of Policy Transformation

All that has been said so far relates the origin of policy challenge and subsequent transformation to the nature of economic circumstances and the effectiveness of the existing policy strategy. We conclude our substantive analysis with some brief observations on the political process by which challenge becomes actualized as a transformed policy agenda.

The first point to be made is negative. Contrary to much of the writing which has sought to reflect on the new policy patterns presaged by the Thatcher and Reagan governments, the impetus to policy transformation in the 1980s was not exclusively the philosophy of the New Right, nor its carrier exclusively of Conservative provenance. Clearly, the economic rationalism preached by the New Right found an audience both amongst those who diagnosed their present discontents in terms of the size of the state and those who saw the problem as undue regulative fetters on the economy, but the experience of Australia and New Zealand in the latter part of the 1980s shows that labour movements and Labour parties could be the agents of change to as great a degree as Conservative parties.

That parties with diverse ideologies should espouse policy transformation is just as one might expect given that the impetus to challenge the status quo appears to have been the character of economic performance and the effectiveness of policy responses to it, rather than the role of the state as an agency of social protection. Perhaps the only sign that ideology may have shaped responses to some degree is in the immediate focus of the challenge to existing policy strategy. The Labour governments of the Antipodes did not couch their rhetoric in terms of root and branch opposition to the big state in the manner of the Conservative regimes in the UK and the US. But the Canadian case, where the real Conservative challenge was to big government and economic nationalism rather than to the welfare state, makes even this ideological distinction tentative at best.[4]

A second point concerns the mechanism by which discontent with existing policy strategy becomes a platform for a party capable of achieving power and, hence, capable of effecting a policy transformation. It is arguable that it is this political aspect of the dynamic of policy change which explains why countries as similar in economic performance as the English-speaking nations and Denmark should have had rather dissimilar outcomes in terms of the success of challenges to existing policy orthodoxies. The Danish experience is different in two important ways: (1) the challenge to the welfare state and all its doings came early and from outside the circle of established parties, and, (2) rather than leading to a wholly transformed policy agenda, it petered out into the politics of rationalizing and reformulating a mature welfare state.

A key to this diversity of outcomes lies in differences between the party and electoral systems of Denmark and the English-speaking nations. Whereas the former was characterized by moderate and (since the early 1970s) extreme multi-partism, based on a highly proportional system of voting, the latter have two or two and a half party systems based on first-past-the-post or modified plurality electoral arrangements. Denmark's low electoral threshold (parties gaining more than 2 per cent of the national vote are guaranteed representation) was the factor which permitted a party espousing a single-issue, tax-backlash challenge to mobilize more than 20 per cent of the vote at its first outing into electoral politics in 1973. But at the same time, the fact that, under proportional electoral arrangements, parties are very closely tied to particular constituencies of electoral support made it quite impossible for such a challenge to capture an existing party capable of forming a government. What happened in Denmark was that the established parties which had presided over prevailing policy strategy simply shut out the Progress Party, condemning it to policy futility and eventual attrition of electoral support. In the English-speaking countries, the high effective electoral threshold implicit in single-member, plurality arrangements prohibits the formation of new parties that can successfully conquer power in less than a generation (witness the abortive British Social Democrat experiment of the 1980s). On the other hand, just because there is no close identification between parties and specific interests in the electorate makes existing parties highly vulnerable to hijack[5] by a vociferous minority of party elites and/or by a particular leadership faction. By the winner-takes-all logic of two-party adversary politics, a hijacked party once elected cannot be prevented from converting challenge into policy.

The contrast between low and high threshold electoral systems in allowing new and potentially destabilizing entrants into the political system has always been a point of faith for the defenders of two-party systems. In terms of the rise of new parties, the contrast between the experience of Denmark and the English-speaking countries goes some way toward confirming that view. On the other hand, in terms of the potentially destabilizing influence of dramatic policy change, the logic of electoral and party systems seems to point in the opposite direction. It was precisely the multi-party character of the Danish system which made it possible to moderate the impact of an anti-statist challenge and direct it through normal party channels,[6] whereas the two-party systems of the English-speaking nations provided a mechanism for the rapid transformation of the existing policy pattern.

A final point on the political dynamics of policy transformation concerns the reason why in some countries Conservative parties were the agency of challenge and in others Labour. On the basis of Downsian logic (Downs, 1957), it is not immediately apparent why either party in a two-party system should foresee electoral advantage in departing from an established policy consensus. In order to maximize electoral advantage, both parties must seek to slant their appeals to the median voter. The impact of economic crisis in discrediting the existing policy orthodoxy is clearly the prime factor impelling a shift in position, but then we are faced with an alternative difficulty: failures associated with a policy strategy held in common ought, by the same logic, to lead to retreat from that strategy by both parties in roughly the same measure. So why does one party rather than the other become the challenger to policy orthodoxy at a particular juncture, even if, after a number of successful elections, the other may accommodate to its views, thereby creating a new policy orthodoxy to replace the old?

Here we advance a very simple hypothesis: that the party most implicated in the failures of the existing policy strategy finds it most difficult to attack its premises. Even though the general theme of policy consensus throughout the post-war Western world was Keynesian, the specific national variants of that strategy were presided over by parties with a wide range of political complexions. As already noted, both in Australia and, to a somewhat lesser degree, in New Zealand, Labour had been the architect of the politics of 'domestic defence', but for most of the post-war period had been out of office, with the policy stance they had helped to shape being administered by their Conservative opponents. In Britain, Labour had created the welfare state and presided over it for much of the 1960s and 1970s. In the US, an uninterrupted Democratic congressional hegemony could be blamed for all that was wrong with the existing policy pattern, even if that pattern had been the template for many of the policy initiatives of occasional Republican presidents. Similarly, economic nationalism was firmly nailed to the masthead of the hegemonic Canadian Liberal Party.

This long-term identification between a consensual policy stance and a particular party is exactly the outcome that party leaders seek when times are good. Under those circumstances, the party most associated in the common mind with the prevailing policy strategy is likely to remain electorally successful. But, in times of crisis, such an identification is far more problematic and may be quite disastrous in circumstances where the party is actually in office when unemployment and/or inflation is rampant, so that its specific application of that strategy is blamed for policy failure. Under these latter circumstances, a party is trapped: it may want to disavow a policy strategy that seems to be getting nowhere and has unpopular consequences, but to do so involves admitting past mistakes and present incompetence. Usually, for the short term at least, a defence of the government's record involves some defence of the basic policy strategy that motivated it.

Of course, it is not always the case that an incumbent party is defeated in times of crisis (see Schmidt, 1983). It may survive or merely 'muddle through' if any or all of the following circumstances apply: (1) if the party is an avowed opponent of the policy strategy blamed for the crisis (e.g. the Social Democrats in Denmark during the Great Depression); (2) if it is perceived as economically competent and/or managing the crisis as well or better than any likely replacement (e.g. Japan, Austria and Germany in the crisis of the 1970s and 1980s); (3) if it exists in the context of a multi-party coalition system where blame for policy is intrinsically hard to allocate and government formation is not directly determined by the electorate, and (4) if economic issues are less salient to the electorate than other issues. Absolutely none of these circumstances pertained in the English-speaking nations during the economic crisis of the late 1970s and early 1980s. Policy effectiveness was low and was popularly perceived as such; socio-economic problems were overwhelmingly the main source of political cleavage, and two-party systems focused blame directly on the government of the day. Above all, the parties in office at the onset of crisis were in every case those that were most popularly associated with the existing policy orthodoxy. Under these circumstances, party labels were irrelevant and the Conservative governments of the Antipodes suffered precisely the same fate as the Labour and progressive governments in the Anglo-American nations.

However, for parties condemned to the outer field of opposition politics for any period of time and hence less immediately implicated in policy failure, policy challenge and transformation constitute a comparatively low risk strategy, and economic crisis a great opportunity. At worst, the party offering new ideas can add one more failure to the long list of those that went before. At best, it can capitalize on popular discontent concerning present economic policy and use it as a wedge to create a new policy strategy, the eventual success of which might, at last, change the political terms of trade in its favour, enabling it to become the new 'natural' party of government. That was the political gamble taken by Thatcher, Reagan, Hawke, Mulroney and Lange. As of the early 1990s, it is one which appears to have reaped huge political dividends[7] even if it has, as yet, produced rather little evidence of any major reversal of adverse economic performance.

Early Family Ties?

To demonstrate, as we have attempted here, that the nations which most vigorously departed from post-war policy orthodoxies concerning the role of the state in the economy had certain features in common does not establish that they were, in any meaningful sense, a 'family of nations'. It will be noted that we have studiously avoided the use of that term as a conceptual designation of the English-speaking nations in our account so far. To establish the existence of such familial ties in any but a very weak sense would require, in addition, that we show that these common structural antecedents of policy transformation – slow economic growth, economic policy ineffectiveness and high electoral thresholds – were, at least in part, a consequence of the English-speaking nations' sharing of certain historical and/or cultural characteristics.

To make that case adequately would require an historical study far beyond the scope of anything that can be presented here. In concluding, all that is possible is the merest sketch of the argument that such a study might advance. Presented in barest outline, such a sketch remains contestable at many points, but can make an important contribution to an exploration of the concept of families of nations by illustrating that the frequently supposed dichotomy between structural and historico-cultural explanations is a false one. Our view is that the common structural antecedents of policy challenge and transformation in the 1980s are themselves to be explained in terms of a series of interlinked historical sequences which shaped the institutions, economy, culture and experience of the English-speaking nations in a distinctive manner.

The first point to be made is the obvious one that, irrespective of whether the policy transformations of the 1980s are, or are not, attributable to common historical and cultural characteristics, the English-speaking countries do possess significant shared national attributes in this sense. Quite apart from a common language and a culture transmitted through that medium, the four non-European nations in the group largely owe their national identity to settlement by the UK. Historically, the settler capitalist states of the Antipodes and the Americas share a common heritage of colonial development under British tutelage and also trading links with the imperial centre which persisted long after their colonial status had been replaced by democratic sovereignty.

The question then becomes one of whether there are plausible links between these 'familial' attributes and the structural antecedents of contemporary policy transformation. The answer is that there are and that, in respect of each of the identified common antecedents, a link can be traced to the timing of sequences of historical development that differentiate the experience of the English-speaking countries from the other nations of advanced capitalism. The argument is simply that slow economic growth, policy ineffectiveness and high threshold electoral systems are all, in some degree, consequences of the relative *earliness* of economic, social and political modernization in Britain and in the countries largely settled by British migration.

The convergence thesis, which (as we saw previously) substantially accounts for post-war patterns of economic growth, is a theory about the effects of timing: the countries which modernize and become richest earliest subsequently grow more slowly and are gradually overtaken by those setting out on the path of modernization later. Britain was, of course, the first nation to embark on a process of industrial modernization and, by establishing overseas settlements, which were attractive to British investors as sources of extensive pastoral and agricultural production and in which there was a tendency to labour shortage relative to capital, she created the conditions for early prosperity in her new dominions and the independent nations that subsequently developed from them.[8] By the late 19th century, the English-speaking nations, along with Argentina and Denmark, which also experienced early prosperity as sources of agricultural commodities for the British market, were the richest nations in the world (see Clark, 1957; Maddison, 1977). They were such partly because they were tied by bonds of colonial status, trade and indebtedness (see Schwartz, 1989, 30–48) to the world's first industrial giant; however, they were foredoomed to losing their early advantage to the degree that technological catch-up and/or increasing preferences for leisure led to progressive convergence over the next century. By the early 1980s, the English-speaking family of nations found it easier to dwell on thoughts of past grandeur than to entertain great expectations for the future.

A structural precondition for the kind of corporatist arrangements that led to reasonably high degrees of policy effectiveness in the economic crises of the 1970s was the prior existence of a set of sectoral blocs, the mutual acquiescence of which was required for successful policy implementation.[9] A number of the smaller European countries – Belgium, the Netherlands and Switzerland – were characterized by such a bloc structure, due to their historical and cultural legacy of religious and/or cultural fragmentation. In others, particularly in Scandinavia, late industrialization led to industry and class-wide mobilization by a wide variety of producer groups. But, with the partial exception of Canada, which was fragmented by a major linguistic cleavage, neither precondition of corporatist arrangements was present to any marked degree in the English-speaking family of nations.

In respect of forms of economic organization, earliness was again the crucial factor in differentiating the development of the English-speaking nations. Early British and American capitalism was small enterprise capitalism, while the capitalist agriculture of the dominions was to no lesser degree based on relatively small-scale production. Small-scale modernization led to the articulation of craft and trade interests rather than to more encompassing sectoral organizations.[10] Arguably, in societies characterized by the former, policy coordination could only proceed through the voluntary and autonomous aggregation of particularistic interests (laissez-faire markets and liberal, pluralist politics) or by regulation from above (as, for instance, in the regulative strategies of 'domestic defence' which had earned the Antipodean settler societies the title of 'colonial socialism' by the late 19th century), whilst, in societies characterized by the latter, effective policy-making required the incorporation of most major organized sectors.

The argument here is that, in the absence of major cultural cleavages and because of early modernization, the English-speaking nations were unlikely to be those in which corporatist forms of interest mediation would develop spontaneously. In addition, they were likely to be those in which deliberately manufactured corporatist arrangements of the kind engineered by many governments in the 1960s and 1970s would sit uneasily with long-established laissez-faire ideas and pluralist forms of representation.[11] This argument from the historical conditions under which industrialism emerged may be seen as a variant of Marxist historicism, but that is not the intention. There is, in fact, nothing here which excludes the possibility of cultural causation as considerable as may be established by historical scholarship. Apart from the impact of attitudinal cleavages already mentioned, it may well be that the ideas and institutional forms of interest representation which first developed in Britain, and which unquestionably owed something to the form of early capitalist development, had a major impact through their diffusion and perpetuation in those nations in which British influence had privileged access by virtue of language or hegemonic power. To the extent that this proved to be the case, it would merely give a cultural dimension to the commonality of the English-speaking family of nations, already clearly defined by virtue of early colonial and trade dependency ties.

If early economic modernity in the English-speaking nations was an inhibitor of economic and political arrangements now regarded as particularly conducive to successful policy management, it may, on the other hand, and more immediately, be regarded as a factor stimulating modern institutional development of a different kind. In comparison with the majority of European nations, the emergence of responsible government in Britain, the US and the British dominions was extremely precocious. Responsible government first emerged in the US in the late 18th century and in Britain in 1832. It was established in all the dominions well before the end of the 19th century and, in contrast to many of the European nations, was in none of these countries subject to reactionary reversal. This earliness, in turn, meant that the English-speaking countries largely escaped the common European experience of a superimposition of the political and constitutional issues raised by democratization and of the social issues inherent in the mobilization of the working class. In consequence, they were less subject to intense pressure for formal electoral equality in the context of broader constitutional struggles for popular sovereignty, and were not forced, as were most European regimes, to abandon traditional territorial forms of representation with high electoral thresholds. Just as in Europe, the English-speaking countries experienced a 'freezing' of party systems and electoral arrangements (Lipset and Rokkan, 1967), but the earliness of their democratic development froze the political landscape into the two-party pattern that persists to this day.

Our story then is that the structural conditions conducive to the policy transformations of the 1980s can plausibly be seen as having their origins in distinctive sequences of historical development manifested in their clearest form in the English-speaking world. In this sense and in respect to this dimension of policy development, the families of nations concept does seem to be applicable. Because these nations were linked to Britain, the pioneer of industrial modernization, by ties of power, trade and cultural transmission of ideas, their patterns of economic and political development – the preconditions for their subsequent strategies of state intervention – were decisively different from those of nations that embarked on modernization in a later era. In other words, quite irrespective of whether the formative influences were historical sequences of events or culturally transmitted ideas and attitudes, the consequences of either or both shaped behaviour patterns and/or became the directing principles of institutional arrangements. Thus, in turn, they became structured constraints on the future development of public policy strategies. Whether there is any deeper developmental logic in the fact that it was the English-speaking family of nations, the pioneer of early economic and democratic modernization, which, more recently, has been in the vanguard of a reappraisal of the proper relationship between state and economy in the late 20th century, only time will tell.

Notes

1. Earlier unsuccessful British Labour attempts at policy reform had taken the alternative course of seeking to create prices and incomes policies in part modelled on the experience of the democratic corporatist states.
2. They are Austria, Belgium, Denmark, Finland, France, Germany, Ireland (except for public employment), Italy, Japan, the Netherlands, Norway, Sweden and Switzerland.
3. France, despite its low degree of policy effectiveness, did not experience an anti-statist challenge comparable to that of the English-speaking nations, although it seems highly probable that economic problems were an important factor in contributing to the first socialist victory in that country since the advent of the Vth Republic in 1958. Although the leftist policy programme envisaged in the first few years of the Mitterand period was a conspicuous failure, it too is testimony to the impetus of policy ineffectiveness in promoting schemes for transforming the relationship between state and economy.
4. The Canadian case is possibly best explained in terms of a different political variable. Of the three English-speaking federal states - Australia, Canada and the US – Canada is the only one in which welfare policy-making responsibilities are divided between provincial and federal levels and in which a social democratic culture persists in a large segment of the population. This combination makes it extremely difficult for governments to attack the principle of 'universality' underlying the Canadian welfare system. I am indebted to Professor Robert Jackson of Carleton University for this interpretation.
5. An apposite term used in a recent book on how the Australian Labor Party was captured by leaders wishing to transform it into a catch-all party of sound economic management (see Jaensch, 1989). Bruce Jesson uses the same term to describe what happened in New Zealand, although he has in mind the influence of the Treasury on the incoming Labour government. He suggests that his book, *Fragments of Labour* (1989, 11) 'is the story of a small and unsophisticated nation hijacked by extremists'.
6. In the 1980s, Denmark experienced a substantial political realignment, with minority Conservative-led governments replacing the Social Democrats as the 'normal' party of government. Minority status prohibited any fundamental departure from the Social Democratic consensus established in the immediate post-war decades, but the Danish Conservatives nevertheless succeeded in constraining public expenditure to some degree, not least by the curtailment of welfare provision on a scale greater than elsewhere in Scandinavia (see Marklund, 1988).
7. The Australian Labor Party in 1990 for the first time in its history won four consecutive federal elections; Mulroney's government as of late 1992 was Canada's longest lived post-war Conservative administration; New Zealand Labour, although going down to defeat in 1990, had its longest period of office since the 1940s; Margaret Thatcher, although ultimately not quite as indestructible as her supporters believed, was the longest serving British Prime Minister this century; and the Republicans last held the US presidency for three successive terms between 1921 and 1933.
8. Black (1966, 90–91) dates Britain and then the US as being the first two nations to

consolidate modernizing political leadership and the remaining English-speaking nations as achieving that status extraordinarily early after British settlement.

9. The structural preconditions of corporatist intermediation must be distinguished from the factors conducive to a search for socially protective solutions, whether corporatist or otherwise, to problems of economic crisis. In this latter respect, the concept of economic vulnerability has been usefully applied to the experience of both the smaller corporatist nations of Western Europe (see Katzenstein, 1985) and the Antipodean nations employing the strategy of 'domestic compensation' (see Castles, 1989).
10. See Ingham, 1974, for an exemplification of these differences as between Britain and Denmark on one side and Norway and Sweden on the other.
11. Indeed, as noted elsewhere, the use of a dummy variable for Englishness (the English-speaking nations) often simply produces a mirror image of the results found in statistical analyses using the concept of corporatism or neocorporatism (Castles and Merrill, 1989, 183–4).

References

Black, C.E. (1966), *The Dynamics of Modernization: A Study of Comparative History*, New York: Harper & Row.

Briggs, A. (1965), 'The Welfare State in Historical Perspective' in M.N. Zald, (ed.), *Social Welfare Institutions*, New York: John Wiley & Sons.

Bruno, M. and Sachs, J. (1985), *Economics of Worldwide Stagflation*, Cambridge, Mass.: Harvard University Press.

Butlin, N.G., Barnard, A. and Pincus, J.J. (1982), *Government and Capitalism*, Sydney: George Allen & Unwin.

Castles, F.G. (1985), *The Working Class and Welfare: Reflections on the Political Development of the Welfare State in Australia and New Zealand, 1890–1980*, Sydney: Allen & Unwin.

Castles, F.G. (1988), *Australian Public Policy and Economic Vulnerability*, Sydney: Allen and Unwin.

Castles, F.G. (1989), 'Big Government in Weak States: The Paradox of State Size in the English-speaking Nations of Advanced Capitalism', *Journal of Commonwealth and Comparative Politics*, **XXVII** (3), 267–93.

Castles, F.G. (1991), 'Democratic Politics, War and Catch-up: Olson's Thesis and Long-term Economic Growth in the English-speaking Nations of Advanced Capitalism', *Journal of Theoretical Politics*, **3** (1), 5–25.

Castles, F.G. and Merrill, E.V. (1989), 'Towards a General Model of Public Policy Outcomes', Journal of Theoretical Politics, **1**, No. (2), 177–212.

Clark, C. (1957), *The Conditions of Economic Progress*, London: Macmillan.

Corden, W.M. (1974), *Trade Policy and Economic Welfare*, London: Oxford University Press.

Crouch, C. (1985), 'Conditions for Trade Union Wage Restraint' in L.N. Lindberg and C.S. Maier (eds), *The Politics of Inflation and Economic Stagnation*, Washington: The Brookings Institution.

Cusack, T.R., Notermans, T. and Rein, M. (1989), 'Political-Economic Aspects of Public Employment', *European Journal of Political Research,* **17** (4), 471–500.

Davidson, A. (1989), *Two Models of Welfare: The Origins and Development of the Welfare State in Sweden and New Zealand, 1888–1988*, Stockholm: Almqvist & Wiksell International.

Downs, A. (1957), *An Economic Theory of Democracy,* New York: Harper & Row.

Dowrick, S. and Nguyen, D.T. (1989), 'OECD Comparative Economic Growth in the Post-war Period: Evidence from a Model of Convergence', *American Economic Review,* **79** (5), 1010–30.

Dunleavy, P. (1989), 'The UK: Paradoxes of an Ungrounded Statism', in Francis G. Castles (ed.), *The Comparative History of Public Policy,* Cambridge: Polity.

Esping-Andersen, G. (1989), 'The Three Political Economies of the Welfare State', *The Canadian Review of Sociology and Anthropology,* **26** (1), 10–36.

Gamble, A. (1981), *Britain in Decline*, London: Macmillan.

Heidenheimer, A.J., Heclo, Hugh and Adams, C.T. (1990), *Comparative Public Policy,* New York: St. Martin's Press, 3rd edition.

Ingham, G.K. (1974), *Strikes and Industrial Conflict*, London: Macmillan.

Jaensch, D. (1989), *The Hawke-Keating Hijack*, Sydney: Allen & Unwin.

Jesson, B. (1989), *Fragments of Labour,* Auckland: Penguin.

Katzenstein, P.J. (1985), *Small States in World Markets*, Ithaca: Cornell University Press.

Klein, R. and O'Higgins, M. (1988), 'Defusing the Crisis of the Welfare State: a New Interpretation' in T. Marmor and J Mashaw (eds), *Social Security: Beyond the Rhetoric of Crisis,* Princeton, N.J.: Princeton University Press, 203–225.

Laxer, J. (1984), 'Taking Stock', *Canadian Forum*, January.

Lehner, F. (1987), 'The Political Economy of Distributive Conflict' in Francis G. Castles, Franz Lehner and Manfred G. Schmidt, *Managing Mixed Economies*, Berlin: De Gruyter, 54–96.

Lipset, S.M. and Rokkan S. (1967), *Party Systems and Voter Alignments*, New York: The Free Press.

Maddison, A. (1977), 'Phases of Capitalistic Development', *Banca Nazionale del Lavoro Review*, **30**, 103–37.

Marklund, S. (1988), *Paradise Lost: The Nordic Welfare States and the Recession 1975–1985*, Lund: Avkiv Förlag.

Marquand, D. (1988), *The Unprincipled Society,* London: Fontana Press.

Mishra, R. (1984), *The Welfare State in Crisis,* Brighton: Wheatsheaf Books.

Myles, J. (1988), 'Decline or Impasse: The Current State of the Welfare State', *Studies in Political Economy*, **26**, 73–107.

O'Connor, J. (1989), 'Welfare Expenditure and Policy Orientation in Canada in Comparative Perspective', *The Canadian Review of Sociology and Anthropology,* **26** (1), 127–50.

OECD (1981), *The Welfare State in Crisis,* Paris.

OECD (1989), *Historical Statistics 1960–67,* Paris.

Offe, C. (1984), *Contradictions of the Welfare State,* London: Hutchinson.

Pempel, T.J. (1989), 'Japan's Creative Conservatism: Continuity under Challenge' in Francis G. Castles (ed.), *The Comparative History of Public Policy,* Cambridge: Polity, 149–91.

Rose, R. (1989), *Ordinary People in Public Policy,* London: Sage Publications.

Sandlant, R.A. (1989), *The Political Economy of Wage Restraint: The Australian Accord and Trade Union Strategy in New Zealand*, M.A. Thesis, University of Auckland.

Scharpf, F.W. (1983), 'Economic and Institutional Constraints of Full-Employment Strategies: Sweden, Austria and Western Germany, 1973–82' in John H. Goldthorpe (ed.), *Order and Conflict in Contemporary Capitalism*, Oxford: Clarendon Press, 257–90.

Schmidt, M.G. (1982), 'The Role of Parties in Shaping Macroeconomic Policy' in Francis G. Castles (ed.), *The Impact of Parties*, London: Sage, 97–176.

Schmidt, M.G. (1983), 'The Welfare State and the Economy in Periods of Economic Crisis', *European Journal of Political Research*, **11** (1), 1–26.

Schmidt, M.G. (1989) 'Learning from Catastrophes: West Germany's Public Policy' in Francis G. Castles (ed.), *The Comparative History of Public Policy,* Cambridge: Polity, 56–99.

Schwartz, H.M. (1989), in the *Dominions of Debt: Historical Perspectives on Dependent Development*, Ithaca: Cornell University Press.

Stockman, D. (1986), *The Triumph of Politics,* New York: Coronet.

Therborn, G. and Roebroek, J. (1986), 'The Irreversible Welfare State: Its Recent Maturation, its Encounter with the Economic Crisis and its Future Prospects', *International Journal of Health Services*, **16** (3), 319–38.

Thomas, N.C. (1988), 'Public Policy and the Resurgence of Conservatism in Anglo-American Democracies' in Barry Cooper, Allan Kornberg and William Mishler (eds), *The Resurgence of Conservatism in Anglo-American Democracies*, Durham: Duke University Press, 96–135.

Varley, R. (1986), *The Government Household Transfer Data Base 1960–84*, Paris: OECD.

Wiener, M. J. (1981), *English Culture and the Decline of the Industrial Spirit 1850–1980*, Cambridge: Cambridge University Press.

Wilensky, H. (1976), 'The 'New Corporatism', Centralization and the Welfare State', *Contemporary Political Sociology Series*, **2** (20), Berkeley: Sage.

2 The Politics of Price Stability: Why the German-Speaking Nations are Different

Andreas Busch

Introduction

The objectives of this chapter are twofold. First, we seek to offer an explanation for the high level of price stability experienced by the Federal Republic of Germany, Austria and Switzerland since World War II and especially in the period after 1973 when, in the face of worsening economic conditions, inflation rates rose markedly throughout the OECD area.[1] Second, we examine the extent to which that explanation is compatible with a families of nations approach, which would attribute the distinctiveness of policy outcomes in the German-speaking nations to antecedent and shared cultural and historical attributes of these nations.

The approach adopted is comparative: the possible commonalities of the German-speaking experience, in respect both of inflationary performance and its antecedents, are established by relating that experience to other OECD nations. Having outlined our research question, we briefly review various explanations for inflation advanced by economists, political scientists and sociologists. This allows us to draw conclusions as to the most appropriate research design for this study and to test some of the more common hypotheses used to explain inflationary performance against empirical evidence. Having discovered that these hypotheses are incapable of accounting for the positive performance of the three countries under consideration, we go on to suggest a set of factors that can explain much of the variation in inflation experienced by the OECD countries in the past two decades.

These factors include the degree of labour unrest, the degree of central bank independence and the degree of fiscal decentralization.

The German-Speaking Family of Nations

The treatment of the Federal Republic of Germany, Austria and Switzerland as a family of nations in the context of this volume rests on a number of distinctive features common to these countries. The first and most obvious are geographical contiguity and the common German language,[2] resulting in a far greater intensity of communications – such as through trading links, the cultural exchange of ideas, views and news – between the German-speaking countries than between them and other nations.

But beyond these apparent points of connection, the three countries also display great similarities in their institutional settings. They are the only countries in Europe that since 1945 have been continuously organized as federal states. Moreover, in all three countries, federal arrangements are of long-standing and deeply rooted in historical tradition. This tradition was drastically disrupted in both Germany and Austria in the period of National Socialism. Whilst that disruption has been a source of emergent differences within the German-speaking family, it also served to strengthen re-federalization in Austria and Germany after World War II.

Federalism aside, there are also great similarities among the three countries at the level of policy formulation and politics. All three are marked by an unusual combination of institutional decentralization, fragmentation and joint decision-making, which Lehmbruch (1989, 19) has found particularly characteristic of the Federal Republic. On the one hand, decision-making power is distributed in such a way as to weaken the central state as an actor; whilst, on the other hand, there are elaborate decision mechanisms that overarch and connect the different levels. These latter involve political actors in arrangements that facilitate strategies of long-term cooperation and conflict resolution. Security of expectations thus produces a high level of political stability which may well translate into security of economic expectations.

A further commonality of the German-speaking nations is that these characteristics are not only revealed within the state structure, but also at the level of labour relations, again with possibly advantageous economic consequences. The combination of overarching arrangements for cooperation and consensus at both state and industry levels provides the institutional basis for Katzenstein's (1984; 1985a, 31, 34) classification of all three countries as corporatist (with the Federal Republic being the only 'big' country labelled in this way).

In summary, it may be suggested that the German-speaking family of nations is marked by *federal decentralization, cooperative to consensus policy-making and a pronounced social partnership*. This combination of features distinguishes it from other families of nations and, as will be demonstrated, has had a profound impact on these countries' post-war economic policy performance.

Price Stability in the OECD Area

The variable to be explained in this chapter is the remarkably high level of price stability in the three German-speaking OECD countries. This stability stands out in an international experience that has been marked by great differences with respect to inflation. Between 1965 and 1988, price stability (or the level of inflation) has varied considerably in the OECD area, both as between different countries and over time. Some statistics can serve to illustrate the extent of this variation (see OECD 1979, 1989).

In the countries studied here, the degree of annual inflation in a single country has varied between figures as diverse as 24.5 per cent (Japan, 1974) and –0.7 per cent (Netherlands, 1987). The highest average inflation for the whole OECD area occurred in 1974, with 13.3 per cent, and the lowest average inflation rate in 1986, when prices rose by only 3.7 per cent. The greatest inflation differential in the OECD could be found in 1975, at 18.2 percentage points, when the UK had an inflation rate of 24.2 per cent and the Federal Republic of Germany only 6.0 per cent. Average inflation rates for 18 OECD countries over different time periods can be found in Table 2.1.

This table shows that the three German-speaking countries performed extremely well throughout the whole period between 1965 and 1988. The Federal Republic ranks first with an average annual inflation rate of only 3.7 per cent, Switzerland second with 4.0 per cent and Austria third with 4.7 per cent. These results are distinctly below the average inflation rate for the whole sample which is 7.1 per cent.

Even more interesting are the results for the sub-periods. Between 1965 and 1973, rates of inflation did not vary much among the OECD countries, as can be seen from the low standard deviation of 0.9. In fact, inflation rates as *between* countries did not vary more than inflation rates *within* a country, for example between different regions of the US (Cassel, 1988, 297). The periods after 1973, however, show a marked rise in the average inflation rate in the OECD area, nearly doubling from 5.2 per cent (1965–73) to 10.2 per cent (1973–80). However, not only did the average rate of inflation rise, but there was also increased international variation, as can be seen from the

Table 2.1: Average rates of inflation in OECD countries, 1965–88

	1965–1988		1965–1973		1973–1980		1973–1986	
	Rate	Rank	Rate	Rank	Rate	Rank	Rate	Rank
Australia	7.9	12	4.6	7	11.6	13	10.2	13
Austria	4.7	3	4.5	5	6.5	3	5.6	3
Belgium	5.6	5	4.3	4	8.1	5	7.2	6
Canada	6.3	8	4.1	2	9.1	8	8.2	8
Denmark	7.9	12	6.7	17	10.8	12	9.3	11
Finland	8.2	14	5.9	13	12.4	14	10.4	14
France	7.4	9	4.8	9	10.7	11	9.7	12
Germany (West)	3.7	1	3.8	1	5.1	2	4.3	2
Ireland	10.0	16	6.7	17	15.0	16	13.3	17
Italy	10.1	17	4.5	5	16.1	18	14.6	18
Japan	5.8	6	6.2	16	10.1	10	6.8	5
Netherlands	5.1	4	5.7	12	7.2	4	5.6	3
New Zealand	10.4	18	5.9	13	13.5	15	13.0	16
Norway	7.6	11	5.6	11	8.8	6	8.8	9
Sweden	7.5	10	5.3	10	9.9	9	9.2	10
Switzerland	4.0	2	4.7	8	4.6	1	4.2	1
UK	8.9	15	5.9	13	15.2	17	11.5	15
US	5.8	6	4.1	2	8.9	7	7.2	6
Average	7.1		5.2		10.2		8.8	
Standard Deviation	2.0		0.9		3.3		2.9	
Coefficient of Variation	0.28		0.17		0.32		0.33	

Source: OECD, 1979, 1989.

tripling in the standard deviation of the sample. It is, therefore all the more impressive that the three countries under consideration suffered only slight increases in their rates of inflation (Switzerland actually managed to *lower* the rate by 0.1 percentage points), ranking first (Switzerland), second (Federal Republic) and third (Austria) in the OECD distribution between 1973 and 1980. The ranking is the same for the period of 1973 to 1986. It would thus seem that these three countries found a uniquely successful way to avoid the general rise in inflation that hit their OECD partners.

If we look at the two other families of nations considered in this volume, quite different pictures emerge. The English-speaking countries form a very heterogeneous group. They occupy places ranging from the middle to the end of the distribution, and their performance worsens considerably after 1973. In contrast, in the earlier period, the Scandinavian countries form a very homogeneous group that is almost invariably to be found at the start of the second half of the rank-distribution. Although their inflation rates also rise after 1973, their relative performance in the OECD-distribution improves slightly.

Although the inflation performance of the three countries under consideration is relatively stable for the whole period between 1965 and 1986, the focus in this chapter will be on the years between 1973 and 1986. There are two reasons which suggest that such a focus is sensible. The first is that the year 1973 marks the end of the almost 30-year-old Bretton Woods system of fixed exchange rates. Under this system, exchange rates were fixed and the monetary authorities of the member countries were obliged to support these exchange rates by monetary policy measures. This imposed severe limitations on national sovereignty in monetary policy and largely shackled the pursuit of national priorities. The Bretton Woods system thus served as an international transmission mechanism for inflation (see e.g. Salant, 1977; Keohane, 1985). This stemmed from the rule of adjusting exchange rates only in the case of 'fundamental disequilibrium' as well as from the dollar's role as the reserve currency. The former allowed some countries (e.g. West Germany) to maintain undervalued currencies, to gain trade advantages and to continue a current-account-surplus, even if this meant importing inflation. The US government, on the other hand, could afford to run a current-account-deficit without risk of losing currency reserves, as the US dollar was the internationally accepted reserve currency. The expansionary monetary policy of the US (the only country able to pursue a sovereign monetary policy under the Bretton Woods system) in the 1960s and early 1970s eventually led to the breakdown of the system. Exchange rates were subsequently allowed to float freely, and a sovereign monetary policy became possible for all states.[3]

A second reason to confine the period of investigation to the period after 1973 is an empirical one. Before 1973, inflation rates in the OECD area were relatively similar, making firm patterns or national profiles hard to recognise. Countries' rates of inflation never deviated much from the average rate of the OECD (see the low standard deviation for the period 1965 to 1973 in Table 2.1) and, for reasons just mentioned, their position slightly above or below the mean was not systematically determined. After 1973, however, when the 'golden age of capitalism' ended and economic difficulties increased, the countries apparently chose different ways of coping with the economic crisis (see Schmidt, 1989a). Rates of inflation (and also other economic indicators) now became widely divergent, and systematic patterns became distinguishable.

As both theoretical and empirical evidence suggests, the period before 1973 differed from the period after 1973. Again, for reasons both of theory and empirical evidence, it seems more promising to try to analyse the political determinants of inflation in the latter period since national policies of price stability were then, in principle, possible.

Inflation can be measured in different ways, with several price indices in existence which measure specific aspects of price increases. The most commonly used indicators are the GNP deflator, the producer price index (PPI) and the consumer price index (CPI). These indicators show quite similar results over longer periods of time, although there may be differences in the short run (see Dornbusch and Fischer, 1987, 41–2). For the purpose of this analysis, however, the CPI seems to be the most appropriate measure and it will therefore be used throughout this chapter.

We prefer this indicator for reasons commonly noted in the literature (Schmidt, 1982, 207; Phelps-Brown, 1990; Scherf, 1988). First, its political relevance: the CPI is the measuring rod for inflation that is best known to the general public and therefore plays a significant role in politics. Second, it also often serves as an indicator in collective bargaining processes or decisions related to the indexing of wages. Last but not least, internationally comparable data for this measure are available for the OECD area.

The Lessons of Past Research

The Literature on Inflation

Here we offer a necessarily brief outline of the main lines of research pursued by economists and social scientists in the field of inflation and draw out the implications for the research design to be employed in this chapter.

Economists have, of course, advanced a variety of theories to explain inflation. However, despite this work, no unitary approach has so far emerged. David Cameron once remarked that 'almost as many causes of inflation are advanced as there are economists' (1985, 225). However, two main groups of theoretical approaches can be distinguished (cf. Frisch, 1977; Woll, 1981; Cassel, 1988; Scherf, 1988). On the one hand, *monetary theories* focus mainly on increases in the money supply (which may be seen to be determined by the actions of the central bank), changes in the velocity of money circulation (for instance, due to financial innovations) and rises in aggregate monetary demand (demand-pull). On the other hand, *non-monetary theories* concentrate on different cost-push factors such as changes in the propensity to consume, strong rises in investment, government expenditure or wages; changes in the economic structure; monopolization of markets or rational expectations.

Application of these approaches has varied among the different schools of economic thought; in addition, their popularity has changed over time, with concomitant effects on the pursuit of economic policy. In the 1960s and early 1970s, for example, cost-push (mainly determined by excessive wage rises) was seen as the main factor causing inflation. This led to many countries pursuing some kind of incomes policy. From the mid-1970s, however, the rising prominence of monetarist ideas among economists (cf. Rothschild, 1986b) led to a nearly complete change of mind: the excessive growth of the money supply was now seen as the (often, sole) cause of inflation which led to cost-push factors being neglected (this may have been enhanced by often frustrating experiences with the implementation and outcomes of incomes policies). Targeting and confining the increase in the money supply were now seen as the 'magic bullet' against inflation.

But economists do not only disagree about theory. The division between theoretical approaches is also reproduced in the econometric tests of competing hypotheses. Some, for example, find a significant effect of the growth of the money supply on inflation in the Federal Republic of Germany (McCallum, 1983; Schlesinger and Jahnke, 1987), whilst others deny such an influence (Woll, 1977; Gerfin et al., 1985; Schöler 1989).

Economists' knowledge about inflation, it can be concluded, is far from complete. It seems therefore justified to approach the explanation of inflation in a way rather different from those suggested by mainstream economics. The justification is the greater since theories stemming from mainstream economics can be criticized on at least four grounds other than their contradictory hypotheses and conflicting results:

1 Institutional factors are only inadequately discussed in the economics literature. The few exceptions (e.g. Alesina, 1989; Grilli et al., 1991) have so far had no detectable influence on the mainstream. Even the so-called 'New Institutional Economics' (e.g. Williamson, 1990) focuses on transaction costs rather than 'real world institutions' such as, for example, the institutional status of the central bank or the structure of the collective bargaining system. But the latter are significant factors that differ from country to country and so can be an important source of international variation in economic performance. These inadequacies have often been noted; because of the similarities of their approaches and their combined critique of the paradigms of mainstream econom-

ics, increased cooperation between political scientists and institutional economists has been advocated (Lindberg, 1982; Lindberg and Maier, 1985).

2 The main reason for neglecting institutional factors is probably the deficiency of systematic international comparison in the repertoire of mainstream economics. However, the prevailing fixation on single countries can cause severe errors. For example, monetarist theories are mainly built upon research about the US (see the work of Milton Friedman and especially Friedman and Schwartz, 1963, 1970). Internationally comparative tests of these hypotheses, however, indicate that with respect to the relationship between budget deficits and the money supply or the money supply and inflation, circumstances in the US are an exception rather than the rule amongst the industrialized countries (cf. Batten, 1981; Cameron, 1985; Giannaros and Kolluri, 1985).

3 Extra-economic factors explaining inflation are seldom incorporated into economic theories, although they dominate the case studies. Inflation performance in West Germany, for example, is explained by economists through variables such as the historical experience of hyperinflation, the lack of conflict in society, the structure of the union system and so on (Fels, 1977; Borchardt, 1982b; Kloten et al., 1985). It is also conceded that inflation is primarily a form of distributive struggle and not simply a problem of monetary economics (cf. Borchardt, 1982b; Scherf, 1988), but this is not built into the economic models. John Goldthorpe (1978, 186–7) has remarked that the introduction of 'residual categories' into economists' analyses points to deficits in the theoretical framework. These are phenomena which are frequently recognized as important, but little attempt is made to incorporate them into the theoretical framework.[4]

4 The approach of mainstream economics can generally be criticized for tracing only the *sources*, but not explaining the underlying socio-political *causes* of economic phenomena. In the words of Mancur Olson (1982, 4): '[T]hey trace the water in the river to the streams and lakes from which it comes, but they do not explain the rain.' Or, as Paul Whiteley (1986, 84–5) puts it with respect to inflation: 'For example, theory might demonstrate a stable relationship between excessive increases in the money supply beyond those warranted by the growth of productive potential and inflation. But this is a rather inadequate theory of inflation, since it does not explain why some governments choose to print money in this way, when others do not. [...] A truly general theory would deal in fundamental causes, which are rooted in the social structure and political organisation of society. The economics paradigm very often chooses to ignore these.' This critique can be summarized as

follows: economic theories alone can explain *how* growth or inflation comes about, but they alone cannot explain *why* (Hirsch, 1978, 263).

In the public policy literature generated from the political science discipline, inflation has not been a very prominent research topic, since its subfield of economic policy research has focused more on unemployment and labour market policy. But some attempts have been made to explain inflation in social science terms, either by identifying social constellations conducive to inflation (Goldthorpe, 1978; Maier, 1978) or by explaining it through the use of political or sociological variables (e.g. the analyses in Lindberg and Maier, 1985). Most often single hypotheses are tested, often in international comparison. These include the influence of party government (Hibbs 1977), the size of the public sector (Peacock and Ricketts, 1978), structures of the interest group and union system (Crouch, 1978, 1985) or the extent of budget deficits (Cameron, 1985). However, due to different sample sizes, results are not consistent and the explained variation is not very high. These studies might well be improved by combining several of the aforementioned variables, by complementing them with findings from studies in the tradition of New Political Economy (e.g. on the behaviour of central banks, as in Alesina (1988)) and by testing such a model against a dataset that includes all OECD countries.

To sum up the argument, and at the same time to characterize the research strategy pursued in this chapter, we would suggest that a combination of economic and political science approaches to the explanation of inflation (understood as a form of distributive struggle) seems particularly promising. What is necessary is to build on economic knowledge about the process of inflation and complement that knowledge with the explanatory power which seems to be offered by tracing the origin of that process in political and social institutions.

Focusing on institutions has important consequences for the explanation of inflation rates. Due to the relatively static character of institutions, *intra* country variation of inflation over time will probably be best explained by the use of intermediary economic variables (such as import prices of certain commodities). But *inter* country variation (for instance, the question of why similar external shocks led to such different rates of inflation in the 1970s) is probably best explained through institutions, by looking at the *causes* of inflation rather than at its *sources*. The objective of this study will be to test a model built around these premises against the evidence provided by comparative data from the OECD nations.

In the composition of the OECD sample, I follow Lijphart (1984, 38), who includes all OECD countries that have been under continuous democratic rule since World War II, excluding only Iceland and Luxembourg for reasons of size. The resulting sample includes the following 18 countries (country codes in brackets): Australia (AUS), Austria (A), Belgium (BEL), Canada (CAN), Denmark (DK), Finland (FIN), France (FRA), the Federal Republic of Germany (GER), Ireland (IRL), Italy (ITA), Japan (J), the Netherlands (NL), New Zealand (NZ), Norway (NOR), Sweden (SWE), Switzerland (SWITZ), the UK (UK) and the US (US).

Some Hypotheses on Inflation

The historical experience of high inflation or hyperinflation Most books that deal with inflation from an empirical perspective include chapters with case studies on Germany (cf. Salant and Krause, 1977; Medley 1982a; Lindberg and Maier, 1985). This is probably so because the German example is indeed extraordinary: in the first half of the 20th century, Germany experienced two large (even hyper-)inflations, whereas in the second half of the century, it has been the country with (on average) the lowest rate of inflation. This striking change has led many scholars to assume a connection between the two incidents, the historical experience of hyperinflation and the social earthquakes triggered by it often being singled out as determinants of the low inflation profile of the Federal Republic after 1950 (e.g. Fels, 1977; Medley, 1982a; Kloten et al., 1985).

There are good grounds for this hypothesis, in particular in terms of an argument from the social consequences of hyperinflation that Germany experienced in the beginning of the 1920s. With an average rate of inflation that in 1923 equalled $2 * 10^{12}$ (Maier, 1978, 46), all monetary assets were practically destroyed. Inflation on this scale had severe consequences for the savings and wealth of much of the population. By the beginning of 1923, the value of the Mark had already sunk to 0.0004 per cent of its 1913 value, and a pre-war bond of 10000 Mark had sunk to the value of only 4 Goldmark (Borchardt, 1982b: 156). These traumatic experiences, and the resulting pauperization of the middle class (further enhanced by the economic depression of the late 1920s) have often been related to the rise of National Socialism, the ultimate defeat of which resulted in another inflation (albeit a suppressed one because of fixed prices). In the period between 1945 and 1948, the German economy was awash with money, but money nearly lost its function as the black market developed more and more into a barter economy. Currency reform in 1948 (the introduction of the D-Mark) again wiped out all monetary assets denominated in the old currency. It is often argued that this expropriation, experienced twice in less than 30 years, led to a deep-rooted aversion to inflation and thus is the cause for the low inflation profile of Germany after 1950.

But although this seems logical at first sight, two points would have to be addressed before the argument could be accepted. First, it remains unclear how the alleged inflation aversion has actually been translated into economic policy and practice. Second, the argument does not stand the test of international comparison. Although it is true that two of the three countries with the lowest rates of inflation after 1960 had lived through the experience of hyperinflation in the 20th century (i.e. Germany and Austria, where the rate in 1922 was 1600 per cent), the third country, Switzerland, did not experience high rates of inflation during this period (Mitchell, 1986).

Moreover, there are a number of countries that *did* experience very high rates of inflation or even hyperinflation in the first half of the 20th century and still are inflation-prone in the second half. Italy and France in the 1940s or Greece, where inflation amounted to a rate of $5 * 10^{10}$, may serve as examples (Maier, 1978; Mitchell, 1986). These experiences shared many of the characteristics of the German inflationary episodes, and Borchardt (1982b: 156) is probably correct in his view that it makes little difference whether one's wealth is reduced to a thousandth or a billionth of its previous level.

This does not mean that the experience of hyperinflation in Germany and Austria is irrelevant to subsequent policy. Rather it means that the mechanisms which transmit these experiences have to be identified with precision. Germany, for example, is a country that has apparently 'learn[t] from catastrophes' (Schmidt, 1989b), and, in consequence, has made a conscious attempt to design anti-inflationary institutions, such as its central bank, the Bundesbank. Indeed, the Bundesbank has sternly objected to the assumption that inflationary experience is a sufficient guarantor of monetary stability, because that might pave the way for attempts to circumscribe its independence (Schlesinger, 1991, 2).

Thus, we may conclude that the historical experience of high or hyperinflation cannot alone explain the low inflation performance of the Federal Republic, Austria and Switzerland. This does not mean that the experience should be regarded as irrelevant. Rather what international comparison tells us is that we must seek further to locate the specific conditions under which it is relevant and the consequences that have or have not been drawn from this experience.

The party-political hypothesis A party-political hypothesis was among the major political science contributions to the explanation of inflationary performance and was first advanced by Douglas Hibbs in an important article in 1977. He built his attempt to provide a combined explanation for both unemployment and inflation on two premises. The first is the existence of the so-called 'Phillips-Curve' – a stable trade-off between inflation and unemployment. Hibbs extended this concept by postulating the existence of a Phillips-Curve relationship not only in one country at different times, but also between different countries at the same time. The second premise is the postulated existence of objective economic interests of different classes which correspond with the subjective preferences of those classes. Thus, according to Hibbs, 'lower income and occupational status groups are best served by a relatively low unemployment-high inflation macroeconomic configuration, whereas a comparatively high unemployment-low inflation configuration is compatible with the interests and preferences of upper income and occupational status groups' (Hibbs, 1977, 1467). Hibbs then argued that interest groups would exert influence on political parties and, for that reason, the respective parties would seek to realize the trade-off preferences of their constituents. On such a basis, it might be assumed that each country's position on the Phillips Curve could easily be derived from the party composition of its government over time.

The argument has two roots. One is empirical research about preferences and target choices of both political parties and interest groups in economic policy; this builds on the work of Etienne Kirschen and others. According to this argument, the primary economic priority of conservative governments is price stability, whereas the priority of leftist governments is full employment, with price stability being clearly less important (Kirschen et al., 1964, 224–5). The second root of Hibbs' argument lies in certain assumptions about the distributive consequences of inflation that mainly seem to depend on the experiences of hyperinflations such as the German one of the early 1920s, when wage earners could make relative gains at the expense of rentier capitalists (which, again, may have influenced the programmes of the parties and interest groups mentioned in Kirschen's work).

Hibbs tested his hypothesis in relation to 12 West European and North American states for the time period from 1960 to 1969 and found empirical support: the relationship between the rate of inflation and the participation of socialist parties in government was positive and amounted to r = 0.74, which seemed to confirm the party-political hypothesis (Hibbs, 1977, 1473). However, analyses by later scholars indicated that this result could not be generalized. Once the sample was extended to include all 21 OECD nations, the relationship between the variables fell drastically to r = 0.31 (Schmidt, 1982, 109). Moreover, if the time period under consideration was changed, the result was actually reversed: for the time period 1974–80, the relationship between the party-political composition of governments and the rate of inflation was r = –0.30, indicating that, during this period, the rate of inflation was lower under leftist than under bourgeois governments (Schmidt, 1983, 24). David Cameron, who also tested this hypothesis, concludes that '[a]n analysis of data on twenty-one countries indicates that the argument that leftist parties are more likely to generate inflation than non-leftist parties is simply wrong – or, at the least, time-bound and true only for an era when inflation was not a significant macroeconomic problem for most nations' (Cameron, 1985, 246). Cameron's findings are quite different from those of Hibbs, as was research undertaken by Kurt Rothschild (1986a).

Given the importance of the argument, we present below the relationship between party political influence on government and rates of inflation for the period under investigation, between 1974 and 1988. The data on partisan control are measured on a monthly basis. The classification of parties is based on Schmidt (1991), who makes minor modifications to the classification presented by Cameron (1985).

Table 2.2: Correlation of partisan control of government and inflation, 1974–88, for 18 OECD countries

	Partisan control (A)		
	Left	Centre	Right
Inflation	–0.05	–0.11	0.17
	Partisan control (B)		
Inflation	0.01	0.00	–0.02

Measurement: (A) head of government; (b) percentage of cabinet seats

Source: Calculated from OECD, 1979, 1989 and Schmidt 1991.

The data in Table 2.2 evidently do *not* support the hypothesis of a clear relationship between rates of inflation and the partisan control of government. For the period under investigation, there is absolutely *no relationship* between these variables.[5]

That the hypothesized relationship does not hold is perhaps best understood in terms of the changing character of the inflationary experience this century and our knowledge of the distributional consequence of different types of inflation. Contrary to the view that certain definable groups gain advantages or disadvantages from distinct economic policies associated with more or less inflation, and the corollary of objective class and group economic interests (Hibbs, 1977; Scharpf, 1988; Alesina, 1989), recent evidence suggests that the distributive consequences of contemporary inflation are by no means so clear-cut. The contemporary experience has been of 'creeping' rather than of 'catastrophic' inflation, and our understanding of the distributive consequences of the former can be summarized as follows (cf. Bach and Stephenson, 1974; Maier, 1978; Piachaud, 1978; Fricke, 1981; Scherf, 1988; Hoffmann, 1990):

- Distributive consequences are very complex, and the 'classical' hypotheses concerning wage lag, and transfer-income lag and redistribution from the creditor to the debtor are no longer valid in respect of the contemporary phenomenon of long-lasting, but relatively low rates of inflation.
- Transfer incomes, which are often determined by political decisions, sometimes even increase in real terms, and wage-lags are not found in empirical research. The relatively low variation in the inflation rate makes it possible to anticipate probable outcomes, which in turn diminishes their economic impact.
- In general, the positions of functional income groups seem to remain stable, and there is no longer an equivalence between functional income groups and social groups as was true, for example, of the rentier capitalists of the early 20th century. Today, most people have multiple economic roles, in some contexts gaining advantages from inflation, in others suffering disadvantages.

Summarizing these points, it may be suggested that the most dramatic political consequences of inflation stem only from the 'catastrophic' type which undercuts the identity of functional and social status. The fact that such an identity is no longer clear-cut in advanced industrial societies makes it unlikely that coalitions for or against inflation will re-emerge as a major cleavage issue; the formation of political coalitions is more likely to be determined by other factors such as occupational or class identification. It therefore comes as little surprise to discover that, contrary to the party-political hypothesis, there is no detectable relationship between party influence on government and rates of inflation. Table 2.3 confirms this further, demonstrating that whilst the Federal Republic, Austria and Switzerland experienced very similar low rates of inflation in the post-war era, the governments of these countries manifested considerable differences in terms of their partisan composition (data in table from Schmidt, 1991, Table 1).

Table 2.3: Long-run partisan composition of government in Austria, the Federal Republic of Germany and Switzerland, 1949–90

	Right	Centre	Left
Austria	1.6	35.2	60.9
Germany (West)	22.2	51.1	26.3
Switzerland	47.0	30.3	22.8
Mean of 18 democratic OECD countries	39.0	30.4	29.2

Note: Partisan composition is measured as share of cabinet seats.
Source: Author's calculations from Schmidt, 1991.

An Institutional Model

The preceding section of this chapter has demonstrated that relatively simple historical or party-political variables cannot contribute very much to the explanation of the difference between inflation rates in the three German-speaking countries and the rest of the OECD. In this section, we seek to locate a set of variables that is capable of explaining this difference. The approach focuses on institutional variables that have an effect on economic outcomes.[6]

Strikes and Social Consensus

Inflation, as has been pointed out above, can be understood as a form of distributive struggle. It is therefore likely to occur in countries that are marked by a high degree of social dissent. But as this dissent is itself hard to measure, the degree of strike activity[7] can usefully serve as a proxy measure of dissent (cf. McCallum, 1983; Jackson et al., 1972). Moreover, the use of this proxy makes sense in economic terms, and particularly in the context of an analysis of price stability, since strike activity is often explicitly designed to exert upward pressure on wage levels and can therefore be interpreted as a cost-push factor, adding to inflationary pressure. The justification of this assumption needs some brief discussion.

Strike activity and increase in earnings Research on the relationship between strike activity and increases in earnings has been conducted at both a micro and a macro level. Micro level tests check the relationship between strike activity and earnings for certain industrial branches or single economies, often using time series data. Studies for the Federal Republic show different results: for the time period 1952 to 1977, Fautz (1979) finds that strike activity makes a significant and relatively stable contribution to the explanation of the rise in standard wages, whereas Schnabel is sceptical about such a systematic contribution, though he does acknowledge the occurrence of such an effect in 1970 (Schnabel, 1989, 89). However, the Federal Republic may be a bad case to test this hypothesis, as it displays low inflation, low strike volume and has a moderate labour movement, so that severe cases of distributive struggle are very unlikely to occur (Medley, 1982a, 145–6). On the other hand, evidence on a micro level from countries that are more strike-prone demonstrates that strikes have a clear impact on increases in nominal wages (Epstein and Schor, 1986, 8–9 for Italy; Stengos and Swidinsky,1990 for Canada).

Studies that approach the question at a macro level (using international comparisons) also clearly demonstrate a positive relationship between strike activity and increase in earnings: McCallum (1983), for instance, discusses the phenomenon of real wage rigidity, which is increased through the lack of social consensus. Under these circumstances, he argues, an external shock leads to inflationary pressure. Strike activity, he concludes, is the 'key-factor accounting for inter-country differences in inflation in the seventies' (1983, 802). David Cameron, in comparing 18 OECD countries, finds a correlation of 0.84 between the strike coefficient (see below) for the time period 1965 to 1981 and the increase in the rate of change in earnings between 1965–67 and 1980–82 (1984, 152–3). In addition, he finds a very strong correlation of 0.93 between the increase in earnings and the increase in the rate of inflation (157).

It can be concluded that support for the hypothesis of a strong relationship between strike activity, on the one hand, and increase in earnings, on the other, is sufficient for us to posit the incidence of strike activity as a pivotal institutional variable for the explanation of cross-national divergences in the rate of inflation.

Measuring strike activity Strike volume data from the International Labour Office (ILO) are only available in the form of lost working days. For the purposes of international comparison, however, it is necessary to make an adjustment for the varying sizes of economies. The most appropriate measure here seems to be the number of employed people in non-agricultural sectors of an economy. The strike indicator used throughout this chapter is therefore calculated as working days lost per annum in industrial disputes per 1000 employees in non-agricultural sectors.[8]

Since this indicator tends to vary significantly over time, at least in some countries (including the FRG, where long periods of nearly complete labour quiescence tend to be interrupted from time to time by significant strike waves), it seems appropriate to use averages over longer time periods in order to exclude distortions in the measurement of the extent of cost-push. Strike coefficients for 18 OECD countries for different time periods are presented in Table 2.4 (data taken from ILO *Yearbook of Labour Statistics*).

Table 2.4: Average rates of the strike coefficient in OECD countries, 1965–85

	1965–85	1965–73	1974–85
Australia	440.06	346.98	544.78
Austria	6.35	15.2	1.92
Belgium	222.6	275.55	192.34
Canada	734.27	711.06	751.68
Denmark	204.89	228.77	183.4
Finland	436	445.26	429.05
France	112.9	190.65	141.30
Germany (West)	36.72	27.55	43.6
Ireland	652.93	674.61	635.19
Italy	1029.55	1124.11	958.63
Japan	70.95	98.8	50.06
Netherlands	25.9	31.13	21.98
Norway	37.7	11.39	57.44
New Zealand	345.87	200.47	454.91
Sweden	89.86	46.25	122.57
Switzerland	1.14	0.68	1.44
UK	450.77	381.5	502.71
US	382.41	563.95	246.26
Average	293.38	298.55	291.91
Standard Deviation	283.80	300.09	284.01

Source: Author's calculations from ILO Yearbook of Labour Statistics, several volumes.

Strikes and rates of inflation We are now ready to test our hypothesis – that a clear correlation exists between strike activity and rates of inflation – against the data for 18 OECD countries.

For the time period of 1974 to 1985, the relationship is a very strong one: r = 0.77. This is very similar to the correlation reported by Cameron (1984, 157) for 18 countries between 1965 and 1981 (0.78).

The resulting scattergram, displayed in Figure 2.1, demonstrates in addition that our hypothesized 'families' of nations show rather similar locations:

- the three German-speaking countries perform best, with very low rates of inflation and very low levels of strike activity. But their inflation performance is even better than the trend would lead us to expect;
- the Anglo-Saxon countries (with the exception of the US) have relatively high rates of strike activity, and there are cases both *above* and *below* trend;
- the Scandinavian countries, Norway, Sweden and Denmark, have low levels of strike activity, but their inflation rates are all *above* trend.

Strikes and inflation: an investigation into causality The correlation between strike activity and rates of inflation alone, however, does not tell us anything about the direction of causality. It could be argued that instead of strikes causing inflation (via cost-push), causality runs the other way: high rates of inflation lead to increased strike activity because inflation intensifies the distributive struggle. If this were the case, countries with high rates of inflation should then experience high and/or increasing strike activity.

Here we argue that there is strong evidence in support of the view that, for the time period under consideration at least, *strikes caused inflation*. This is not to seek to simplify what is admittedly a very complex relationship or to deny either the possibility of feedback processes or the fact that an interactive relationship is likely to exist between strikes and inflation (because high rates of inflation can very well lead to strikes in order to maintain real income). However, if certain stipulated conditions are met, the main impact in the period under consideration runs from strikes to inflation.

Contrary to the effect displayed in Figure 2.1, for the time period from 1965 to 1973, there is no significant relationship between strike activity and the rate of inflation (r = –0.10). Thus the effect we observed above appears to be time-bound. But if inflation caused strikes, we would expect a positive correlation between the average rate of inflation between 1965 and 1973, and the degree of strike activity in a later period, such as the average value for the period 1974 to 1985. This, however, is not the case.

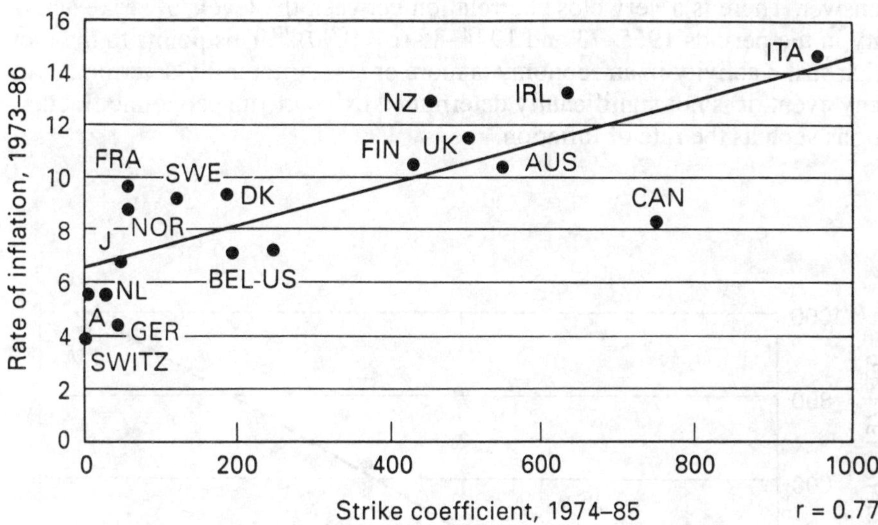

Source: Author's calculations from OECD and ILO data.

Figure 2.1: Strike coefficients and rates of inflation in the OECD, 1974–85

The correlation between these two variables for 18 OECD countries is r = 0.00.

Apparently countries with relatively high rates of inflation between 1965 and 1973 could just as well experience near labour quiescence as marked labour militancy. This does not fit well with the assumption of causality running from inflation to strike activity. But do high rates of inflation at least lead to an increase in labour militancy? Again, there is no empirical evidence for this hypothesis. The correlation between the average rate of inflation from 1965 to 1973 and the change in the strike coefficient between 1965–73 and 1970–79 is r = 0.14. This finding allows us to reject the hypothesis that the amount of strike activity in a country is determined by the rates of inflation experienced earlier and to assume that, at least during the period 1973 to 1985, causality ran from strikes to inflation.[9]

But how then can the amount of strike activity in a country be explained if inflation apparently does not play a major role? Figure 2.2 provides an answer. There is a very close correlation between the levels of strike activity in the periods 1965–73 and 1974–85 (r = 0.90).[10] This points to the fact that strike activity in an economy is more or less structurally determined; in any event, it is not significantly determined by short-run economic fluctuations such as the rate of inflation.

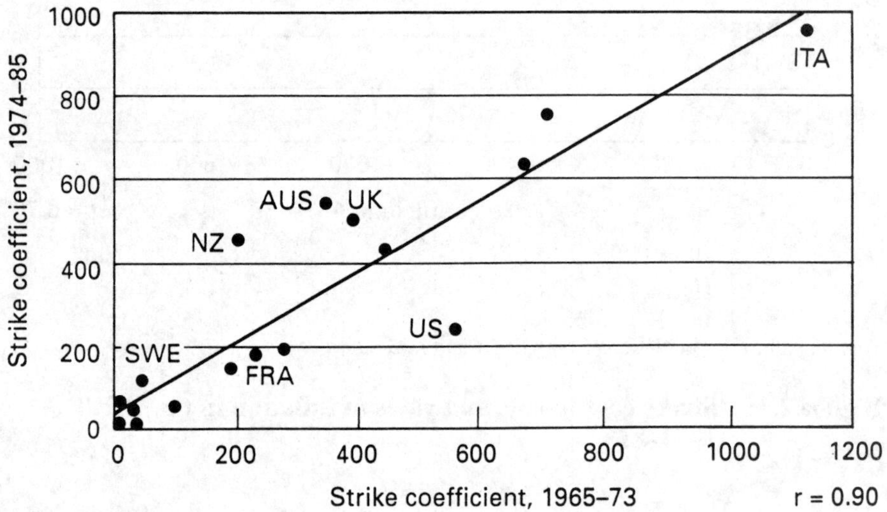

Source: Author's calculations from ILO data.

Figure 2.2: Average strike coefficients in the OECD, 1965–73 and 1974–85

Such an interpretation is compatible with findings produced by research on trade unions and strikes, which suggest that degrees of labour militancy are largely determined by the organizational features of trade unions (degree of centralization, ideological stance, etc.) and the system of wage-bargaining institutions in place (institutionalization of conflict resolution, degree of employer coordination, etc.) (Crouch, 1985; Armingeon, 1992). It is also compatible with findings on the influence of corporatist structures; for instance, there is a consistently high correlation (in the range of approximately –.70), between the corporatism indicator constructed by Schmidt (1982) and the strike coefficients for the different time periods considered in Table 2.4.

How, then, can an explanation be found for the fact that strikes caused inflation in the period after 1973, when, they apparently did not do so before 1973? The solution lies in the change in the exchange rate regime that took place in 1973, when there was a switch to floating rates. Under the old system of fixed exchange rates, with the member countries being obliged to support these rates (via measures of monetary policy), rates of inflation could not differ very much (see above). Under these circumstances, the inflationary pressure of strikes and of large wage increases in any one country were distributed more or less evenly across the entire system and did not, therefore, have much influence on that country's rate of inflation. This changed completely after the Bretton Woods system had collapsed and there was no longer any obligation for monetary authorities to intervene. Each country was now able to choose its own rate of inflation, just as it was allowed to insulate itself through monetary policy from foreign inflation. This resulted in the inflationary pressure emanating from labour militancy now taking effect in the country of origin itself. Under these circumstances, high wage inflation in a country led to high rates of price inflation in that same country. Countries with labour market structures of a particular type fell victim to a vicious circle of high strike volume and high inflation.

Hence, we may conclude that there is strong evidence in support of the hypothesis that, under conditions of flexible exchange rates, labour militancy (and the high wage increases induced by it) create strong inflationary pressure. The three German-speaking countries under consideration experienced low inflationary pressure from this source due to their marked degree of labour quiescence.

However, the systematic deviations of our three families of nations from the trend demonstrated in Figure 2.1 point to the fact that wage increases alone cannot explain inflation performance. This leads to the question of whether these deviations can be explained by reference to further institutional characteristics which vary systematically as between families of nations.

The Institutional Status of the Central Bank

In the parlance of economics, the previous section utilized a cost-push theory to explain inflation, assuming that a high degree of strike activity leads to steeply rising wages, which in turn feed back into rising prices. But such a cost-push effect, as economic theory points out, is not in itself a sufficient condition for the development of inflation. 'It is easily overlooked that a continuing inflation that is caused by non-monetary factors needs maintenance by a rise in monetary demand, which ultimately means a rise in the money supply' (Woll, 1981, 507). Monetary conditions in a country therefore have to be taken into account to complement any explanation of inflation.

Thus another important institutional variable for the explanation of variances in inflation and policies against inflation is the character of a country's central bank (cf. Woolley, 1985; Scharpf, 1987; Alesina, 1988; Kurzer, 1988). By executing a country's monetary policy – through, for example, discount rates, active pressure on the level of interest rates, and the cost and availability of credit – central banks have important macroeconomic instruments at their disposal. It is therefore a matter of some significance whether or not a central bank is independent from the government administration (and thus constitutes an independent actor in economic policy). Since politicians and administrations may well be tempted to use inflation as an instrument for softening distributive conflicts, it may be hypothesized that price stability is better achieved by independent central banks that are not bound by such considerations.

Historical variations in the relative importance of central banks for economic policy-making The importance of central bank independence was already a matter of debate in the 19th century (cf. Goodhart, 1988), and it remains so today. Political and democratic arguments can be advanced both for and against a high degree of independence (cf. Caesar, 1980; Alesina, 1989). Historically, the role of central banks and their importance in economic policy-making have varied considerably depending on the framework within which they operate. This historical development and the conditions determining the importance of central banks will now briefly be reviewed.

Modern central banks generally have two tasks (Goodhart, 1989, 89): they assume responsibility both for the functioning of the banking system and for overall monetary conditions in an economy. Historically, the first aspect is the more important: 'Central banks were not created for the purpose of macroeconomic stabilisation. On the contrary, in every Western setting central banks emerged as a response to needs for a central institution to serve other banks' (Woolley, 1985, 319). The second historical task of central banks, founded as early as 1668 (Sweden), was the provision of credit to the state and the handling of the state's financial matters. The German Reichsbank, for example, emerged from the Prussian Staatsbank that (as the Prussian 'Seehandlung') had been founded and functioned mainly as a state bank to further the financial interests of Prussia (Goodhart,

1988, 105ff.; see also Holtfrerich, 1988). Central banks, therefore, often had an organizational proximity to the state.[11]

The role of central banks as important actors in the macroeconomic policy arena developed only in the course of the 20th century, the importance of this role varying in accordance with the exchange rate system (cf. Caesar, 1980, 348–9). During the period of the gold standard, both the prevailing mechanism and the banks' primary goal of defending a country's gold reserves limited the central banks' economic responsibility and room for manoeuvre. Controversies between the central bank and the administration were hardly imaginable. After the break with the gold standard and the introduction of a more active economic policy in the period between the world wars, claims for increased state influence on the central banks were advanced; this often led to their nationalization.

After World War II, opinions on central bank independence were ambiguous: on the one hand, a need for macroeconomic coordination of monetary and fiscal policy to achieve stabilization goals was acknowledged; on the other hand, there was plenty of experience with the inflationary consequences of excessive growth in the money supply induced by the state. However, in general, insofar as exchange rate adjustments were not acceptable outcomes, the central banks' room for manoeuvre in monetary policy, under the Bretton Woods system, was very limited.

With the end of the pegged exchange rate regime in 1973, it became possible for central banks to embrace a sovereign monetary policy; the importance of such policy grew considerably. This policy transformation was further enhanced by the growing importance of monetarist thought in macroeconomics, amounting to a change in paradigm. Simultaneously, the topic became an interesting one for political science, with a substantial body of the literature assigning a pivotal economic policy role to central banking institutions (e.g. Uusitalo, 1984; Scharpf, 1987; Schmidt, 1988a; Kurzer, 1988; Sturm, 1989).

However, as noted above, the status of a central bank as a political actor depends crucially on its independence from the administration. The problems of measuring the extent of central bank independence will be dealt with in the following sections.

Central bank independence in the Federal Republic, Austria and Switzerland Organizational features are important determinants of central bank independence although, in themselves, they are insufficient (Woolley, 1985, 326). They determine, for example, whether the bank alone is responsible for monetary policy or whether it must coordinate these measures with other institutions, such as the finance ministry. On a personnel level, it makes a difference whether members of the bank's board can be removed only for cause or also for political reasons, since this may discourage the bank's attempts to pursue an independent monetary policy. In this section, the focus is on the organizational features and the policy stance of the central banks in the three countries constituting the German-speaking family of nations.[12]

The members of the governing boards of these nations' central banks are extremely independent: their terms of office last from four to eight years (considerably longer than in many other countries) and they cannot be removed for political reasons. They are also not subject to parliamentary control. The banks' degree of functional autonomy is also high, and no coordination of decisions with other institutions is required.

It is undisputed in the literature that the German central bank, the Bundesbank, enjoys an exceptionally high degree of independence from the administration (Caesar, 1981; Narr-Lindner, 1984; Alesina, 1988, 1989) and that it is a crucial political actor (cf. Scharpf, 1987; Schmidt, 1988a; Emminger, 1986; Sturm, 1989).[13] The institutional organization of the Bundesbank has deliberately been constructed to preserve its independence from influences emanating both from the state apparatus and from interest groups (Bethusy-Huc, 1962; Wildenmann, 1969).

The Swiss Nationalbank is also rated as very independent (Caesar, 1981; Alesina, 1988, 1989), but differing views are advanced in the case of the Austrian Nationalbank. The latter is seen as less independent than the Bundesbank, a fact which is substantiated by its 'institutional subordination' (Kurzer, 1988, 32), its personal integration into the social partnership and its comprehensive obligation to support the government (Scharpf, 1987, 253–4). It may, be argued, however, that a legal commitment to support the government also exists in the Federal Republic and in Switzerland and that *de facto* conditions matter more than legal definitions. In addition, it has been argued that the Austrian Nationalbank enjoys a functional autonomy that is not subject to greater restrictions than those imposed on Germany's or Switzerland's central banks (Wenger, 1979).

Katzenstein (1985b, 240) concludes that the Austrian Nationalbank is, in principle, independent, but, in fact always acts in agreement with the finance ministry. This points to an important fact – the Austrian consensus about a 'hard currency policy' that, from 1974 to the present, has been part of the strategy of 'Austro-Keynesianism'. That strategy consists of the pursuit of a pegged Schilling-DM exchange rate which is the main goal of monetary policy.[14] This policy of importing price stability has been pursued with great constancy even in economically hard times. So even if the Austrian Nationalbank may be rated by some authors as institutionally less independent than its German or Swiss counterparts (cf. Schmidt, 1988b), this does not matter here. What is important with respect to inflation is the ability of the administration to influence day-to-day monetary policy and force the bank, for instance, to pursue an expansionary monetary policy. In Austria, such government manipulation is impossible, since, in effect, Austrian monetary policy is actually made in Frankfurt, and is therefore completely exogenous to the Austrian administration. Thus, for the purposes of this chapter, the Austrian Nationalbank will be considered as being as independent as the Bundesbank.

Measuring the independence of central banks Any systematic indicator for the measurement of central bank independence that can be used in international comparison should include three aspects:

1 the degree of legal independence (veto power of other institutions against measures of monetary policy; an obligation that the bank coordinate its measures with the administration, etc.);
2 the degree of personnel independence (procedure for the nomination of the central bank's board and governor; conditions for their removal, etc.);
3 the degree of economic independence (an obligation to buy government bonds; the ability to control the money market, etc.).

Ideally, an indicator should also take account of the variation of these parameters over time, as these conditions are subject to change and reform.[15]

Unfortunately data that fulfil these demands are not available. Scholars who have undertaken comparative work on central bank independence have used data (often slightly modified) from several unpublished papers by Robin Bade and Michael Parkin of the University of Western Ontario (e.g. McCallum, 1983; Alesina, 1988, 1989). But as the operational criteria of this indicator are unpublished, modifications to allow for reforms cannot be made. On the other hand, this is the only indicator that is available for a sufficiently large number of countries.

Data on central bank independence that meet the demands set out above have been collected by Grilli, Masciandaro and Tabellini (1991), but unfortunately important countries are missing from their dataset. Tests, however, have shown that there is a relatively high correlation ($r = 0.7$ for $n = 13$) between their indicator and Alesina's, which is based mainly on the work of Bade and Parkin (Alesina, 1989). Given such a degree of coincidence between the two measures, we utilize the one with the broader country coverage.

The data are displayed in Table 2.5.[16] It should be emphasized that these figures are at best indicative and do not account for changes over time, although such changes have certainly taken place (e.g. in Italy during the period under consideration). Clearly, the construction of a satisfying indicator of central bank independence for a sufficiently broad range of nations remains an important task for future research.

Table 2.5: Degree of central bank independence (1 = minimum, 4 = maximum)

Australia	1	Italy	1.5
Austria	4	Japan	3
Belgium	2	Netherlands	2
Canada	2	New Zealand	1
Denmark	2	Norway	2
Finland	2	Sweden	2
France	2	Switzerland	4
Germany, West	4	UK	2
Ireland	–	US	3

Source: Alesina, 1989 and author's addition (see text).

Central bank independence and inflation performance In the preceding sections, we have seen that monetary policy has become an important macroeconomic instrument under the system of flexible exchange rates. But this also means that monetary policy can be used for the manipulation of macroeconomic outcomes; politicians could well have an interest in such manipulations to achieve partisan goals or at specific points in the electoral cycle. Theoretical incentives for this behaviour have been much discussed in the literature on the theory of political business cycles (e.g. Alesina, 1988, 1989). Independence of central banks from political influence could thus reduce a country's inclination to inflation: 'If the politicians currently in office do not have direct control over monetary policy, they cannot engage in partisan or electoral policy-making' (Alesina, 1988, 39).

We shall now test this hypothesis against our data. Figure 2.3 shows a strong negative correlation (r = –0.80) between the index of central bank independence and the average rate of inflation between 1973 and 1986. This supports our hypothesis strongly. It shows that an independent central bank can apparently be a strong antagonist to government and is apparently capable of effectively holding down inflation. On the other hand, central banks under strong political influence from an administration can be subject to political manipulation for various reasons and are therefore not as effective in controlling inflation.

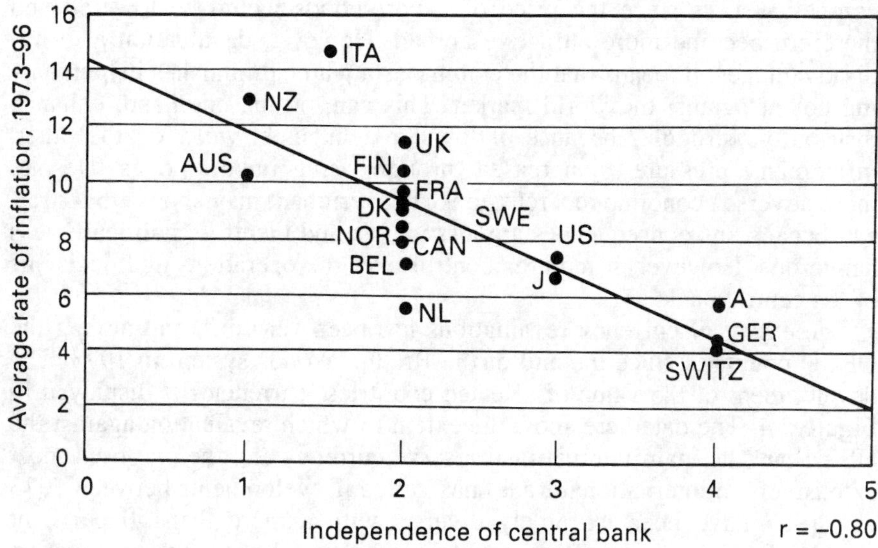

Source: Author's calculations from OECD data and Alesina, 1989 (see above).

Figure 2.3: Central bank independence and inflation performance, 1973–86

Government, central bank non-independence and currency policy It may prove useful to give an illustration of how a government may use a subservient central bank to its own political ends. Let us assume the following situation: unit labour costs in a country are rising much faster than in other countries (e.g. because of high labour militancy and high wage increases). As a result, the country's competitiveness is declining and its exports are decreasing, while its imports are rising. This leads to a current account deficit that cannot be maintained indefinitely. To bring adjustment about, a recession can be induced (e.g. by the central bank using restrictive monetary policy). Rising unemployment will lead to a lowering of wages or a much slower rise, so that the rate of increase in costs is slowed down and international competitiveness improved. But this strategy evidently implies considerable costs (unemployment, low growth, etc.), which may be politically dangerous in an electoral context.

An alternative strategy would be the devaluation of the national currency, which would also lead to an improvement in the country's international competitiveness since the price of export goods would be lowered and therefore become more attractive abroad. However, devaluation also has disadvantages: it means that the country as a whole diminishes its purchasing power against the world market. This can, on the one hand, enhance distributive struggles because of lower real income while, on the other, inflationary pressure is increased through rising import prices. Despite these adverse economic repercussions, a government may choose this strategy because its consequences are less visible and therefore politically less dangerous. However, it requires control over the operations and decisions of the central bank.

The extent of currency revaluations has been very different among the OECD countries since the end of the Bretton Woods system in 1973. The development of the value of selected countries' currencies is displayed in Figure 2.4. The data here show the extent to which revaluation against the US-dollar (the main international reserve currency and the one used most extensively in international trade) has varied. Developments between 1973 and 1987 have been extremely diverse, with a more than 50 per cent appreciation in the case of Japan and a more than 120 per cent depreciation in the case of Italy. The currencies of the three German-speaking countries all appreciated strongly. Switzerland's revaluation, at 60.9 per cent, was the strongest among the OECD countries. The Federal Republic and Austria experienced virtually identical development in their currencies (due to the Austrian hard-currency policy mentioned above and the pegging of the Schilling to the D-Mark). They appreciated by 43.6 per cent (FRG) and 45.3 per cent (Austria) against the Dollar.

The economic implications of devaluation have already been briefly mentioned. A reduction in the international purchasing power of the currency is traded against improved competitiveness, which means that the pressure for adjustment on the domestic economy (especially in the case of external shocks) is lowered. But this also means that the exchange rate can be used as an additional policy instrument – if the administration is capable of directing the central bank's operations and decisions. If it is not able to direct the central bank, the administration has to accept the exchange rate as a given datum for its actions and decisions, leaving no room to soften the adjustment pressure which the domestic economy is facing.

From this argument, we may conclude that the amount (and direction) of revaluation of a country's currency should vary systematically with the independence of its central bank from political interference. Currency depreciation should be higher in countries with less autonomous central banks

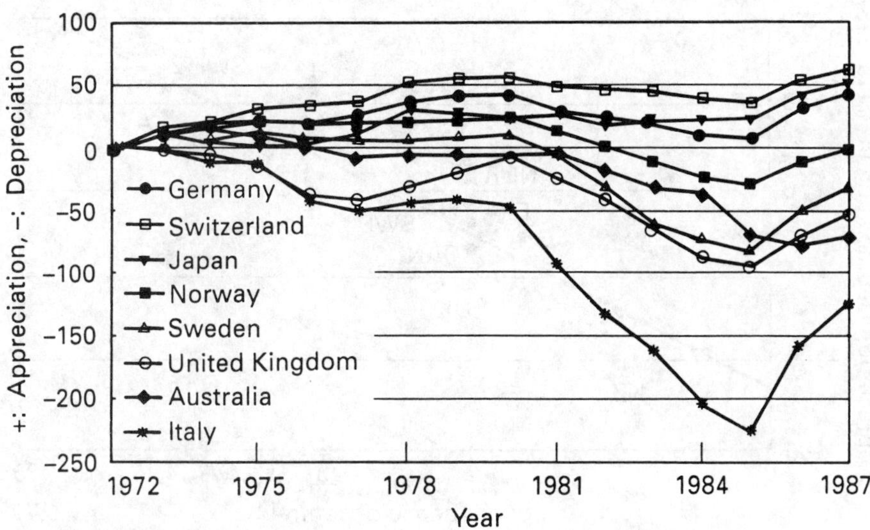

Source: Author's calculations from OECD, 1989a.

Figure 2.4: Appreciation and depreciation of selected currencies against the US-dollar since 1972 (1972 = 0)

than in those countries where central banks are independent. This is indeed the case, as Figure 2.5 demonstrates: the correlation amounts to r = 0.79.

We may conclude from this section that pursuing a strategy of currency devaluation is a 'soft option' for coping with problems of economic adjustment that can be attractive to politicians and administrations. Influence on monetary policy and particularly on the central bank is required for the pursuit of such a strategy.

The argument in the preceding sections can be summarized as follows: central banks, as the most important executor of monetary policy, have become important in economic policy-making under conditions of a regime of floating exchange rates of the kind experienced since 1973. However, the ability of central banks in the OECD area to pursue monetary policy without interference from government varies considerably. There is strong evidence that more independent central banks achieve the goal of checking

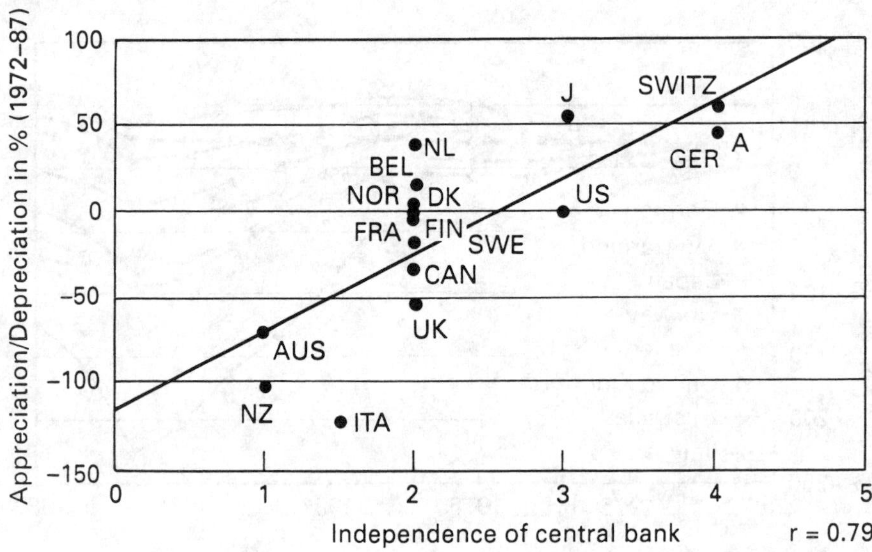

Source: Author's calculations from OECD, 1989a and Alesina, 1989 (see above).

Figure 2.5: Relationship between currency revaluation against the US-dollar and central bank independence

inflation better than do less independent central banks. In the three German-speaking countries, whose low inflation performance is to be explained here, monetary policy is highly independent of political influence because of the institutional autonomy of their central banks (a special case in this respect is Austria with its pegging of the Schilling to the D-Mark, the strong currency of Austria's most important trade partner). Thus, in these three countries, a non-permissive monetary policy has been pursued, a fact also reflected in the strong appreciation of the three countries' currencies since 1973. This appreciation, in turn, reduced inflationary pressure since it lowered the prices of imported goods. Inflationary pressure, on the contrary, was increased in those countries whose currencies have depreciated since 1973.

Fiscal Policy and Inflation

In this section, we will consider state influence on inflation via fiscal policy. Expansionary fiscal policy can, in principle, influence inflation in two ways:

1 via budget deficits, which in turn can lead to an increase in the money supply, and
2 via an increase in aggregate monetary demand, which may exert a cost-push effect on the economy if it is not operating at a very low degree of capacity utilization.

The pursuit of expansionary fiscal policy is central in the Keynesian conception of macroeconomic policy. It is used for stabilization purposes in order to pursue counter-cyclical policies and to dampen recessions caused by insufficient demand. After the oil shock in 1973–74, for example, many administrations tried to replace lost aggregate demand via state spending programmes, thereby creating inflationary pressure. It may thus be hypothesized that the degree of inflation experienced in a country is related to the extent to which expansionary fiscal policy is put into effect.

The pursuit of such an expansionary fiscal policy is, of course, dependent on many factors. These include the reception of Keynesianism, which varied considerably among the industrialized countries (cf. Hall, 1989), and differing partisan priorities (even if there was talk about a 'Keynesian consensus' between different parties). However, institutional variables are also important and, in line with the focus of rest of this chapter, the emphasis here is on political difficulties in the pursuit of expansionary fiscal policy that are rooted in the state structure.

Such an argument has been postulated by Scharpf (1987, 263–4) and builds on three premises:

- First, that the economic impact of an expansionary fiscal policy (both in terms of growth and inflation) depends on the extent to which funds are employed for this purpose (in relation to GNP).
- Second, that active fiscal policy and demand management generally are the tasks of central government.
- And third, that the political difficulty of fiscal policy increases with the volume of change required in the budget relative to the overall volume of that budget.

The initial point to note is the considerable variation in the central government budget share in GNP. This share is influenced by two parameters:

on the one hand, by government spending as a percentage of GNP and, on the other, by the degree of fiscal centralization within a state. The average ratio of the central government budget to GNP for 17 OECD countries in the period between 1974 and 1986 is displayed in Table 2.6.[17]

Table 2.6: Average ratio of central government budget to GNP, 1974–86

Austria	22.64	Italy	28.21
Australia	25.43	Japan	12.46
Belgium	26.97	Netherlands	29.76
Canada	17.27	Norway	32.48
Denmark	36.89	Sweden	29.55
Finland	22.94	Switzerland	9.29
France	20.93	UK	30.16
Germany, West	14.53	US	14.11
Ireland	32.38		
		Mean	23.12

Source: Author's calculations from OECD, 1988.

It can be seen that this ratio varies from more than 35 per cent to less than 10 per cent of GNP. As we would expect, the ratio tends to be lower in federal states (such as the US or Germany) than in unitary ones (like the Netherlands or the UK).

In order to achieve a certain economic impact, varying degrees of difficulty have to be overcome; according to the hypothesis, the greater the degree of difficulty, the lower, *ceteris paribus*, will be the increase in inflation. Given Scharpf's third premise above, it is appropriate to measure this difficulty by calculating the percentage by which the central government budget has to be raised in order to achieve an additional demand stimulus of 1 per cent of GNP (Scharpf, 1987, 265). This 'degree of difficulty' is displayed for selected countries in Figure 2.6 below. It is largely invariant over time because its components change only very slowly.

Once again, there is considerable variation among the countries (with federally organized states displaying higher degrees of difficulty), whereas variation over time is relatively small. According to our hypothesis, countries with a higher degree of 'fiscal difficulty' should experience less inflationary pressure from the state and therefore have lower rates of inflation. But before testing this hypothesis against the data, one reservation has to be

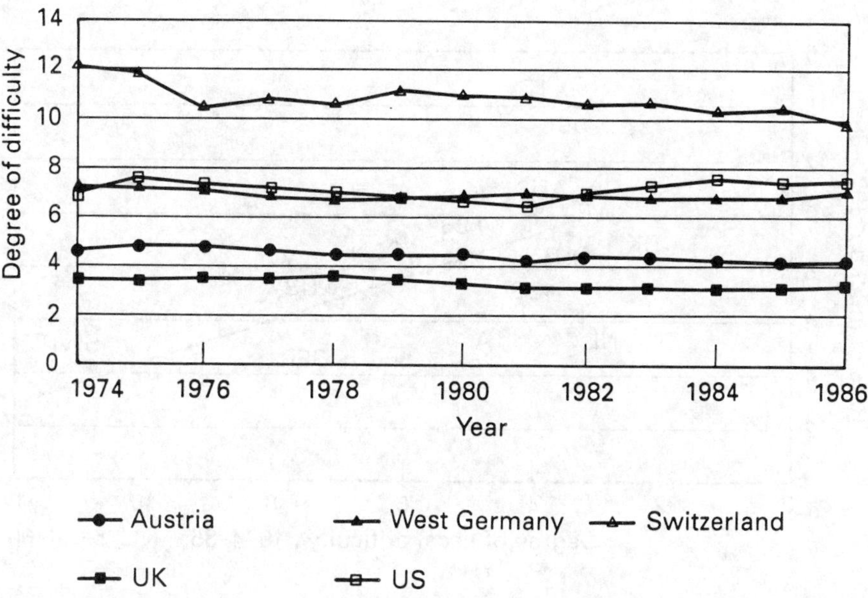

Source: Author's calculations from OECD, 1988.

Figure 2.6: Degree of difficulty of fiscal policy, 1974–86

made. The degree of 'fiscal difficulty' is, clearly, a rather crude measure. It apparently varies little over time, yet we know that, within countries, there has been considerable variation in the extent to which expansionary fiscal policy has been used. That is illustrated by the case of the UK where, despite a continuously low degree of fiscal difficulty, expansionary fiscal policy was used in the 1970s, but not in the 1980s (cf. Busch, 1989). That demonstrates what is clearly true of all areas of economic policy-making: that there is always, room for 'political will and skill'. Nevertheless, despite such changes over time, our hypothesis presumes that institutional factors should have an impact over longer time periods and in international comparison.

This does indeed turn out to be the case, as Figure 2.7 shows. The correlation between the two variables amounts to r = –0.60, offering substantial support for the institutional hypothesis.

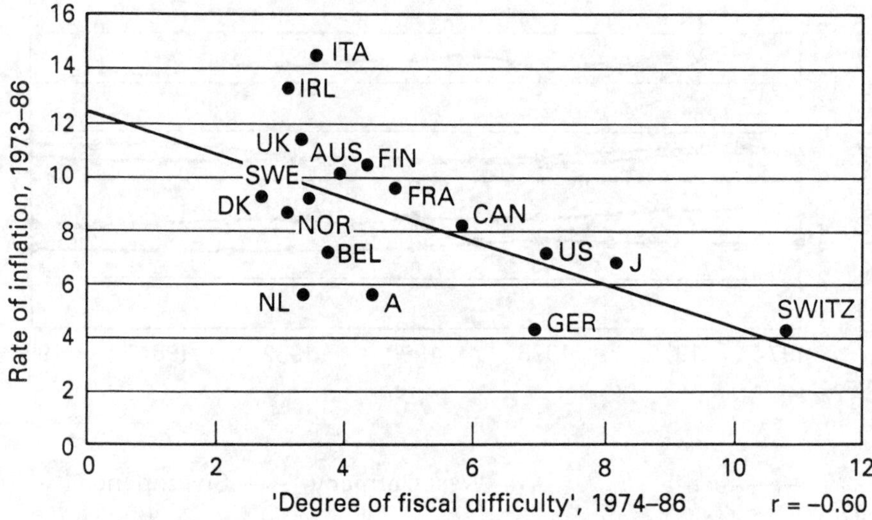

Source: Author's calculations from OECD, 1979, 1988 and 1989.

Figure 2.7: Average 'difficulty' of fiscal policy, 1974–86, and average rate of inflation in the OECD, 1973–86

Furthermore, we can see from the scattergram, that four out of five countries with high measures of difficulty are federally organized. The only unitary country in this group, Japan, shows a rather low degree of fiscal centralization (see the Appendix to this chapter for data). On the other hand, those with low degrees of difficulty tend to be unitary countries, with two exceptions: Austria and Australia, both federal countries with relatively high levels of fiscal centralization.

As to our 'families' of nations, we can see that the Scandinavian countries display a very similar pattern, with low degrees of difficulty. Two of the three German-speaking countries are among those with the highest difficulty. In the third case, Austria, a potential for easy fiscal expansion is probably not used to an extent that has inflationary consequences, because of the 'hard currency policy' outlined earlier in this chapter. Among the

English-speaking countries, there is considerable diversity, but inflation rates vary in line with fiscal difficulty.

With regard to the German-speaking countries, it should be added that further mechanisms exist to prevent the state from pursuing a policy incompatible with monetary stability. This is true of labour-market policy, for instance, where the mechanisms of funding (insurance contributions instead of taxes) work as a disincentive for a full-employment policy (cf. Schmid and Reissert, 1988).

To conclude this section, we can say that the probability of the state exerting inflationary pressure on the economy via expansionary fiscal policy varies strongly among the OECD countries. For the German-speaking countries, it is unlikely that such pressure will occur over longer periods of time as their administrations would then have to face considerable political difficulties.

Reinforcing Effects Between the Variables

In the preceding sections of this chapter, a range of institutional variables have been examined which, on their own, could influence the inflationary performance of a country. But besides these direct effects, there is also a degree of mutual reinforcement between the variables. Two such mechanisms can be noted.

First, in the period here examined, there is strong negative correlation between strike activity and the existence of central bank independence ($r = -0.59$), the point being that, in countries lacking an independent bank, militant trade unions face no institutional guarantor of monetary policy and consequently find it easier to push for higher wages. Furthermore, the countries of high militancy tend to be characterized by a relatively low degree of fiscal difficulty ($r = -0.30$), suggesting that militant labour movements seeking to exert pressure for programmes of economic stimulation are that much less likely to encounter barriers to the achievement of their objectives.

The corollary is, of course, that countries with low levels of strike activity have often had politically independent central banks. We know from the above discussion that both institutional features are likely to lower inflationary pressure in their own right. However, their combination enhances this effect. Low levels of strike activity, as has been pointed out above, are often associated with (and caused by) a high degree of aggregation in the system of collective bargaining – both on the trade union and the employer side. When, after 1973, many central banks began to announce targets for the growth of the money supply at the beginning of each year, this could be interpreted in game-theory terms as the privilege of the first move (Scharpf,

1987, 176), markedly strengthening the position of the central banks – at least of those independent enough to make fulfilment of the announced target likely. To respond to this externally-set constraint in a rational way, a high level of aggregation of the partners in collective bargaining proved to be vital.

It can be shown that these changed circumstances affected the level of strike activity. In countries with weak central banks, strike activity grew – both because the policy of the central bank was permissive and because the trade unions reacted with increased militancy to the crisis. Inflation was the consequence. In countries with strong central banks, however, strike activity was already comparatively low and now diminished still further. This can be attributed to the fact that restrictive monetary policy, executed by independent central banks, could only lead to recession and rising unemployment under circumstances of any major rise in the overall wage level. Given this ineluctable constraint, relatively strong and centralized trade unions in these countries responded to this situation with a still lower degree of militancy and greater wage restraint (for a study of the German case, see Scharpf, 1987, 165–6 and Soskice, 1990, 45).

After 1973, the correlation between central bank independence and strike activity became stronger as reactions to changing circumstances took place in each country. The relationship between both variables for the time period 1965 to 1973 is r = –0.40. In the next time period, 1970 to 1979, the correlation rises to r = –0.50, and for the time period 1974 to 1985, the correlation increases to r = –0.59.[18] Another indication of this effect is the high correlation between central bank independence and the *change* in the level of strike activity between 1965–73 and 1970–79, which amounts to r = –0.54.

Another reinforcement effect involving these institutional variables is that between the degree of central bank independence and characteristics of state structures, for the more decentralized a state is, the more likely it will be to have an independent central bank.[19] The correlation between these two variables is r = –0.56. This could be explained with reference to a tradition of power sharing in decentralized states. Power here is often distributed over several layers of government, with more 'checks and balances' mechanisms – diminishing monopoly power – than in highly centralized states. These nations seem to be far more ready to remove important tasks from the ambit of central government, even if this makes the occurrence of differences in opinion more likely. The conscious construction of the German central bank, the Bundesbank, as a *contre-gouvernement* (Wildenmann, 1969) may serve as an example; so do the renunciation of nationalization of the central banks in both Austria and Switzerland.

The degree of centralization is, of course, strongly influenced by the existence of federalism. A federal state is much more likely to be decentralized (r = –0.60) although there are exceptions, as has been pointed out above. Decentralization thus works in two ways to reduce inflation: on the one hand, it makes an independent central bank more likely and, on the other, it strongly influences the degree of 'fiscal difficulty'. The less centralized a state is, the more likely it will be to have a high degree of 'fiscal difficulty' (r = –0.69). This effect also explains the correlation between the level of central bank independence and the degree of 'fiscal difficulty', which is as high as r = 0.70.

But the existence of an independent central bank further enhances the difficulty of an expansionary (and deficit) fiscal policy. The likelihood of the state being able to reduce its debt-burden through inflation is severely diminished, because it cannot count on a future accommodative monetary policy via the central bank monetizing the deficit by buying government bonds (see Cameron, 1985, 269–70). Empirical evidence of such an effect has been found by economic studies (Burdekin and Laney, 1988). The simultaneous occurrence of a high degree of 'fiscal difficulty' and of an independent central bank thus leads to a very low degree of inflationary pressure on the part of the state in such countries.

In summary, the simultaneous occurrence of factors inhibiting inflation is likely to have major mutually reinforcing effects. Independent central banks exert a dampening effect both on the inflationary potential of labour unrest and of the state. The inflation record of the three German-speaking countries stands as testimony to the way this institutional set-up operates to curb inflation over the long term.

Concluding Interpretation

Price stability in the German-speaking nations The initial question to be answered in this chapter was why the three German-speaking countries manifested such comparatively good inflation performance in the period after 1973. This period was marked by growing economic difficulties and at the same time by growing differences between the industrialized countries with respect to major macroeconomic indicators such as growth, unemployment and inflation. The question therefore is: 'How and why did essentially common global economic forces lead to such divergent patterns in the behaviour of national inflation rates?' (Solomon, 1984,VII).

Focusing on political-institutional variables in a broad sense, we are now in a position to answer this question with regard to the Federal Republic of Germany, Austria and Switzerland. Examining the economic 'sources' of inflation (in the sense used by Mancur Olson, 1982, 4), we concede that inflation can in principle come from only three sources: either from *foreign influence* or from the domestic economy, and in the latter case either from the *private sector* or from the *state sector*. Looking at the *private sector*, inflationary pressure in the three countries is low because of a low degree of labour militancy, which reflects a high degree of consensus. This can be attributed to organizational factors in the system of collective bargaining, but also to recent historical experience, such as hyperinflation in Germany or civil war in Austria. With regard to the trade union system, relatively highly organized and centralized unions and employer organizations together with the existence of a system of arbitration dominate the picture in Austria and (to a lesser degree) in Germany, whereas a decentralized system of trade unions with an absolute no-strike obligation yields the same result in Switzerland, with labour trading high real wage flexibility against high employment security.[20] A high share of exports in GNP emphasizes the importance of maintaining international competitiveness in all three countries.

With regard to the *state sector*, inflationary pressure emanating from expansionary fiscal policy is low in all three countries, albeit for slightly different reasons. In Germany and in Switzerland, this is due to the comparatively high degree of decentralization, which makes the costs or 'difficulty' of expansionary fiscal policy very high. Furthermore, a strong and independent central bank is a powerful counterweight to a central government that is not omnipotent and, in the case of Switzerland, rather weak. Furthermore, the receptivity to Keynesian ideas (and with it conceptions of demand management and deficit spending) has been 'underdeveloped' in Germany (Allen, 1989), empirical inquiries among economists confirming the rejection of these economic ideas in both Germany and Switzerland (Frey et al., 1984). The Austrian case is somewhat different, but we encounter policies which amount to a functional equivalent: here a more centralised state, with a higher formal degree of control over its central bank, has not used its potential for expansionary fiscal policy to the point of inflationary consequences, but from 1974 has embarked on a 'hard currency policy' by pegging the Schilling to the D-Mark and thus importing price stability.

As far as *foreign economic influence* is concerned, all three countries were subject to the oil price shocks of the 1970s and experienced considerable inflationary pressure on this score. But compared to the other OECD countries which suffered the same shocks, in the three German-speaking countries, these pressures were dampened through a marked (and relatively the strongest) appreciation of their currencies against the US-Dollar. Again central banks' independence from political pressure was an important determinant in this development.

Is inflation a family of nations phenomenon? Our analysis demonstrates the existence, in all three German-speaking countries, of the institutional conditions for a maximization of price stability. That being so, the crucial question (in terms of the focus of this volume on the distinctive policy outcomes of families of nations) is the extent to which these institutional features stem from common cultural and historical experiences.

With respect to decentralization (and, derived from it, fiscal difficulty), we have already noted at the beginning of this chapter that the three German-speaking countries share a long and deep tradition of federalism. All three consist of self-confident sub-entities with their own identities and traditions, which have collectively founded the central state (instead of having been granted a limited self-responsibility by the centre). This helps us to understand the mechanisms of '*Politikverflechtung*' (joint decision-making) so typical of these countries. At the same time, the historical roots and institutional embodiment of that style of decision-making suggest that decentralization as a technique to enhance the performance of a political system will probably not yield the same results.

As far as the independence of the central banks is concerned, there are differences between the countries. Germany and Austria had negative experiences with hyperinflation. This and pressure from abroad[21] led to the institutionalization of independent central banks which were then quickly accepted and became, most notably in the case of Germany, important actors in economic policy making. Switzerland is different in this respect, ultimately due to its being a country of early industrialization, whereas both Germany and Austria were late industrializers. This led to different economic structures and roles for the state in economic policy-making. The traditionally liberal Swiss state does not interfere with the central bank.

There are also differences in explanation for the high degree of labour quiescence in the three German-speaking countries, which derive from a similar source. In Switzerland, early industrialization gave rise to a decentralization of industry, which, together with early democratization and the absence of a militant ideology in the labour movement, led to peaceful labour relations (cf. Katzenstein, 1984). Germany and Austria, on the other hand, have experienced massive social and political shocks in the 20th century: they have lost wars, the countries have been occupied and divided (Austria for 10 years, Germany for 40 years) and, in the case of Germany, there has been a massive influx of expellees from the east. These experiences, which led to a thorough shake-up of the two countries' societies and again – in the case of Germany – influence from the occupying forces (in this case Britain, which led to the installation of a trade union system organized along industry lines) paved the way for labour quiescence. In addition, the experience of the breakdown of their respective first republics, which ended in fascist dictatorships, led to a consensus-oriented mode of policy-making in both the second German and Austrian republics. This is more visible in the grand coalitions of Austria, but also has clear resonances in the German political system (Katzenstein, 1987). The mode is very similar to that of 'low voltage politics' characteristic of Switzerland (Katzenstein, 1985a, 32).

The evidence for a family of nations interpretation of the inflation performance of the German-speaking nations is thus mixed. Clearly, there is a commonality in terms of policy outcomes which derives from the existence of common institutional features; however, with the exception of federal arrangements, the routes by which the countries have arrived at those institutional commonalities are rather different. The fairest conclusion is probably that inflationary performance is not a policy area in which a families of nations approach has its strongest explanatory value. That is perhaps not surprising when we consider the extent to which, institutional constraints aside, inflation is driven by the operation of external economic forces.

On the other hand, two glosses are appropriate which may suggest some greater relevance of the concept. First, as noted previously, there are strong reinforcing effects amongst the institutional variables. Hence it could be argued that the decentralization that the German-speaking nations have in common is a prior influence, constraining other institutional arrangements in a direction favouring price stability. Second, the institutional routes to low inflation taken by Austria and Germany are much more similar than those of the German-speaking group as a whole. In terms of the former nations, it could possibly be appropriate to think of a 'family' emergent in the post-war era, shaped by a common legacy of decentralization conjoint with experiences of economic disaster and reflexive institution-building, themselves consequent on a shared experience of military defeat and foreign occupation.

Does the model apply to other families? Here we broaden the analysis to see whether the policy and institutional commonalities identified amongst the German-speaking nations are to be found in the other putative families discussed in this volume. For this purpose, the three explanatory variables (strike activity, central bank independence and fiscal difficulty) are dichotomized at the median, so that, for each variable, two groups of the same size emerge, with one incorporating 'low' values of the variable and the other 'high' values. In line with the earlier analysis, it is assumed that 'low' values with respect to strike activity and 'high' ones with respect to central bank independence and fiscal 'difficulty' will serve as inhibitors to inflation.[22] The result is shown in Table 2.7.

Table 2.7: Inhibitors to inflation in 18 OECD countries, 1973–85

	Strikes	Central bank	Fiscal policy	Number of inhibitors
Australia	0	0	0	0
Austria	1	1	1	3
Belgium	0	0	0	0
Canada	0	0	1	1
Denmark	1	0	0	1
Finland	0	0	1	1
France	1	0	1	2
Germany (West)	1	1	1	3
Ireland	0	–	0	0
Italy	0	0	0	0
Japan	1	1	1	3
Netherlands	1	0	0	1
New Zealand	0	0	–	0
Norway	1	0	0	1
Sweden	1	0	0	1
Switzerland	1	1	1	3
UK	0	0	0	0
US	0	1	1	2

Source: Author's calculations from ILO Yearbook (several volumes); Alesina, 1989 (see above) and OECD, 1988.

It can be seen that the explanation advanced for the three German-speaking countries apparently also fits the rest of the OECD. The only countries where three inhibitors to inflation exist are Austria, Germany, Switzerland and Japan. Japan also has a very good average inflation performance: for the time period 1973 to 1986, it ranked fifth in the OECD, after the three German-speaking countries and the Netherlands. On the other hand, countries with a very bad inflation performance have only one inhibitor to inflation or none at all. The latter is the case in relation to both Italy and the UK (that rank 18th and 15th respectively).[23]

In Table 2.8, we present a cross-tabulation of the number of institutional inhibitors to inflation and inflation rates, 1973–86. This shows a strong relationship between the two variables ($r = -0.77$)[24] and demonstrates that our model is also applicable to the OECD nations in general – capable not only of explaining the good inflation performance of the German-speaking nations, but also the worse performance of countries like Italy, New Zealand and Ireland.

Table 2.8: Number of inhibitors to inflation and average rates of inflation in 18 OECD countries

Average rate of inflation, 1973–86, in per cent	Number of inhibitors			
	3	2	1	0
>12				Italy New Zealand Ireland
10–12			Finland	Australia UK
8–10		France	Canada Norway Sweden Denmark	
6–8	Japan	US		Belgium
4–6	Switzerland Germany Austria		Netherlands	

Source: Author's calculations.

We have so far advanced a model to explain inflation performance in the three German-speaking countries and have seen that it also fits the rest of the OECD members quite well. The common profile of the German-speaking 'family' of nations thus has been satisfactorily explained. But are there also commonalities amongst the Scandinavian and English-speaking families?

The Scandinavian 'family' clearly does display interesting commonalities. All four countries are located in the worse half of the inflation ranking. In all four of them only one inhibitor to inflation is operating: in three it is the strike variable, whereas in the case of Finland it is fiscal difficulty. But none has an independent central bank. All in all these countries appear very similar with respect to inflation and the variables that explain it. Speculatively, one might argue that the absence of any decentralizing tendency or of an independent central bank are both linked to the historical continuity of strong central institutions fostered by a Lutheran belief which, more than elsewhere in Europe, has reinforced the authority of the centralized state.

The English-speaking 'family', in contrast, manifests a much more dispersed picture. Two of the five countries rank in the better half of the inflation table (the US and Canada) and three in the worse half (the UK, Australia and New Zealand). With respect to inhibitors to inflation, the picture is similar. Whereas four countries have non-independent central banks, one of them has an independent one (the US); two of the countries have high degrees of 'fiscal difficulty' (Canada and again the US), two show low degrees of difficulty (data for New Zealand were not available). But one commonality with respect to the third inhibitor does not operate in any of the Anglo-Saxon countries: they are all in the group with higher levels of strike activity. This commonality is again of historical origin, stemming from an early industrialization which fostered the emergence of a labour movement along craft lines.

This brief analysis shows that the Scandinavian family of nations does have a distinctive pattern of inflation outcomes and that, in part, at least, both families share institutional features rooted in historical experience which favour particular outcomes. Again, it would appear that whilst, as in the case of the German-speaking nations, familial commonalities are far from being a decisive 'cause' of contemporary policy outcomes, they may make some contribution towards understanding patterns of cross-national diversity.

It has been pointed out in the course of this chapter that the three explanatory variables considered here are strongly linked to the existence of two other political variables which can be seen as underlying them. These are the existence of corporatist arrangements in the case of strike activity, and the existence of federalism in the case of central bank independence and the degree of difficulty of an expansionary fiscal policy. As a multiple regression analysis demonstrates,[25] the combined effects of corporatism and federalism are highly relevant and can explain roughly two-thirds of the variation in inflation rates in the period under consideration. Moreover, there are again distinctive patterns in the three 'families' with regard to these variables: the German-speaking countries are all federally organized, and in all of them corporatist arrangements exist. In addition, they are the only OECD countries which combine these variables.

The Scandinavian countries all have corporatist arrangements, but none of them is a federal state. Again, the picture is more dispersed in the English-speaking family, some of which are federal and some of which are unitary states. But they share the absence of corporatist arrangements (with the slight exception of the UK, which Lehmbruch (1984, 66) ranks under 'weak corporatism').

These findings illuminate the inflationary experience of the diverse families of nations identified in this study. A low level of inflation can be expected in a country where corporatist arrangements contribute to a more coordinated (and less conflict-laden) way of running the economy and where a decentralized state has insufficient strength to manipulate economic outcomes for political reasons. This is the route taken by the three German-speaking countries. Another route is the one by which corporatist arrangements lead to reduced conflict in the economy; here the role of a strong and centralized state in facilitating these arrangements results in a moderate, but relatively stable, rate of inflation. This is the experience of the Scandinavian countries. The third configuration, which is that typical of the English-speaking countries, is characterized by the absence of corporatist arrangements and, consequently, greater conflict in the economy. Within this group, the federally organized countries (and especially those with a high degree of fiscal decentralization, such as the US and Canada) have much less opportunity to interfere with the economy, both in terms of monetary and fiscal policy. It is therefore not surprising that inflation in this group of nations varies in line with the degree of centralization evident.

Towards a single European family of nations? At the end of this chapter, a final, highly speculative remark is appropriate. This analysis has focused primarily on the effects of institutional variables and their interaction. It could be argued that institutions do not determine political decisions completely and that more allowance should be made for political 'will and skill'. Clearly, however, this is well beyond the scope of this chapter and a task for further research, building on the findings advanced here. On the other hand, increasing economic and financial integration has diminished the room for manoeuvre for national strategies considerably, often to the discontent of political actors. So the room for political 'will and skill' may have been small and has probably been shrinking over time.

This trend towards increased integration also has an effect on the working of the variables set out in this chapter. The Single European Market, due in 1993, has led to more countries pegging their currencies either to the ECU or directly to the D-Mark, the EMU's anchor currency. This amounts to a voluntary abandonment of one part of economic sovereignty and diminishes the influence ascribed above to central bank independence. The model therefore seems to be confined to the time period under consideration in this chapter. Whether these states will stick to their decision even in the face of economic adversity (as has been the case with Austria) remains to be seen.*

The fascinating speculation is that, faced with the inflationary experiences of the 1970s and 1980s and now with the new challenges of the 1990s, the European nations at least are deliberately creating economic structures in which there is an institutionalized divide between national governments and monetary authorities, along lines pioneered by Austria's earlier policies. It could well be that an historian of monetary policy of a later era will look back at the experience of the core countries of the German-speaking family of nations (Austria and Germany) at the subsequent development of the ERM and at the foundation of the single market, as formative stages in the gradual emergence of a single European family of nations.

Notes

1. For comments on an earlier draft of this paper, I am grateful to Klaus von Beyme, Dietmar Braun, Frank Castles, Wolfgang Merkel, Manfred G. Schmidt, Jürgen Siebke and Göran Therborn.
2. Switzerland, of course, is officially a quadrilingual country, but German speakers, who comprise nearly three-quarters of all Swiss, are by far the largest and politically and economically the dominating group (Weibel, 1988).
3. The several European attempts to create new exchange rate systems should be briefly mentioned. However, they never affected the main source of difficulty in the Bretton Woods system – the varying exchange rate of the US$ against different European currencies – and they never again included a strict obligation for monetary intervention; moreover, exchange rate adjustments remained quite frequent until the middle of the 1980s.
4. An example is the concluding sentence of Giannaros and Kolluri's article on deficits, money and inflation (1985, 415), where the authors find differences between the US

* The problems with this strategy encountered by the Scandinavian EFTA-countries in the early nineties are illustrative of the emerging dilemmas and constraints (cf. *The Economist*, 14.12.1991, 12.9.1992, 26.9.1992): Finland, impaired by the economic collapse of its main trading partner, the Soviet Union, was forced to devalue the Finmark against the ECU both in 1991 and 1992 and had to give up the peg in September 1992, suffering a 16% devaluation within hours of floating the currency. The Swedish currency, in its wake, had also come under speculative attack in 1991 and September 1992, but had managed to fight it off by spectacular rises in interest rates (at one point the marginal lending rate was raised to an unprecedented 500%). But in November 1992 the growing economic crisis in Sweden led to a massive outflow of foreign currency which eventually forced a floating of the currency, leading to an 11% devaluation. Norway, in December 1992, was also forced to give up the link between its currency and the ECU and float the currency, which led to a 5% devaluation on the first day.

and the nine other OECD countries but make no attempt to explain these differences: 'In general, differences observed between the U.S. and the rest of the industrial countries on the propositions tested may be a reflection of the different institutional structures and the different policy priorities of these countries'.

5. For illustrative purposes, some cases which clearly contradict Hibbs' hypothesis may be noted: New Zealand has a consistent record of rightist party government and a very high rate of inflation, whereas Austria's inflation is very low, as is its share of rightist party government. Italy is another case of strong divergence, with almost no left participation, but consistently high levels of inflation.
6. Institutions have an important impact on policy outcomes, because they define restrictions and potentials for action and 'circumscribe the room to manoeuvre that is open to policy-makers' (Schmidt 1989b, 77). It should be made clear, however, that they do not influence policy outcomes in a deterministic way.
7. As this is meant to be an institutional model, it should be pointed out that strike activity in itself is not an institutional variable. However, it will be demonstrated below that such activity may well be regarded as an outcome of certain institutional structures.
8. Virtually the same indicator is used by McCallum (1983). Cameron (1984, 153) uses working days lost per 1000 of the total labour force. But inter-country variation should only be marginally affected by this slight difference. It should be noted, however, that this definition involves a systematic bias in favour of countries with a high level of part-time employment.
9. This is also the result of a test of time series data for selected cases in the sample. Cross correlations were performed for time series (yearly data from 1973 to 1985) of strike coefficients and lagged time series of rates of inflation for the UK, Italy and Germany, using first differences. If strikes induced inflation, we would expect the highest correlations for positive lags; if inflation caused strikes, for negative lags. We found by far the strongest correlations at lag 1 for the cases of Italy and the UK (0.65 and 0.38). Correlations at lag –1 were, in both cases, negative. It is interesting that correlations for Germany were practically zero for all lags from –3 to 3, indicating that there is no correlation at all between the two time series.
10. McCallum (1983, 787) reports very similar correlations between strike activity in the 1950s, 1960s and 1970s. His correlations fall between 0.87 and 0.90.
11. In trying to explain contemporary differences in central bank independence, it can be argued that this proximity continued if there were no major breaches in political continuity in a country. Such breaches could, for instance, be caused by political regime changes or by currency reforms. If a breach occurred together with a negative experience of state influence on the central bank, then it can be argued that a shift to more central bank independence was likely. This was the case of Germany in 1923, for example, when a combination of such experience and pressure from the Allies led to independence for the German Reichsbank (cf. Holtfrerich, 1988).
12. The following account is based on Woolley, 1985; Wenger, 1979 and Caesar, 1982. For organizational details of the central banks in the UK, France, the US, the Federal Republic, Sweden and Switzerland, see Woolley 1985, 321.
13. On procedures for the appointment of the Bundesbank's board, see Kloten et al., 1985, 371; on its composition and personnel continuity, see Sturm, 1990.
14. For an account of the strategy of the 'hard currency policy', see Rhomberg, 1985. An evaluation of Austrian economic policy can be found in Rothschild, 1985.
15. For example, the reforms in the relationship between the Italian central bank and the

treasury (Epstein and Schor, 1986) or the institutional reforms of the central bank in New Zealand that took place still more recently.

16. Source of the data for all countries except Austria and Ireland is Alesina, 1989; for the classification of Austria see the text above.
17. Author's calculation from OECD data. Time periods for Denmark are 1977 to 1986, for Ireland 1974 to 1984 and for Italy 1983 to 1986, since data for the other years are not available for these countries. But as year-to-year variation in the ratios is small, it seems acceptable to use these averages nevertheless. Data for New Zealand were not available from the OECD.
18. These correlations remain quite stable even if Italy, which is something of an outlier, is dropped from the distribution. The coefficients for the consecutive time periods are –0.37, –0.49 and –0.59 respectively.
19. Centralization is measured as the central state's share in tax receipts. In this I follow Lijphart (1984), from which the data are taken.
20. For an account of these systems see, for Germany: Scharpf, 1987; Katzenstein, 1987; for Austria: Butschek, 1985 and for Switzerland: Danthine and Lambelet, 1987. For a comparative account including both Austria and Switzerland, see Katzenstein, 1984.
21. In the 1920s, the League of Nations demanded security for its stabilization loan; after 1945, the role of the US military government in Germany was similar (cf. Holtfrerich 1988 and Polster and Voy, 1990, 178).
22. Dividing groups at the median is only useful for continuous variables. For the discrete variable, of 'central bank independence', the sample is divided into (a) the two classes with low independence (1 and 2) and (b) the two classes with high independence (3 and 4).
23. As data for New Zealand and Ireland are missing, no statement can be made for them. For a ranking of the average inflation rates, 1973–86, see Table 2.1.
24. This correlation would be even stronger (–0.88) were it not for the two outliers Netherlands and Belgium. Their relatively low rates of inflation can best be explained by their intensive economic interlinking with Germany. As Katzenstein (1985a) points out, these small states have developed a specific form of corporatism to deal with problems arising from their size.
25. Using the classification of corporatism developed by Lehmbruch (1984) (which does not include France and Japan), the result for 16 countries is (t-values in parentheses): Inflation 1973–86 = 15.31 – 4.94 Federalism (–4.76) – 1.73 Corporatism (–3.83), R^2 adj. = 0.64.

References

Alesina, Alberto (1988), 'Macroeconomics and Politics' in Stanley Fischer (ed.), *National Bureau of Economic Research Macroeconomics Annual 1988*, Cambridge (MA): MIT Press, 13–52.

Alesina, Alberto (1989), 'Politics and Business Cycles in Industrial Democracies', *Economic Policy*, 8, 55–98.

Allen, Christopher S. (1989), 'The Underdevelopment of Keynesianism in the Federal Republic of Germany' in Peter A. Hall (ed.), *The Political Power of Economic Ideas. Keynesianism across Nations*, Princeton (NJ): Princeton University Press, 263–90.

Armingeon, Klaus (1992), 'Streiks' in Manfred G. Schmidt (ed.), *Lexikon der Politik*, Vol. 3, München: Beck, 431–5.

Bach, G.L. and Stephenson, James B. (1974), 'Inflation and the Redistribution of Wealth', *Review of Economics and Statistics*, **56** (1), 1–13.

Barry, Brian (1985), 'Does Democracy Cause Inflation? Political Ideas of Some Economists' in Leon N. Lindberg and Charles S. Maier (eds), *The Politics of Inflation and Economic Stagnation. Theoretical Approaches and International Case Studies*, Washington D.C.: The Brookings Institution, 280–317.

Batten, Dallas S. (1981), 'Money Growth Stability and Inflation: An International Comparison', *Federal Reserve Bank of St. Louis Review*, **63** (8), 7–12.

Bethusy-Huc, Viola Gräfin von (1962), *Demokratie und Interessenpolitik*, Wiesbaden: Franz Steiner.

Borchardt, Knut (1982a), *Wachstum, Krisen, Handlungsspielräume der Wirtschaftspolitik. Studien zur Wirtschaftsgeschichte des 19. und 20. Jahrhunderts*, Göttingen: Vandenhoeck & Ruprecht.

Borchardt, Knut (1982b), 'Die Erfahrung mit Inflationen in Deutschland' in Knut Borchardt: *Wachstum, Krisen, Handlungsspielräume der Wirtschaftspolitik. Studien zur Wirtschaftsgeschichte des 19. und 20. Jahrhunderts*, Göttingen: Vandenhoeck & Ruprecht, pp.151–61.

Borchardt, Knut (1985), *Grundriss der deutschen Wirtschaftsgeschichte*, Göttingen: Vandenhoeck & Ruprecht.

Budd, Alan and Dicks, Geoffrey (1982), 'Inflation: A Monetarist Interpretation', in Andrea Boltho (ed.), *The European Economy*, Oxford: Oxford University Press, 104–31.

Burdekin, Richard C.K. and Laney, Leroy O. (1988), 'Fiscal Policymaking and the Central Bank Institutional Constraint', *Kyklos*, **41** (4), 647–62.

Busch, Andreas (1989), *Neokonservative Wirtschaftspolitik in Großbritannien. Vorgeschichte, Problemdiagnose, Ziele und Ergebnisse des 'Thatcherismus'* [Beiträge zur Politikwissenschaft, Bd. 41], Frankfurt am Main u.a.: Peter Lang.

Butschek, Felix (1985), *Die österreichische Wirtschaft im 20. Jahrhundert*, Stuttgart: Gustav Fischer.

Caesar, Rolf (1980), 'Die Unabhängigkeit der Notenbank im demokratischen Staat. Argumente und Gegenargumente', *Zeitschrift für Politik*, **27**, 347–77.

Caesar, Rolf (1981), '*Der Handlungsspielraum von Notenbanken. Theoretische Analyse und internationaler Vergleich* [Schriften zur Monetären Ökonomie Bd. 13], Baden-Baden: Nomos.

Caesar, Rolf (1982), 'Notenbanken im Spannungsfeld der Politik', Wirtschaftsdienst, **62** (11), 569–76.

Cameron, David R. (1984), 'Social Democracy, Corporatism, Labour Quiescence, and the Representation of Economic Interest in Advanced Capitalist Society' in John H. Goldthorpe (ed.), *Order and Conflict in Contemporary Capitalism*, Oxford: Clarendon Press, 143–78.

Cameron, David R. (1985), 'Does Government Cause Inflation? Taxes, Spending, and Deficits' in Leon N. Lindberg and Charles S. Maier (eds), *The Politics of Inflation and Economic Stagnation. Theoretical Approaches and International Case Studies*, Washington D.C.: The Brookings Institution, 224–79.

Cassel, Dieter (1988), 'Inflation' in Dieter Bender et al., *Vahlens Kompendium der Wirtschaftstheorie und Wirtschaftspolitik*, Band 1, 3. Auflage, München: Vahlen, 257–314.

Castles, Francis G. (ed.) (1989), *The Comparative History of Public Policy*, Cambridge: Polity Press.

Crouch, Colin (1978), 'Inflation and the Political Organization of Economic Interests' in Fred Hirsch and John H. Goldthorpe (eds.), *The Political Economy of Inflation*, Cambridge (MA): Harvard University Press, 217–39.

Crouch, Colin (1985), 'Conditions for Trade Union Wage Restraint' in Leon N. Lindberg and Charles S. Maier (eds), *The Politics of Inflation and Economic Stagnation. Theoretical Approaches and International Case Studies*, Washington D.C.: The Brookings Institution, 105–39.

Danthine, Jean Pierre and Lambelet, Jean Christian (1987), 'The Swiss Recipe. Conservative Policies Ain't Enough', *Economic Policy*, **2** (2) (A Special Report: The Conservative Revolution), 147–79.

Deutsche Bundesbank (ed.) (1988), *40 Jahre Deutsche Mark. Monetäre Statistiken 1948–1987*, Frankfurt a.M.: Fritz Knapp.

Dornbusch, Rudiger and Fischer, Stanley (1987), *Macroeconomics*, 4th edition, New York: McGraw-Hill.

Emminger, Otmar (1986), *D-Mark, Dollar, Währungskrisen. Erinnerungen eines ehemaligen Bundesbankpräsidenten*, Stuttgart: DVA.

Epstein, Gerald A. and Schor, Juliet B. (1986), 'The Divorce of the Banca d'Italia and the Italian Treasury: A Case Study of Central Bank Independence' [Harvard Institute of Economic Research, Discussion Paper Number 1269], Cambridge (MA): Harvard University.

Fautz, Wolfgang (1979), 'Gewerkschaften, Streikaktivität und Lohninflation. Mit empirischen Ergebnissen für die Bundesrepublik Deutschland, 1952–1977', *Zeitschrift für die gesamte Staatswissenschaft*, **135** (4), 605–28.

Fels, Gerhard (1977), 'Inflation in Germany' in Walter S. Salant and Lawrence B. Krause (eds), *Worldwide Inflation. Theory and Recent Experience*, Washington D.C.: The Brookings Institution, 589–629.

Frey, Bruno S.; Pommerehne, Werner; Schneider, Friedrich and Gilbert, Guy (1984), 'Consensus and Dissension among Economists: An Empirical Inquiry', *The American Economic Review*, **74** (5), 986–94.

Fricke, Dieter (1981), *Verteilungswirkungen der Inflation*, Baden-Baden: Nomos.

Friedman, Milton and Schwartz, Anna Jacobson (1963), *A Monetary History of the United States, 1867–1960*, Princeton: Princeton University Press.

Friedman, Milton and Schwartz, Anna Jacobson (1970), *Monetary Statistics of the United States*, New York: Columbia University Press.

Frisch, Helmut (1977), 'Inflation Theory 1963–1975: A "Second Generation" Survey', *Journal of Economic Literature*, **15**, 1289–1317.

Fürstenberg, Friedrich (1985), 'Kulturelle und traditionelle Faktoren der Arbeitsbeziehungen aufgrund der Sozialstruktur' in Günter Endruweit, Eduard Gaugler, Wolfgang H. Staehle and Bernhard Wilpert (eds), *Handbuch der Arbeitsbeziehungen. Deutschland. Österreich. Schweiz*, Berlin/New York: de Gruyter, 3–12.

Gerfin, Harald; Horn, Gustav Adolf and Siebeck, Karin (1985), 'Zur Bewährung inflationstheoretischer Hypothesen. Empirische Befunde für die Bundesrepublik Deutschland', *Hamburger Jahrbuch für Wirtschafts- und Gesellschaftspolitik*, **30**, 155–69.

Gerschenkron, Alexander (1966), 'Economic Backwardness in Historical Perspective' in Alexander Gerschenkron, *Economic Backwardness in Historical Perspective. A Book of Essays*, Cambridge (MA): Harvard University Press, 2. Auflage, 5–30.

Giannaros, Demetrios S. and Kolluri, Bharat R. (1985), 'Deficit Spending, Money, and Inflation: Some International Empirical Evidence', *Journal of Macroeconomics*, **7** (3), 401–17.

Goldthorpe, John H. (1978), 'The Current Inflation: Towards a Sociological Account' in Fred Hirsch and John H. Goldthorpe (eds), *The Political Economy of Inflation*, Cambridge (MA): Harvard University Press, 186–214.

Goldthorpe, John H. (ed.) (1984), *Order and Conflict in Contemporary Capitalism. Studies in the Political Economy of Western European Nations*, Oxford: Clarendon Press.

Goodhart, Charles (1988), *The Evolution of Central Banks*, Cambridge (MA): MIT Press.

Goodhart, Charles (1989), 'Central Banking' in John Eatwell, Murray Milgate and Peter Newman (eds), *The New Palgrave: Money*, London: Macmillan, 88–92.

Green, Steven L. (1987), 'Theories of Inflation: A Review Essay', *Journal of Monetary Economics*, **20** (1), 169–75.

Grilli, Vittorio; Masciandaro, Donato and Tabellini, Guido (1991), 'Political and Monetary Institutions and Public Financial Policies in the Industrial Countries', *Economic Policy*, **13**, October 341–92.

Hall, Peter A. (1986), *Governing the Economy. The Politics of State Intervention in Britain and France*, Cambridge: Polity Press.

Hall, Peter A. (ed.) (1989), *The Political Power of Economic Ideas. Keynesianism across Nations*, Princeton (NJ): Princeton University Press.

Hallett, Graham (1990), 'West Germany' in Andrew Graham and Anthony Seldon (eds), *Government and Economics in the Postwar World. Economic Policies and Comparative Performance, 1945–85*, London, New York: Routledge, 79–103.

Hardach, Karl (1980), 'Deutschland 1914–1970' in Carlo M. Cipolla and Knut Borchardt (eds), *Europäische Wirtschaftsgeschichte, Band 5: Die europäischen Volkswirtschaften im zwanzigsten Jahrhundert*, Stuttgart, New York: Fischer, 47–99.

Heidenheimer, Arnold J., Heclo, Hugh and Adams, Carolyn Teich (1990), *Comparative Public Policy. The Politics of Social Choice in America, Europe, and Japan*, 3rd ed., New York: St. Martin's Press.

Herr, Hansjörg (1986), *Weltgeld und Währungssystem* [WZB disc. paper IIM/LMP 86–25], Berlin: Wissenschaftszentrum.

Hibbs, Jr., Douglas A. (1977), 'Political Parties and Macroeconomic Policy', *American Political Science Review*, **71**, 1467–87.

Hibbs, Jr., Douglas A. (1985), 'Inflation, Political Support, and Macroeconomic Policy' in Leon N. Lindberg and Charles S. Maier (eds), *The Politics of Inflation and Economic Stagnation. Theoretical Approaches and International Case Studies*, Washington D.C.: The Brookings Institution, 175–95.

Hirsch, Fred (1978), 'The Ideological Underlay of Inflation' in Fred Hirsch and John H. Goldthorpe (eds), *The Political Economy of Inflation*, Cambridge (MA): Harvard University Press, 263–84.

Hirsch, Fred and Goldthorpe, John H. (eds) (1978), *The Political Economy of Inflation*, Cambridge (MA): Harvard University Press.

Hoffmann, Rainer-W. (1990), 'Implikationen von Inflationen. Notizen zu verborgenen Verzweigungen eines globalen Problems', *Universitas*, **4**, 310–21.

Holtfrerich, Carl-Ludwig (1988), 'Relations between Monetary Authorities and Governmental Institutions: The Case of Germany from the 19th Century to the Present' in Gianni Toniolo (ed.), *Central Banks' Independence in Historical Perspective*, Berlin/New York: de Gruyter, 105–59.

International Labour Office (ILO), *Yearbook of Labour Statistics* (various years), Geneva.

Jackson, Dudley, Turner, H.A. and Wilkinson, Frank (1972), *Do Trade Unions Cause Inflation?*, Cambridge: Cambridge University Press.

Katzenstein, Peter J. (1984), *Corporatism and Change. Austria, Switzerland, and the Politics of Industry*, Ithaca N.Y., London: Cornell University Press.

Katzenstein, Peter J. (1985a), *Small States in World Markets. Industrial Policy in Europe*, Ithaca N.Y., London: Cornell University Press.

Katzenstein, Peter J. (1985b), 'Small Nations in an Open International Economy: The Converging Balance of State and Society in Switzerland and Austria' in Peter B. Evans, Dietrich Rueschemeyer and Theda Skocpol (eds), *Bringing The State Back In*, Cambridge: Cambridge University Press, 227–51.

Katzenstein, Peter J. (1987), *Policy and Politics in West Germany. The Growth of a Semisovereign State*, Philadelphia: Temple University Press.

Keohane, Robert O. (1985), 'The International Politics of Inflation' in Leon N. Lindberg and Charles S. Maier (eds), *The Politics of Inflation and Economic Stagnation. Theoretical Approaches and International Case Studies*, Washington D.C.: The Brookings Institution, 78–104.

Kirschen, Etienne S. et al. (1964), *Economic Policy in Our Time*, Vol. 1: General Theory, Amsterdam: North-Holland.

Kloten, Norbert; Ketterer, Karl-Heinz and Vollener, Rainer (1985), 'West Germany's Stabilization Performance' in Leon Lindberg and Charles Maier (eds), *The Politics of Inflation and Economic Stagnation*, Washington D.C.: The Brookings Institution, 353–402.

Kriesi, Hanspeter (1980), *Entscheidungsstrukturen und Entscheidungsprozesse in der Schweizer Politik*, Frankfurt/New York: Campus.

Krul, Nicolas (1984), 'Switzerland' in Ezra Solomon (ed.), *International Patterns of Inflation: A Study in Contrasts*, New York: The Conference Board, 161–76.

Kurth, James R. (1982), 'Economic Sectors and Inflationary Policies: The Politics of Inflation in Historical Perspective' in Richard Medley (ed.), *The Politics of Inflation. A Comparative Analysis*, New York: Pergamon, 44–64.

Kurzer, Paulette (1988), 'The Politics of Central Banks: Austerity and Unemployment in Europe', *Journal of Public Policy*, **7** (1), 21–48.

Lehmbruch, Gerhard (1967), *Proporzdemokratie. Politisches System und politische Kultur in der Schweiz und in Österreich*, Tübingen: J.C.B.Mohr (Paul Siebeck).

Lehmbruch, Gerhard (1984), 'Concertation and the Structure of Corporatist Networks' in John H. Goldthorpe (ed.), *Order and Conflict in Contemporary Capitalism*, Oxford: Clarendon Press, 60–80.

Lehmbruch, Gerhard (1989), 'Marktreformstrategien bei alternierender Parteiregierung: Eine vergleichende institutionelle Analyse – Theodor Eschenburg zum 85. Geburtstag gewidmet' in Thomas Ellwein, Joachim Jens Hesse, Renate Mayntz and Fritz W. Scharpf (eds), *Jahrbuch zur Staats- und Verwaltungswissenschaft*, Bd.3/1989, Baden-Baden: Nomos, 15–45.

Lijphart, Arend (1984), *Democracies. Patterns of Majoritarian and Consensus Government in Twenty-One Countries*, New Haven, London: Yale University Press.

Lindberg, Leon N. (1982), 'The Problems of Economic Theory in Explaining Economic Performance', *The Annals of the American Academy of Political and Social Science*, **459**, January, 14–27.

Lindberg, Leon N. and Maier, Charles S. (eds) (1985), *The Politics of Inflation and Economic Stagnation. Theoretical Approaches and International Case Studies*, Washington D.C.: The Brookings Institution.

Lipsey, Richard G. (1985), 'What Have We Learned about Inflation in the Past 300 Years?', *Atlantic Economic Journal*, **13** (1), 5–18.

Maier, Charles S. (1978), 'The Politics of Inflation in the Twentieth Century' in Fred Hirsch and John H. Goldthorpe (eds), *The Political Economy of Inflation*, Cambridge (MA): Harvard University Press, 37–72.

McCallum, John (1983), 'Inflation and Social Consensus in the Seventies', *The Economic Journal*, December, 784–805.

McNabb, Robert and McKenna, Chris (1990), *Inflation in Modern Economies*, Hemel Hempstead: Harvester Wheatsheaf.

Medley, Richard (1982a), 'Inflation Policy in Germany: The Institutional and Political Determinants' in Richard Medley (ed.), *The Politics of Inflation. A Comparative Analysis*, New York: Pergamon, 127–53.

Medley, Richard (ed.) (1982b), *The Politics of Inflation. A Comparative Analysis*, New York: Pergamon.

Mitchell, Brian R. (1986), 'Statistischer Anhang 1920–1970' in Carlo M. Cipolla and Knut Borchardt (eds), *Europäische Wirtschaftsgeschichte. Band V: Die europäischen Volkswirtschaften im zwanzigsten Jahrhundert*, Stuttgart/New York: Fischer, 413–92.

Müller, Wolfgang C. (1988), 'Österreichs Regierungssystem. Institutionen, Strukturen, Prozesse', *Der Bürger im Staat*, **38** (2,) 121–7.

Narr-Lindner, Gudrun (1984), *Grenzen monetärer Steuerung. Die Restriktionspolitik der Bundesbank 1964–1974*, Frankfurt/New York: Campus.

Neidhart, Leonhard (1988), 'Die Schweizer Konkordanzdemokratie. Elemente des schweizerischen Regierungssystems', *Der Bürger im Staat*, **38** (1), 44–52.

OECD (1979), *OECD Economic Outlook*, Paris: OECD.

OECD (1988), *OECD National Accounts 1974–1986*, Vol. II, Paris: OECD.

OECD (1989), *OECD Economic Outlook*, Paris: OECD.

OECD (1989a), *OECD Economic Outlook. Historical Statistics 1960–1987*, Paris: OECD.

Olson, Mancur (1982), *The Rise and Decline of Nations. Economic Growth, Stagflation, and Social Rigidities*, New Haven, London: Yale University Press.

Panic, Milivoje (1978), 'The Origin of Increasing Inflationary Tendencies in Contemporary Society' in Fred Hirsch and John H. Goldthorpe (eds), *The Political Economy of Inflation*, Cambridge (MA): Harvard University Press, 137–60.

Peacock, Alan T. and Ricketts, Martin (1978), 'The Growth of the Public Sector and Inflation' in Fred Hirsch and John H. Goldthorpe (eds), *The Political Economy of Inflation*, Cambridge (MA): Harvard University Press, 117–36.

Phelps-Brown, Henry (1990), 'The Control of Cost Push', *The Political Quarterly*, **61** (1), 8–22.

Piachaud, David (1978), 'Inflation and Income Distribution' in Fred Hirsch and John H. Goldthorpe (eds), *The Political Economy of Inflation*, Cambridge (MA): Harvard University Press, 88–116.

Polster, Klaus and Voy, Werner (1990), 'Von der politischen Regulierung zur Selbstregulierung der Märkte – Die Entwicklung von Wirtschafts- und Ordnungspolitik in der Bundesrepublik' in Klaus Voy, Werner Polster and Claus Thomasberger (eds), *Marktwirtschaft und politische Regulierung. Beiträge zur Wirtschafts- und Gesellschaftsgeschichte der Bundesrepublik Deutschland (1949–1989)*, Band 1, Marburg: Metropolis, 169–226.

Rhomberg, Rudolf R. (1985), 'Von der "kontrollierten Inflation" zur "Hartwährungspolitik" – Wandlungen der Stabilitätspolitik', in Helmut Kramer and Felix Butschek (eds), *Vom Nachzügler zum Vorbild (?) – Österreichische Wirtschaft 1945–1985*, Stuttgart: Fischer, 49–58.

Rothschild, Kurt W. (1985), 'Felix Austria? Zur Evaluierung der Ökonomie und Politik in der Wirtschaftskrise', *Österreichische Zeitschrift für Politikwissenschaft*, **14** (3), 261–74.

Rothschild, Kurt W. (1986a), '"Left" and "Right" in "Federal Europe"', Kyklos, **39** (3), 359–76.

Rothschild, Kurt W. (1986b), 'Der Wechsel vom keynesianischen zum neoklassischen Paradigma in der neueren Wirtschaftspolitik. Versuch einer soziologisch-historischen Einordnung' in H.-J. Krupp, B. Rohwer, und K.W. Rothschild (eds), *Wege zur Vollbeschäftigung*, Freiburg, 107–23.

Salant, Walter S. (1977), 'International Transmission of Inflation' in Lawrence B. Krause and Walter S. Salant (eds), *Worldwide Inflation. Theory and Recent Experience*, Washington D.C.: The Brookings Institution, 167–242.

Salant, Walter S. and Krause, Lawrence (eds) (1977), *Worldwide Inflation. Theory and Recent Experience*, Washington D.C.: The Brookings Institution.

Scharpf, Fritz W. (1987), *Sozialdemokratische Krisenpolitik* in *Europa. Das 'Modell Deutschland' im Vergleich* [Theorie und Gesellschaft, Band 7], Frankfurt: Campus.

Scharpf, Fritz W. (1988), 'Inflation und Arbeitslosigkeit in Westeuropa. Eine spieltheoretische Interpretation', *Politische Vierteljahresschrift*, **29** (1), 6–41.

Scherf, Harald (1988), 'Inflation' in *HdWW*, Band 4: Han - Kre, Stuttgart usw., 159–84.

Schlesinger, Helmut (1991), 'Deutsche Währungsgeschichte als Lehrstück für eine Europäische Währungsunion' in *Deutsche Bundesbank. Auszüge aus Presseartikeln*, Nr. 85, 11. November, 1–4.

Schlesinger, Helmut and Jahnke, Wilfried (1987), 'Geldmenge, Preise und Sozialprodukt: Interdependenzzusammenhänge im Lichte ökonometrischer Forschungsergebnisse für die Bundesrepublik Deutschland', *Jahrbücher für Nationalökonomie und Statistik*, **203** (5/6), 576–90.

Schmid, Günther and Reissert, Bernd (1988), 'Machen Institutionen einen Unterschied? Finanzierungssysteme der Arbeitsmarktpolitik im internationalen Vergleich' in Manfred G. Schmidt (ed.), *Staatstätigkeit. International und historisch vergleichende Analysen*, Opladen: Westdeutscher Verlag, 284–305.

Schmidt, Manfred G. (1982), *Wohlfahrtsstaatliche Politik unter bürgerlichen und sozialdemokratischen Regierungen. Ein internationaler Vergleich*, Frankfurt/New York: Campus.

Schmidt, Manfred G. (1983), 'The Welfare State and the Economy in Periods of Economic Crisis: A Comparative Study of Twenty-three OECD Nations', *European Journal of Political Research*, **11**, 1–26.

Schmidt, Manfred G. (1988a), 'West Germany: The Policy of the Middle Way', *Journal of Public Policy*, **7** (2), 135–77.

Schmidt, Manfred G. (1988b), 'The Politics of Labour Market Policy. Structural and Political Determinants of Rates of Unemployment in Industrial Nations' in Francis G. Castles, Franz Lehner and Manfred G. Schmidt (eds), *Managing Mixed Economies* [Rudolf Wildenmann (ed.), *The Future of Party Government*, Vol. 3], Berlin, New York: de Gruyter, 4–53.

Schmidt, Manfred G. (1989a), 'The Political Management of Mixed Economies: Political Aspects of Macroeconomic Performance in OECD Nations (1960–1984)' in Burkhard Strümpel (ed.), *Industrial Societies after the Stagnation of the 1970s – Taking Stock from an Interdisciplinary Perspective*, Berlin, New York: de Gruyter, 101–27.

Schmidt, Manfred G. (1989b), 'Learning from Catastrophes. West Germany's Public Policy' in Francis G.Castles (ed.), *The Comparative History of Public Policy*, Cambridge: Polity Press, 56–99.

Schmidt, Manfred G. (1991), 'Structures and Trends in the Party-Political Composition of Governments in Western Democracies' [Paper prepared for publication in Mauro Calise (ed.), *Come cambiano i partiti*, Bologna: il Mulino 1992].

Schmölders, Günther (1975), 'The German Experience' in C. Lowell Harris (ed.), *Inflation. Long-term problems*, Proceedings of The Academy of Political Science, **31** (4), New York: S. 201–11.

Schnabel, Claus (1989), *Zur ökonomischen Analyse der Gewerkschaften in der Bundesrepublik Deutschland. Theoretische und empirische Untersuchungen von Mitgliederentwicklung, Verhalten und Einfluß auf wirtschaftliche Größen*, Frankfurt a.M.: Peter Lang.

Schöler, Klaus (1989), 'Zu den Kausalitätsbeziehungen zwischen Geldmenge,

Sozialprodukt und Preisniveau', *Zeitschrift für Wirtschafts- und Sozialwissenschaften*, **109** (2), 287–301.

Seidel, Hans (1986), 'Der österreichische Weg der Inflationsbekämpfung' in Josua Werner (ed.), *Nationale Wege der Inflationsbekämpfung* (Schriften des Vereins für Socialpolitik, N.F. 157), Berlin: Duncker & Humblot 29–50.

Shannon, Russell and Wallace, Myles S. (1985), 'Wages and Inflation: An Investigation into Causality', *Journal of Post-Keynesian Economics*, **8** (2), 182–91.

Siegenthaler, Hansjörg (1980), 'Schweiz 1910–1970', in Carlo M. Cipolla and Knut Borchardt (eds), *Europäische Wirtschaftsgeschichte, Band 5: Die europäischen Volkswirtschaften im zwanzigsten Jahrhundert*, Stuttgart: Fischer, 245–75.

Solomon, Ezra (ed.) (1984), *International Patterns of Inflation: A Study in Contrasts*, New York: The Conference Board and the American Council of Life Insurance.

Soskice, David (1990), 'Wage Determination: The Changing Role of Institutions in Advanced Industrialized Countries', *Oxford Review of Economic Policy*, **6** (4), 36–61.

Stengos, T. and Swidinsky, R. (1990), 'The Wage Effects of the Strike: A Selectivity Bias Approach', *Applied Economics*, **22**, 375–85.

Strümpel, Burkhard and Scholz, Joachim (1987), 'The Comparative Study of the Economy: Dimensions, Methods and Results' Meinolf Dierkes, Hans N. Weiler and Ariane B. Antal (eds), *Comparative Policy Research. Learning from Experience*, Aldershot: Gower, 264–346.

Sturm, Roland (1989), 'The Role of the Bundesbank in German Politics', *West European Politics*, **12**, 1–11.

Sturm, Roland (1990), 'Die Politik der Deutschen Bundesbank' in Klaus von Beyme and Manfred G. Schmidt (eds), *Politik in der Bundesrepublik Deutschland*, Opladen: Westdeutscher Verlag 255–82.

Tichy, Gunther (1988), 'Soziale Marktwirtschaft in Österreich: Ergebnis einer Evolution, nicht eines theoretischen Konzepts', *WiSt*, **17**, 289–94.

Tilly, Richard H. (1990), *Vom Zollverein zum Industriestaat. Die wirtschaftlich-soziale Entwicklung Deutschlands 1834 bis 1914*, München, dtv.

Uusitalo, Paavo (1984), 'Monetarism, Keynesianism and the Institutional Status of Central Banks', *Acta Sociologica*, **27** (1), 31–50.

Vicarelli, Fausto (1988), 'Central Bank Autonomy: A Historical Perspective' in Gianni Toniolo (ed.), *Central Banks' Independence in Historical Perspective*, Berlin/New York: de Gruyter, 1–16.

Weibel, Ernest (1988), 'Sprachgruppen und Sprachprobleme in der Schweiz. Konflikte und Konfliktregelungsmodelle' in *Der Bürger im Staat*, 38. Jg., Heft 1: 'Die Schweiz', 26–33.

Wenger, Karl (1979), 'Die Notenbankautonomie der österreichischen Nationalbank', in Werner Clement and Karl Socher (eds), *Empirische Wirtschaftsforschung und monetäre Ökonomik. Festschrift für Stephan Koren zum 60. Geburtstag*, Berlin: Duncker & Humblot, 265–84.

Whiteley, Paul (1986), *Political Control of the Macroeconomy. The Political Economy of Public Policy Making*, London: Sage Publications.

Wildenmann, Rudolf (1969), *Die Rolle des Bundesverfassungsgerichts und der Deutschen Bundesbank in der politischen Willensbildung. Ein Beitrag zur Demokratietheorie*, Stuttgart usw.: Kohlhammer.

Williamson, Oliver E. (1990), *Die ökonomischen Institutionen des Kapitalismus: Unternehmen, Märkte, Kooperationen*, Tübingen: J.C.B. Mohr (Paul Siebeck).

Wittendal, Frank (1984), 'West Germany', in Ezra Solomon (ed.), *International Patterns of Inflation: A Study in Contrasts*, New York: 197–221

Woll, Artur (1977), 'Beschäftigung, Geld und Preisniveaustabilität. Empirische Untersuchungen zum Inflationsproblem', *Wirtschaftsdienst*, **57** (11), 562–5.

Woll, Artur (1981), *Allgemeine Volkswirtschaftslehre. 7., völlig überarbeitete und ergänzte Auflage*, München: Vahlen.

Woll, Artur (ed.) (1979), *Inflation. Definitionen, Ursachen, Wirkungen und Bekämpfungsmöglichkeiten*, München: Vahlen.

Woolley, John T. (1985), 'Central Banks and Inflation' in Leon N. Lindberg and Charles S. Maier (eds), *The Politics of Inflation and Economic Stagnation. Theoretical Approaches and International Case Studies*, Washington D.C.: The Brookings Institution, 318–48.

Appendix: Data

	Infl7386	Infl6585	Infl6573	Infl7079	Currency	StrCo6585	StrCo6573	StrCo7485
AUS	10.2		4.6	9.8	–70.28	440.06	346.98	544.78
A	5.6	5.18	4.5	6.1	45.3	6.35	15.2	1.92
BEL	7.2		4.3	7.2	15.17	222.6	275.55	192.34
CAN	8.2	6.66	4.1	7.4	–33.95	734.27	711.06	751.68
DK	9.3	8.43	6.7	9.2	1.56	204.89	228.77	183.4
FIN	10.4	8.79	5.9	10.4	–6.01	436	445.26	429.05
FRA	9.7	8.05	4.8	8.9	–19.15	162.08	190.65	141.30
GER	4.3	4.15	3.8	4.9	43.63	36.72	27.55	43.6
IRL	13.3	11	6.7	12.8	–68.06	652.93	674.61	635.19
ITA	14.6	10.85	4.5	12.3	–122.22	1029.55	1124.11	958.63
J	6.8	6.61	6.2	9.1	52.29	70.95	98.8	50.06
NL	5.6		5.7	7	36.88	25.9	31.13	21.98
NOR	8.8	7.55	5.6	8.4	–2.26	37.7	11.39	57.44
NZ	13		5.9	11.5	–102.5	345.87	200.47	454.91
SWE	9.2	7.84	5.3	8.6	–33.13	89.86	46.25	122.57
SWITZ	4.2	4.4	4.7	5	60.95	1.14	0.68	1.44
UK	11.5	9.61	5.9	12.6	–52.82	450.77	381.5	502.71
USA	7.2	6.14	4.1	7.1	0	382.41	563.95	246.26

	StrCo7079	CBudgGNP	FisDif7486	SD74856573	SD70796573	CtrBkIndep	Federalism	Centralism
AUS	583.18	25.43	3.95	197.8	236.2	1	1	80
A	8.93	22.64	4.43	–13.28	–6.27	4	1	70
BEL	238.03	26.97	3.72	–83.21	–37.52	2	0	93
CAN	862.36	17.27	5.81	40.62	151.3	2	1	50
DK	234.52	36.89	2.72	–45.37	5.75	2	0	71
FIN	602.72	22.94	4.37	–16.21	157.46	2	0	70
FRA	196.48	20.93	4.78	–43.35	–5.83	2	0	88
GER	48.81	14.53	6.88	16.05	21.26	4	1	71
IRL	705.44	32.38	3.12	–39.42	30.83		0	92
ITA	1242.82	28.21	3.55	–165.48	118.71	1.5	0	96
J	98.93	12.46	8.09	–48.74	0.13	3	0	65
NL	39.47	29.76	3.36	–9.15	8.34	2	0	98

	StrCo7079	CBudgGNP	FisDif7486	SD74856573	SD70796573	CtrBkIndep	Federalism	Centralism
NOR	42.17	32.48	3.11	46.05	30.78	2	0	70
NZ	349.97			254.44	149.5	1	0	93
SWE	44.23	29.55	3.4	76.32	−2.02	2	0	62
SWITZ	1.92	9.29	10.8	0.76	1.24	4	1	41
UK	581.69	30.16	3.32	121.21	200.19	2	0	87
USA	441.84	14.11	7.1	−317.69	−122.11	3	1	57

Definitions and sources:

Inflxxyy: Average rate of inflation between 19xx and 19yy (CPI). Source: *OECD Economic Outlook*, 1979 and 1989

Definitions and sources:

Inflxxyy: Average rate of inflation between 19xx and 19yy (CPI). Source: *OECD Economic Outlook*, 1979 and 1989.

Currency: Depreciation (–) or appreciation (+) of national currency against the US-Dollar between 1972 and 1987. Source: Author's calculations from *OECD Historical Statistics 1960–1987*.

StrCoxxyy: Average strike coefficient between 19xx and 19yy (working days lost per 1000 employed in non-agricultural sectors). Source: Author's calculations from *ILO Yearbook*, several volumes.

CBudgGNP: Average ratio of central government budget to GNP (per cent), 1974–86. Source: Author's calculations from *OECD National Accounts 1974–1986*, Volume II.

FisDif7486: Average fiscal difficulty, 1974–86. For definition, see text. Source: same as for CBudgGNP.

SDvvwwxxyy: Change in strike coefficient between 19xx–19yy and 19vv–19ww. Source: same as strike coefficient.

CtrBkIndep: Degree of central bank independence. Source: Alesina, 1989 plus author's addition for Austria (see text).

Federalism: Dummy variable: federal states = 1, non-federal states = 0. Source: Lijphart, 1984.

Centralism: Central government's share in total tax receipts. Source: Lijphart, 1984, 178, 213.

3 Worlds of Welfare and Families of Nations

Francis G. Castles and Deborah Mitchell

Introduction

In terms of direct state intervention, the two main forms of social protection in the nations of advanced capitalism are the provision of social services and of social security cash transfers. Viewed from a 'families of nations' perspective, the English-speaking nations' record on transfers expenditure appears to be straightforward enough, but is, in reality, distinctly puzzling. On the one hand, the *a priori* case for similar outcomes under circumstances of similar cultural and historical stimuli seems extraordinarily strong when we consider the data provided in Table 1.1 above, demonstrating that transfer spending levels, both in the 1960s and 1980s, were about 50 per cent lower in the English-speaking nations than in the OECD in general. Moreover, the adjustment of transfer spending levels to reflect need presented in Table 1.2 markedly reinforces the impression of the English-speaking nations as a family of welfare laggards. Whereas between 1960 and 1983 other OECD nations increased their relative generosity to those in need by almost exactly a quarter, over the same period, the English-speaking nations experienced no increase whatsoever. Nor is this just a matter of averages, with one or two English-speaking nations bringing down the mean performance of the group as a whole. In 1983, of 18 OECD members, the six English-speaking nations (here including Ireland) exhibited the six lowest ratios of expenditure to need.

Puzzlement arises for two reasons. First, the case for an English-speaking family of nations united by the common 'status' of welfare state laggards sits very uneasily with the historical record. Several of these nations – conspicuously Australia, New Zealand and the UK – have at various times been regarded as social policy innovators on a major scale. Admittedly,

Australia's period as a social laboratory was as long ago as the first decade of the 20th century (see Reeves, 1902; Métin, 1977) and rested as much on regulation of the labour market as on the kind of cash transfers and services now regarded as characteristic of contemporary social security programmes (see Castles, 1985), although it should be pointed out that Australia was a pioneer of invalidity pensions in 1908 and was the first country in the world to introduce a maternity benefit in 1912. However, New Zealand and the UK were welfare state leaders in an entirely modern sense. The New Zealand Social Security Act of 1938 was regarded by the ILO as having 'more than any other law, determined the practical meaning of social security, and so has deeply influenced the course of legislation in other countries' (Briggs, 1965). One of those countries was the United Kingdom which, on the basis of both the wartime national consensus around the Beveridge Report and the reform impetus of Britain's first majority Labour government, became the international exemplar of the comprehensive welfare state in the decades following World War II. That several of the English-speaking nations have so conspicuous a place in the welfare state's role of honour makes it inappropriate to consign them without further investigation to the same category of welfare laggards as a nation such as the US which has eschewed interventionist welfare activism as a basic tenet of its political belief structure (King, 1974).

A second source of puzzlement is the fact that in a number of the English-speaking nations, the issue of the relative extent of welfare expenditure does not appear to have been a source of undue disquiet to those who might have been expected to be most concerned about issues of social protection and income redistribution. In both Australia and New Zealand, Labour governments and the broad mass of their supporters have rarely seen the expansion of welfare expenditure as an important policy priority. The prevailing view has been that, by selective policies designed to focus expenditure on those most in need, it was possible to achieve a substantial alleviation of poverty and a considerable degree of income redistribution without, in the process, necessarily contributing to the growth of an 'over-mighty' state in expenditure terms. In essence, the argument has been that the means-tested and flat-rate benefits characteristic of these nations' social security systems, and often criticized as contributing to welfare state laggardliness, are, in reality, policy instruments designed to achieve higher levels of welfare efficiency (i.e. a greater diminution of poverty and inequality per dollar expended). To the extent that nations do, indeed, vary along this dimension of welfare efficiency (see Mitchell, 1990, for a complete discussion of the evidence), it would imply that expenditure alone is an inappropriate measure of the success or otherwise of the socially protective activities of the state. It would also suggest that the apparent similarity of the English-speaking nations in welfare expenditure terms might well co-exist with substantial variations in redistributive outcomes.

Although such issues have been at the heart of the long-running theoretical debate on the rival merits of universal and selective social policy instruments, until quite recently it has not been possible to address them by means of cross-national empirical analysis. Indeed, the comparative social policy research agenda of the past two decades has been almost exclusively pre-occupied with understanding the determinants of social spending either in aggregate or for particular programmes (i.e. what Wilensky (1975) has called 'welfare effort'). That has not been because of the particular intrinsic interest of expenditure measures of this kind, but rather because they have been the most easily available (or the only available) quantitative indicators of state intervention in the field of income redistribution (see Castles, 1989). The relative contributions to redistributive outcomes of the quantum of social expenditure and the targeting of that expenditure through particular policy instruments have not been open to empirical investigation because comparative data on both income distribution and policy instruments have been lacking. Hence, it could be that the only reason we tend to assume a fundamental similarity of welfare performance in the English-speaking 'family of nations' is that systematic comparative research has only been conducted in those areas in which they are similar.

Today, that situation is changing. Where, earlier, we had no reliable cross-national indicators of policy outcomes in terms of measured levels of poverty and inequality, these are now becoming available through the microdata-sets being assembled by the Luxembourg Incomes Study (LIS), allowing us to contrast the redistributive performance of some 10 OECD nations on the basis of the first wave of data for the early 1980s, and eventually permitting comparison of more nations on the basis of later waves. Moreover, renewed interest has emerged in a comparative analysis of the ways in which welfare is delivered and their distributional implications (see Esping-Andersen, 1985b and 1990; Jones, 1985). Where, earlier, discussion of the impact of policy instruments, other than the crude quantum of expenditure, rested on implications drawn from ideal typical characterizations (for instance, Titmuss' (1974) distinction between residual, industrial-achievement and institutional types of welfare state, and Marshall's (1975) categorization of stages in the development of citizenship rights), research on the institutional characteristics of welfare programmes conducted at the Swedish Institute of Social Research since 1981 (organized by Walter Korpi and Gøsta Esping-Andersen) has now begun to make possible a quantitative assessment of the impact of such particular instruments as contributory insurance, the extent of coverage, the degree of benefit equality and the operation of means tests.

These new sources of data permit us to take the initial steps towards the elaboration, operationalization and testing of a comparative model of the linkages between welfare effort, welfare instruments and welfare outcomes. In this chapter we seek to locate some of these linkages, to map their incidence in cross-national terms and to explore the factors which condition their operation. These are all necessary preliminaries to addressing the central question of whether the English-speaking nations really do share a common pattern of linkages between the welfare state and equality once the focus of analysis is extended beyond expenditures to the policy instruments that target spending to particular groups of recipients.

One of the authors of this chapter has been prominent amongst those who have sought to understand the dynamic of welfare provision through a comparative and quantitative analysis of welfare effort (Castles, 1982); the other is a researcher whose focus of analysis has been the new data emerging from the Luxembourg Incomes Study (Mitchell, 1990). We take our title from Gösta Esping-Andersen's pioneering volume, *The Three Worlds of Welfare Capitalism* (1990), on the distributional consequences of choosing between diverse types of policy instruments. In our analysis, we question his conclusions, not because we doubt that the three worlds of Liberal, Conservative or corporatist, and Social Democratic welfare capitalism he identifies have strong empirical referents, but rather because our empirical analysis of the linkages between effort, instruments and outcomes suggests, in addition, the existence of a fourth 'radical' world, the characteristics of which help to explain some of the puzzles arising from the welfare performance of the English-speaking nations.

Linkages of the Welfare State

The availability of reliable cross-national microdata on the incidence of poverty and inequality is going to alter the entire character of comparative social policy analysis. The centrality of the welfare state in the comparative public policy literature has until now drawn its rationale from plausible inferences concerning the impact of government intervention on distributional outcomes in advanced societies. However, in the absence of any independent measure of outcomes, both aggregate expenditures and types of instruments necessarily became proxies for distributional consequences, making any serious distinction between means and ends impossible. The debate about the linkage between the extent and type of government intervention and social justice became a matter of demonstrating what nations, for which reasons, spent most on social policy objectives and then of devising a quasi-moral calculus by which it could be shown that some types of instruments for achieving those objectives were more welfare-conferring than others.

The inadequacies of aggregate expenditure as a proxy for outcomes have always been recognized by practitioners of comparative policy analysis but, understandably, since stressing them without an alternative would have implied the need to abandon comparative social policy research altogether, they have not, until quite recently, been strongly emphasized. Now, with the LIS providing a series of reasonably reliable, cross-national measures of such outcomes as poverty head-counts (the number in poverty), poverty gaps (the aggregate expenditure required to remove measured poverty) and various indices of income inequality, locating those inadequacies can become part of a process of model-building by which we can better explain the forces contributing to social policy outcomes. Such a model will still necessarily include expenditure – the extent of resources a society is willing to transfer from some groups of citizens to others clearly remains an important limiting condition of the extent to which it can modify existing outcomes – but it must also include at least three other factors generally neglected in aggregate expenditure studies.

The first of these factors is precisely the character of the existing outcomes which social policy interventions seek to modify. *Ceteris paribus*, an identical input of expenditure will lead to quite different observed levels of poverty and inequality depending on the distribution of income prior to income maintenance expenditures and taxes. One crucial determinant of that initial distribution is the extent of 'need' in a particular society (see Gilbert and Moon, 1988). Leaving aside the much argued topic of the extent to which institutional arrangements, such as incomes policies and practices of corporatist intermediation, can modify primary income distribution, it is quite apparent that demographic and social structural features have a major impact on the need for government interventions to redistribute income. The greater the percentage of the aged, the unemployed, of single parents and of children dependent on any other of these categories, the greater the inputs a government will have to make to obtain a high level of post-transfer, post-tax, equality.

A second inadequacy of the expenditure approach is that it ignores the way in which the welfare dollar is spent. As Esping-Andersen puts it (1990, 19–20):

> By scoring welfare states on spending, we assume that all spending counts equally. But some welfare states, the Austrian one, for example, spend a large share on benefits to privileged civil servants. This is normally not what we would consider a commitment to social citizenship and solidarity. Others spend disproportionately on means-tested social assistance. Few contemporary analysts

would agree that a reformed poor-relief tradition qualifies as a welfare-state commitment.

The final remark illustrates the tendency to shift to a quasi-moral calculus in debates of this kind but, stripped of such connotations, the point being made is the wholly correct one that the redistributive consequences of a given quantum of expenditure depend on the instruments through which it is delivered. Earnings-related (or status-related) benefits will clearly have a less equalizing effect, all other things being equal, than flat-rate benefits; universalism (the provision of benefit to all members of a categorical group – the aged, the unemployed, etc.) will, other things being equal, lead to greater equality of treatment of citizens than means-tested or targeted benefits. As already noted, however, since these latter are directed to the less well-off, they are inherently more redistributive in income terms. Because Esping-Andersen's account is less immediately concerned with redistribution than with the rights-conferring aspects of welfare provision – his organizing problematic is a notion of welfare 'de-commodification', defined in terms of welfare 'rendered as a matter of right' (1990, 22) – he is unwilling to concede the welfare-conferring potential of means-tested benefits in redistributive terms. As we shall see subsequently, this has important implications for his categorization of worlds of welfare capitalism.

A third deficiency of the aggregate expenditure approach is that it has largely ignored linkages between taxation and the various components of welfare provision. At least four important points should be made here. First, that the capacity to spend for social purposes depends on the capacity to extract for social purposes; some tax instruments – in particular, dedicated social security contributions – appear to be far more closely associated with high levels of welfare effort than others (see Castles, 1990). Second, tax expenditures, representing tax revenues foregone by governments through the operation of deductions, concessions and rebates, in themselves constitute a significant welfare instrument, increasing the household disposable incomes of particular groups of 'beneficiaries' *vis-à-vis* others (Gilbert and Moon, 1988). Third, and systematically unnoticed by those who laud the virtues of the big-spending welfare state, many of those nations providing the most generous direct benefits are also most assiduous in 'clawing-back' benefits through taxation (Mitchell, 1990, 113–25). Targeting, in the sense of making sure that most benefit goes to the poor, is a phenomenon by no means restricted to the nations conventionally labelled as providing 'residual' social provision; it is rather that, in these systems, targeting takes place through the direct benefit system, whereas, in many European nations, targeting occurs through taxation and, often (in a no less intrusive and stigmatizing way) as officials inquire into taxpayers' patterns of spending to establish their probable 'true' income levels. Fourth, it must be noted that in outcome terms, and other things being equal, the more progressive the tax structure, the greater is likely to be the extent of income redistribution.

The model of welfare linkages presented here is a very simple one. To understand the genesis of welfare outcomes, we have to start from the way in which the different incidence of need in different countries leads to variation in the distribution of market incomes. Thereafter, the redistributive policy process begins, whereby market income is modified by a series of inputs consisting of the level of expenditure devoted to social policy goals and the level of revenues extracted to finance these expenditures. The final distribution of income will also depend on the characteristics of the transfer and tax instruments, for example, the extent to which expenditures and revenues are targeted. Changes in needs, the distribution of market incomes from employment or any one of these policy instruments will necessarily modify the distribution of post-transfer, post-tax, incomes.

The model is simple because it ignores a variety of reciprocal linkages which may also substantially influence final poverty and inequality outcomes. For instance, it ignores the possibility of the 'shifting' behaviour resulting from the fact that high rates of progressive taxation may be taken into account in negotiations leading to pay relativities and, hence, in initial market income distributions (see Dernberg, 1974). It also ignores the fact that some aspects of the private provision of welfare (i.e. benefits procured through private insurance provision) are already included in the initial distribution of incomes and that the extent of such private provision is itself likely to be inversely related to the public provision of transfers. Moreover, the model does not take account of the possible ambiguity of the interaction between social insurance contributions and redistribution, with the contributory principle serving as a stimulus to the expenditure that makes possible welfare generosity, whilst simultaneously biasing that expenditure in a regressive direction. Finally, it further neglects the possibility, strongly argued by the protagonists of universal and generous welfare benefits, that means-testing will have a double knock-on effect on the extent of welfare expenditure: first, by its automatic effect of non-provision for the better-off and, second, because it will dissuade the better-off from supporting adequate benefits for the poor. If this indirect effect could be empirically demonstrated to outweigh the direct redistributional impact of means tests, the redistributional case for targeted instruments would be much weakened.

Whilst the model is simple, it does go well beyond the mere identification of expenditure levels or instruments with outcomes. It also has the strong policy implication of alternative routes to similar redistributive goals, so that, for instance, those who wish simultaneously to offer equality of citizen status and a measure of redistribution may, arguably, have their cake and eat it by providing universal benefits, whilst financing them from a highly progressive tax system.

Basically, the model transforms the research task of comparative social policy analysis from an account of the factors determining the nature of inputs of whichever kind to a threefold endeavour: (1) of establishing the precise nature of the linkages operating in particular countries and policy areas, (2) of locating the broad configurations of welfare linkages that characterize contemporary welfare states and (3) of seeking reasons why particular configurations occur in particular nations. The first task involves detailed empirical analysis of the income distribution process in as large a number of countries as possible and constitutes the research agenda of the LIS project. The second involves typology construction, and the third a search for explanations. This chapter, in a necessarily preliminary way, attempts to make some headway with these latter tasks.

A focus on characterizing and understanding patterns of welfare linkages is anything but irrelevant to our brief of identifying the extent to which English-speaking nations really do constitute a single family of nations in respect of welfare outcomes. The elaboration of a typology of worlds of welfare capitalism, defined by the degree to which particular patterns of expenditure and instruments lead to particular distributional outcomes, allows us to assess the similarity or otherwise of the English-speaking nations on the basis of criteria far more comprehensive and far more relevant to distributional issues than those utilized in previous comparative analysis. Were we to discover that the English-speaking nations are characterized by a similar range of social policy instruments and distributional outcomes, as well as by similar expenditure levels, that might indeed be regarded as *a priori* evidence of strong 'family' likeness in respect of the role of the state in social protection. If, on the other hand, similarity of expenditure levels is conjoint with systematic dissimilarities in these other respects, the 'family' metaphor might be rather less appropriate and our task would be one of explaining why it is that the English-speaking nations, despite ostensible similarities in respect of spending, seek to provide social justice in different ways and with different consequences.

Types of Typologies

The logic of our model implies that categorizations of welfare states on the basis of any single linkage component are unlikely to have the same explanatory potential as those based on two or more components. Modifying the familiar categorization of expenditure leaders and laggards by additional information (about the extent of needs, the character of transfer instruments and the structure of taxation) should lead to typologies which are better able to predict redistributive outcomes than those based on expenditure alone. In this section, we explore a number of possible typologies that relate to the way in which policy-making contributes to such outcomes. Although some categories of need can be altered by policy-action – reducing unemployment by an 'active' labour market policy is a prime example – that is not generally the case. We concentrate instead on the direct policy mechanisms of social security and taxation, which aim to transform the distribution of market incomes.

Esping-Andersen's work is an obvious starting-point in the search for relevant criteria by which to classify transfer instruments. Not only does he elaborate a typology of worlds of welfare capitalism on the basis of the index of de-commodification mentioned earlier, but he also creates three further measures which supposedly tap salient dimensions of welfare-state stratification, that term being used to denote ways in which the welfare state serves to structure the quality of social citizenship (Esping-Andersen, 1990, 57). Because he is quite explicitly critical of comparative research based on expenditure criteria, he seeks to derive each of these classifications substantially from quantitative data on transfer instruments or their impact. The findings of the de-commodification index and measures of stratification are seen as being mutually reinforcing. Nations fall into three groupings on the criterion of degree of de-commodification; these three configurations are argued by Esping-Andersen to correspond reasonably closely to the groupings located by strong adherence to particular principles of stratification. These classifications are presented in Table 3.1.

Table 3.1: Esping-Andersen's worlds of welfare capitalism

De-commodification			Principles of stratification*		
Low	Medium	High	Liberal	Conservative	Socialist
Australia	Italy	Austria	Australia	Austria	Denmark
US	Japan	Belgium	Canada	Belgium	Finland
New Zealand	France	Netherlands	Japan	France	Netherlands
Canada	Germany (West)	Denmark	Switzerland	Germany (West)	Norway
Ireland	Finland	Norway	US	Italy	Sweden
UK	Switzerland	Sweden			

Source: Esping-Andersen, 1990, Tables 2.2 and 3.3.
* Only countries classified as strong exponents of particular stratification principles are shown here.

First, there is a Liberal world of welfare capitalism in which de-commodification (measured in terms of the replacement rates of benefits, length of contribution periods and the individual's share of benefit financing) is low, and where Liberal principles of stratification (measured by the extent of means-tested poor relief, private pensions and private expenditure on health) are prevalent. This is the world of the selectivist and residual welfare state, limiting 'the realm of social rights' and providing 'a blend of a relative equality among state-welfare recipients, market-differentiated welfare among the majorities, and a class-political dualism between the two' (Esping-Andersen, 1990, 27). On the basis of the de-commodification typology, the Liberal world is exclusively English-speaking. All six English-speaking nations fall into the low de-commodification category and no others. Moreover, three of the six English-speaking nations are amongst the five strongest exemplars of the Liberal stratification principle – Australia, Canada and the US being joined in this by Japan and Switzerland.

Second, there is a world of moderate de-commodification described by Esping-Andersen as 'corporatist'. This is associated with the contributory and earnings-related characteristics of continental European welfare states and is mirrored by a Conservative stratification principle resting on corporatism and etatism in welfare provision. This world is shaped by the twin historical legacy of corporatism and Catholic social policy, limiting the direct role of the state to the provision of income maintenance benefits related to status-position (Esping-Andersen, 1990, 27). It is important to note that, in Esping-Andersen's view, the Conservative welfare state is not inherently more egalitarian than its Liberal counterpart, since the 'state's emphasis on upholding status differences means that its redistributive impact is negligible' (ibid.). Italy, France, Germany, Japan, Finland and Switzerland are corporatist in de-commodification terms; the first three also feature as Conservative in terms of stratification.

Finally, there is a Social Democratic world of welfare capitalism in which de-commodification is high, and there is a corresponding Socialist principle of stratification, resting on universal benefits and a high degree of benefit equality. This world is seen as the product of a Social Democratic ideology, which eschewed 'a dualism between state and market [and] between working class and middle class … [and sought to] promote an equality of the highest standards, not an equality of minimal needs as was pursued elsewhere' (Esping-Andersen, 1990, 27). Esping-Andersen clearly sees this world as being much the most redistributive in terms of both objectives and achievements. The Netherlands, Denmark, Norway and Sweden feature as both Social Democratic and ultra-Socialist, with Austria and Belgium fitting this classification in de-commodification terms, but adhering to Conservative principles of stratification.

Esping-Andersen's finding – that the countries which manifest the least de-commodification of social rights comprise precisely that grouping of English-speaking nations demonstrated in our own and other studies to be simultaneously the most conspicuous expenditure laggards – appears at first glance to be a major step in establishing a fundamental family likeness in the character of social protection in these nations. However, although we strongly support the logic of Esping-Andersen's attempt to improve the classificatory power of welfare state analysis by locating the impact of diverse social policy instruments, it is necessary to query both the theoretical and empirical status of his de-commodification typology.

Theoretically, Esping-Andersen's typologizing rests on the insight that 'not all spending counts equally' and yet his classifications rest on composite indices which are heavily influenced by expenditure considerations. This is particularly true of the de-commodification index, where both minimum benefit rates and standard benefits for an average worker feature as major components of the index. But such replacement rates are inherently related to the aggregate expenditures which Esping-Andersen otherwise rejects as a basis for comparative social policy analysis. As OECD statisticians have pointed out (OECD, 1985), aggregate expenditures can be decomposed in terms of the size of the population in need (demography), coverage of that population and average real benefit. Replacement rates are, in different ways and to varying degrees, proxies for average real benefit, with high average benefits being aggregated to contribute in an important way to high national welfare expenditures. Hence, it is not surprising that there are statistically significant relationships between both transfers as a percentage of GDP and the ratio of transfers to need and the de-commodification index (see Table 3.6 below); nor that the six nations scoring bottom on aggregate expenditures are also bottom in de-commodification terms. In justifying his double weighting for replacement rates in the index, Esping-Andersen points to their 'singular importance ... for people's welfare-work choices' (1990, 54). By doing so, he in effect undermines his own contention that aggregate expenditure is largely irrelevant to the distributional outcomes of the welfare state.

Moreover, turning to more detailed empirical matters, both the de-commodification index and the Socialist stratification index are highly influenced by somewhat idiosyncratic decisions about the import of means testing of benefits in two of the English-speaking nations, Australia and New Zealand. In both cases, index scores are adjusted well below actual coverage ratios on the grounds that such 'programs are highly conditional in terms of offering rights' (Esping-Andersen, 1990, 54). That is as may be, but what Esping-Andersen fails to note is that, insofar as rights are affected, it is not the poor and disadvantaged who lose out – their right to benefit in these countries is absolute (and, in some instances, appreciably greater than in the nations of income-related benefits) – but rather those coming from middle and upper echelons of income and wealth. Esping-Andersen's operationalization makes absolutely no sense in terms of a Socialist principle of stratification and only a sort of sense in the case of de-commodification, assuming that that principle is absolutely unrelated to redistributive outcomes.

The real problems of this classification are made blatantly apparent by Esping-Andersen's treatment of unemployment benefits. Both Australia and New Zealand score 'exceedingly low … because they offer only means-tested benefits' (1990, 51). Yet these nations, perhaps more than any others, may be seen as having provided a genuine 'work-welfare choice' (Esping-Andersen's decisive criterion for the presence of de-commodification) since unemployment benefits were, at least until recently, available irrespective of the duration of unemployment and without contribution. Since, in these nations, as in all others, the unemployed come substantially from the lower income ranges, the exclusions that derive from means testing are not very considerable. Means tests exclude the better-off and stigmatize the less well-off, but they have little direct effect on the income replacement rights of production workers earning poor or average wages. It is arguable whether or not unemployment benefits in Australia and New Zealand meet Esping-Andersen's critical criterion of de-commodification – that 'individuals or families can uphold a socially acceptable standard of living independently of market participation' (1990, 37) – but that is not because of the operation of means-tests, but because of the level of benefits. That is, once again, not a consideration independent of the extent of welfare expenditure and, in any case, is already adequately captured in the construction of the de-commodification index without requiring further adjustment.

Given these problems of theory and operationalization, as well as our explicit concern with the distributional rather than the status-conferring aspects of the welfare state in the English-speaking nations, it seems inappropriate to rest our analysis on any of Esping-Andersen's composite indices. On the other hand, the instrument measures from which those indices are constructed are potentially valuable indicators of the redistributional thrust of given choices of policy instruments. This is particularly true of the instruments – universalism and benefit equality – which go to make up the Socialist stratification index. Both are in principle related to the redistributive potential of the welfare state although, as we have noted, there is real disagreement as to whether universal benefits enhance or impede the achievement of greater equality. In fact, because Esping-Andersen's measure of universalism is not a true coverage ratio, but is arbitrarily adjusted to fit with theoretical preconceptions about the impact of means testing, it suffers from flaws similar to those in some of his composite indices.

That is not the case in respect of average benefit equality, however, which does appear to be a valuable quantitative indicator of the radical thrust of income maintenance policy, radicalism being interpreted here in terms of the equalizing potential of a given policy instrument. In Table 3.2 we present the typology that emerges from cross-classifying 18 OECD nations (the same 18 that feature in Esping-Andersen's study) in terms of high and low aggregate expenditure levels and high and low degrees of benefit equality.

Table 3.2: Welfare expenditure and benefit equality

		Household transfers as a percentage of GDP			
		Low		High	
Average benefit equality	Low	Canada Japan Switzerland US	**A**	Austria France Germany (West) Italy Netherlands	**B**
	High	Australia Finland Ireland New Zealand UK	**C**	Belgium Denmark Norway Sweden	**D**

Sources: Data on 1980–84 household transfers from Varley, 1986, 11, and on average benefit equality in 1980 from Esping-Andersen, 1990, 70–71.

It should be noted that the Varley data-set for transfer expenditure used here is derived from OECD sources and suffers from any defects therein. In particular, OECD transfers do not include occupational pensions mandated by legislation, but paid directly by employers. In Finland, this is a major item of transfer expenditure and might, if included, alter that country's classification in this and subsequent tables. It is also now becoming a major item in Australia, but in no way sufficient to alter that country's classification here or subsequently. The case for adjusting OECD data to take account of these exclusions is an arguable one, but we prefer to use the unadjusted data, noting that the major Finnish source advocating such an inclusion simultaneously complains of 'the large inequalities among pensioners ... partly due to the relatively large differences in the benefit levels of pension schemes' (Alestalo and Uusitalo, 1986, 229). In our view, the exclusion of employer-funded occupational schemes is justified precisely because they are likely to translate or magnify the inequalities of working life beyond pensionable age to a degree greater than would be acceptable to publicly-funded schemes.

Subject to this caveat, what is fascinating about this typology, based explicitly on the combination of aggregate expenditure and a single welfare instrument, is the degree to which it reproduces the worlds of welfare capitalism identified by Esping-Andersen in terms of his stratification principles. With the exception of Australia, Quadrant **A** consists of precisely those countries which most strongly manifest the Liberal principle. Quadrant **B** contains four of the five nations scoring highest on the Conservative principle, while three of the four nations contained in Quadrant **D** are firm exponents of the Socialist principle. What is different about our typology is the existence of a fourth type – Quadrant **C** – which is largely, but not exclusively, constituted by English-speaking nations. The crucial question is whether this fourth world of welfare is merely an artefact of this mode of typology construction, or whether it has a coherence similar to the other types in terms of its consequences for outcomes and its historical and structural origins. Much of the remainder of this chapter deals with these issues.

Here we simply note that, with the exception of Finland, conceivably to be explained in terms of the caveat concerning occupational pensions discussed above, the cases included in Quadrant **C** are those which fit least easily in to Esping-Andersen's own framework. Australia, as has been pointed out, is almost certainly misclassified by Esping-Andersen. Whilst the strong Liberal label is apposite in terms of the elements constituting his index of Liberal stratification, adjusting for the anomalous scoring in respect of universalism would make Australia a nation of strong Socialist stratification as well, the only instance in which a single nation scored strongly on two principles. Ireland, New Zealand and the UK are, by contrast, cases which Esping-Andersen does not classify as adhering strongly to any single principle of stratification. Ireland is medium on Conservatism and low on Liberalism and Socialism. New Zealand is medium on Socialism (it too would be high with a rescoring of universalism that was not artificially biased against means testing) and low in other respects. The UK is medium on Liberalism and Socialism and low on Conservatism. That four of the five nations identified as potentially constituting an additional type or world of welfare capitalism are difficult or impossible to label using Esping-Andersen's typology suggests the possibility that the grouping in Quadrant **C** may capture a reality undiscovered by his study.

That impression is strongly reinforced when we turn our attention to questions of taxation, a component influencing welfare outcomes much neglected in comparative social policy research. Reliance on different tax instruments as a means of influencing the redistribution of income is analogous to the use of diverse transfer instruments to distribute social security expenditures. Whether progressivity is considered as a principle directing the provision of tax benefits, as a means of 'clawing-back' benefits accorded to the better-off or, more generally, as a principle that higher income earners should contribute a greater proportion of their income to social purposes, it will, in varying ways, reduce poverty and increase income equality. Since taxes on income and profits are ostensibly based on the principle of progressivity in most nations, and since most other taxes are levied on a proportional or even regressive basis income and profits, taxes as a percentage of GDP may be taken as a very crude proxy of the redistributive potential of a nation's tax system. Like the earlier measure of average benefit equality, it may be regarded as an alternative, and perhaps more fundamental, indicator of the radicalism of redistributive instruments. In Table 3.3 we present the typology that emerges from cross-classifying aggregate expenditure and aggregate income and profits tax revenues.

Very little comment is required concerning this typology. Except that Ireland and Canada have changed place between Quadrants **A** and **C**, Tables 3.2 and 3.3 are identical in their location of cases. It would appear that the same radical principle which leads to the equalization of benefits also leads to a high proportion of national income being extracted in the form of progressive taxes. It is this radical principle which clearly distinguishes between Esping-Andersen's high-spending Conservative and Social Democratic worlds. The fact that it also consistently discriminates between groups of low welfare spenders suggests that we should take the notion of a fourth world very seriously indeed – a world in which the welfare goals of poverty amelioration and income equality are pursued through redistributive instruments rather than by high expenditure levels. In that world, English-speaking nations are conspicuous. At the same time, however, the notion of a tightly-knit family of nations becomes less persuasive because the US and, to a lesser extent, Ireland and Canada (depending on whether one looks at benefit equality or taxation), appear to inhabit a world of welfare in which substantial redistribution by either route is unlikely.

Table 3.3: Welfare expenditure and taxes

		Household transfers as a percentage of GDP			
		Low		High	
Income and profits taxes as a percentage of GDP	Low	Ireland Japan Switzerland US	**A**	Austria France Germany (West) Italy Netherlands	**B**
	High	Australia Canada Finland New Zealand UK	**C**	Belgium Denmark Norway Sweden	**D**

Sources: Data on 1980–84 household transfers from Varley, 1986, 11, and on average income and profits tax revenues 1980–84 from OECD, 1986.

Before turning to evidence concerning the redistributional profiles of the four worlds of welfare identified here, it is worth briefly noting an additional point supportive of the notion of a distinct radical dimension of state activity, essentially independent of a nation's expenditure propensity. In Chapter 1, we noted that the one area of state intervention about which the English-speaking nations could boast was in respect of their high degree of government employment. Australia, Canada, New Zealand, the UK and the US were the five biggest employers of labour in 1960 and, although by 1983 the profile of the English-speaking nations was not markedly different from the OECD mean, only the US had dropped out of the top half of the distribution. What was not explicitly noted in Chapter 1 was that at both dates the other countries featuring as large employers were primarily Scandinavian: Sweden, Norway and Denmark in 1960 and in 1983 Finland also. At both dates, the only non-English-speaking and non-Scandinavian nation to feature as a large employer was Austria. This means that, by 1983, the distribution of these nations in respect of state employment was almost identical to the distribution of income and profits taxes presented in Table 3.3 above, the only difference being that, in respect of state employment,

Austria was in the top half of the distribution and, in respect of taxes, Belgium was in the top half. It follows from our previous discussion that state employment and benefit equality are only to a slightly lesser degree associated.

The strength of the associations between these variables is more formally demonstrated by the correlation matrix appearing in Table 3.4.

Table 3.4: Correlation matrix for radical state and expenditure variables

	(1)	(2)	(3)	(4)
(1) 1980 Benefit Equality	1			
(2) 1980–84 Income + Profits Tax	.70	1		
(3) 1983 State Employment	.61	.72	1	
(4) 1980–84 Transfers	.19	–.04	.04	1

Sources: For benefit equality, taxes and transfers, as in Tables 3.2 and 3.3. For state employment, see Cusack et al., 1989, 474. Since Ireland is excluded from the state employment data-set, correlations refer to 17 cases only.

Apart from the highly significant associations between benefit equality, taxes and state employment, it will be noted that none of these variables is in any degree associated with the expenditure dimension of welfare. It would therefore appear that the first three of these attributes covering a wide range of important activities of the modern state – the targeting of its welfare system, the structure of its tax system and its role as employer – are clustered together in a manner quite different from the spending activities of the state.[1] Moreover, the thrust of this dimension is unequivocally radical insofar as it expresses traditional socialist demands of equality of treatment, financing of common purposes by those who can most afford it, and ownership by the state of utilities and welfare services.

Redistribution and Types of Welfare Capitalism

An important step in establishing the validity of our 'four worlds' of welfare model is to contrast its power to explain outcomes with that of other potential explanatory paradigms. Here, the availability of the LIS dataset is invaluable, although with only ten OECD nations included in the first wave for the early 1980s, the conclusions of any analysis necessarily remain somewhat tentative. In this section, we use measures pertaining to the distribution and redistribution of incomes in order to ascertain whether each of the four worlds of welfare we have identified corresponds to distinctive outcomes and whether our model's explanatory power is greater than that of other models.

In Table 3.5, we present data on the pre-transfer and post-transfer, post-(income) tax Gini coefficients of inequality for the ten nations in the first wave of the LIS data, together with a measure of the net redistribution occurring as a consequence of the impact of diverse types of tax-transfer systems on the distribution of market income.

Table 3.5: Ranks based on Gini coefficients pre-transfer, post-transfer, post-tax and net redistribution, circa 1980–81

Rank	Pre-transfer Gini		Post-tax Gini		Net redistribution (per cent)	
1	Norway	.385	Sweden	.197	Sweden	53
2	Canada	.387	Norway	.234	Norway	39
3	UK	.393	Germany (West)	.252	Germany (West)	38
4	Germany (West)	.407	UK	.264	Netherlands	37
5	Switzerland	.414	Australia	.287	France	35
6	Australia	.414	Canada	.293	UK	33
7	Sweden	.417	Netherlands	.293	Australia	31
8	US	.425	France	.307	US	25
9	Netherlands	.467	US	.317	Canada	24
10	France	.471	Switzerland	.336	Switzerland	19

Source: Calculated from LIS datafiles.

Looking first at pre-transfer Gini coefficients, which reflect both the inequality of income from employment and the existence of diverse degrees of need, we note the absence of any obvious connection between levels of inequality and either our four worlds or Esping-Andersen's three worlds of welfare capitalism. Of the Socialist nations, Norway ranks as the most equal nation, whilst Sweden ranks seventh; of the Conservative nations, Germany ranks fourth and France tenth, and of the Liberal (or low de-commodification) nations, Canada ranks second and the US eighth. Only the nations located in Quadrant **C** fit somewhat more closely, with all of them being at or above the median level of equality. Similarly, there is no association between the fact of a nation being English-speaking and the extent of its pre-transfer income inequality, with two such nations ranking near the top of the distribution and two in the bottom half. The absence of any link between pre-transfer inequality and configurations of welfare linkages is, of course, not very surprising. Redistributive effort is designed to redress prior inequalities and might well be expected to demonstrate an inverse relationship to primary income distribution. The single most important factor contributing to such prior inequalities is unquestionably the age structure of the population, in particular, the percentage above working age. In addition, to the degree that high levels of state-provided welfare have squeezed private insurance provision, we would expect high expenditure states to be those with the most unequal initial distribution of income.

Post-transfer, post-tax Gini coefficients manifest an utterly different picture and one in which the impact of diverse configurations of welfare instruments begins to be apparent. In this respect, Sweden and Norway rank first and second and, at the other end of the distribution, the US and Switzerland (two LIS countries that are Liberal in Esping-Andersen's classification and feature in Quadrant **A** in ours) rank ninth and tenth. This is precisely the result that would be predicted on the basis of our own typology and is also compatible with Esping-Andersen's interpretation. However, since Esping-Andersen classifies the Quadrant **C** nations appearing in the LIS dataset – Australia, Canada and the UK – as nations of low decommodification and largely adhering to Liberal stratification principles, he would presumably predict that these nations would have less favourable equality outcomes than the Netherlands which, according to his classification, is a Socialist high de-commodification system.

The data do not, however, support such a contention. The UK, Australia and Canada all manifest lower levels of post-transfer, post-tax inequality than the Netherlands. On the other hand, the fact that these three English-speaking nations – Liberal in Esping-Andersen's classification and inhabitants of a distinctive world of low expenditures but targeted instruments in ours – manifest a higher level of post-transfer, post-tax equality than France and a lower level than Germany (the two Conservative nations in the LIS dataset) contradicts neither exercise in typologizing. Esping-Andersen is explicit in pointing out that higher de-commodification in Conservative nations has no inherent redistributive implications. Our own position is that high welfare expenditures (characteristic of the Conservative welfare states) and targeting through either the transfer or tax systems (characteristic of the nations in Quadrant **C**) are alternative or complementary mechanisms of income redistribution, and we do not venture an *a priori* theoretical judgement about which is likely to be more effective. What the finding does seem to contradict is the notion that the English-speaking countries can be readily identified as a coherent family of nations in terms of final outcomes, for, despite similar welfare expenditure outcomes, a number of them fall in the middle rather than at the bottom of the income redistribution range.

At first glance, the net redistribution findings are nicely poised between Esping-Andersen's interpretation and our own and do show a real clustering of the English-speaking nations in terms of the overall policy-impact of expenditure and instruments. In favour of Esping-Andersen's thesis, should be counted the fact that his three Socialist nations rank in the first four in redistribution terms; also, it now becomes apparent that the one reason for the Netherlands to be so seriously misclassified *vis-à-vis* the nations of Quadrant **C** in post-transfer, post-tax terms is because of its high level of pre-tax inequality. Against his interpretation, should be counted only the fact that the Netherlands and Germany exchange ranks. Turning to the four worlds interpretation, support comes from the almost perfect clustering of types: Quadrant **D** first, **B** second, **C** nations third and **A** fourth and last. Against, should be counted the one exception, Canada, which is situated in Quadrant **C** according to the income tax-based typology (although not in terms of benefit equality, where the clustering is wholly perfect), but is ranked behind the US in redistributional terms. In favour of the thesis of 'English awfulness' (a more than somewhat evaluative designation deriving from the earliest work on the families of nations project – see Castles and Merrill, 1989) is the fact that four of the five lowest ranks go to the four English-speaking countries, and against only that Switzerland ranks lowest of all.

But the similar degree of support for the various explanations is only apparent. Because Esping-Andersen's does not distinguish the redistributional effects of Conservative and Liberal welfare states, his prediction amounts only to an expectation that Sweden, Norway and the Netherlands will manifest more equalizing policies than the other seven nations. That is true for Sweden and Norway, whilst the Netherlands achieves a greater equalization than all other nations except Germany. On the other hand, we predict a rather more differentiated hierarchy, with Quadrant **D** nations being the most equalizing, Quadrant **A** nations the least and Quadrant **B** and **C** nations falling in between. Although in our case there is also one departure from the expected hierarchy (i.e. Canada), the degree of fit of the four worlds model is appreciably greater simply because its detailed predictive power is greater. The same applies to a contrast between the 'English awfulness' thesis and the more differentiated four worlds model.

The analysis so far has rested on contrasting the degree of fit of various categorizations of welfare state – our four worlds model, Esping-Andersen's de-commodification types and English-speaking and non-English-speaking states. Although re-emphasizing the caveats inherent in the analysis of only ten cases, it is worth cross-checking these findings with those which emerge from a more formal statistical analysis. Table 3.6 presents a correlation matrix that locates the strength of the association between net redistribution and five other variables: (1) 1981 transfers as a percentage of GDP (the most familiar measure of expenditures); (2) 1981 income plus profits taxes as a percentage of GDP (our favoured measure of redistributive instruments – see Table 3.3); (3) an index of redistributive potential (simply the additive function of (1) plus (2) and, hence, a crude test variable for the four worlds model based on the joint effect of expenditure and redistributive instruments); (4) Esping-Andersen's de-commodification index, and (5) Englishness (English-speaking nations scored 1; others 0).

Table 3.6: Correlation matrix for variables predicting net redistribution

	(1)	(2)	(3)	(4)	(5)	(6)
(1) 1981 Transfers	1					
(2) 1981 Income + Profits Taxes	–.16	1				
(3) 1981 Redistributive Potential	.76	.52	1			
(4) De-commodification (circa 1980)	.58	.35	.73	1		
(5) English-speaking	–.70	.02	–.59	–.83	1	
(6) Net Redistribution	.69	.50	.92	.62	–.47	1

Sources: as in Table 3.3 and Esping-Andersen, 1990, 52.

Much that has been argued or implied in the previous analysis is supported by the findings of Table 3.5. Harking back to our suggestion that Esping-Andersen's de-commodification index is contaminated by expenditure considerations, we note the moderately strong association between transfers and de-commodification. We further note the existence of strong to moderately strong associations between both expenditure and taxation and net redistribution of the kind implied by our linkages model, with the former significant even in a sample this small. There is, however, no link between expenditure and taxation, suggesting that these two predictors of redistribution are largely independent of each other – that the choice to redistribute by one route has no implications in respect of the other. That being so, it is not surprising that the combined index of redistributive potential that these measures jointly constitute should be so massively related to net redistribution, explaining more than 80 per cent of the variance. In comparison, de-commodification and the common attributes of the English-speaking nations, at least as potential explanations of redistribution, fade into relative unimportance. Indeed, neither is as strong a predictor of redistribution as expenditure alone.

Ideally, we would wish to test the degree of fit of all these competing explanations against complete data from all 18 cases included in the typologies of Tables 3.1, 3.2 and 3.3, but that must necessarily await the further expansion of the LIS dataset. In the meantime, we wish merely to note that the four worlds model is a better predictor of redistributive outcomes than a conventional expenditure 'leaders and laggards' model, better than Esping-Andersen's typology based on social policy instruments and better than a model premised on the unique 'awfulness' of the English-speaking nations in social protection terms. Although the evidence is as yet insufficient to come to definitive conclusions as to the relative potential for vertical redistribution of different types of welfare states, we are surely entitled, *pro tem* at least, to prefer that which rests on an affirmation of two intuitively obvious social policy principles: that more expenditure on the poor and greater targeting of what expenditure there may be to the poorest are **both** factors likely to enhance vertical redistribution.

That also is the message of a multiple regression of net redistribution on both total transfer expenditure and progressive taxes as percentages of GDP.[2] Here, as previously, ten cases provide a basis for only interim conclusions, but the finding that both expenditures and our proxy for the progressivity of taxes are highly significant predictors of outcomes and of rather similar explanatory power offers some further substantiation of the case argued in these pages.[3] Certainly, that finding is enough to justify the final stages in our enquiry: first, an effort to locate the historical and political antecedents of the four worlds of welfare identified here and, second, a brief and somewhat speculative discussion of the reasons why a number of the English-speaking nations seem to cluster in a radical world in which redistribution is sought through targeted social policy instruments and progressive taxation rather than by means of generous welfare expenditures.

The Political Foundations of Welfare Outcomes

Much of the comparative literature on aggregate welfare expenditure has been concerned with the extent to which spending is a function of socio-economic variables and the extent to which it reflects political partisanship and class politics, in particular, the opposed interests of working class and bourgeois parties and organizations. We concede what is now the consensus position that this debate was far too extreme: expenditure levels are the outcome of a complex process in which myriad social, demographic, economic and political factors interact, sometimes with different results under diverse historical circumstances (see Castles, 1990). In this section, we do not intend to disinter these old quarrels about the ultimate causes of welfare development (see Wilensky, 1975; Castles, 1982), but rather seek to explore whether class politics and its partisan manifestations, now widely agreed to be amongst the important determinants of expenditure, also play a role in distinguishing worlds of welfare defined not only in expenditure terms, but also in terms of the character of the redistributive instruments they utilize.

There are good *a priori* reasons for believing this could well be so. Expenditure reflects class politics and party despite the fact that, as a measure of resources, it is necessarily immediately constrained by the availability of such resources (economic factors) and by the demand for such resources (need or demographic factors). But the choice between diverse types of instruments – the equality of benefits, their selectivity and the progressivity of taxes – has rather fewer immediate direct economic or demographic implications. It is a choice, first and foremost, about who (amongst potential recipients and potential financers of the welfare burden) is most worthy of favourable treatment by the political community and that makes it an intensely political choice. The underlying ideologies of partisanship in the advanced capitalist nations have a direct bearing on that choice in terms of their differing evaluations of state intervention to effect a greater or lesser degree of redistribution amongst classes and citizens. Hence, it is not surprising that Esping-Andersen finds that the three worlds of welfare capitalism, which he seeks to differentiate in terms of instruments, correspond to partisan political affiliations – Liberal, Conservative and Social Democratic – and to the underlying class historical configurations on which they rest. In effect, what we seek to do here is to establish whether the political logic which implies these three worlds of welfare capitalism simultaneously presupposes a fourth world to which a substantial number of the English-speaking nations belong.

The deliberate decision not to disinter the outworn polemics of the comparative public policy literature corresponds with a desire to avoid getting caught up in the quite possibly no less acrimonious debate likely to follow the publication of Peter Baldwin's (1990) brilliant historical analysis of the critical role of bourgeois parties in shaping welfare state reform. That book has already been seen as fundamentally challenging the predominantly social democratic historiography of the advanced welfare state (see Olsson, 1990). Baldwin's analysis rests on the proposition that certain policy instruments – in particular, universal benefit provision – may favour middle-class interests in horizontal redistribution through a widening of the pool of insured risk sharing, and that bourgeois parties will fight for extensions of the welfare state that have such characteristics. That middle-class parties may well be the protagonists of welfare reform we readily concede, but focus here substantially, although not exclusively, on the role of class politics as expressed through the strength of trade unionism and of leftist or non-right parties (the latter being an alternative categorization that sits rather more easily with Baldwin's thesis).

Our belief that class politics and its partisan manifestations remain the basic key to understanding important facets of the welfare state derives from our concern with vertical redistribution and the obviation of poverty, which clearly are goals which one might expect would distinguish the social policy stance of parties and groups ostensibly espousing lower-class interests. The one caveat we would propose to the Baldwin thesis is the extent to which he underplays the potential for and the politics of vertical redistribution in advanced capitalist societies. As Table 3.5 above demonstrates, that potential is not inconsiderable. Sweden succeeds in reducing income inequality by around 50 per cent, and all but three of the LIS nations reduce it by more than 30 per cent. On this count, it would appear that the tax-transfer state is on occasions rather more than merely the instrument of horizontal risk reallotment that Baldwin (1990) conceives it to be. Most certainly, it cannot be regarded as a part of that perverse exploitation of the disadvantaged by the advantaged that certain revisionist writers have identified as the crowning irony of welfare state development in the area of direct service provision (Le Grand, 1982).

We start our analysis by examining the political correlates of the differentiating criteria of expenditure and instruments and then proceed to more focused delineations of individual types. In each instance, our conclusions are stated as propositions locating strong tendencies, with any important exceptions noted in the text. In line with our intention of avoiding monocausal interpretation, we do not seek to explain those exceptions away, our only objective being to show whether or not a convincing case can be made for a broad correspondence between distinct political configurations and the four worlds of welfare identified in the prior analysis. In light of the case we are making for the distinctiveness of the world of welfare captured in Quadrant **C** of Tables 3.2 and 3.3, we devote a somewhat greater space to a discussion of the political configuration which emphasizes the primacy of equalizing instruments. Data sources for the judgements made are Paloheimo (1984) for cabinet incumbency, Mackie and Rose (1984) for electoral support, and Stephens (1979) and Bain and Price (1988) for trade union density.

Proposition 1. High expenditure countries (those on the right hand side of Tables 3.2 and 3.3) are nations in which the political right has not been in office for long periods in the post-war era. Counting Christian Democratic,

democratic socialist and centrist agrarian parties as non-right, this generalization holds for all these nations except France under the Fifth Republic.

Proposition 2. Low expenditure countries (those on the left-hand side of Tables 3.2 and 3.3) are nations in which the political right has enjoyed long periods of political office. Japan, the US, Australia, New Zealand and the UK are countries in which the right has ruled through a major dominant party for more than half the post-war era, and Ireland and Switzerland are ones in which either rightist factions have alternated or ruled in coalition. Canada is a case which defies easy classification. The until recently hegemonic Canadian Liberal Party is clearly to the left of the Conservative Party but, over time, its adherence to progressive causes has varied quite markedly. Some writers, deriving their classification from a neo-Marxist perspective, count both Canadian parties, as both American ones, as 'bourgeois' in partisan complexion (see Schmidt, 1982, 135). The operational definition of non-right parties (used as the differentiating criterion for the typology of political configurations which appears below in Table 3.7) rests on partisan control by Christian Democratic, democratic socialist and centrist agrarian parties. Canada does not constitute an exception to Proposition 2 on this basis.

We remind readers that Finland's location in Quadrant **C** rather than **D** depends to some extent on an operational choice concerning the classification of employer-paid occupational pensions. Finland is only an exception if, as here, we use OECD data excluding such pensions as a component of public expenditure. The Finnish right is unquestionably weak (see Alestalo, Flora and Uusitalo, 1985), but it is arguable that Finland's relatively low level of aggregate welfare spending when occupational pensions are excluded – and, indeed, the very fact that the choice was made to mandate the private sector to provide such pensions – stem from strong divisions on the left. These mean that democratic socialist and agrarian parties, though frequently in office, are usually in coalition with one or more parties with a much weaker ideological commitment to welfare state expansion.

Proposition 3. Countries which do not adopt equalizing instruments (those at the top of Tables 3.2 and 3.3), whether in respect of benefits or taxes, are ones in which the labour movement has been weak. Weakness here is measured in terms of union membership (the countries in the top half of Table 3.3 had an average level of union membership of 34 per cent of the labour force in 1984, whilst the countries in the bottom half averaged 60 per cent), in terms of parliamentary support for Social Democracy or Labour, and of cabinet incumbency of such parties. Only Germany and Austria are partial exceptions to this generalization. The German Social Democrats, however, only broke the 40 per cent barrier of voter support in the late

1960s, and the Austrian Party, although historically stronger, had to wait until 1970 before taking office outside the framework of a Proporz arrangement with its Christian Democratic rival.

Proposition 4. Countries which adopt equalizing instruments (those at the bottom of Tables 3.2 and 3.3) are predominantly those in which the labour movement has been strong. This is not always recognized by European scholars looking at the countries of the Antipodes (assuming they bother), but it should be noted that, taking the average vote from the beginning of this century, Australia's Labor Party has been more strongly supported than Sweden's Social Democrats; also that the New Zealand Labour Party's period of one-party majority rule from 1935–49 is second only to that of Norway's Social Democrats from 1945–63. In both Australia and New Zealand, the trade union movement has been historically strong, with the Scandinavian nations only decisively overtaking them in the post-war period. Canada is apparently again an exception, although the much greater strength of the social democratic NDP at the provincial level (in power in as many as three out of ten provinces at one time) than federally, mitigates the usual impression that Canada, like the US, is wholly lacking in a politically powerful labour movement. Belgium may be seen as an exception by some, but whether that is so depends on which criteria of labour movement strength are used. Belgium has manifested appreciably higher levels of union density than any country in the top half of the tables (in 1982, 78.6 per cent contrasted with the highest in the top half of the table, Austria, at 58.2 per cent), but Social Democratic party electoral support has been lower than in Germany and Austria. During the period 1950–80 the Belgian Social Democratic party was in office for longer, although usually as the subordinate coalition partner, than its equivalent in any of these nations except Austria.

Proposition 5. Low expenditure, low equalizing instruments countries (those in Quadrant A) are nations in which the role of the labour movement has been vestigial and in which rightist liberal parties have been dominant. The only possible partial exception might be Canada in respect of average benefit equality, depending on one's ideological classification of the Canadian Liberal Party. In ideological terms, this world of welfare capitalism is quite appropriately described as **Liberal**.

It is worth noting, however, that this world could as easily be distinguished in terms of party structures as of political ideologies, for what the otherwise very disparate American, Japanese, Irish and Swiss political systems have in common are democratic structures substantially untouched by the advent of modern mass parties, whether organized on the basis of working class mass mobilization and counter-mobilization or of 'catch-all' people's parties. To the degree that this is the case, one might speculate that an important political factor conditioning the achievement of redistributional outcomes in advanced capitalist states is the extent to which political structures have been modernized in such a way as to facilitate the articulation of the welfare demands of the democratic electorate.

Proposition 6. High expenditure, low equalizing instruments countries (those in Quadrant **B**) are nations in which the main political divide is between Catholicism and Socialism. In these countries, electoral competition between the people's parties representing these diverse strands of social thought has involved competitive pressure for greater expenditure, but the Catholic input has prevented any substantial equalizing thrust. Only in France does the structure of partisan conflict not reflect this basic cleavage division, although the input of Catholic social policy ideas in France is well established (Ashford, 1986). Labels here are not so obvious. Esping-Andersen offers both 'corporatist' and Conservative, though Christian Democratic or Catholic would be equally well merited. Our choice of **Conservative** simply reflects a wish to maintain continuity with that aspect of Esping-Andersen's analysis, his typologies of stratification principles, which has most resemblance to our own.

Proposition 7. Low expenditure, high equalizing instruments countries (those in Quadrant **C**) are nations in which a strong labour movement has found it difficult to translate popular support into cabinet incumbency during the post-war era. The mechanisms operating here are not wholly transparent and the directions of causality less than certain. That long-term incumbency is required to increase expenditure seems obvious enough, but how strong labour movement support can be translated into equalizing instruments is more difficult to understand.

The influence of a powerful trade union movement is clearly involved, with highly significant associations with all aspects of what we have earlier described as the radical dimension of state activity – with benefit equality .64, with taxes .73 and with state employment .76. The question is how, in the absence of democratic socialist governments, such an influence is exerted to promote equality. At least two possibilities can be discerned: first that the trade unions operate as an extra-parliamentary veto group opposed to reversals of existing egalitarian policies and, second, that the trade union density variable serves as a proxy for a strong solidaristic sentiment within the population which governments of whatever complexion must take into account in their decision-making. On either count, the world of welfare captured by Quadrant **C** must be regarded as a manifestation of the effects of class politics unalloyed by the influence of party. The impact of trade unionism or of solidarity expressed through trade unionism could perhaps best be likened to a ratchet effect by which reforms once in place are difficult to reverse, despite long periods in office of parties with little or no attachment to egalitarian principles. That leaves open the question of the mechanism by which equalizing instruments are first initiated as state policy.

Another probable contributory factor, and one which does offer a clue to the origin of such instruments, is the legacy of radical egalitarianism on the part of new social forces that emerged around the turn of the century and which strongly influenced the initial choices concerning how to structure welfare benefits and welfare financing. Such a legacy is common to Scandinavia and a number of the English-speaking nations, in the former deriving its impetus from the ideas of the 'people's movements' of the late 19th century (see Therborn, 1989), and in both Britain and the Antipodes from an admixture of social liberalism and trade union-inspired political organization (labourism). In much of Scandinavia, the coincidence in the early post-1945 era of Social Democratic hegemony and rapid economic growth led to the supplementation and partial usurpation of social protection through equalization by massively expanded welfare state expenditure. In the English-speaking countries, a labour movement which rarely succeeded in obtaining office has had to rest content with defending those equalizing reforms already enacted.

Finland's radical credentials are as profound as any of these nations, Scandinavian or English-speaking. Finland was the first country in Europe to confer female suffrage (New Zealand and Australia were the first in the world; perhaps this constitutes a criterion as good as any other of a radical commitment to citizen equality) and had a strongly peasant-based Social Democratic Party which was the first in Europe to achieve majority status (see Alapuro, 1988). What distinguishes Finland from the other Scandinavian countries to some extent and makes for similarity with some of the English-speaking nations is a greater reluctance on the part of the labour movement to move beyond an equalizing instruments approach to social policy. The ideology of workers' parties and organizations in the countries of early social radicalism was originally strongly imbued with an emphasis on the egalitarian virtues of selective social policy and flat-rate benefits. That changed in much of Scandinavia and in the UK in the early post-war years, but remains manifestly true of Australia and New Zealand throughout the post-war era. Significantly (and a pointer to a welfare difference between Finland and the other Scandinavian countries which is not solely dependent on the operational classification of occupational pensions), that is also the case in Finland. Here 'the most distinctive spokesman for universalism has been the Agrarian Party, while the Social Democrats have been stubborn supporters of the income test' (Kangas and Palme, 1989, 10).

That there is a connection between a continuing emphasis on an equalizing instruments approach to social policy and the relative weakness of Social Democracy seems clear, but the direction of causality is by no means self-evident. A strong argument can be mounted that structural impediments to democratic socialist incumbency in Australia, Britain, Finland and New Zealand are the fundamental determinants of a failure to obtain the governmental status required to legislate more generous welfare benefits. In the case of Australia, New Zealand and the UK, Labour parties have not fared well against unified parties of the Right in the context of plurality electoral systems. In the case of Finland, a strong cleavage line dividing Social Democrats and Communists has made it impossible for the left to rule except in coalition with a variety of middle-class parties with quite diverse social policy stances. However, the linkage between social policy stance and Social Democratic strength may also, in some part, be a matter of strategic choice by political actors. Seen in these latter terms, the abandonment of some aspects of the equalizing instruments approach in Denmark, Norway and Sweden – selectivity; to a more limited degree, benefit equality; and, only in the late 1980s, a major move away from reliance on progressive incomes and profits taxes as a means of financing the welfare state – and their replacement by an emphasis on expenditure generosity can be regarded as a deliberate response by Social Democratic parties in these countries to the problems of winning political support in the context of the rapidly changing social structure of a post-industrial society (see Esping-Andersen, 1990, 31). In this view, the failure of democratic socialist parties to obtain a strong purchase on government in the UK, Australia, New Zealand and Finland can, at least in some part, be attributed to these parties' social policy choices. Almost certainly, the direction of causality is both ways simultaneously, including a vicious circle by which structural conditions in some nations impede certain strategic options and a virtuous one in others where the two are mutually reinforcing. In any case, the direction is irrelevant to the basic contention of this section that a distinct political configuration corresponds to a distinct set of social policy outcomes in the nations located in Quadrant **C**. The only issue in question here is whether political causality is a matter of political structure or of political choice.

The combination of equalizing social policy instruments and low welfare expenditure identified in Quadrant **C** and the political configuration of a strong labour movement denied corresponding political power demands a label that provides clear differentiation from the other worlds of welfare capitalism located by Esping-Andersen's typologizing. The social liberal and 'laborist' (McIntyre, 1985) movements in the English-speaking nations in the early part of the century and the 'popular movements' of Scandinavia at the end of the 19th were frequently described as **Radical** rather than socialist by contemporaries. It seems wholly appropriate to use that term to denote a political configuration identified with the persistence of egalitarian social policies of precisely the kind that such movements sought to initiate and to arrogate the title of the radical dimension of state activity to the nations that adhere to it in its purest form.

Proposition 8. High expenditure, high equalizing instruments countries (those in Quadrant **D**) are nations in which a weak right is conjoint with a powerful trade union movement. In the three Scandinavian nations appearing in this quadrant in both Tables 3.2 and 3.3, we can be more specific and locate the prevailing political configuration in terms of the dominance or hegemony of Social Democracy. This suggests that Esping-Andersen's 'Socialist' label might be the appropriate one, but that clearly does not apply to Belgium,[4] where the most that can be argued is that a Social Democratic party, averaging around 32 per cent of the vote in the three decades 1950–80, and in coalition with the Christian Centre for approximately half that period, supplied a centre-left complexion to government for much of the post-war period. Of course, what the Social Democratic countries have in common with Belgium and what sets them apart from Germany and the Netherlands, is that the weakness of the political right in government is reinforced by labour movement support in the population expressed through trade union membership.[5] Under these circumstances, we adopt the label **Non-Right Hegemony (N-RH)** to express the political impetus shaping the world of welfare located in Quadrant **D**.

Table 3.7 provides a summary presentation of the political configurations described by these eight propositions. The underlined cases are those which do not fit precisely with the earlier observed configurations of aggregate expenditure and equalizing instruments, while the abbreviations in brackets indicate to which of our four worlds of welfare they properly belong in these terms. The labels in bold are the designations of the four worlds and appropriately describe the combination of aggregate expenditure and equalizing instruments for all but the underlined cases in each quadrant. In 14 cases the political configuration predicts the welfare configuration precisely and in no case is there a complete discontinuity between politics and welfare (i.e. expenditure may be lower (Finland) or higher (France) than predicted and income tax may be lower (Austria) or higher (Canada), but no country is misclassified on both counts).

Because of the lack of full LIS data, we do not, of course, know how all the countries in the typology of political configurations in Table 3.7 would perform in terms of redistributive outcomes. For the ten nations for which we do have such data (Table 3.4), only France is misclassified. With a

Table 3.7: Political configurations and worlds of welfare

		Non-Right incumbency			
		Low		High	
Trade union density	Low	*Canada* (Rad) *France* (Con) Ireland Japan Switzerland US	**Liberal**	Germany (West) Italy Netherlands	**Conservative**
	High	Australia New Zealand UK	**Radical**	*Austria* (Con) Belgium Denmark *Finland* (Rad) Norway Sweden	**N-RH**

Sources: Data on union density 1984 from Bain and Price (1988). Non-Right incumbency defined as the number of years between 1960–84 that the chief executive came from a Christian Democratic, democratic socialist or centrist agrarian party. Data from Paloheimo (1984).

strong political right and a weak labour movement, its degree of redistribution should be low, when in fact it is medium. With that exception, the three LIS countries sharing the same political configuration as France do manifest low degrees of redistribution; Norway and Sweden the two nations combining a weak right and strong labour movement exhibit a strong equalising tendency and the remaining cases fall in between the extremes.

Overall, the impression is of an extraordinarily close fit between political structure and the character of welfare provision; indeed, the degree of congruence is more apparent when instruments are taken into account than when expenditure is considered alone. Moreover, it is clear that our fourth world of Radical welfare capitalism corresponds closely to a particular configuration of political preconditions, consisting of a labour movement unable to obtain a degree of partisan control commensurate with its political support base in the community and of an historical legacy of radical egalitarianism. Three of the six English-speaking nations – Australia, New Zealand and the UK – are unequivocally located in this world. Two others – Canada and Ireland – have characteristics which cross-cut the Radical and

Liberal worlds. The US alone is clearly an inhabitant of the Liberal world. Whether under these circumstances it remains appropriate to think of a distinctive pattern of social protection somehow deriving from the common historical and cultural experience of an English-speaking family of nations is the subject of our concluding remarks.

On Degrees of Consanguinity

Family relationships can, of course, vary in their degree of closeness. In the case of our earlier analysis of the role of the state in the economy (see Chapter 1), they appeared to be rather close, with a similar policy dynamic emerging from common economic and political circumstances conditioned by a distinctive pattern of historical development. Here, in respect of the state's socially protective role, particularly insofar as that is directed towards redistribution, the relationship, if such there be, appears to be more distant. If the English-speaking nations of the Radical world of welfare capitalism are kin to the Liberal US or the ambivalent cases of Canada and Ireland, the relationship is perhaps more analogous to that of cousins than of siblings in that they share only to a limited degree in a common historical inheritance.

That shared component is most clearly manifested on the expenditure side, posing the question of whether or not the determinants of low aggregate expenditure in these nations share a common historical origin. A plausible argument might proceed from the fact noted in the earlier discussion of the state and the economy: that the early emergence of responsible government in all these nations (other than Ireland) led to the preservation of territorial forms of representation with high electoral thresholds, resulting in essentially two-party systems. Clearly, that would contribute to the explanation of why all these countries have been characterized by the relative strength of rightist governments inhibiting the incremental expansion of aggregate welfare expenditure.

At least two routes leading from high electoral thresholds to the strength of the right are arguable. First, in terms of historical priority, there is a route by which parties, entrenched by the difficulty of mounting a third-party challenge in a plurality voting system, could fight off the mobilizational challenge of new class forces. This makes comprehensible the absence of a socialist party in the US and the weakness of a socialist challenge at the federal level in Canada. Second, there is a route whereby socialist parties once mobilized were prevented from reaping the sort of electoral gains that could accrue from divisions of interest (not least, as Baldwin (1990) convincingly demonstrates, in the field of welfare) amongst the bourgeoisie.

As both Castles (1978) and Esping-Andersen (1985a) have argued, the Scandinavian Social Democrats gained decisively from a fragmentation of the right from which the Labour parties of the English-speaking nations with two-party systems could not benefit. Ireland too has had predominantly rightist government, not as a consequence of high electoral thresholds or a two-party system, but rather because the party system was mobilized around 'revolutionary' issues irrelevant to class concerns. Ireland has shared in the English-speaking nations' expenditure laggardliness, but not because it was part of a common family of nations.

Where family likeness tends to evaporate is on the egalitarian instruments side. Australia, New Zealand and the UK, together with Finland, form the central core of the radical world, sharing all the features characteristic of that cluster: high benefit equality, high progressive taxation, a large state sector in employment, strong trade unionism and a relatively poor record of democratic socialist incumbency. In the early 1980s, the US manifested none of these characteristics, although it is interesting to note that in the 1960s, and presumably earlier, it was in the top half of the distribution in respect of both progressive taxes and state employment. Contemporary Canada and Ireland share some features of the Radical and some of the Liberal world. Explaining the ultimate historical reasons for this diversity amongst the English-speaking nations across both time and space is far beyond the scope of this chapter, involving, amongst other things, an account of the reasons for the divergent pace and extent of labour movement mobilization in the six nations under review. That no easy conclusions are available is, perhaps, best indicated by the long decades of unresolved debate as to the reasons for the failure of the socialist enterprise in America, an issue almost certainly germane to why the US alone of the English-speaking countries finds itself unequivocally in the camp of Liberal welfare states today.

Perhaps equally mystifying are the reasons why any of the English-speaking nations, other than Britain (with its mass proletariat born of the first industrial revolution), should have experienced mass lower-class political mobilization at all. Countries like Australia and New Zealand, which together with Britain form the core of the Radical world of welfare capitalism, were the acknowledged home of labour activism at the turn of the century, yet almost entirely lacked an industrial working class that was to be the basis of such movements in Europe later in the century. These countries' early democratic and economic progress, as noted in Chapter 1, could be relevant, but not in a way which readily distinguishes them from the US. Possibly, the structural imperative for massive state intervention to establish the economic and social infrastructure of the Antipodean colonies supplies a part of the answer, and perhaps the fact that the 'fragments' of the British population exported to found these new nations were imbued with the newly burgeoning radicalism of the English working class (see Rosecrance, 1964) supplies another part. The latter argument at least would contribute a cultural and historical component to explain why a significant number of the English-speaking countries feature so conspicuously as the core nations of a Radical world of welfare capitalism.

Notes

1. Factor analysis of the four variables appearing in Table 3.4 demonstrates the existence of two quite distinct factors: the first loading on benefit equality, taxes and state employment and the second almost wholly on transfers.
2. 1981 Net Redistribution = –7.0 + 1.4. 1981 Social Security Expenditures (5.26) + 1.5. 1981 Incomes & Profit Taxes (4.21). **Adj R2 = .81.** (Figures are unstandardized regression coefficients; figures in parentheses are t-values. Data sources and definitions are those cited in Tables 3.3 and 3.4.) The quite fortuitous fact that the explained variation is almost identical to the crude additive index of potential redistribution in Table 3.6 is a function of the similarity of both the unstandardized regression coefficients (with a per cent of GDP expended on transfers being worth a 1.4 per cent reduction in inequality and a per cent of GDP extracted in income and profits taxes leading to a 1.5 per cent reduction) and the magnitudes of transfers and taxes.
3. For reasons of space, we have restricted our analysis to overall measures of distribution and redistribution, but it is worth noting that the conclusions which would have emerged from an analysis of poverty reduction would have been essentially similar. Using expenditure and benefit equality (i.e. the variables defining the typology in Table 3.2) as regressors of the reduction of the poverty head-count after transfers, we obtain the following equation: 1981 Poverty Reduction = 16.6 + 2.03. 1981 Social Security Expenditures (3.80) + 41.24. 1980 Benefit Equality (3.06). **Adj R2 = .72**. The definition of poverty reduction is the percentage change in the poverty head-count after transfers, using a poverty line of 50 per cent of median income adjusted by the OECD equivalence scale (see Mitchell, 1990).
4. Esping-Andersen uses the Socialist label to describe the stratification system of the Netherlands. That is at least as inappropriate as using the same label to describe Belgium. In the period 1950–80, the Dutch Social Democratic party supplied the Prime Minister more often than in Belgium and was in government for only a marginally shorter length of time, but it consistently enjoyed lower electoral support while the degree of union mobilization was approximately 50 per cent that achieved in Belgium.
5. A possibly significant difference remains in that in Belgium, unlike Scandinavia, the unions are divided on religious and political lines. Whether that difference has any implications for the equalizing thrust of social policy cannot be ascertained in the absence of LIS data for Belgium. It should be noted, however, that we have earlier mentioned that Belgium, whilst manifesting both high benefit equality and high levels of income and profits taxes, does not share all the aspects of the radical dimension of state activity in that its level of state employment falls in the bottom half of the OECD distribution.

References

Alapuro, R. (1988), *State and Revolution in Finland*, Berkeley: University of California Press.

Alestalo, M., Flora, P. and Uusitalo, H. (1985), 'Structure and Politics in the Making of the Welfare State: Finland in Comparative Perspective' in Risto Alapuro et al. (eds), *Small States in Comparative Perspective: Essays for Erik Allardt*, Oslo: Norwegian University Press, 188–210.

Alestalo, M. and Uusitalo, H. (1986), 'Finland' in Peter Flora (ed.), *Growth to Limits: The Western European Welfare States Since World War II*, Vol. 1, Berlin: de Gruyter.

Ashford, D. (1986), *The Emergence of Welfare States*, New York: Blackwell.

Bain, G.S. and Price, R. (1988), *Trade Union Density Data Set 1970–85*, University of Warwick: mimeo.

Baldwin, P. (1990), *The Politics of Social Solidarity: Class Bases of the European Welfare State 1875–1975*, Cambridge: Cambridge University Press.

Briggs, A. (1965), 'The Welfare State in Historical Perspective' in M.N. Zald (ed.), *Social Welfare Institutions*, New York: John Wiley & Sons.

Castles, F.G. (1978), *The Social Democratic Image of Society*, London: Routledge & Kegan Paul.

Castles, F.G. (1982), 'The Impact of Parties on Public Expenditure' in F.G. Castles (ed.), *The Impact of Parties: Politics and Policies in Democratic Capitalist States*, London: Sage Publications.

Castles, F.G. (1985), *The Working Class and Welfare: Reflections on the Political Development of the Welfare State in Australia and New Zealand, 1890–1980*, Sydney: Allen & Unwin.

Castles, F.G. (1989), 'Puzzles of Political Economy' in F.G. Castles (ed.), *The Comparative History of Public Policy*, Cambridge: Polity Press.

Castles, F.G. (1990),'Australian Welfare State Expenditure Revisited: Some Implications for Change', *Politics*, **25** (2).

Castles, F.G. and Merrill, E.V., (1989), 'Towards a General Model of Public Policy Outcomes', *Journal of Theoretical Politics*, **1** (2), 177–212.

Cusack, T.R., Notermans, T. and Rein, M. (1989) 'Political-Economic Aspects of Public Employment', *European Journal of Political Research*, **17** (4), 471–500.

Dernberg, T.F. (1974), 'Personal Taxation, Wage Retaliations, and the Control of Inflation', *International Monetary Fund, Staff Papers*, **31** (3), November, 758–88.

Esping-Andersen, G. (1985a), *Politics Against Markets*, Princeton, N.J.: Princeton University Press.

Esping-Andersen, G. (1985b) 'Power and Distributional Regimes', *Politics and Society*, **14** (2).

Esping-Andersen, G. (1990), *The Three Worlds of Welfare Capitalism*, Cambridge: Polity.

Gilbert, N. and Moon, A. (1988), 'Analyzing Welfare Effort: An Appraisal of Comparative Methods', *Journal of Policy Analysis and Management*, **7** (2).

Jones, C. (1985), *Patterns of Social Policy*, London: Tavistock Publications.
Kangas, O. and Palme, J. (1989), *Public and Private Pensions: The Scandinavian Countries in Comparative Perspective*, Stockholm: Swedish Institute for Social Research.
King, A. (1974), 'Ideas, Institutions and the Policies of Governments: A Comparative Analysis (Part II)', *British Journal of Political Science*, **4**, 409–23.
Le Grand (1982), *The Strategy of Equality*, London: George Allen and Unwin.
McIntyre, S (1985), *Winners and Losers*, Sydney: Allen & Unwin.
Mackie, T.T. and Rose, R. (1984), *The International Almanac of Electoral History*, London: Macmillan, 2nd edition.
Marklund, S. (1988), *Paradise Lost? The Nordic Welfare States and the Recession 1975–1985*, Lund Studies in Social Welfare, Arkiv förlag.
Marshall, T.H. (1975), *Social Policy*, London: Hutchinson, revised edition.
Métin, A. (1977), *Socialism without Doctrine*, Chippendale, NSW: Alternative Publishing Cooperative Ltd.
Mitchell, D. (1990), *Income Transfer Systems: A Comparative Study Using Microdata*, Ph.D., Australian National University .
OECD (1985), *Social Expenditure 1960–1990*, Paris.
OECD (1986), *Revenue Statistics of OECD Member Countries 1965–1985*, Paris.
Olsson, S. (1990), *Social Policy and the Welfare State in Sweden*, Lund Studies in Social Welfare, Lund: Arkiv.
Paloheimo, H. (1984), *Governments in Democratic Capitalist States 1950–1983*, Studies in Political Science: University of Turku.
Reeves, P. (1902), *State Experiments in Australia and New Zealand*, 2 vols, London: Grant Richards.
Rosecrance, R.N. (1964), 'The Radical Culture in Australia' in L. Hartz (ed.), *The Founding of New Societies*, New York: Harcourt Brace.
Schmidt, M.G. (1982), 'The Role of Parties in Shaping Macroeconomic Policy' in F.G. Castles (ed.), *The Impact of Parties: Politics and Policies in Democratic Capitalist States*, London: Sage Publications.
Stephens, J.D. (1979), *The Transition From Capitalism to Socialism*. London: Macmillan.
Therborn, G. (1989), 'Pillarization and Popular Movements' in Francis G. Castles (ed.), *The Comparative History of Public Policy*, Cambridge: Polity.
Titmuss, R. (1974), *Social Policy*, London: George Allen & Unwin.
Varley, R. (1986), *The Government Household Transfer Base 1960–1984*, Paris: OECD.
Wilensky, H. L. (1975), *The Welfare State and Equality*, Berkeley: University of California Press.

PART II
THE POLITICS OF LABOUR SUPPLY

4 Coping with Economic Crisis: Labour Supply as a Policy Instrument

Gaby von Rhein-Kress

Introduction

Germany, Austria and Switzerland are countries which have maintained a striking degree of price stability. Even under the difficult economic conditions of the 1970s and 1980s, their inflation rates were extremely low in comparison with the rest of the OECD (Busch, this volume). However, the standard account of the full employment-inflation dilemma[1] suggests that a high level of price stability can only be achieved by sacrificing full employment. According to this view, the German-speaking countries should have had to pay for their low inflation by suffering high unemployment. However, this was not the case. Between 1973 and 1989, the average unemployment rate was, in fact, lower in the German-speaking countries than the OECD average (Table 4.1). Austria and Switzerland rank with Japan as the only three nations to combine exceptionally low levels of inflation and unemployment, while Germany's overall macro performance was also much better than the OECD norm.

The success of the German-speaking countries appears even more impressive when one looks more closely at the economic conditions under which it took place. Dividing the period after 1973 into two parts, that of severe economic recession (1973–83) and that of slow but steady economic recovery (1984–89),[2] one sees that the combination of low inflation and low unemployment uniquely characterized the German-speaking nations in the former part. Thus, Germany, Austria and Switzerland were successful in realizing the supposedly unrealizable combination of low inflation and low unemployment precisely at the time when Western industrialized nations in general suffered most severely from economic stagnation and declining employment. In the period of economic recovery, from 1984 to 1989, Germany was unable to maintain its earlier performance. Although still successfully curbing inflation, it was no longer able to keep pace with Switzerland and Austria in managing problems in the labour market. Germany then joined those countries having an unemployment rate higher than the OECD average.

Table 4.1: Rates of unemployment and inflation in OECD countries, 1973–89 (average rates in per cent)

	1973–89		1973–83		1984–89	
	Rate of unemployment	Rate of inflation	Rate of unemployment	Rate of inflation	Rate of unemployment	Rate of inflation
Australia	6.3	9.8	5.5	11.2	7.7	7.2
Austria	2.6	4.9	2.1	6.1	3.5	2.7
Belgium	8.7	6.3	7.2	8	11.3	3.1
Canada	8.3	7.5	7.8	9.3	9.2	4.3
Denmark	6.9	8.4	6.9	10.4	6.9	4.7
Finland	4.6	9.5	4.5	11.8	4.7	5.3
France	7.1	8.6	5.5	10.9	10	4.2
Germany	5.3	3.8	4	5	7.6	1.5
Ireland	11.4	11.5	8.5	15.3	16.7	4.5
Italy	8.5	12.9	7.1	16.2	11.1	7
Japan	2.2	5.8	2	8.2	2.6	1.3
Netherlands	7.6	4.7	6.3	6.6	10	1.1
New Zealand	3	12.3	1.8	13.4	5.1	10.5
Norway	2.3	8.4	2	9.5	3	6.5
Sweden	2.3	8.5	2.3	9.9	2.2	6
Switzerland	0.5	3.9	0.3	4.7	0.8	2.3
UK	7.2	10.5	5.8	13.3	9.8	5.2
US	6.9	6.6	7.1	8.2	6.4	3.7
Mean	5.7	8	4.8	9.9	7.1	4.5

Sources: OECD, 1986 and OECD, 1991a.

This chapter focuses on the period of economic recession from 1973 to 1983, when the singularity of the German-speaking nations was at its clearest, and asks why their maintenance of price stability did not lead to the ‘costs’ which the full employment-inflation dilemma predicts to be a natural consequence. In other words, how did the German-speaking countries manage to keep unemployment low under such difficult economic conditions and, is there any sense in which this record of macroeconomic success is attributable to the German-speaking nations’ character as a distinct ‘family of nations’?

Previous research on full employment and unemployment offers both economic and political models of explanation. Basic economic models explain the phenomena of full employment and unemployment mainly by means of economic variables (see Dornbusch and Fischer, 1987). Both in the neoclassical and the Keynesian school, population labour supply and labour demand by business are defined as functions of the level of real wages;[3] imbalances in the labour market are seen as the result of an inappropriate level of long-run real wages. According to classical theory, imbalances in the labour market do not persist because they can be removed by adjusting highly flexible wages. According to Keynesian theory, a wage level exists below which prospective workers are not willing to supply their labour. If the lowest wage level is reached, further adjustments in wages will not help to re-establish the balance between labour supply and labour demand. If an expansion in the total demand for goods does not take place, unemployment will continue to rise.

Political models of full employment and unemployment – most of them stemming from the 1970s and 1980s – focus on specific weaknesses in the economic theories (Schmidt, 1987): (1) the exclusive concentration on economic variables and the particular emphasis on microeconomic cost-benefit considerations, (2) the disregard of social, political, and political-institutional factors that can determine individual decisions, and (3) the systematic difficulty of economic theories in accounting for cross-national differences in labour markets. According to the political science analysts of public policy (see, e.g. Scharpf, 1987; Schmidt, 1988a), important variables associated with unemployment include the following:

1 the degree of coordination in monetary, fiscal and wage policies, or the extent to which institutional circumstances support such a coordination;
2 the availability of appropriate policy instruments for managing economic problems;
3 the distribution of power between capital and labour, or the power of trade unions;
4 the political party composition of the government, or the dominant political ideology; and
5 the preferences of the electorate regarding economic policy, or the political reaction to mass unemployment.

Analyses of the relationships between these variables and the level of unemployment or changes in the level of unemployment suggest two very interesting conclusions. First, low unemployment may occur where full employment is the most important goal of economic policy, and where the political-institutional circumstances support cooperation among important actors in determining economic policy; this may be called the 'labour-dominated road to full employment' (Schmidt, 1988a, 17). Second, low rates of unemployment also occur where the private economy takes the leading role in ensuring full employment, and where the state either only partially intervenes or, alternatively, acts within the framework of institutionalized relationships to the economy; this may be called the 'conservative-reformist road to full employment' (Schmidt, 1988a, 25).

The following analysis recognizes the value of both economic and political insights in explaining full employment and unemployment. However, it differs from exclusively economic or political models in several significant respects. It differs from the former by recognizing the explanatory role of political and political-institutional variables and by assuming a cross-nationally comparative perspective, i.e. by its political-scientific character. It differs from the latter by emphasizing the relevance of both socio-cultural variables and political and political-institutional variables. This approach is based on the view that the socio-cultural circumstances of a society can have a quasi-institutional character (Heinelt, 1991), with a major impact on labour supply decisions at the individual level. Finally, it differs both from the economic and the political approaches by concentrating on the importance of labour supply – i.e., the extent of integration of the population in working life – as a means of understanding imbalances in the labour market.

This focus on labour supply stems from two main considerations. First, in terms of the level of labour demand (measured by the growth in employment) and in terms of the level of unemployment in OECD countries in the period studied (Table 4.2), the German-speaking countries are distinguished by a striking peculiarity. They were the only countries, other than France, which manifested an extremely unfavourable pattern of employment change, without a concomitant increase in unemployment or a high level of unemployment in 1983. This is not only contrary to what one would expect, but also supports the view that something happened on the supply side of the labour market which prevented a strong increase in unemployment. Second, the supply side of the labour market has not yet been the focus of a comprehensive cross-national, comparative analysis of labour market imbalances, although the importance of changes in labour supply for the development of unemployment has often been pointed out (e.g. Biffl, 1986, 25; McMahon, 1986,10; Schettkat, 1987a, 257; Scharpf, 1987, 292; Wagner, 1985, 101).

In what follows, we demonstrate the need to incorporate the supply side of the labour market into research on the determinants of labour market imbalances. First, it is necessary to test whether the pattern of changes in labour supply in the German-speaking countries was in some way distinctive; in other words, to compare the development of labour supply in these countries with what was typical of other OECD countries.[4] The main part

Table 4.2: Growth of employment and unemployment (1973–83) and level of unemployment (1983) in OECD countries

	Growth of employment 1973–83	Growth of unemployment 1973–83	Level of unemployment in 1983
Australia	medium	strong	high
Austria	low/negative	low	low
Belgium	low/negative	strong	high
Canada	strong	medium	high
Denmark	low/negative	strong	high
Finland	medium	low	medium
France	low/negative	medium	medium
Germany	low/negative	medium	medium
Ireland	medium	strong	high
Italy	medium	low	medium
Japan	medium	low	low
Netherlands	medium	strong	high
New Zealand	medium	medium	medium
Norway	strong	low	low
Sweden	medium	low	low
Switzerland	low/negative	low	low
UK	low/negative	strong	high
US	strong	medium	medium

Source: Calculated from OECD 1989a.
Low/negative growth in employment: less than 3.5 per cent, strong growth in employment: more than 12.9 per cent. Low increase in unemployment: less than 4.1 percentage points, strong increase in unemployment: more than 10.6 percentage points. Low unemployment: less than 5.3 per cent, high unemployment: more than 9.6 per cent. The values between these form middle categories.

of the study then seeks to explain the changes in labour supply in German-speaking countries. Our consideration of labour supply focuses on four groups within the labour market: the young, older workers, foreigners, and women.[5] Finally, we consider the effects which changes in labour supply in the German-speaking countries had on the unemployment rate in those countries in 1983.

The principal indicator for labour supply is the change in the rate of participation in the labour force. This is defined as the proportion of the total labour force in the overall working-age population (15-64 years) or within a specific age cohort or a specific social grouping. The labour force here consists of persons holding or seeking employment – all those who fulfil the requirements for inclusion among the employed or the unemployed (OECD, 1989a).[6] In cases where unavailability of data precludes the use of the labour force participation rate, we use the size of the overall labour force or the number of those employed.[7] Independent variables here are those which previous research has suggested to be decisive determinants of labour supply for different groups in the population. Whilst it follows from the current approach that these are above all political, political-institutional and political-cultural, we also take various socio-economic variables into consideration.

Data for these independent variables are mainly from OECD statistics, publications of the United Nations and UNESCO, and various national sources. The period of economic recession from 1973 to 1983 is chosen as a focus for two reasons: first, because of the striking changes in the labour market of the German-speaking countries between 1973 and 1983,[8] and second, because of our assumption that political, political-institutional and socio-cultural variables are relevant to changes in the labour supply. The validity of this assumption should be most clearly demonstrated during periods of economic recession when regulative intervention in the labour market is particularly necessary in order to minimize severe imbalances.

Changes in Labour Supply in OECD Countries, 1973–83

The course of changes in the labour supply in OECD countries between 1973 and 1983 can best be demonstrated by distinguishing the labour force participation rates of the different countries into their component features – the overall labour force and the working-age population – and comparing the changes in these components in relation to one other. The data are presented in Figure 4.1; on the x-axis is the average growth rate of the working age population ('potential labour supply') and on the y-axis the average growth rate of the overall labour force ('real labour supply').

Figure 4.1 shows the expected positive correlation between growth in potential labour supply and growth in real labour supply (r = .75). An unexpected finding here concerns the respective positions of the individual countries. While the Scandinavian countries lie clearly above the trendline and are consequently characterized by a growth in the overall labour force that is 'too high' in relation to the growth in the working-age population, the German-speaking countries are situated clearly below the trendline and thus show a growth in the overall labour force that is 'too low' in relation to the growth in the working age population. These groupings of nations appear, *a priori*, to be characterized by broad patterns of labour market

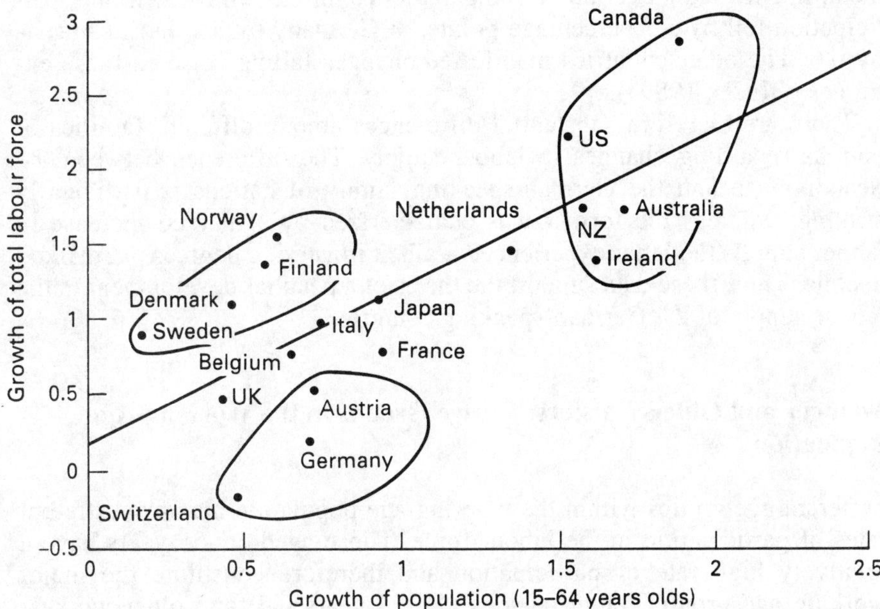

Source: Calculated from OECD, 1989a.

Figure 4.1: Correlation between the average growth rate of the working-age population and the average growth rate of the overall labour force, OECD countries 1973–83

outcomes that are congruent with the 'families of nations' perspective. On the other hand, the English-speaking countries do not form anything like such a tightly defined grouping. Admittedly, with the exception of the UK, they are all situated in the upper right quadrant of the figure (i.e. they experienced a strong increase in the working age population and a strong increase in the overall labour force), but the US and Canada are clearly above the trendline, while New Zealand and Australia are close to it, and Ireland falls below.

OECD statistics indicate the consequences of these developments for changes in labour force participation rates. The Scandinavian countries, the

US and Canada experienced a sharp increase, with a rise of between 4.7 and 7.8 percentage points. The German-speaking countries, on the other hand, manifested a decline of comparable magnitude: in Switzerland, participation fell by 5.7 percentage points, in Germany by 3.7 and in Austria by 0.6. The other countries manifested changes falling between these extremes (OECD, 1989a).

There are therefore substantial differences among different families of nations regarding changes in labour supply. The difference between the Scandinavian and the German-speaking family of nations is particularly striking; whereas the former was characterized by a marked increase in labour supply, the latter experienced – albeit in varying degrees – a marked decline. Thus, these data support the thesis of a peculiar development in the labour supply of the German-speaking countries.

Younger and Older Workers: Fringe Groups in the Working-Age Population

Different age groups within the working-age population manifest different rates of participation in the labour force. Those aged 25–55 years have a relatively high rate of participation and therefore constitute the major working age group. Young persons (15–24 years old) and older workers (55–64 years old)[9] manifest lower rates and therefore represent more marginal groups in the labour market. The differing labour force participation rates of various age groups in the working-age population can be explained by the fact that specific age cohorts have socially accepted alternatives to working life (Offe, 1977). The young, for example, have the possibility of working or remaining in education, while older workers may be able to retire.

The factors leading younger and older workers to choose alternatives to work are highly disputed. In the case of the young, economic labour supply theory assumes that the voluntary decision to remain in education depends on the benefits expected to accrue.[10] More institutional and comprehensive approaches, however, refer to other factors such as institutional regulations (e.g. structural reforms in the educational system), more or less autonomous social developments (e.g. the increased value of 'education' within society) and specific economic situations (e.g. a high level of unemployment) to explain different levels of continued participation in the educational system (Blien and Tessaring, 1989; Schneider, 1983). In the case of older workers, there are a variety of theories on the determinants of the decision to continue working or to retire (see below).

The questions we seek to answer here are whether or not these groups, with age-specific alternatives to work, contribute to the peculiar course of labour supply in German-speaking countries? And if so, how can this be explained? To find answers, we need to examine changes in the labour force participation rates of these groups as well as changes in the proportion of these groups in the working age population. The latter is necessary because the overall labour force participation rate – the rate of those aged 15–64 years – is the weighted average of group-specific participation rates. Thus a change in the overall participation rate may be explained either by changes in the structure of the population or by changes in the behaviour[11] of the labour force within specific groups of population. For example, men generally show a higher rate of labour force participation than women, so that an increase in the proportion of men in the working-age population raises the overall labour force participation rate without the behaviour of either men or women having changed. Similarly, an increase in the proportion of those aged 15–24 or 55–64 would (because of the relatively low participation rates of these groups) reduce the overall participation rate without any change in the behaviour of the population.[12]

Tables 4.3 and 4.4 present the labour force participation rates amongst younger and older workers in the OECD countries for which data are available. The rate amongst the young developed quite differently in the various OECD countries. Half experienced an increase (including the English-speaking countries and, with the exception of Finland, the Scandinavian ones), while the other half experienced a decline. Importantly for the present analysis, all the German-speaking countries were amongst those manifesting a decline in the labour force participation rate of the young.

There are also great differences regarding the extent of changes in the participation rate within the two groups of countries. However, here the above groups are not characterized by any uniformity. In those countries showing an increase in the participation rate amongst the young, one Scandinavian country (Norway) shows the greatest increase, followed by the English-speaking countries and Italy; another Scandinavian country (Sweden) manifests only a marginal increase. The countries with a decline in the participation rate amongst the young offer slightly more, if not unequivocal, evidence of a pattern. One of the German-speaking countries, Germany, manifested the most pronounced decline in youth participation, while Austria and Switzerland showed a similar trend of rather lesser magnitude, ranking fourth and fifth behind Japan and France.

Labour force participation rates amongst those aged 55–64 years developed differently from those amongst the young. The male population is the group of greater importance regarding labour force participation; interestingly, all of the countries experienced a decline in the labour force partici-

Table 4.3: Labour force participation rates of those aged 15–24, 1973 and 1983, and change in percentage points

	1973	1983	Change in percentage points
Australia	67.0	69.1	2.1
Austria	65.3	61.5	–3.8
Canada	58.4	66.1	7.7
Finland	60.6	57.1	–3.5
France	51.3	46.1	–5.2
Germany	65.4	56.3	–9.1
Ireland[1]	61.9	58.6	–3.3
Italy	40.5	44.6	4.1
Japan	52.8	44.2	–8.6
Netherlands	55.0	51.5	–3.5
Norway	49.1	60.9	11.8
Sweden	64.1	65.4	1.3
Switzerland[2]	70.7	67.0	–3.7
UK	69.9	72.4	2.5
US	64.9	67.5	2.6
Mean	59.8	59.2	–0.6

[1] 1975 and 1983

[2] Participation rates in 1970 and 1980. Hence the values are not strictly comparable with those of the other countries.

Sources: Calculated from OECD, 1989a; Biffl, 1988; *Bundesamt für Statistik, 1985* and United Nations: *Demographic Yearbooks*.

pation of older male workers. The extent of this decline, however, varied greatly. In the Netherlands, Australia, France and the UK, the participation rate among older workers fell considerably; in Finland, Germany, Austria and Canada, it fell to a moderate extent, while Ireland, Sweden, Norway, Switzerland and Japan experienced only a minor fall in participation amongst older workers.

Thus, the German-speaking countries were not distinguished by a particularly strong decline in the labour force participation of older male workers. At –13.2 percentage points, Germany almost reached the level in countries with a striking exit of older workers; however, Austria showed only an average decline (–11.1 percentage points) while Switzerland (dis-

Table 4.4: Labour force participation rates of men and women aged 55–64, 1973 and 1983, and change in percentage points

	Men			Women		
	1973	1983	Change in percentage points	1973	1983	Change in percentage points
Australia	82.6	62.0	–20.6	24.5	20.5	–4.0
Austria[1]	63.5	52.4	–11.1	25.5	20.2	–5.3
Canada	81.3	72.3	–9.0	31.0	33.7	2.7
Finland	67.6	54.1	–13.5	44.6	47.4	2.8
France	72.1	53.6	–18.5	37.2	32.6	–4.6
Germany	73.4	60.2	–13.2	25.6	24.7	–0.9
Ireland[2]	83.8	78.0	–5.8	20.9	20.2	–0.7
Japan	86.8	84.7	–2.1	44.7	46.1	1.4
Netherlands	77.2	54.2	–23.0	14.8	14.4	–0.4
Norway	84.0	78.8	–5.2	41.6	52.2	10.6
Sweden	82.7	77.0	–5.7	46.3	59.7	13.4
Switzerland[3]	91.2	88.8	–2.4	34.7	33.8	–0.9
UK	87.7	71.7	–16.0	39.8	35.1	–4.7
US	76.9	68.8	–8.1	41.1	41.2	0.1
Mean	79.3	68.3	–11.0	33.7	34.4	0.7

[1] Calculated from Biffl, 1988, 245–53.
[2] Participation rates in 1975 and 1983.
[3] Participation rates in 1970 and 1980. Hence the values are not strictly comparable with those of the other countries.

Sources: Calculated from *OECD*, 1989a and c; Biffl, 1988 and United Nations: *Demographic Yearbooks.*

regarding the limited comparability of data) experienced the second lowest decline.

Changes in the proportion of younger and older workers in the working-age population are presented in Tables 4.5 and 4.6. Here the German-speaking countries assume a special position, at least with regard to the young. Whereas their proportion in the working-age population generally declined, in German-speaking countries (particularly Germany and Austria) it rose. Furthermore, among the six countries that experienced an increase in the proportion of the young in the working-age population, Austria and Germany were those with the greatest increase.

Table 4.5: Levels of and changes in the proportion of younger workers (15–24) in the working age population, 1973–83

		Levels	Change in percentage points
Australia	t1: 1973	27.4	
	t2: 1983	26.0	–1.4
Austria	t1: 1973	22.8	
	t2: 1983	25.5	2.7
Belgium	t1: 1973	24.2	
	t2: 1983	23.6	–0.6
Canada	t1: 1973	29.7	
	t2: 1983	26.8	–2.9
Denmark	t1: 1973	23.4	
	t2: 1983	23.4	0
Finland	t1: 1973	26.7	
	t2: 1983	22.7	–4.0
France	t1: 1972	26.3	
	t2: 1983	24.0	–2.3
Germany	t1: 1973	21.7	
	t2: 1984	24.2	2.5
Ireland	t1: 1974	28.9	
	t2: 1983	29.3	0.4
Italy	t1: 1974	22.3	
	t2: 1984	24.2	1.9
Japan	t1: 1973	24.9	
	t2: 1983	20.5	–4.4
Netherlands	t1: 1974	26.5	
	t2: 1984	25.6	–0.9
New Zealand	t1: 1974	29.1	
	t2: 1983	28.6	–0.5
Norway	t1: 1973	24.5	
	t2: 1983	24.3	–0.2
Sweden	t1: 1973	21.6	
	t2: 1983	21.5	–0.1
Switzerland	t1: 1974	23.1	
	t2: 1982	23.3	0.2
UK	t1: 1973	22.6	
	t2: 1982	25.0	2.4
US	t1: 1974	29.2	
	t2: 1984	25.6	–3.6
Mean	t1:	25.3	Mean:
Mean	t2:	24.7	–0.6

Source: Calculated from United Nations: *Demographic Yearbooks*.

Table 4.6: Levels of and changes in the proportion of older workers (55–64) in the working-age population, 1973–83

		Levels	Change in percentage points
Australia	t1: 1973	13.6	
	t2: 1983	14.0	0.4
Austria	t1: 1973	16.6	
	t2: 1983	16.4	–0.2
Belgium	t1: 1973	15.2	
	t2: 1983	17.0	1.8
Canada	t1: 1973	12.7	
	t2: 1983	13.3	0.6
Denmark	t1: 1973	17.1	
	t2: 1983	16.0	–1.1
Finland	t1: 1973	14.9	
	t2: 1983	14.9	0
France	t1: 1972	14.6	
	t2: 1983	15.6	1.0
Germany	t1: 1973	16.0	
	t2: 1984	16.2	0.2
Ireland	t1: 1974	16.4	
	t2: 1983	13.7	–2.7
Italy	t1: 1974	15.4	
	t2: 1984	17.1	1.7
Japan	t1: 1973	11.7	
	t2: 1983	14.2	2.5
Netherlands	t1: 1974	14.0	
	t2: 1984	14.0	0
New Zealand	t1: 1973	13.9	
	t2: 1983	13.5	–0.4
Norway	t1: 1973	18.1	
	t2: 1983	17.2	–0.9
Sweden	t1: 1973	18.6	
	t2: 1983	17.8	–0.8
Switzerland	t1: 1974	14.9	
	t2: 1982	15.0	0.1
UK	t1: 1973	18.0	
	t2: 1982	17.1	–0.9
US	t1: 1974	14.4	
	t2: 1984	14.3	–0.1
Mean	t1:	15.3	Mean:
Mean	t2:	15.4	0.1

Source: Calculated from United Nations: *Demographic Yearbooks*.

Changes in the proportion of those aged 55–64 years in the working age population were less striking in the German-speaking countries. As in the majority of OECD members, this proportion hardly changed. However, at the beginning of this period, the proportion was larger in German-speaking countries – at least, in Germany and Austria – than the average among all OECD states. Thus, in Germany and Austria, the working population was comparatively older than elsewhere, a characteristic shared with the Scandinavian countries, but not with most English-speaking countries, for example.

Three points can be made on the basis of these results for our present purposes. First, in the period examined here, the German-speaking countries were distinguished by a demographic structure (or rather a demographic development) that had a dampening effect on the labour force participation rate. Because of the relatively strong increase in the proportion of the young in the working-age population and the relatively advanced age in the working-age population, the relatively low labour force participation rate of the youthful age cohort and of those aged 55–64 years had a particularly strong influence. Second, the German-speaking countries were distinguished by a clear decline in the labour force participation rate of the young. Third, in Germany and Austria, the labour force participation of those aged 55–64 years also declined but, in comparison with other OECD countries, the decline was not particularly strong.

Education and Deferred Labour Market Entry

There are two ways to explain the striking decline in labour force participation of the young in German-speaking countries. The first supposes a direct relationship between that decline and changes in the labour market. This can be summarized as follows. The more difficult the labour market situation is in general, and especially for the young, the higher the age at which the young enter the labour market, and the lower the labour force participation of the young (see Blien and Tessaring, 1989). This thesis implies that the countries which experienced a decline in the labour force participation of the young (including the German-speaking countries) should have been those in which the labour market situation for the young had deteriorated most substantially.

Table 4.7 presents the development of youth unemployment in those OECD countries for which data are available and shows that this was not the case. There is no relationship between the development of youth unemployment and the development of the labour force participation among the young in the period under examination here. Youth unemployment increased not only in those countries where there was a decline in the labour force participation young among the young, but also in those in which there was an increase (the UK and Italy are the best examples). Moreover, among those countries which experienced a pronounced decline in the labour force participation of the young, only two show a striking increase in youth unemployment: the Netherlands and France. The others experienced either a moderate increase, as in Germany, Ireland and Finland, or a relatively low increase (as in Japan, and presumably Switzerland and Austria, where the data are unfortunately insufficient to draw definite conclusions). There-

Table 4.7: Youth unemployment in OECD countries, 1973–83, and change in percentage points

	1973	1975	1977	1979	1981	1983	Change in percentage points
Australia	3.3	9	12.2	12.2	10.8	17.9	14.6
Austria[1]					2.2	4.9	
Canada	10.1	12	14.4	12.9	13.3	19.9	9.8
Finland[2]	4.5	5.1	12.3	10.8	9.2	10.5	6.0
France[3]	4	7.9	11.1	13.3	17	19.7	15.7
Germany	0.9	5.2	5	3.4	6.5	10.7	9.8
Ireland[4]	9.1		13.2	9.2	14.7	20.1	11.0
Italy[5]	12.6	12.8	23.9	25.6	25.8	30.5	17.9
Japan	2.3	3	3.5	3.4	4	4.5	2.2
Netherlands	2.8	6.3	7.3	8.1	13.4	24.9	22.2
Norway[6]	5.6	7.8	5	6.6	5.7	8.9	3.3
Sweden[6]	5.2	3.7	4.4	5	6.3	8	2.8
Switzerland[7]				0.6	0.3	1.3	
UK[8]	3.1	8.7	12.7	10.3	17.9	23.4	20.3
US[6]	9.9	15.2	13	11.3	14.3	16.4	6.5
Mean	5.6	8.1	10.6	9.5	10.8	14.8	9.5

[1] from *Bundesministerium für soziale Verwaltung*, 1984
[2] 1976 break in series
[3] 1982 break in series
[4] 1971 instead of 1973
[5] 14–24 years old; 1977 break in series
[6] 16–24 years old
[7] 20–24 years old; calculated from data of BIGA
[8] 16–24 years old; 1982 break in series
Sources: OECD, 1989a; *Bundesministerium für Soziale Verwaltung*, 1984; *Bundesamt für Industrie, Gewerbe and Arbeit* (BIGA).

fore the thesis of difficult labour market conditions does not explain the decline in the labour force participation of the young, which the German-speaking countries – particularly Germany – and a number of other OECD members experienced between 1973 and 1983.

The second approach to explaining the striking decline in the labour force participation amongst the young in the German-speaking countries focuses on the alternative to work which the young enjoy – continued participation in education. In the view of Offe, the educational system provides a 'substitute' function with regard to the labour market, inasmuch as it absorbs parts of the population which cannot be integrated into the employment system (Offe, 1975, 246). Further, Blien and Tessaring have analysed the relationship between school-leaving and the labour market situation and described a 'maintaining function' of the educational system: if the education system does not offer the young a refuge from the labour market, more of them will seek jobs (Blien and Tessaring, 1989, 93). According to this thesis, there is likely to be a strong correlation between changes in labour force participation of the young and changes in their participation in education. In this view, the striking decline in labour force participation of the young in the German-speaking countries could be accounted for by a particularly strong increase in educational participation.

Because of the great differences in educational systems and in the statistical registration of pupils and students (see Statistisches Bundesamt, 1988, 709), only a partial test of this hypothesis is possible. However, one can use UNESCO statistics on changes in the number of students in relation to the population to estimate international differences in youth participation in education. Data are available for the period 1970–1985 (Table 4.8) and are compatible with the hypothesis. Between 1970 and 1985, the German-speaking countries show the strongest increase in the proportion of students in the population. In Germany and Austria, the increase was more than twice the OECD average; in Switzerland, the proportion rose somewhat less, although more than in most other OECD countries. Thus, falling labour force participation in the German-speaking countries seems to have been associated with a strong increase in educational participation.

However, for the OECD countries in general, there was no correlation between changes in labour force and in educational participation. Between 1970 and 1985, the proportion of students in the population increased not only in those countries which experienced a decline in the labour force participation of the young after 1973, but also in those which experienced an increase. In particular, the English-speaking countries (with the exception of Ireland), but also Norway, Italy and Sweden, experienced a parallel increase in the labour force participation of the young and their participation in education.[13]

Table 4.8: Number of students per 100,000 inhabitants (OECD countries, 1950–85) and change in percentage points

	1950	1955	1960	1965	1970	1975	1980	1985	1950–60	1960–70	1970–85
Australia	441	485	785	1159	1431	2016	2203	2348	78	82.3	64.1
Austria	358	275	547	680	803	1286	1811	2309	52.8	46.8	187.5
Belgium	234	426	568	888	1296	1735	2111	2499	142.7	128.2	92.8
Canada	593	565	793	1651	2999	3600	4057	5100	33.7	278.2	70.1
Denmark	428	402	618	1010	1542	2179	2074	2271	44.4	149.5	47.3
Finland	361	393	532	841	1298	2425	2577	2611	47.4	144	101.2
France	334	446	595	1049	1581	1971	1998	2318	78.1	165.7	46.6
Germany	256	350	499	632	830	1684	1987	2540	94.9	66.3	206
Ireland	296	378	439	759	965	1440	1610	1979	48.3	119.8	105.1
Italy	310	288	386	583	1283	1762	1981	2074	24.5	232.4	61.7
Japan	471	617	750	1140	1744	2017	2065	1944	59.2	132.5	11.5
Netherlands	603	674	923	1209	1774	2108	2544	2795	53.1	92.2	57.6
New Zealand	742	636	837	962	1502	2143	2463	2950	12.8	79.5	96.4
Norway	231	161	258	525	1291	1663	1937	2280	11.7	400.4	76.6
Sweden	241	312	493	923	1756	1985	2062	2200	104.6	256.2	25.3
Switzerland	353	322	398	554	821	1010	1346	1702	12.7	106.3	107.3
UK					1084	1304	1468	1824			68.3
US	1508	1606	1983	2840	4148	5179	5311	5118	31.5	109.2	23.4
Mean	456	490	671	1024	1564	2084	2311	2603	54.7	152.3	80.5

Source: UNESCO *Statistical Yearbooks*.

How can we explain the strong increase in participation in education in the German-speaking countries? The data and the results of previous studies suggest at least two answers to this question. First, in the 1970s the German-speaking countries had a 'pent-up' demand for educational participation. Second, as in other Western industrialized countries, they felt the 'after-pains' of an 'educational mobilization' which took place in the 1960s and can be seen as a political reaction to continuing economic growth and the resulting increased demand for qualified labour, as well as to the progressive levelling out of differences in living conditions and the increasing discussion of continuing inequalities in society (Schneider, 1983, 68).

The thesis of pent-up demand for educational participation in the German-speaking countries is supported by the data in Table 4.8. These demonstrate that, in the 1960s, two of the German-speaking countries – Austria and Germany – had the lowest increase among the OECD countries in the proportion of students in the population. They also show that in 1970 the German-speaking countries had the lowest number of students in relation to the population.

The thesis of the continuing educational mobilization of the 1960s – that political determinants were responsible for the increase in educational participation – is founded on the parallel expansion in public expenditures on education and in educational participation. The substantial increase in the latter in the 1960s (see Table 4.8) was associated with a particularly strong expansion in public expenditure on education. The average proportion of educational expenditures in the gross national product in OECD countries rose from 3.8 per cent in 1960 to 6.1 per cent in 1975 (OECD, 1985c),[14] an increase of some 50 per cent.

Thus, in the 1960s and early 1970s, there was a clear correlation between government education policies and participation in education. The data on changes in the numbers of students in the 1970s and 1980s confirm that the expansive educational policies in the 1960s had long-term effects.

The variable of educational participation thus makes a greater contribution to understanding the striking decline in labour force participation among the young in the German-speaking countries than does the labour market situation of these countries. Between 1973 and 1983, Germany, Austria and Switzerland experienced a striking decline in labour force participation among the young because that group substantially increased its participation in education. This strong increase in educational participation resulted, in part, from a pent-up demand in the German-speaking countries *vis-à-vis* other OECD countries, as well as from the after-effects of the educational mobilization of the 1960s. Although the latter was not peculiar to the German-speaking countries, it was probably the most decisive variable. This is because the educational mobilization of the 1960s was one of the main reasons for the considerable expansion in educational participation which the majority of the OECD countries experienced in the 1960s but which the German-speaking countries enjoyed in the 1970s and early 1980s.

The Welfare State and Early Exit from the Labour Market

How can we explain the decline in the labour force participation among older workers in the German-speaking countries? The literature again suggests two possible approaches. One is economic and emphasizes the impact of deteriorating labour market conditions (see Kühlewind, 1986). The other relies on political variables and emphasizes the retirement policy of the state, its institutional conditions and the basic social policy principles on which the retirement policy is based (Esping-Andersen and Sonnberger, 1989; Esping-Andersen, 1990; Heinelt, 1991).

Following Esping-Andersen and Sonnberger, the two types of explanation can also be distinguished in terms of 'push' and 'pull' effects. The term 'push' effect refers to the fact that, in periods of economic recession, older workers are among the first to be pushed out of the labour market because they cannot compete with younger workers. This reasoning provides the basic rationale of the economic approach. The term 'pull' effect refers to the fact that attractive retirement schemes, as an aspect of social policy, may encourage older workers to leave the labour market earlier than otherwise. This offers a political approach to the question, based on choices built into social policy legislation (Esping-Andersen and Sonnberger, 1989).

In analysing the changes in unemployment among older workers,[15] we first identify the importance of 'push' effects. Table 4.9 shows that, between 1973 and 1983, there was a positive correlation between the strength of the 'push' effect and the extent of decline in the labour force participation of older workers in OECD countries. On the one hand, those countries that showed the strongest decline – the Netherlands, Australia, France, the UK and Germany – are also those with the strongest increase in the unemployment rate among older workers. On the other hand, most of the countries that manifested only weak decline – Japan, Switzerland, Norway, Sweden and Ireland – are also those with the lowest increase in unemployment among older workers.

The decline in the labour force participation among older workers in the German-speaking countries can therefore be understood, at least partly, as a consequence of 'push' effects. In Germany, the labour force participation of older workers clearly fell because the labour market conditions for older workers deteriorated; in Switzerland, their participation fell only slightly because the labour market conditions for older workers deteriorated only

Table 4.9: Unemployment rates of 55 to 64 year-old men (OECD countries, 1973–83) and change in percentage points

	1973	1975	1977	1979	1981	1983	Change in percentage points
Australia[1]	0.8	2.5	2.5	2.7	3.5	6.5	5.7
Austria[2]		0.6	0.5	0.5	0.5	1	
Canada	4.7	3.9	5	4.4	4.3	8.2	3.5
Finland	1.4	1.6	3.6	3.6	5	5.1	3.7
France	1.9	2.6	3.6	4	4.8	6	4.1
Germany	1.6	3.9	3.7	4.3	5.4	8.5	6.9
Ireland[3]	9.4		8.5	6.5	8.8	11.2	1.8
Italy[4]	0.7	0.7	2.5	2	2.3	1.9	1.2
Japan	1.8	3.2	3.8	4.4	4.3	5	3.2
Netherlands	2.5	3.3	3.5	3.3	4.4	14.9	12.4
Norwegian[5]	0.7	0.7	0.7	0.7	0.7	1.4	0.7
Sweden	2.1	1.5	1.1	1.8	2.2	4	1.9
Switzerland[6]				0.2	0.1	0.4	
UK[7]	5.7	6.3	7.8	8.1	15.2	13.9	8.2
US	2.4	4.3	3.5	2.7	3.6	6.1	3.7
Mean	2.7	2.7	3.3	3.3	4.3	6.3	4.4

[1] 55 and over
[2] 60 and over; calculated from data of *Bundesministerium für Arbeit und Soziales* and Biffl, 1988
[3] 1971 instead of 1973
[4] 60 to 64 year olds; 1977 beak in series
[5] 60 and over
[6] 60 and over; calculated from data of *Bundesamt für Industrie, Gewerbe und Arbeit*
[7] 1982 break in series
Sources: OECD, 1989a; Biffl, 1988; *Bundesministerium für Arbeit und Soziales*; *Bundesamt für Industrie, Gewerbe and Arbeit* (BIGA).

marginally. In Austria, however, there was a clear discrepancy between the weakness of the 'push' effect and the strong decline in labour force participation of older workers. Consequently, in the case of Austria, the variable of deteriorating labour market conditions does not help to explain the departure of older workers from the labour market.

Understanding the role of 'pull' effects requires a more detailed analysis. Here we must not only find out whether there is a relationship between the decline in labour force participation among older workers and early retirement measures, but also the extent to which the basic principles of social policy support or hinder such early retirement measures. It is convenient to start the analysis with the latter: the relation between the basic principles of social policy and the decline in labour force participation among older workers. According to Esping-Andersen and Sonnberger, the basic principles of social policy in OECD countries – the various types of welfare states – are related to the pattern of changes in labour force participation among older workers since the middle of the 1960s. In social-democratic welfare states (e.g. Sweden), the degree of participation declined relatively little; in conservative welfare states (e.g. Germany) relatively strongly, and in liberal welfare states (e.g. the US) only moderately (Esping-Andersen and Sonnberger, 1989; Esping-Andersen, 1990).

The reason for these differences is that certain types of welfare states are more likely than others to use 'demographic instruments' such as early retirement schemes for regulating the labour market (Esping-Andersen and Sonnberger, 1989; Schmidt, 1988b). The early retirement possibilities of social-democratic welfare states are relatively far-reaching. However, their use is seldom necessary because the state pursues a comprehensive full employment policy. The conservative welfare state also possesses far-reaching early retirement possibilities, and these are used extensively because of the limited obligation assumed by the state for ensuring full employment in a deteriorating labour market situation. The liberal welfare state, finally, is characterized neither by attractive early retirement schemes, nor by an obligation to support labour market conditions. In these latter countries, the declining labour force participation of older workers is a function principally of deteriorating labour market conditions and the existing structure of regular benefits provided by pension systems.

Does this differentiation help to explain changes in the labour force participation of older workers in OECD countries between 1973 and 1983? What is the value of this approach for explaining the case of German-speaking countries? The model appears to correspond very well to patterns in the data, especially when one adds a fourth type – the 'radical' welfare state. This type is identified by Castles and Mitchell in testing the explanatory power of the model for English-speaking countries (Castles and Mitchell, this volume). In this view, the radical welfare state is distinguished from the social-democratic and conservative types by a relatively low level of social expenditure, and from the liberal type by its emphasis on equalizing policy instruments. In fact, a clear correlation can be discerned between the types of welfare state and the extent of decline in the labour force participation of older workers (Table 4.10). The seven countries that experienced a relatively strong decline in their participation belonged to either conservative or radical welfare state types, whereas the seven countries that

Table 4.10: Correlation between the types of welfare states and the decline in labour force participation of older workers

Rank respecting the decline of labour force participation* of older workers	Nation	Type of welfare state
1	Netherlands	conservative
2	Australia	radical
3	France	conservative
4	UK	radical
5	Finland	radical
6	Germany	conservative
7	Austria	conservative
8	Canada	(liberal)
9	US	liberal
10	Ireland	(liberal)
11	Sweden	social-democratic
12	Norway	social-democratic
13	Switzerland	liberal
14	Japan	liberal

* 1: strongest decline; 14: lowest decline
Source: OECD, 1989a and c; Esping-Andersen, 1990; Biffl, 1988; United Nations: Demographic Yearbooks; Castles and Mitchell, Chapter 3 of this volume.

experienced a relatively low decline belonged to either the social-democratic or liberal types.

Thus, the decline in labour force participation among older workers in the various OECD countries between 1973 and 1983 was associated with the respective types of welfare states existing in these countries. This correlation is precisely as described by Esping-Andersen and Sonnberger. In the social-democratic welfare states of Scandinavian countries, the relatively low decline in labour force participation among older workers was related to a relatively low increase in unemployment among them; attractive early retirement possibilities existed (e.g. Heinelt, 1991), but because of the low risk of unemployment there was no reason to use them. In the liberal welfare states of the US, Switzerland, Japan, Canada and Ireland,[16] the relatively low decline in labour force participation among older workers was related to a different set of factors in the unemployment risk: the lack of attractive early retirement possibilities hindered their leaving the labour market (e.g. Bruche and Casey, 1982b, 170; Casmir, 1989, 354; Tschudi, 1989, 91). In the conservative welfare states of Germany, France, the Netherlands and Austria, the relatively strong decline in labour force participation among older workers – at least in Germany, the Netherlands and France – was related to a strong increase in unemployment among these workers; comprehensive early retirement measures supported the exit of older workers from the labour market (see Heinelt, 1991; Internationale Chronik zur Arbeitsmarktpolitik, 1981b; Talos, 1985, 1987). In the radical welfare states of Australia, Finland and the UK, the relatively strong decline in labour force participation among older workers was associated with a strong increase in the unemployment rate; attractive early retirement possibilities did not exist, at least in the case of the UK (Internationale Chronik zur Arbeitsmarktpolitik, 1981b). However, one still needs to examine the extent to which exit from the labour market was supported by the equalizing social policy instruments of the radical welfare states or by other factors, such as widespread private home ownership and the resulting relative financial security for the retired, which were characteristic of these countries.

The varying degree of decline in labour force participation among older workers that OECD countries experienced between 1973 and 1983 was therefore a function of the respective types of welfare states in two respects. On the one hand, the degree of responsibility assumed by the state for conditions in the labour market and for protecting individuals from loss of income (see Schmidt, 1988b, 162) determined the aspects of public policy concerning older workers. In those countries in which the state bore an obligation to ensure full employment, the attempt was made to integrate older workers into the labour market. In those, however, in which the state assumed no such obligation but afforded the individual relatively high protection in the case of income losses, the exit of older workers from the labour market was supported by expanding the existing early retirement possibilities or by creating new ones. Finally, in the countries in which the state assumed no responsibility for ensuring full employment and afforded the individual little protection in the case of income losses, policy was more passive.

One might also consider to what extent the respective pension systems – i.e. differing institutional conditions – determined pension policy. In social-democratic and conservative welfare states, the creation and expansion of early retirement possibilities were facilitated by public insurance systems, as these systems help to externalize the costs of early retirement measures. In liberal welfare states, however, the creation and expansion of early retirement possibilities were hindered by the weakness of public insurance systems, making the externalization of early retirement costs largely impossible (Heinelt, 1991).

We can therefore conclude that the type of welfare state was the major factor determining the degree of decline in labour force participation of those aged 55–64 years in German-speaking countries. In Germany and Austria, the decline in labour force participation of older workers was determined by the conservative stance of the welfare state regarding its obligation to ensure full employment and to pursue a comprehensive early retirement policy. In Switzerland, the low decline in labour force participation by older workers was determined by the liberal stance of the welfare state and by the lack of early retirement possibilities.

Foreign Workers: A 'Reserve Army' in the Labour Market

In most Western European countries, the period of the late 1950s and 1960s was characterized by labour market conditions that were appreciably different from those of more recent decades. There was no surplus of labour and, indeed, on occasions there were extreme shortages (see Dietz, 1987). To ensure high economic growth and an increase in prosperity, it was necessary to search for additional labour. This search focused on southern European countries, where rapid growth in population had produced high labour supply (Butschek, 1984, 5).

A number of international recruitment agreements[17] led to an enormous migration from southern to western Europe. Switzerland, Germany, Austria, Belgium, France, the Netherlands and Sweden 'imported' foreign workers in an attempt to bridge the gap between high labour demand and scarce labour supply. Until the 1970s and in some cases even beyond, the proportion of foreigners in the labour force rose continuously in these countries.

The extent to which the various western European countries employed foreign workers varied substantially. In 1973, the proportion of foreign workers in the labour force was 4.9 per cent in Sweden, 5.7 per cent in France, 7.0 per cent in Belgium, 7.4 per cent in Austria, 9.3 per cent in Germany, and 27.9 per cent in Switzerland (OECD, 1985b, 40). Thus, it was the German-speaking countries – particularly Switzerland – in which foreign workers constituted the largest proportion of the labour force.

Did these foreigners, however, contribute to the striking decline in the labour supply in the years 1973 and 1983? In terms of Offe's model of acceptable alternatives to labour market participation (see above), this could be a plausible explanation, for foreigners always potentially have the possibility of returning home and supplying their labour in their native lands (Sesselmeier and Blauermel, 1990, 176).

Unfortunately, cross-nationally comparative data on the level of foreign worker participation in the labour force are not available for all OECD countries (see OECD, 1985a). However, one can use the data that are available on the inflow of foreigners into the major regions of the OECD countries to provide a view concerning tendencies in foreign labour supply. Migration movements in the West have always been either labour market oriented – as in southern and west Europe – or have become so to an increasing extent – as in the US (see OECD, 1985a, 57).

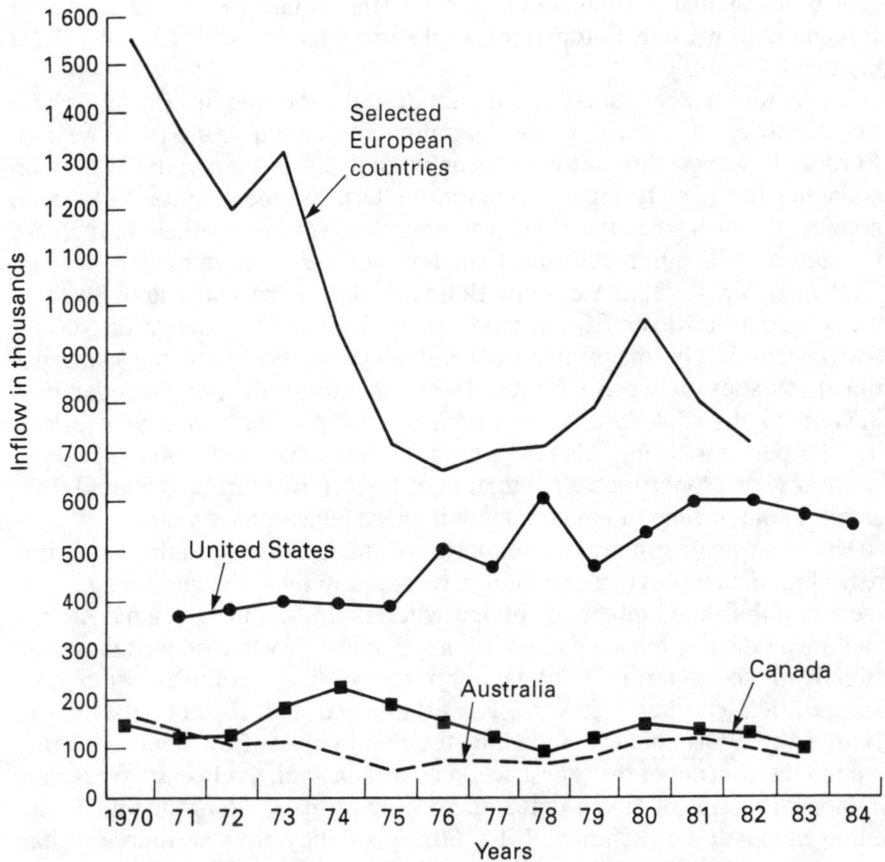

Source: OECD, 1985a, 58.

Figure 4.2: Inflow of foreigners, 1970–84 (in thousands)

As Figure 4.2 makes clear, the pattern of such migration over time indicates the contribution that foreigners made to the decline in labour supply in the German-speaking countries. While the inflow of foreigners to the US after 1973 showed an increasing tendency, and while Canada and Australia experienced only low declines, the inflow to European countries fell dramatically. In contrast to the 1.3 million foreigners who had moved to Switzerland, Germany, the Netherlands, Belgium, France or Sweden by 1973,[18] there were only 700,000 by 1976. This figure was 200,000 more than that for the US. In 1971, however, the European countries had absorbed four times as many foreigners as the US. In the late 1970s, the inflow of foreigners to western Europe increased somewhat, but in 1981 and 1982 it again fell.

These highly aggregated data do not describe the role of German-speaking countries in absorbing this migration of foreign workers to western Europe; however, this becomes clear in analysis of the available data on changing levels of foreign workers in western Europe (Figure 4.3). Three countries, which since the 1960s had employed foreign workers to increase the supply of labour, manifested a modest increase in the number of foreign workers after 1973; these were Belgium, the Netherlands and Sweden. Three others, however, experienced a sharp decline – Germany, Austria and Switzerland.[19] The magnitude of this decline can be calculated using national statistics: between 1973 and 1976, the number of foreigners declined in Germany by 25.4 per cent, in Austria by 23.4 per cent and in Switzerland by 22.7 per cent.[20] Here, then, is strong evidence that the German-speaking countries' disproportionate population of foreign workers contributed massively to the decline in labour supply in these recessionary years.

How can one explain the peculiarity of the German-speaking countries regarding the employment of foreign workers? Why at the beginning of the recession did the numbers of foreign workers decline in Germany, Austria and Switzerland, while they remained more or less constant or even increased slightly in other countries? The answer lies in political – political-institutional and political-cultural – factors. The established and distinctive policy in German-speaking countries regarding the employment of foreigners, centring around the concept of the 'guest-worker', makes it relatively easy to regulate numbers in terms of labour demand. Seeking primarily to protect the indigenous labour force (Schmidt, 1985, 56), this policy aims at a more or less continuing rotation of foreign labourers. Work and residence permits are issued only on a temporary basis, the immigration of relatives is strictly controlled, and the possibilities of naturalization are minimized (e.g. Bruche, 1983; Castles, 1984; Castles and Kosack, 1985; Leitner, 1986; Therborn, 1985; Tichy, 1990). Thus, as long as economic conditions permit, foreign

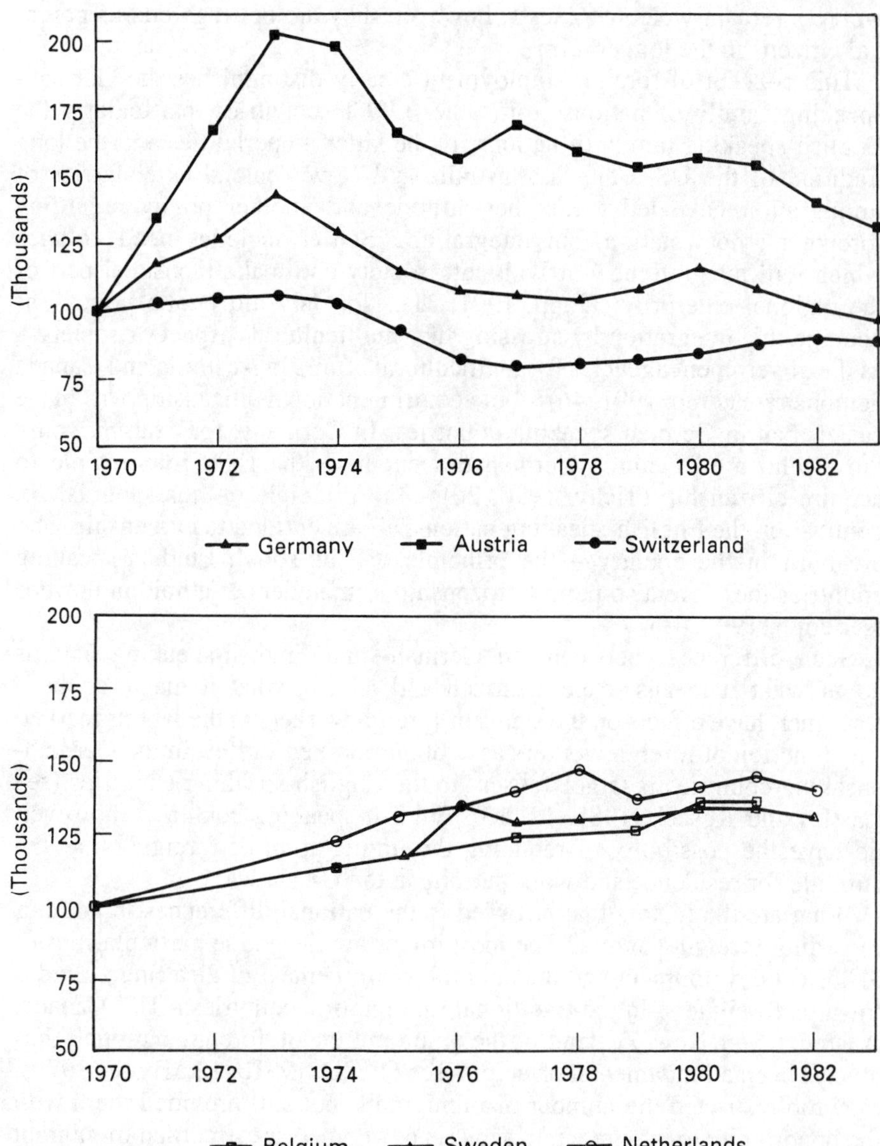

Source: Calculated from Statistical Yearbooks of individual nations and Werner and König, 1984.

Figure 4.3: Changing levels of foreign workers in selected Western European countries, 1970–82 (1970 = 100)

workers remain welcome guests; however, they are not regarded as potential citizens in the longer term.

This concept of foreign employment clearly distinguishes the German-speaking family of nations from other OECD countries, particularly the English-speaking family of nations. In the latter, imperial ties and the long tradition of the US, Canada, Australia and New Zealand as countries of immigration have led to another attitude and another policy regarding foreigners: not rotation, but integration. 'Settler societies need policies which will integrate new arrivals into society and make them feel part of the national enterprise' (Jupp, 1991, 31). Not only did public policy encourage this integration by stressing the 'multicultural' aspect of society – as the government agencies for multicultural affairs in Australia and Canada demonstrate (Jupp, 1991, 46) – but acquiring national citizenship was made easier than in German-speaking countries. In Germany, for example, only those who are of ethnic German descent have the right in principle to acquire citizenship (Tichy, 1990, 20) – the principle of 'jus sanguis'. In contrast, in the English-speaking nations, all are entitled to citizenship who are born in the country – the principle of 'jus solis'. English-speaking countries therefore also permit citizenship to members of ethnic minorities (see Jupp, 1991, 41).

Such differences between the German- and English-speaking nations about what it means to be a citizen and, hence, what it means to be a foreigner, have effects on the status of foreign workers in the labour market. The function of foreign workers as a labour market 'buffer' in the German-speaking countries is largely absent in the English-speaking countries (see Castles and Kosack, 1985, 12, 13). English-speaking countries, however, do have the possibility of reducing the immigration of foreigners, as the struggle for residence and work permits in the US shows.

What are the factors that have led to the national differences in policies regarding foreign workers? The most important lies in the particularities of historical development and the cultural reinforcement of differing attitudes towards foreigners. In the traditional immigration countries – US, Canada, Australia and New Zealand – the immigration of foreign nationals has always been a fundamental principle (see OECD, 1991b, 12). By the 1970s, they too restricted the number of immigrants, but still provided them with the opportunity to integrate into society: newcomers are accorded immigrant status, the right of permanent settlement and free entry to the labour market (Hammar and Lithman, 1987). The UK, France and the Netherlands, as well as the German-speaking countries, know the phenomenon of 'guest worker'. However, because of their past as colonial powers, most of their immigrants come from countries with earlier imperial ties and towards whose nationals they therefore feel some obligation. To these immigrants they have long allowed the right of permanent settlement, often also the right of acquiring full citizenship (see Castles, 1984). Since the 1970s the UK, France and the Netherlands – as the other Western nations – have pursued more restrictive immigration procedures, whilst in general maintaining the parameters of earlier immigration and integration policies. This is seen in the granting of full political rights to immigrants from Commonwealth countries in the UK (Hammar and Lithman, 1987, 242), the relatively liberal naturalization laws in France (Castles, 1984, 56) and the measures of the Netherlands government concerning the legal and social status of immigrants at the end of the 1970s and the beginning of the 1980s (see Castles, 1984, 60ff).

In contrast, however, the German-speaking countries have neither a tradition as countries of immigration nor as important colonial powers, and therefore do not assume such obligations regarding the integration of immigrants. While the inflow of foreigners has a long tradition in Germany, Austria and Switzerland (Mertens and Kühl, 1977; Thränhardt, 1975; Wimmer, 1986), it always resulted from economic factors – i.e. labour shortages – and was consequently seen as a temporary phenomenon. The 'employment' of foreign workers during the Second World War in Germany is a well-known and notorious example of this phenomenon.

The peculiarity in the way in which German-speaking countries deal with prospective immigrants derives not only from their different historical development and traditions regarding the employment of foreigners. In comparison with the classical immigration countries, the German-speaking countries' capacity to absorb additional population is substantially restricted by their smaller size, particularly in the case of Austria and Switzerland.[21] Furthermore, after the Second World War, Germany and Austria faced a huge immigration of refugees from eastern parts of Germany and other eastern regions. This 'domestic' immigration limited their ability to pursue a generally liberal immigration policy.

In Austria and Switzerland, specific political-institutional circumstances supported a restrictive foreign worker policy. In Austria, the institutionalized integration of the various industrial actors in economic policy-making allowed the trade unions to exert strong influence in the area of foreign-worker policy (Wimmer, 1986). Trade unions above all seek to protect the interests of their members, particularly in ensuring jobs and high wages; this tends to militate against expansion in the labour supply by employing large numbers of foreign workers (see Leitner, 1986, 202). A number of studies on the early controversies over employing foreigners in the Austrian economy in the early 1960s demonstrate that the attitude of trade unions was determined by such considerations. Here the Austrian trade unions supported a restrictive handling of approval procedures for employing foreign workers (Bauboeck and Wimmer, 1988; Misslbeck, 1983).

In Switzerland, one of the four 'pillars of political representation and participation' (Neidhart, 1988, 48) – direct democracy – supports such a restrictive attitude in foreign worker policy. Direct democracy procedures make it relatively easy for the opponents of a liberal foreign worker policy – especially the right-wing 'Alienization Opponents' (see Schmidt, 1985, 54) – to conduct nationwide campaigns for a restrictive policy and to put pressure on crucial political actors (Schmitter-Heisler, 1988, 54). These procedures were undoubtedly substantially responsible for the restrictive foreign worker policy of Switzerland in the 1970s and 1980s (Castles, 1984, 71).

In summary, the strong decline in the supply of foreigners in German-speaking countries since 1973 has historical, cultural and political-institutional causes. Lacking a tradition as havens of immigration or former colonial powers, permanent cohabitation with foreigners does not belong to the historical ethos shaping the experiences of German-speaking countries. The result is a specific attitude towards prospective immigrants and a typical way of dealing with foreigners already resident in the country. As long as economic conditions allow, foreigners are accepted as welcome guests, but there are no efforts to integrate them into the society. Hence, foreigners serve as a 'reserve army' in the labour market which can be called up when labour demand is excessive – as in 1970–73 (see Figure 4.3) – and whose employment is ended or restricted when labour demand falls.

Women: The Under-utilized Labour Potential

In Western countries, the participation of women in the labour force has increased significantly over recent decades. While, in 1960, an average of 45.8 per cent of women were integrated into the labour market in OECD countries, in 1989 the figure was 58.9 per cent (OECD, 1991a, 39). This is a highly significant development, especially since it was accompanied by a declining participation of men in the labour force from 94.2 to 82.9 per cent during the same period. It led to far-reaching change in relations between men and women at work – a 'feminization' of the labour force participation (Hagen, Jenson and Reddy, 1988). This section very briefly examines this development and seeks to determine differences among the OECD countries and the extent to which these differences contribute to our present analysis: do the German-speaking countries show a peculiar development in female labour force participation, and does that development help to explain the striking decline in their labour supply?

Statistics for the OECD countries allow a clear answer to this question. The German-speaking countries do show a peculiar development in the female labour supply. They 'bring up the rear', as it were, regarding the influx of women into the labour market (Table 4.11). While in the Scandinavian countries, Canada and the US, the labour force participation rate of women increased by over 10 percentage points, and while other countries experienced increases between 3.2 and 9.3 percentage points,

Table 4.11: Labour force participation of women (OECD countries, 1973 and 1983) and change in percentage points

	1973	1983	Change in percentage points
Australia	47.7	52.1	4.4
Austria[1]	48.5	49.0	0.5
Belgium	42.5	49.8	7.3
Canada	47.2	60.3	13.1
Denmark	61.9	74.2	12.3
Finland	63.6	72.7	9.1
France	50.1	54.4	4.3
Germany	49.6	49.7	0.1
Ireland	34.1	37.8	3.7
Italy[2]	33.5	40.3	6.8
Japan	54.0	57.2	3.2
Netherlands[3]	31.0	40.3	9.3
New Zealand	39.2	45.7	6.5
Norway	50.6	65.5	14.9
Sweden	62.6	76.6	14.0
Switzerland	54.1	53.3	–0.8
UK	53.2	57.2	4.0
US	51.1	61.8	10.7
Mean	43.9	52.7	6.9

[1] 1973 and 1981;
[2] 1971 and 1983;
[3] 1975 and 1983

Source: OECD, 1989a.

there was almost no change in Germany or Austria. In Switzerland the rate even decreased by 0.8 percentage points.

The importance of these results for answering our question becomes clear when one recalls Figure 4.1 and considers its counterpart dealing only

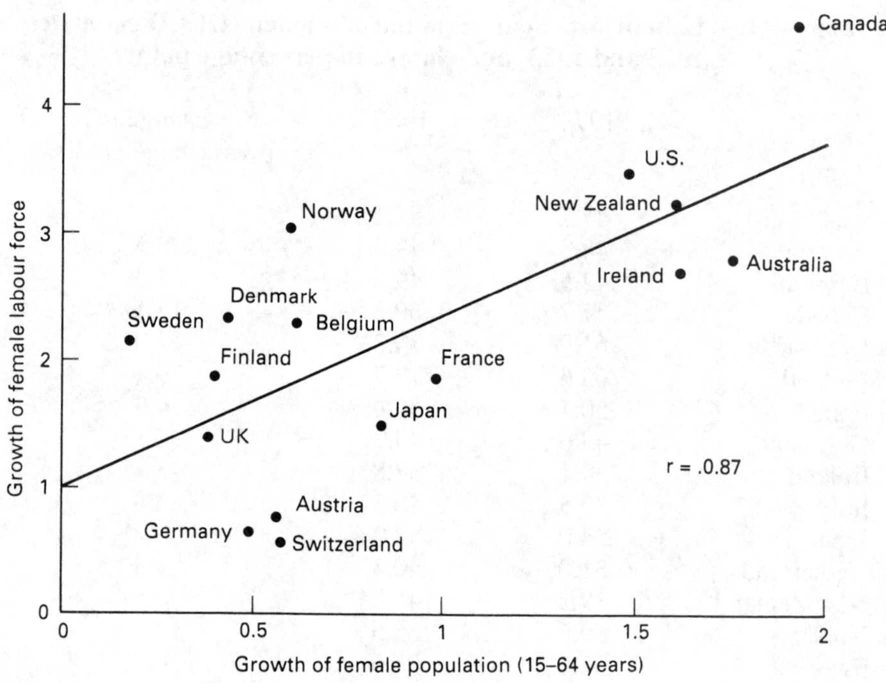

Source: OECD, 1989a.

Figure 4.4: Correlation between the average growth rate of the female labour force and the average growth rate of the female population, OECD countries, 1973–83

with women (Figure 4.4). One sees here how trends in the German-speaking countries converged. Each showed an average increase in the female working-age population of roughly 0.5 per cent and an average increase in the female labour supply of 0.5 per cent. The decline or lack of increase in female labour force participation is clearly an important determinant of the decline in labour supply in the German-speaking countries. Without the absence of women from the labour market, the labour supply could not have declined in Austria, Germany and Switzerland in the way it did.

In contrast to our previous analysis of the determinants of downward labour market flexibility in the German-speaking countries, we do not seek to discuss the reasons for this vastly important transformation in the conditions of labour supply in Western nations. That topic demands a full-scale analysis in its own right, which is provided in the next chapter. What is of interest here is the impact of the transformation and how it shaped the diverse response of the OECD nations to the recession beginning in 1973. That is the subject to which we now turn.

The Effect of Labour Supply on the Unemployment Rate

This section deals with the effect which the decline in labour supply in German-speaking countries had on the level of unemployment at the end of the period under investigation. We ask here what the unemployment rate in Austria, Germany and Switzerland would have been in 1983 if the labour supply of the groups analysed above had developed in terms of the average for OECD countries. In other words, to what extent did the peculiar development of labour supply among these groups retard the potential rate of unemployment?

More specifically, we pose four questions. First, to what extent would the rate of unemployment have been higher if the labour force participation of women had not remained constant or declined, but had increased to the extent typical of other OECD countries? Second, to what extent would the rate of unemployment have been higher if foreign worker employment had not been reduced to such an extent, but had developed as in other OECD countries? Third, to what extent would the rate of unemployment have been higher if the labour force participation of the young had not declined to such an extent, but had developed at the OECD average rate? Fourth, to what extent would the rate of unemployment have been higher if the labour force participation of those aged 55–64 years had not declined in the way described here, but only to an extent comparable with other OECD countries?

We should note, first, that the following calculations are based on two assumptions. The first is that of *ceteris paribus*, or otherwise comparable circumstances – particularly an unchanged labour demand. Second, with the assumption of an unchanged labour demand, we assume that all those who additionally would have entered the labour market if the labour supply had developed at the OECD average rate would have become unemployed and registered as such.[22] Moreover, we can calculate only single dampening effects, not an overall dampening effect. Since we analyse the labour supply in terms of three dimensions of the working age population – age, sex and native/foreigner – we are considering throughout the same set of individuals. A 59-year-old foreign woman, for example, is the subject of analyses of the labour force participation of women, the labour supply of foreigners, and the labour force participation of older workers. This overlapping precludes the calculation of an overall dampening effect on labour supply.

Considering first the hypothetical labour force participation of women, the total labour force in 1983 would have included 1.5 million more in Germany, and 165,000 more in both Austria and Switzerland, if the trends here had been in terms of the OECD average. On the assumption of unchanged labour demand, the number of unemployed would thus have increased by the same extent. Consequently, the resulting unemployment rate would have been much higher: in Germany 12.8 per cent instead of 8.2 per cent, in Austria 8.3 instead of 3.8, and in Switzerland 5.9 instead of 0.9.[23] Hence, the constant or declining level of the female labour supply reduced the unemployment rate in Germany by 4.6 percentage points, in Austria by 4.5, and in Switzerland by 5.0 (Table 4.12).

In the case of foreign workers, we observe lesser but still considerable dampening effects. If the number of foreign workers had developed at the 1983 average of those OECD countries which employ foreign workers,[24] in 1983, the total labour force would have been higher by 716,000 in Germany, 67,000 in Austria and 95,000 in Switzerland. In the case of un-

Table 4.12: Reductions in the rate of unemployment in German-speaking countries in 1983 compared with the OECD average in percentage points

	Women	Foreigners	The young	Older workers
Austria	4.5	1.9	1.2	0
Germany	4.6	2.3	2.8	0.2
Switzerland	5.0	2.9	(1.0)	(–0.8)

changed labour demand, this would have increased the rate of unemployment by 2.3 percentage points in Germany, 1.9 in Austria and 2.9 in Switzerland.[25]

The higher than average decline in labour force participation among the young had dampening effects on the unemployment rate, particularly in Germany. If the labour force participation of younger workers had declined at the OECD average, the total labour force in 1983 would have included 876,000 more in Germany, 41,000 more in Austria and 32,000 more in Switzerland. With an unchanged labour demand, the unemployment rate would therefore have been higher by 2.8 percentage points in Germany, 1.2 in Austria and 1.0 in Switzerland.[26]

The decline in labour force participation among older workers, on the other hand, did not reduce the unemployment rate in German-speaking countries more than in other OECD countries. Under hypothetical conditions as above, only in the case of Germany does one find a dampening effect – by 0.2 percentage points. Since the labour force participation of older workers in Austria declined almost as much as the OECD average (see Table 4.4), there was no such effect there. In Switzerland, there was an enhancing rather than a dampening effect. The unemployment rate here would have been lower by 0.8 percentage points in 1983 if labour force participation had not declined by 2.4 percentage points but by the OECD average of 11 points.[27]

In summary, we can conclude that the specific development of labour supply in the German-speaking countries significantly reduced the rates of unemployment. In particular, the lack of an increase in female labour force participation, the rapid decline in foreign worker employment, and the marked decline in labour force participation by the young contributed to the improvement in the labour market. Although we cannot draw conclusions as to the overall dampening effect on labour supply, the unemployment rates would undoubtedly have been substantially higher in Germany, Austria and Switzerland without the specific pattern of changes in labour supply that characterized these countries.

Summary and Conclusions

This analysis has dealt with the reasons for the comparatively low unemployment rates in the German-speaking countries during the period of economic crisis from 1973 to 1983. The principal finding is that low unemployment was a function of the decline in labour supply which distinguished the family of the German-speaking countries from the Scandinavian and English-speaking countries. The causes of this decline in labour supply are to be found in the policy treatment of, and the responses by, those groups in the population which, according to Offe, have socially accepted alternatives to work: women, foreigners, the young and older workers. Though not always altogether voluntarily, women, foreigners and the young withdrew to these alternatives more frequently in the German-speaking nations than in other OECD countries. Labour force participation among older workers was not reduced to a striking extent, but there was some tendency in that direction in both Austria and Germany.

The determinants of this striking withdrawal from the labour market were principally political, political-institutional, historical and cultural in nature. In the case of the young, the educational mobilization of the 1960s and the greater pent-up demand than in other OECD countries led to a particularly strong increase in educational participation in the 1970s and 1980s. Together with demographic developments, this increase caused a marked decline in the number of young workers entering the labour market. In the case of older workers, the basic stance of the welfare state made itself felt. Against the background of a deteriorating labour market situation in Germany and Austria, the lack of state responsibility for ensuring full employment, together with the relatively far-reaching protection of the individual in the case of income loss and the comprehensive early retirement measures typical of the conservative welfare state, led to an increasing exit of older workers from the labour market. In Switzerland, the lack of far-reaching protection of individuals suffering income loss and the lack of early retirement possibilities typical of the liberal welfare state led to a lower decline in labour force participation among these workers who were, in any case, more than somewhat protected by Switzerland's maintenance of full employment for Swiss nationals. Foreign workers became the victims of a restrictive policy after 1973. According to the historically determined view of foreigners as 'guest workers', the governments reduced the inflow and work opportunities of prospective immigrants and, in some degree, took steps which made it harder for existing guestworkers to find jobs. Finally, women were effectively kept out of the labour market by the lack of economic, social and political incentives to participate in the labour force (see Schmidt, Chapter 5). Above all, the male-oriented employment structure and the traditional division of labour between men and women that dominated public policy in these countries made female entry into the labour market more difficult.

It was therefore a combination of the after-effects of earlier policies, demographic developments, principles of the welfare state, deep-seated cultural attitudes, and active political regulation which led to the striking decline in labour supply in the German-speaking countries.

Finally, we consider three questions that arise directly from this analysis. First, were the pro-cyclical development and political regulation of labour supply in German-speaking countries peculiarities of the period of economic crisis from 1973 to 1983, or are they general characteristics of labour market conditions in the German-speaking countries? Second, what are the consequences of this analysis for labour market research? Third, what are the implications of this study for the utility of the families of nations concept?

Regarding the first question, the data presented here, together with other studies on the subject and developments in the recent past, suggest that the pro-cyclical development and political regulation of labour supply are general characteristics of labour market conditions in German-speaking countries. Comparing changes in labour demand and labour supply across OECD countries in the 1960s, one finds that only in Germany, Austria and Switzerland was a decline in labour demand associated with a clear decline in labour supply (see OECD, 1984, 1989a). This parallel development between labour demand and labour supply was also largely the result of political regulation (see Bruche and Casey, 1982a; Dietz, 1987; Leitner, 1986; Lutz, 1988). After 1983, the regulation of labour supply also played an important role in German-speaking countries. This became particularly obvious in the developments after German unification. On the one hand, the German government largely displaced older workers from the former East Germany by creating far-reaching early retirement possibilities (Sachverständigenrat zur Begutachtung der wirtschaftlichen Entwicklung, 1990; Deutsches Institut für Wirtschaftsforschung, 1991). On the other hand, East German women, who had previously been highly integrated into the labour market, have been increasingly eliminated from it by the imposition of institutional structures imported from West Germany which hinder the participation of women in the labour force (Maier, 1991).

The answer to the second question supports a stronger integration of the supply side of the labour market into cross-national comparative labour market research. One of the most important findings of this study is that analysis of the supply side of the labour market makes an important contribution to understanding unemployment. Concentration on the demand side of the labour market, as is typical of earlier labour market research, prevents a comprehensive understanding of routes to full employment and mass unemployment.

A positive answer can be given to the question as to the utility of the families of nations concept. Its heuristic value is demonstrated in the present analysis by the fact that a common peculiarity of German-speaking countries was identified which had gone unnoticed in previous research. The families of nations approach helps to identify common developments and common public policies. It has a very marked utility in explaining common labour supply developments in German-speaking countries by integrating common characteristics of these countries. Understanding the restrictive foreign employment policies of German-speaking countries after 1973 is not possible without considering the historically-determined and deeply-rooted view of foreign labourers as 'guest-workers' both in society and in public policy.

Nevertheless, one should not accord such cultural factors the status of comprehensive explanations of common developments and common policy outcomes. While this analysis has demonstrated the relevance of culturally defined families of nations, it has also noted the role of variables traditionally regarded as significant in cross-national comparative policy research, namely socio-economic and political-institutional conditions.

Notes

1. In the literature, the full employment-inflation dilemma is also known as the 'Phillips curve' relationship, named after the British economist A.W. Phillips. This describes an inverse association between the level of unemployment and the level of inflation (see Gahlen et al., 1983, 132).
2. The period was divided on the basis of the average economic performance and average employment growth of OECD countries.
3. The real wage level is defined as the nominal wage level divided by a price index, such as the index of consumer prices (Sellien and Sellien, 1979, 921).
4. The analysis focuses on the 18 countries of the OECD which have been democratic and capitalist throughout the period studied, and for which comparable data are available. These are Australia, Austria, Belgium, Canada, Denmark, Finland, France, Germany, Ireland, Italy, Japan, the Netherlands, New Zealand, Norway, Sweden, Switzerland, the UK and the US.
5. The separate analysis of different groups in the labour force is necessary because the labour supply varies by sex, age and nationality (or for citizens versus foreigners), and because the labour supply of the different groups depends on different factors (see e.g. Sorrentino, 1983; Schettkat, 1987a). It is also convenient as it reduces the complexity of the object of study.
6. The labour force participation rate does not measure the total volume of labour in a society, as it takes no account of variations in working time. Nevertheless, it is the appropriate indicator for the integration of the population in the formal economy because it measures the relative number of persons who supply or are prepared to supply their labour (Schettkat, 1987b).
7. This applies especially in the case of foreigners, because cross-national comparative data are available only for the number of foreign workers.
8. See note 2.
9. To speak of the labour force participation of older workers is imprecise because older workers always participate in working life. We use this term because it is customary in the literature and for the sake of brevity.

10. Among economic labour supply theories, the life-cycle hypothesis, in particular, deals with this problem. According to this hypothesis, the individual tries to optimize his labour market value over his life by seeking the path which maximizes his benefit; this benefit is a function of consumption and leisure (Schettkat, 1987a, 92). Because the future consumption of the individual depends on his future wages, and his future wages depend on his educational attainment, the individual has an incentive to extend the period of schooling (for details on the life-cycle hypothesis, see e.g. Franz, 1986).
11. The term 'labour force behaviour' refers to the individual decision to participate in the labour force or not; it does not imply anything whether this decision is voluntary.
12. In the technical literature, that part of the change in the labour force participation rate resulting from changes in the structure of the population is termed as the structural effect; that part resulting from changes in the labour force behaviour is referred to as the behavioural effect. One method for distinguishing these effects is component analysis. For the technique of component analysis, see Schettkat, 1987a; McMahon, 1986; for a critique, see von Knorring, 1978; Görzig, 1980.
13. This study cannot evaluate the extent to which this phenomenon is associated with the fact that students who have a job while still in education are registered as employed. However, there are grounds for this assumption, at least in the case of some English-speaking countries.
14. The data are those on the following countries: Australia, Finland, France, Germany, Italy, Japan, the Netherlands, New Zealand, Norway, Sweden, the UK and the US. For the other OECD countries, corresponding data are not available.
15. For Belgium, Denmark, Italy and New Zealand the corresponding data are not available; these countries were therefore excluded from the present analysis.
16. For the somewhat ambiguous characterization of Canada and Ireland as 'liberal' welfare states, see Castles and Mitchell (this volume, Chapter 3).
17. Between 1955 and 1968, for example, Germany concluded recruitment agreements with Italy and with seven countries outside the European Community (Dietz, 1987, 72).
18. The values for Austria are not available.
19. For France, the data on the number of foreign workers are extremely contradictory. Consequently, France was excluded from this analysis.
20. Calculated from *Statistical Yearbooks* of Germany, Austria and Switzerland.
21. It should be noted, however, that their small size does not necessarily lead to a rigid policy towards foreign workers. The fact that in Belgium and the Netherlands the employment of foreigners did not decline during the economic recession of the 1970s and early 1980s demonstrates this.
22. These assumptions are not uncontroversial. We do not know exactly what the German, Austrian or Swiss unemployment rates would have been if the labour supply had increased at the OECD average. We also do not know whether the assumption of an increase in labour supply at the OECD average is actually realistic in the cases of Germany, Austria and Switzerland. However, the only possibility of estimating the extent to which changes in the labour supply of the German-speaking countries influenced their rates of unemployment is to make certain explicit assumptions. On the other hand, comparing the developments of single countries or families of nations with the average levels in OECD countries is certainly valid.
23. Calculated from Table 4.11; OECD, 1989a; United Nations, *Demographic Yearbooks*.

24. These are Switzerland, Germany, Austria, Belgium, France, the Netherlands, Luxembourg and Sweden.
25. Calculated from Werner and König, 1984; EUROSTAT, 1979, 1983, 1988; *Statistical Yearbooks* of Germany, Austria and Switzerland; OECD, 1989a.
26. Calculated from Table 4.3; OECD, 1989a; United Nations, *Demographic Yearbooks*. Because of limited data in the case of Switzerland, we have had to use data in part for the years 1970 and 1980. One must therefore assume that the result is somewhat inaccurate.
27. Calculated from Table 4.4; United Nations, *Demographic Yearbooks*; OECD, 1989a. For the case of Switzerland, see note 26.

References

Aichholzer, Georg (1982), 'Arbeitsmarktpolitik in Österreich. Zum Verhältnis von Eingliederungs- und Ausgliederungsstrategien', *Österreichische Zeitschrift für Soziologie*, **3/4**, 69–80.

Appelbaum, Eileen (1982), 'Der Arbeitsmarkt' in Alfred Eichner (ed), *Über Keynes hinaus*, Köln: Bund.

Bach, Hans-Uwe and Brinkmann, Christian (1986), 'Erwerbsbeteiligung von Frauen im internationalen Vergleich', *Mitteilungen aus der Arbeitsmarkt- und Berufsforschung*, **3.**

Bach, Hans-Uwe, Brinkmann, Christian and Kohler, Hans (1987), 'Zur Arbeitsmarktsituation der Ausländer in der Bundesrepublik', *Mitteilungen aus der Arbeitsmarkt- und Berufsforschung*, **3**.

Bäcker, Gerhard and Nägele, Gerhard (1981), 'Arbeitsmarkt, Altersgrenze und die Ausgliederung älterer Arbeitnehmer', *WSI-Mitteilungen*, **11**.

Bauboeck, Rainer and Wimmer, Hannes (1988), 'Social Partnership and "Foreigners Policy", On Special Features of Austrian's Guest Worker System', *European Journal of Political Research*, **16**, 659–81.

Bender, Dieter (1977), 'Angebot des Haushalts I: Arbeitsangebot' in W. Albers et al. (eds), *Handwörterbuch der Wirtschaftswissenschaften*, Stuttgart-New York: Fischer, Volume 1, 223–32.

Bernabe, Franco (1982), 'The Labour Market and Unemployment' in A. Boltko, (ed.), *The European Economy. Growth and Crisis*, New York: Oxford University Press.

Biffl, Gudrun (1979), 'Die Entwicklung der Erwerbsbeteiligung unter veränderten Arbeitsmarktbedingungen', *Österreichisches Institut für Wirtschaftsforschung Monatsberichte*, **11**, 512–23.

Biffl, Gudrun (1984), 'Der Strukturwandel der Ausländerbeschäftigung in Österreich', *Österreichisches Institut für Wirtschaftsforschung Monatsberichte*, **11/12**, 649–64.

Biffl, Gudrun (1985), 'Die Entwicklung der Ausländerbeschäftigung in den wichtigsten europäischen Industriestaaten', *Österreichisches Institut für Wirtschaftsforschung Monatsberichte*, **8**, 480–93.

Biffl, Gudrun (1986), 'Unterschiedliche Entwicklung der Arbeitslosigkeit in

Österreich und in der BRD', *Österreichisches Institut für Wirtschaftsforschung Monatsberichte*, **4**, 211–16.

Biffl, Gudrun, Guger, Alois and Pollan, Wolfgang (1986), *Some reasons for low unemployment in Austria*, unpublished manuscript.

Biffl, Gudrun (1988), *Arbeitsmarkt 2000*, Forschungsberichte aus der Sozial- und Arbeitsmarktpolitik, 21, Wien: Bundesministerium für Arbeit und Soziales.

Biffl, Gudrun (1989), 'Arbeitsmarktpolitik in Österreich' in H. Abele et al. (eds), *Handwörterbuch der österreichischen Wirtschaftspolitik*, Wien:Manzsche Verlags- und Universitätsbuchhandlung, 333–46.

Blien, Uwe and Tessaring, Manfred (1989), 'Abgangsalter aus dem Bildungswesen und Arbeitsmarktsituation. Ergebnisse der Bildungsgesamtrechung des IAB', *Mitteilungen aus der Arbeitsmarkt- und Berufsforschung*, **1**, 85–99.

Blot, Daniel (1990), 'The Demographics of Migration', *The OECD Observer 163*, April–May, Paris: OECD, 21–5.

Brinkmann, Christian and Reyher, Lutz (1985), 'Erwerbspersonenpotential und Stille Reserve', *Mitteilungen aus der Arbeitsmarkt- und Berufsforschung*, **1**, 4–10.

Bruche, Gert (1983), 'Ausländische Arbeitnehmer' in Manfred G. Schmidt (ed.), *Westliche Industriegesellschaften. Wirtschaft-Gesellschaft-Politik*, München-Zürich: Piper, 40–6.

Bruche, Gert and Casey, Bernard (1982a), 'Arbeitsmarktpolitik unter Stagflationsbedingungen', *Mitteilungen aus der Arbeitsmarkt- und Berufsforschung*, **3**, 232–50.

Bruche, Gert and Casey, Bernard (1982b), *Arbeit oder Rente? Beschäftigungs- und sozialpolitische Manahmen für ältere Arbeitnehmer in Frankreich, Grobritannien, den Niederlanden, Schweden und den USA*, Frankfurt a.M.-New York: Campus.

Bruno, Michael and Sachs, Jeffrey D. (1985), *Economics of Worldwide Stagflation*, Cambridge, Mass.: Harvard University Press.

Bundesamt für Industrie, Gewerbe und Arbeit (BIGA) (1980), *Gründzüge der schweizerischen Arbeitsmarktpolitik*, 2 volumes, Bern: BIGA.

Bundesamt für Statistik (1985), *Eidgenössische Volkszählung 1980, Schweiz, Erwerbstätigkeit*, Vol. 9, Statistische Quellenwerke der Schweiz, Vol. 709.

Bundesministerium für Arbeit und Soziales (ed.) (1990), *Programmbudget der Arbeitsmarktverwaltung*, Wien: Bundesministerium für Arbeit und Soziales.

Busch, Andreas (this volume), 'The Politics of Price Stability. Why the German-speaking Nations are Different'.

Butschek, Felix (1981), *Vollbeschäftigung in der Krise. Die österreichische Erfahrung 1974–1979*, Wien: Wirtschaftsverlag Orac.

Butschek, Felix (1982a), 'Full Employment during Recession' in Arndt, S.W. (ed.), *The Political Economy in Austria*, Washington D.C./London: American Enterprise Institute for Public Policy Research.

Butschek, Felix (1982b), 'Versteckte Arbeitslosigkeit von Frauen und Jugendlichen', *Österreichisches Institut für Wirtschaftsforschung Monatsberichte*, **11**, 666–74.

Butschek, Felix (1984), 'Determinanten und Problematik der Ausländerbeschäftigung' in Österreichisches Institut für Wirtschaftsforschung (ed.),

Untersuchung über ausländische Arbeitnehmer in Österreich, Vol. 1, Wien, 1–28.

Casmir, Bernd (1989), *Staatliche Rentenversicherungssysteme im internationalen Vergleich*, Frankfurt a.M.: Lang.

Castles, Francis G. and Mitchell, Deborah (this volume), 'Worlds of Welfare and Families of Nations'.

Castles, Stephen (1984), *Here for Good. Western Europe's New Ethnic Minorities*, London et al.: Pluto Press.

Castles, Stephen and Kosack, Godula (1985), *Immigrant Workers and Class Structure in Western Europe*, London: Oxford University Press (2nd edition).

Chaloupek, Günther and Swoboda, Hannes (1975), 'Sozialpartnerschaft und Wirtschaftsentwicklung in den fünfziger und sechziger Jahren', *Österreichische Zeitschrift für Politikwissenschaft*, **3**, 333–43.

Christl, Josef and Potmesil, Stefan (1984), 'Beschäftigungs-und Arbeitsmarktpolitik in Österreich', *Österreichische Zeitschrift für Politikwissenschaft*, **13**, 279–94.

Cornetz, Wolfgang (1985), *Determinanten der Erwerbsbeteiligung. Eine theoretische und empirische Analyse sozio-ökonomischer Einflufaktoren des Arbeitsangebots*, Frankfurt–Bern–N.Y.: Lang.

Deutsches Institut für Wirtschaftsforschung (DIW) (1990), 'Vereintes Deutschland – geteilte Frauengesellschaft? Erwerbsbeteiligung und Kinderzahl in beiden Teilen Deutschlands', *DIW Wochenbericht*, **41**.

Deutsches Institut für Wirtschaftsforschung (DIW) (1991), *DIW Wochenbericht*, **12**.

Dietz, Frido (1987), 'Entwicklung und Struktur der beschäftigten ausländischen Arbeitnehmer in der Bundesrepublik Deutschland – Ein Vergleich zwischen Deutschen und Ausländern' in E. Hönekopp, (ed.), *Aspekte der Ausländerbeschäftigung in der Bundesrepublik Deutschland*, Beiträge aus der Arbeitsmarkt- und Berufsforschung, **114**, Nürnberg: 67–143.

Dornbusch, Rüdiger and Fischer, Stanley (1987), *Makroökonomik*, München-Wien: Oldenbourg.

Eidgenössische Konsultativkommission für das Ausländerproblem (1977), 'Auswirkungen der Rezession auf die Ausländer', *Die Volkswirtschaft*, **10**, 557–63.

Esping-Andersen, Gösta (1990), *The Three Worlds of Welfare Capitalism*, Princeton, New Jersey: Princeton University Press.

Esping-Andersen, Gösta and Sonnberger, Harald (1989), *The Demographics of Age in Labor Market Management*, European University Institute, Working Papers, 89/414, Florence.

Franz, Wolfgang (1986), 'Neuere mikroökonomische Analysen des Arbeitsmarktgeschehens: Ein Überblick' in Schelbert-Syfrig et al. (eds), *Mikroökonomik des Arbeitsmarktes*, Bern-Stuttgart: Haupt.

Gahlen, Bernhard et al. (1983), *Volkswirtschaftslehre*, Tübingen: Mohr.

Gerfin, Harald (1987), 'Die Bundesrepublik Deutschland in und nach derweltweiten Stagflationsperiode' in Rudolf Henn (ed.), *Festschrift für Lothar Späth*, Heidelberg: Springer, 737–56.

Görzig, Bernd (1980), 'Einige Bermerkungen zu v.Knorrings Kritik an der statistischen Ermittlung von Strukturfaktoren', *Jahrbücher für Nationalökonomie und Statistik*, **195**, 557–9.

Grande, Edgar (1988), 'Sozialpartnerschaft' in Landeszentrale für politische Bildung (ed.), *Österreich*, Der Bürger im Staat, **2**, 145–50.

Hagen, Elisabeth, Jenson, Jane and Reddy, Calleigh (eds) (1988), *Feminization of the Labour Force*, Cambridge: Polity Press, 3–16

Hammar, Thomas and Lithman, Yngve G. (1987), 'The Integration of Migrants: Experiences, Concepts and Policies' in *The Future of Migration*, Paris: OECD, 234–52.

Heinelt, Hubert (1991), *Frühverrentung als politischer Prozeß*, Wiesbaden: Deutscher Universitätsverlag.

Hönekopp, Elmar (1987), 'Rückkehrförderung und die Rückkehr ausländischer Arbeitnehmer und ihrer Familien' in E. Hönekopp (ed.), *Aspekte der Ausländerbeschäftigung in der Bundesrepublik Deutschland*, Beiträge zur Arbeitsmarkt- und Berufsforschung, **114**, Nürnberg.

Jeschek, Wolfgang, 1984: 'Der Einfluß von Demographie und Bildungsverhalten auf das Bildungssystem und die Auswirkungen auf das Angebot von Arbeitskräften in der Bundesrepublik Deutschland', *Vierteljahresschrift für Konjunkturforschung*, **3**, 331–43.

Jupp, James (1991), 'Managing Ethnic Diversity: How does Australia Compare?' in F.G. Castles (ed.), *Australia Compared. People, Policies and Politics*, Sydney: Allen & Unwin.

Kelly, John J. (1987), 'Improving the Comparability of International Migration Statistics: Contributions by the Conference of European Statisticians from 1971 to Date', *International Migration Review*, **4**, 1017–37.

Killingsworth, Mark R. (1983), *Labor Supply*, Cambridge: Cambridge University Press.

Knorring, Ekkehard von (1978), 'Die statistische Ermittlung von Strukturfaktoren. Einige kritische Anmerkungen', *Jahrbücher für Nationalökonomie und Statistik*, **193**, 558–63.

Kohl, Jürgen (1988), 'Altersicherung in Westeuropa: Strukturen und Wirkungen' in M.G. Schmidt (ed.), *Staatstätigkeit. International und historisch vergleichende Analysen*, PVS Sonderheft 19/88, Opladen: Westdeutscher Verlag, 221–50.

Krupp, Hans-Jürgen (1988), 'Entwicklungen am Arbeitsmarkt und Veränderungen des Erwerbsverhaltens' in W. Schmähl (1988), 114–27.

Kühlewind, Gerhard (1986), 'Beschäftigung und Ausgliederung älterer Arbeitnehmer. Empirische Befunde zu Erwerbsbeteiligung, Rentenübergang, Vorruhestandsregelung und Arbeitslosigkeit', *Mitteilungen aus der Arbeitsmarkt- und Berufsforschung*, **2**, 209–32.

Kühlewind, Gerhard (1988), 'Erfahrungen mit dem Vorruhestand aus beschäftigungspolitischer Sicht' in W. Schmähl (1988), 54–63.

Kuhn, W.E. (1978), 'Guest Workers as an Automatic Stabilizer of Cyclical Unemployment in Switzerland and Germany', *International Migration Review*, **2**, 210–24.

Leitner, H. (1986), 'The State and the Foreign Worker Problem. A Case Study of the Federal Republic of Germany, Switzerland, and Austria' in *Environment and Planning C: Government and Policy*, Vol. 4, 199–219.

Lever-Tracy, Constance (1983), 'Immigrant Workers and Postwar Capitalism: In Reserve or Core Troops in the Front Line?', *Politics and Society*, **12**, 127–57.

Lutz, Burkart (1988), 'Notwendigkeit und Ansatzpunkte einer angebotsbezogenen Vollbeschäftigungspolitik' in L. Reyher and J. Kühl (eds), *Resonanzen. Arbeitsmarkt und Beruf – Forschung und Politik*, Beiträge aus der Arbeitsmarkt- und Berufsforschung, 111, Nürnberg: 275–89.

Maier, Friederike (1991), 'Erwerbstätigkeit von Frauen – Geschlechtsspezifische Umbrüche im Arbeitsmarkt und Beschäftigungssystem' in A. Westphal et al. (eds), *Wirtschaftspolitische Konsequenzen der deutschen Vereinigung*, Frankfurt-New York: Campus, 295–318.

McMahon, Patrick J. (1986), 'An International Comparison of Labor Force Participation, 1977–84', *Monthly Labor Review*, **5**, 3–12.

Mertens, Dieter and Kühl, Jürgen (1977), 'Arbeitsmarkt I. Arbeitsmarktpolitik' in W. Albers et al. (eds), *Handwörterbuch der Wirtschaftwissenschaft*, Stuttgart-New York: Fischer, Vol. 1, 279–93.

Misslbeck, Johannes (1983), *Der Österreichische Gewerkschaftsbund. Analyse einer korporatistischen Gewerkschaft*, Frankfurt/a.M.: Wisslit.

Mordasini, Bruno (1985), *Das Erwerbsverhalten in der Schweiz. Eine empirische Analyse*, Basel: Institut für Sozialwissenschaften, Universität Basel.

Naegele, Gerhard (1985), 'Aktuelle Trends und Probleme des Ausscheidens aus dem Erwerbsleben in der Bundesrepublik Deutschland', *Soziale Arbeit*, **9**, 425–8.

Neidhart, Leonhard (1988), 'Die Schweizer Konkordanzdemokratie' in Landeszentrale für politische Bildung Baden-Württemberg (ed.), *Die Schweiz*, Der Bürger im Staat, 1, 44–52.

OECD (1984), *OECD Main Economic Indicators. Historical Statistics 1964–1983*, Paris: OECD.

OECD (1985a), *OECD Employment Outlook*, Paris: OECD.

OECD (1985b), *OECD Economic Surveys: Switzerland*, Paris: OECD.

OECD (1985c), *Social Expenditure 1960–1990. Problems of Growth and Control*, Paris: OECD.

OECD (1986), *OECD Economic Outlook. Historical Statistics 1960–1984*, Paris: OECD.

OECD (1987), *OECD Economic Surveys: Switzerland*, Paris: OECD.

OECD (1988a), *Reforming Public Pensions*, Paris: OECD.

OECD (1988b), *OECD Economic Surveys: Austria*, Paris: OECD.

OECD (1989a), *Labour Force Statistics 1967–1987*, Paris: OECD.

OECD (1989b), *Economies in Transition. Structural Adjustment in the OECD Countries*, Paris: OECD.

OECD (1989c), *OECD Economic Surveys: Switzerland*, Paris: OECD.

OECD (1991a), *OECD Economic Outlook. Historical Statistics 1960–1989*, Paris: OECD.

OECD (1991b), *Migration. The Demographic Aspects*, Paris: OECD.

Offe, Claus (1975), 'Bildungssystem, Beschäftigungssystem und Bildungspolitik. Ansätze zu einer gesamtgesellschaftlichen Funktionsbestimmung des Bildungswesens' in H. Roth and D. Friedrich (eds), *Bildungsforschung. Probleme-Perspektiven-Prioritäten*, Stuttgart: Klett, Vol. 1, 217–52.

Offe, Claus (ed.) (1977), *Opfer des Arbeitsmarktes: Zur Theorie der strukturierten Arbeitslosigkeit*, Neuwied-Darmstadt: Luchterhand.

Offe, Claus and Hinrichs, Karl (1977), 'Sozialökonomie des Arbeitsmarktes und die Lage "benachteiligter" Gruppen von Arbeitnehmern' in C. Offe (1977), 3–61.

Peinemann, Holger (1990), *Regulierung der Arbeitskräftestruktur – 'Early-Retirement' im europäischen Vergleich*, Berlin: Diplomarbeit, Freie Universität Berlin.

Sachverständigenrat zur Begutachtung der Gesamtwirtschaftlichen Entwicklung (1990), *Jahresgutachten*, Stuttgart: Metzler-Poeschel.

Scharpf, Fritz W. (1987), *Sozialdemokratische Krisenpolitik in Europa*, Frankfurt-New York: Campus.

Schelbert-Syfrig, H. et al. (eds) (1986), *Mikroökonomik des Arbeitsmarktes. Theorie, Methoden und empirische Ergebnisse für die Schweiz*, Bern-Stuttgart: Haupt.

Schettkat, Ronald (1987a), *Erwerbsbeteiligung und Politik*, Berlin: Edition Sigma.

Schettkat, Ronald (1987b), *Die Erwerbsquote, ein geeigneter Indikator zur Analyse der Erwerbsbeteiligung? Zur internationalen und intertemporären Vergleichbarkeit der Erwerbsbeteiligung*, Wissenschaftszentrum Berlin für Sozialforschung (WZB), Discussion Paper, Berlin: WZB.

Schmähl, Winfried (ed.) (1988), *Verkürzung oder Verlängerung der Erwerbsphase?*, Tübingen: Mohr.

Schmid, Günther (1975), *Steuerungssysteme des Arbeitsmarktes*, Göttingen: Schwarz.

Schmid, Günther (1987), *Arbeitsmarktpolitik im Wandel. Entwicklungstendenzen des Arbeitsmarktes und Wirksamkeit der Arbeitsmarktpolitik in der Bundesrepublik Deutschland*, WZB Discussion Paper, Berlin: WZB.

Schmid, Günther (1990a), 'Arbeitsmarktpolitik: Zum Verhältnis von Marktsteuerung und staatlicher Beschäftigungssicherung' in U. Sarcinelli (ed.), *Demokratische Streitkultur. Theoretische Grundpositionen und Handlungsalternativen in Politikfeldern*, Bonn: Bundeszentrale für Politische Bildung.

Schmid, Günther (1990b), 'Beschäftigungs- und Arbeitsmarktpolitik' in K.v. Beyme and M.G. Schmidt (eds), *Politik in der Bundesrepublik Deutschland*, Opladen: Westdeutscher Verlag, 228–54.

Schmidt, Manfred G. (1985), *Der Schweizerische Weg zur Vollbeschäftigung*, Frankfurt-New York: Campus.

Schmidt, Manfred G. (1987), 'Politikwissenschaftliche Arbeitsmarktforschung' in H. Abromeit and B. Blanke (eds), *Arbeitsmarkt, Arbeitsbeziehungen und Politik in den 80er Jahren*, Opladen: Westdeutscher Verlag, 12–19.

Schmidt, Manfred G. (1988a), 'The Politics of Labour Market Policy. Structural and Political Determinants of Rates of Unemployment in Industrial Nations' in F.G. Castles, F. Lehner and M.G. Schmidt (eds), *Managing Mixed Economies*, Berlin-New York: de Gruyter.

Schmidt, Manfred G. (1988b), *Sozialpolitik. Historische Entwicklung und internationaler Vergleich*, Opladen: Leske & Budrich.

Schmidt, Manfred G. (1989), 'Arbeitslosigkeit und Vollbeschäftigung in der Bundesrepublik', designated for H.-D. Klingemann and W. Lutkardt (eds), *Wohlfahrtsstaat, Sozialstruktur und Verfassungsanalyse*, Opladen: Westdeutscher Verlag.

Schmidt, Manfred G. (this volume), 'Gendered Labour Force Participation'.

Schmitter, Barbara E. (1981), 'Trade Unions and Immigration Politics in West Germany and Switzerland', *Politics and Society*, **10**, 317–34.

Schmitter-Heisler, Barbara (1988), 'From Conflict to Accommodation: The "Foreigners Question" in Switzerland', *European Journal of Political Research*, **16**, 683–700.

Schneider, Reinhard (1983), 'Bildungspolitik' in M.G. Schmidt (ed.), *Westliche Industrigesellschaften. Wirtschaft-Gesellschaft-Politik*, München-Zürich: Piper, 61–71.

Schüle, Ulrich (1987), *Der gleitende Übergang in den Ruhestand als Instrument der Sozial- und Beschäftigungspolitik*, Europäische Hochschulschriften, Frankfurt–Bern–N.Y.–Paris: Lang.

Sellien, Reinhold and Sellien, Helmut (eds) (1979), *Gablers Wirtschaftslexikon*, Wiesbaden: Gabler.

Sesselmeier, Werner and Blauermel, Gregor (1990), *Arbeitsmarkttheorien*, Heidelberg: Physica.

Siegenthaler, Jürg K. (1988), *Ältere Arbeitnehmer, Austritt aus dem Erwerbsleben und Arbeitsmarkt: Forschungsresultate über die langfristige Entwicklung – Anwendungen auf den Fall Schweiz*, Bericht im Auftrag des BIGA.

Sorrentino, Constance (1983), 'International Comparisons of Labour Force Participation, 1960–1981', *Monthly Labour Review*, **2**, 23–36.

Statistisches Amt der Europäischen Gemeinschaft (EUROSTAT) (1979) (1983) (1988), *Beschäftigung und Arbeitslosigkeit*, Luxembourg: EG.

Statistisches Bundesamt, *Statistisches Jahrbuch für die Bundesrepublik Deutschland*, Stuttgart-Mainz: Metzler-Poeschel (various volumes).

Statistisches Bundesamt (1989), *Statistisches Jahrbuch für das Ausland*, Stuttgart: Metzler-Poeschel.

Strahm, Rudolf H. (1984), 'Wie die Schweizer mit der Arbeitslosigkeit fertig geworden sind', *Mitteilungen aus der Arbeitsmarkt- und Berufsforschung*, **1**, 88–93.

Talos, Emmerich (1985), 'Krise der sozialen Sicherung in Österreich', *Österreichische Zeitschrift für Politikwissenschaft*, **3**, 275–94.

Talos, Emmerich (1987), 'Arbeitslosigkeit und Beschäftigungspolitische Steuerung: Problemwahrnehmung/Problemartikulation, Zielsetzungen, Strategien und Maßnahmen in Österreich seit Mitte der 70er Jahre' in E. Talos and M. Wiederschwinger (eds), *Arbeitslosigkeit. Österreichs Vollbeschäftigungspolitik am Ende?*, Wien: Verlag für Gesellschaftfskritik.

Therborn, Göran (1985), *Arbeitslosigkeit. Strategien und Politikansätze in den OECD-Ländern*, Hamburg: VSA.

Therborn, Göran (1987), 'Nationale Politik der internationalen Arbeitslosigkeit. Der Fall Bundesrepublik im Lichte der OECD-Daten von 1973–1985' in H. Abromeit and B. Blanke (eds), *Arbeitsmarkt. Arbeitsbeziehungen und Politik in den 80er Jahren*, Opladen: Westdeutscher Verlag.

Thränhardt, Dietrich (1975), 'Ausländische Arbeiter in der Bundesrepublik, in Österreich und der Schweiz', *Neue Politische Literatur*, **22**, 68–88.

Thränhardt, Dietrich (1988), 'Die Bundesrepublik Deutschland – ein unerklärtes Einwanderungsland' in *Aus Politik und Zeitgeschichte*, **24**, 3–13.

Thränhardt, Dietrich (1990a), *Einwanderungspolitik in der Bundesrepublik Deutschland*, contribution to '40 Jahre Bundesrepublik Deutschland zwischen Kontinuität und Wandel', 21–23 July 1990, Berlin.

Thränhardt, Dietrich (1990b), 'Bildungspolitik' in K.v. Beyme and M.G. Schmidt (eds), *Politik in der Bundesrepublik Deutschland*, Opladen: Westdeutscher Verlag, 177–202.

Tichy, Gunther (1984), 'Strategy and Implementation of Employment Policy in Austria' , *Kyklos*, **37**, 363–86.

Tichy, Roland (1990), *Ausländer rein! Warum es kein 'Ausländerproblem' gibt*, München-Zürich: Piper.

Tschudi, Hans-Peter (1989), *Entstehung und Entwicklung der schweizerischen Sozialversicherung*, Basel: Helbing/Lichtenhahn.

Tuchtfeldt, Egon (1978), 'Die schweizerische Arbeitsmarktentwicklung – ein Sonderfall?' in O. Issing (ed.), *Aktuelle Probleme der Arbeitslosigkeit*, Berlin: Duncker & Humblot, 165–99.

United Nations (UN), *Demographic Yearbook*, New York: UN (various volumes).

United Nations Educational, Scientific and Cultural Organization (UNESCO), *Statistical Yearbooks*, Paris: UNESCO (various volumes).

Wagner, Antonin (1975), 'Die sozial Schwachen in der Rezession', in *Schweizer Monatshefte*, **55**, 541–53.

Wagner, Antonin (1985), *Wohlfahrtsstaat Schweiz*, Bern-Stuttgart: Haupt.

Walterskirchen, Ewald (1977), 'Arbeitsmarktpolitik in Österreich', *Institut für Wirtschafts- und Sozialforschung (WSI), Mitteilungen*, **5**.

Webber, Douglas (1982), 'Zwischen programmatischem Anspruch und politischer Praxis: Die Entwicklung der Arbeitsmarktpolitik in der Bundesrepublik Deutschland von 1974–1982', *Mitteilungen aus der Arbeitsmarkt- und Berufsforschung*, **15**, 261–75.

Werner, Heinz (1987), 'Die Entwicklung der Ausländerbevölkerung in einigen westeuropäischen Ländern – eine Analyse der Komponenten der Bevölkerungsentwicklung', in E. Hönekopp (1987), 343–60.

Werner, Heinz and König, Ingeborg (1984), 'Ausländerbeschäftigung und Ausländerpolitik in einigen westeuropäischen Industriestaaten', *Mitteilungen aus der Arbeitsmarkt- und Berufsforschung*, **4**, 506–10.

Wimmer, Hannes (1986), 'Zur Ausländerbeschäftigungspolitik in Österreich' in H. Wimmer (ed.), *Ausländische Arbeitskräfte in Österreich*, Frankfurt/a.M.-New York: Campus, 5–32.

Wissenschaftszentrum Berlin für Sozialforschung (WZB) (ed.) (1981a), 'Ausländerbeschäftigung und Arbeitsmarktpolitik', *Internationale Chronik zur Arbeitsmarktpolitik*, **4**, Berlin: WZB, 1–4.

WZB (ed.) (1981b), 'Frühverrentung im internationalen Vergleich', *Internationale Chronik zur Arbeitsmarktpolitik*, **5**, Berlin: WZB, 1–4.

5 Gendered Labour Force Participation

Manfred G. Schmidt

Introduction

The political economies of the German-speaking democracies in the post-World War II period are widely regarded as success stories (Shonfield, 1965; Katzenstein, 1985). Austria, West Germany and Switzerland have been more successful than most other nations in maintaining relative price stability; moreover, relative to the long-run misery index – an additive index of the rate of inflation and the rate of unemployment – their performance has also been good (Schmidt, 1989). At the same time, despite relatively high income levels, the economies of Switzerland, West Germany and, to a lesser extent, Austria have both maintained high wage levels and have remained keenly competitive (see, for example, Katzenstein, 1989). Moreover, most of the citizens of the German-speaking family of nations are covered by high levels of social protection; this is through welfare state provision in Germany and Austria, and in Switzerland through a combination of market income with job security for nationals together with a more parsimonious welfare state, complemented by large-scale private social insurance.

However, in contrast to the expertise on the part of these countries' policy-makers in manipulating the macroeconomy and providing social security, the level of social and economic gender inequality in Austria, Switzerland and West Germany has remained remarkably high and the impetus to reduce the degree of sexual inequality through public policy intervention has been weak (see, for example, Norris, 1987; OECD, 1988a). The dominant approach of the public authorities to gender issues in the German-speaking nations has long rested upon a conservative family policy in conjunction with social security schemes for male and female workers, and social security coverage for married or widowed housewives. Moreover, relatively high levels of gender inequality have also characterized other important policy areas in the German-speaking nations. These include levels of educational attainment (Bundesanstalt für Arbeit, 1989), female-male ratios of hourly earnings and changes in these ratios (OECD, 1988a), female-male ratios of unemployment rates, and political representation of women in parties, parliament and government (see, for example, Kolinsky, 1989; Eidgenoessische Kommission, 1984 and 1990; Norris, 1987; Castles and Marceau, 1989).

Even more striking is the relatively high level of inequality in the labour market revealed by data on female-male ratios of labour force participation in the OECD countries in the 1980s. On this indicator, the German-speaking nations are all below the OECD mean, whereas all the Nordic countries are located at the top of the distribution (see Table 5.1, column 1). Moreover, the data arrayed in this table are indicative of the extent to which sexual differences in labour force participation have stagnated in Austria, Switzerland and West Germany in a period in which dramatic improvements in job opportunities for women relative to those for men have been reported from most other OECD nations. Whereas the female-male ratio of labour force participation rose in most OECD countries in the period from 1960 to 1985 to a truly dramatic extent – with a 40 percentage point change in Sweden, Norway and Denmark – the change in Austria, Switzerland and West Germany was modest and, indeed, as slow as in countries which have long been notorious for their conservative stance in gender-related policies, including Ireland, Italy and Japan (see Table 5.1).

By definition, changes in the sex ratio of participation rates mirror the impact of levels (and the change in the level) of male and female participation rates. Decomposing the gross change in the sex ratio of labour force participation reveals a striking configuration in Austria, Switzerland and West Germany. In these countries, the modest increase in the level of gender equality, as measured by the sex ratio in Table 5.1, has mainly been the result of declining male participation rates (see Table 5.1, columns 3–5, and Table 5.2). This is in marked contrast to the trends in gender inequality that characterize the Nordic countries and the English-speaking family of nations (except for Ireland) in which the increase in the level of gender equality is mainly attributable to rising rates of labour force participation of women.

The male participation rate has declined in almost all OECD countries in the period studied, the German-speaking nations being no exception to this trend (see Table 5.2). However, the behaviour of the female participation rate in Austria, Switzerland and West Germany has been anomalous. While most other Western nations have experienced an intensification of women's

Table 5.1: Gender inequality in labour force participation, 1960–85[1]

	1985	1960	1985–1960[2]	Of which due to… female component	male component[3]
Australia	.63	.35	.28	.20	.08
Austria	.63	.57	.06	–.01	.07
Belgium	.67	.43	.24	.16	.07
Canada	.73	.37	.36	.32	.05
Denmark	.85	.44	.41	.31	.10
Finland	.90	.72	.18	.09	.09
France	.72	.49	.23	.09	.14
Germany, West	.63	.52	.11	.01	.10
Ireland	.43	.35	.08	.02	.06
Italy	.52	.42	.10	.01	.09
Japan	.65	.65	.0	–.03	.03
Netherlands	.54	.27	.27	.15	.12
New Zealand	.57	.33	.24	.17	.06
Norway	.79	.39	.40	.34	.05
Sweden	.92	.51	.41	.28	.13
Switzerland	.60	.51	.09	.02	.07
UK	.68	.47	.21	.14	.07
US	.75	.47	.28	.23	.05
Mean	.68	.46	.22	.14	.08

[1] The data presented are ratios of the female and male labour force participation rates. Low values indicate high levels of inequality. *Source*: OECD, *Employment Outlook*.

[2] First differences (ratio in 1985 minus ratio in 1960).

[3] The estimate of the female labour force component of the gross change in the ratio of female-male workforce participation between time point (t) and timepoint (t+1) is based on the hypothetical change in the female-male ratio of labour force participation that would have been generated if the male workforce participation rate had remained at the level reached at the beginning of the period. The male labour force component of the gross change in the sex ratio is based on the hypothetical change in the female-male ratio that would have been generated if the female labour force participation rate had remained throughout the period at the level reached at (t+1). *Source*: see Table 5.2.

More formally: Gross change G = F + M.

G is, by definition, $G = ((W\ t{+}1)/(M\ t{+}1)) - (W\ t)/(M\ t)$,

and can be transformed into a decomposed sex ratio change:

$G = ((W\ t{+}1)/M\ t) - ((W\ t)/(M\ t)) + ((W\ t{+}1/M\ t{+}1) - (W\ t{+}1/M\ t)$,

with the female component F given by $F = ((W\ t{+}1)/M\ t) - ((W\ t)/(M\ t))$, and the male component M given by $M = ((W\ t{+}1/M\ t{+}1) - (W\ t{+}1/M\ t)$.

W = labour force participation of women,

M = male labour force participation rate,

t = time point t (beginning of period) and

t+1 = time point t+1 (end of period).

participation in the paid labour force in the post-1960 period, the female participation rate in the German-speaking nations remained at the level it had reached in 1960. Whilst other modern nations have moved towards an increased 'feminization of the labour force' (Jenson, Hagen and Reddy, 1988) beyond the 70 per cent mark in female participation, as in the Nordic countries, the paradox of the German-speaking nations has been that of a stagnating female participation rate at a level of 50 per cent (see Table 5.2).

The data arrayed in Table 5.1 and in Table 5.2 provoke a wide variety of questions. Why has the female labour force participation rate in the German-speaking family of nations changed so little in the 1960–85 period? How is

Table 5.2: Male and female labour force participation rates, 1960–85

	Female 1960	Male 1960	Female 1985	Male 1985	Change 1960–85 Female	Change 1960–85 Male
Australia	34.1	97.2	54.1	85.2	20.0	–12.0
Austria	52.1	92.0	51.0	81.2	–1.1	–10.8
Belgium	36.4	85.5	50.5	75.9	14.1	–9.6
Canada	33.7	91.1	62.4	84.9	28.7	–6.2
Denmark	43.5	99.5	74.5	87.4	31.0	–12.1
Finland	65.6	91.4	73.7	81.8	8.1	–9.6
France	46.6	94.6	54.9	76.7	8.3	–17.9
Germany, West	49.2	94.4	50.3	80.0	1.1	–14.4
Ireland	34.8	99.0	36.6	85.5	1.8	–13.5
Italy	39.6	95.3	41.0	79.3	1.4	–16.0
Japan	60.1	92.2	57.2	87.8	–2.9	–4.4
Netherlands	26.2	97.8	40.9	75.8	14.7	–22.0
New Zealand	31.3	93.8	47.6	83.2	16.3	–10.6
Norway	36.3	92.2	68.0	86.6	31.7	–5.6
Sweden	50.1	98.5	77.6	84.2	27.5	–14.3
Switzerland	51.0	100.4	53.2	89.4	2.2	–11.0
UK	46.1	99.1	60.2	88.4	14.1	–10.7
US	42.6	90.5	63.8	84.6	21.2	–5.9
Mean	43.3	94.7	56.5	83.2	+13.2	–11.5

Source: OECD, *Employment Outlook*. Labour force participation rates are measured as employed and unemployed persons as a percentage of population of working age from 15–64. Change in participation rate was measured by first differences (participation rate in 1985 minus participation rate in 1960).

the rapid increase in the female participation rate in Scandinavia, and also in the larger Anglo-American democracies, to be accounted for? Why has the female-male labour force participation ratio been lower in Austria, Switzerland and West Germany and, hence, the level of sexual inequality in economic participation been higher than in most other developed OECD nations? Why have the labour force participation rates of men and women in the OECD varied as much as they have? These are the questions to which this chapter seeks answers.

Research Design and Theoretical Framework

The Dependent Variable

Because we are primarily concerned in this chapter with gender differences in workforce participation, the *explanandum* is ultimately the level of the female-male ratio of labour force participation in the mid-1980s and the change in this ratio over a period for which comparable data for 18 OECD nations are available (1960–85). The explanation will be advanced in four steps. This section introduces the research design and the theoretical frame of reference adopted in this study. The second section presents a descriptive account of factors that are associated with the sex ratio of labour force participation in the mid-1980s. In this part, the non-decomposed sex ratio will be the dependent variable. What we are seeking to do here is to map broad patterns in the correlates of gender inequality. However, a more detailed analysis of the determinants of changes in levels of gender inequality requires the decomposition of the dependent variable and separate analysis of the underlying changes in male and female participation rates. For this reason, the dependent variable in later sections is the change in the female participation rate, or the change in the rate of labour force participation of men.

Participation rates of men and women are measured by the share of the male labour force in the male population of working age from 15 to 64 and, conversely, by the female labour force as a percentage of the female population of working age from 15 to 64. The data are taken from OECD sources and they may, broadly speaking, and despite some contaminating factors, be regarded as sufficiently comparable.[1]

Families of Nations and the Sample of this Study

The effort to account for gender inequality in the family of German-speaking nations in this chapter is premised on the view that a satisfactory answer to the research question must be based on a comparison of the German-speaking family of countries with other Western democracies – regardless of whether or not they have familial characteristics in the broad sense defined in the Introduction to this study. The assumption is that a convincing explanation of the relatively high level of gender inequality in the labour market of the German-speaking nations requires a model which, in principle, is applicable to all other democratic capitalist nations. It is for this reason, that the analysis focuses on those 18 countries of the OECD area which have been democratic and capitalist throughout the period studied and for which comparable data have been available (for the list of countries in the sample, see Table 5.1).

It should be noted that, whilst this chapter proceeds from the assumption that the family of nations concept is potentially valuable for exploring variation in gender-related inequalities in the labour market, we consciously embrace the methodology of comparative inquiry favoured by Przeworski and Teune (1970) of seeking to substitute variables for the proper names of countries or groups of countries. In other words, we start from the most minimal definition of a family of nations – that of a group of countries sharing a common cultural tradition – and only after full-scale comparative analysis, according to the standard methodology, offer conclusions as to the possible validity of any more encompassing definition.

Nature of the Data

The data utilized in this study are macro-political and macro-sociological (and some of them also macroeconomic) in nature. The choice of a macro perspective has been dictated by the non-availability of comparable micro-level data for the 18 nations in our sample. However, the macro perspective also promises to generate a more parsimonious account of cross-national and cross-time variation in labour force participation rates of men and women. On theoretical grounds, it can also be argued that a macro-political and macro-sociological perspective can potentially shed more light on underlying institutional determinants of cross-national variation in labour force participation than studies which focus on micro-level data. This expectation rests on the assumption that decisions taken by female and male workers on entry to, or withdrawal from, the labour force are to a significant extent shaped by institutions on the meso and macro level of the economic, social and political order.

Comparative Institutionalism

The perspective adopted in this study and the emphasis that it places on macro-sociological factors, political-institutional variables and political-cultural traditions differ radically from the economic paradigms that have dominated the field of labour force participation research hitherto (see, for example, Ashenfelter and Layard, 1986). Within the context of the dominant paradigms, the major emphasis has been on microeconomic studies of labour supply and demand for labour, complemented by macroeconomic research and socio-demographic analysis. Valuable as these contributions are, they have very rarely (and, if at all, highly selectively) investigated the impact of deep-seated institutional factors – such as cultural traditions, political norms, beliefs and attitudes, political institutions and policy – on workforce participation in general and gender-related labour force participation in particular. Moreover, the dominant paradigms in labour force participation research are marked by a serious sample bias: most of the theory is based on empirical data taken from a small number of larger OECD economies, mainly the US, the UK and, to a lesser extent, West Germany, whereas the large cross-country differences in female and male participation rates across the range of OECD nations tend to be ignored in both empirical and theoretical work. What is largely missing from this paradigm (see, for example, Pencavel, 1986, and Killingsworth and Heckman, 1986) is a truly comparative framework and a satisfactory explanation – or at least a set of hypotheses relevant to an explanation – of the large cross-country differences in labour force participation of men and women (for exceptions, see Mincer, 1985).

That systematic cross-national comparative analysis is largely absent from research conducted within the context of leading paradigms of labour economics may have serious consequences. Following cross-cultural studies in the sociology of work, it is plausible to argue that cultural differences in attitudes and behaviour towards paid and unpaid work will affect labour force participation, and that the neglect of political and social factors thus impairs a fuller understanding of entry to, and exit from, the labour market (see, for example, Youssef, 1972).

Hypotheses

A comparative perspective on male and female participation rates and a greater emphasis on institutional determinants have been the trade-mark of a relatively small school of thought, comprising political-sociological studies (see, for example, Norris, 1987), political-institutionalist contributions to the study of labour market policy (such as Schmid and Weitzel, 1984;

Schmid, 1984a and 1984b; Schettkat, 1987a), and the more recent comparative studies on the part of Bureau of Labor Statistics and OECD experts on labour force participation of men and women (see Sorrentino, 1983; McMahon, 1986; OECD, 1988a). Although political and social factors have not yet been systematically tested against comparative labour force participation rates in all OECD nations, empirical evidence from smaller samples suggests that an institutionalist approach is potentially fruitful in the study of cross-country and cross-time variations of sex differences in economic activity. For example, C. Sorrentino's comparison of labour force participation trends in 11 countries in the period from 1960 to 1981 has suggested that the underlying factors in recent increases in female participation rates are the 'expansion of the service sector; increased availability of part-time work; extension of higher education for women; abating job discrimination against women and changing attitudes towards women's role in society' (Sorrentino, 1983, 27). In a major OECD study of economic activity by women in Western nations in recent decades, it has further been argued that the large cross-country variation in female participation rates 'can be properly appreciated only in the light of the deep-seated institutional differences between countries' (OECD, 1988a, 29).

A variety of hypotheses proceeding from this institutional perspective can be identified. Comparative studies of political aspects of labour supply have pointed to incentives that the structure of taxation can create for female labour supply (Gustavsson, 1984; Schettkat, 1987a). Other studies have suggested that the level and the change in female participation rates are influenced by economic policy regimes, social policy, the wage policy stance of trade unions, part-time employment (Jensen, Hagen and Reddy 1988), party-political factors, such as the political composition of government (Norris, 1987), the degree of political representation of women (Norris 1987), political-cultural factors, such as religious traditions (Schmidt, 1984) as well as attitudes to gender issues (Norris, 1987).

Moreover, sociologists and historians have pointed to the role of economic modernization and the level of economic wealth in shaping the occupational structure and the level of job opportunities for women (see, for example, Wilensky, 1968; Jensen, Hagen and Reddy, 1988), while social policy studies suggest that the welfare state functions as an important labour market for men and, to a larger extent, for women (Rein, 1985). Family sociologists have argued that the supply of female and male labour is also influenced by the socio-economic characteristics of the household, by marital status, by the degree of responsibility for work inside the home, by the number and age of children, and by access to public or semi-public child care (see, for example, Paukert, 1984; Ruggie, 1984; OECD, 1988a). Last but not least, research by scholars in the human capital school suggests that characteristics of workers, such as work experience and, above all, levels of qualification, will influence the supply of labour. In contrast to this, demand-oriented approaches to the study of labour economics emphasize the impact of macroeconomic policy on the demand for labour (for overviews of supply side and demand side factors in labour force participation, see Pencavel, 1986; Killingsworth and Heckman 1986; Weck-Hannemann and Frey, 1989).

In seeking to contribute to a better understanding of cross-national differences in female and male participation rates, these hypotheses and others which can be derived from more detailed country studies (see, for example, Farley, 1985; Antal and Kernsbach-Gnath, 1985; Jenson, Hagen and Reddy, 1988) will be tested against cross-national data. However, it must be emphasized that what follows is guided by a comparative-institutionalist approach to the study of labour markets (see, for example, Schmidt, 1987). It is for this reason that a major part of the analysis is centred on the impact of social and political factors on the supply of, and the demand for, male and female labour. While this approach promises to redress some of the imbalance that has been created by the neglect of social and political variables in labour force participation research, it is essential to emphasize that it needs to be complemented in future work by a micro-level oriented reconstruction of choices on entry to, and exit from, the labour market on the part of workers and firms.

Correlates of Female-Male Ratios of Labour Force Participation in 1985: The 'Level of Industrial Development' School and More Recent Contributions

What comparative research there has been on labour market gender inequality has tended to focus on the impact of economic modernization. For example, Klein (1963) and Wilensky (1968) have suggested that the female participation rate and the sex ratio of labour force participation vary with levels of economic development; that poor countries are marked by high levels of inequality in the labour market and rich nations by low levels of gender inequality. To quote from Semyenov's discussion of this view, economic development 'brings females to the work place through changes in the occupational structures and educational opportunities, coupled with declining fertility and the changing functions of the family unit (from a production to a consumption unit)' (Semyonov 1980: 535). There has also been a strong tendency in the 'logic of industrialism' school of thought to regard levels of development as a purely economic variable and as the major determinant of female participation rates. An example of that position can be found in the work of Wilensky (1968), who argues that the 'level of economic development is far more important than ideology as a determinant of female participation in the urban economy' (Wilensky, 1968, 236).

The latter type of 'industrialism' theory has rightly been criticized for adopting an economistic and mechanical view and for underestimating the importance of political and cultural factors. However, it can be argued that the 'industrialism' perspective points to a high level of economic development as a necessary, although not sufficient, condition for high levels of gender inequality.

Defined in these terms, the 'level of economic development' view receives some support from cross-sectional comparisons (although we will later point out that this does not apply for change measures). Consider, for example, the correlation that exists between the female-male ratio of workforce participation in 1985 and GDP per capita in 1985. The statistical relationship between these variables suggests that rich countries tend to be marked by lower levels of gender inequality on the labour market than poor countries (Pearson's $r = .62$; regression equation: $Y= 0.45 + 0.022$ (GDP per capita, in 1000 US$); $t = 3.13$; GDP data from Summers and Heston, 1988).

However, there are deviant cases. Particularly striking is the extent to which two families of nations deviate from the trend. The level of gender equality in Switzerland, for example, is far 'too low' relative to the trend in the data for the OECD nations as a whole, and West Germany and Austria exhibit the same tendency, although to a lesser degree. In contrast, all the Nordic nations are above the trend and hence are characterized by a level of sexual equality in labour force participation which is 'too high' relative to the trend for the OECD area as a whole. The countries of the English-speaking family of nations tend to fall within the area closely above or below the regression line (with the major exception of Ireland). Statistically, the English-speaking countries, except for Ireland, behave in a way which is most consistent with the prediction to be derived from the level of industrialization school of thought.

Why are there family-specific clusters of nations? What variables strengthen or, conversely, weaken the links that exist between economic development and labour force participation? At least a partial answer to this can be derived from bivariate correlation coefficients. These coefficients show that six groups of variables were significantly related to female-male ratios of labour force participation in the mid-1980s (significance level $p < .05$). According to these results, a high level of gender equality is associated with the following:

- high levels of equality in the economic activity rates of men and women in the early 1960s ($r = .46$);

- demand-related factors such as a high level of economic development (r = .62 for 1985) (data from Summers and Heston 1988) together with a high share of employment in the service sector in general (r = .41) and in the public sector in particular (r = .60) (OECD data);
- factors on the supply side, such as a high female-male ratio of enrolment in higher education (r = .63) (data from Castles and Marceau, 1989) and in educational attainment (OECD, 1989b, 53–5), and low rates of fertility (r = –.48) (data are taken from OECD, 1988a);
- the effect of certain policies explicitly designed to reduce gender inequality or which have functioned tacitly as inequality reducing mechanisms; these include strong growth of child-care facilities for working women with children (r = .56), powerful taxation incentives for women's labour force participation (OECD, 1990b, 166) (r = .58), availability of part-time jobs in 1985 (OECD, 1988a) (r = .43) and liberal abortion laws (r = .55, N = 17);
- a wide variety of genuinely political variables, such as government by left-wing parties in 1960–85 (r = .63) and, in particular, left-wing parties' participation in the government of Protestant countries (r = .68), highly organized trade unions (r = .49, N = 17, data from Cameron, 1984), and a high level of political representation of women in parliaments in the early 1980s (r = .60, data from Norris, 1987); and
- cultural variables, such as the share of the Protestant population (r = .61) or, conversely, the share of the Catholic population (r = –0.62).

Countries which score high on the variables listed above (except for fertility and Catholicism, for which the reversed order applies) are marked by high levels of gender equality in labour force participation, while countries which score low on these variables (except for fertility and Catholicism) are characterized by low levels of gender equality. For example, the relatively high level of gender equality in the Nordic countries is not attributable to their being Nordic *per se*, but can rather be regarded as a consequence of the particular configuration of economic, social and political factors that has prevailed in the Scandinavian countries. The female-male ratio of labour force participation in the Nordic nations is high, the analysis so far suggests, because the Scandinavian countries score high on the critical determinants of the demand for, and the supply of, female labour, and because policy, the political process and cultural traditions have all facilitated a more egalitarian policy stance on the part of government.

In contrast, the low score of the German family of nations on our measure of gender equality can largely be attributed to a particular configuration of labour supply and labour demand characteristics, policy, politics and culture. In the German-speaking countries, the level of gender inequality inherited from the past tends to be stabilized by a wide variety of factors operating on both the demand and supply sides, such as a high share of industrial employment in total employment, a low share of service sector employment and lower levels of child care, to mention just a few of the critical variables.

The findings reported have shed light on the correlates of female-male ratios of labour force participation in the mid-1980s. However, the major drawback of this kind of data analysis and the interpretations based on it is the limited degree to which a cross-sectional research design allows for causal inferences. In order to establish causality, a cross-time design is required, or in some cases a design with lagged variables, and that demands the extension of the analysis to determinants of change in the female-male ratios of labour force participation. Moreover, in order to account fully for the change in the sex ratio of labour force participation, it is necessary to decompose the dependent variable and study the variation in the female participation rate separately from that of the male participation rate.[2] It is to these tasks that we now turn.

Social and Political Determinants of Changes in the Rate of Female Labour Force Participation, 1960–85

A Summary of the Findings

A wide range of variation marks the change in female participation rates in the period from 1960 to 1985. For example, a dramatic increase in the female rate of labour force participation has characterized Sweden, Norway, Denmark and Canada in this period. Also remarkable has been the increase in workforce participation of women in the US and in Australia. In contrast to this, the rate of economic activity of women has stagnated or declined in the German-speaking countries, in Ireland, Italy and Japan and the Catholic nations of Southern Europe (see Table 5.2).

How is the large cross-country variation in change in female participation rates to be explained? Broadly speaking, a matching of hypotheses from the literature with cross-national data suggests that the change in female participation rates in the period from 1960 to 1985 can be attributed to five sets of factors summarized in Table 5.3.

Table 5.3: Correlates of change in the female rate of labour force participation, 1960–85[1]

I.	*Historical rate of female labour force participation, 1960*	–43*
II.	*Modernization and occupational structure*:	
	Level of economic development (GDP per capita) 1960	.55*
	Long-run rate of growth of real GDP, 1960–85	–.21
	Employment in agriculture 1960 (% total employment)	–.46*
	Decline of agricultural employment (% total employment) 1960–85	.43*
	Employment in industry 1960 (% total employment)	.04
	Change in industrial employment (% total employment) 1960–85	–.57*
	Employment in service sector 1960 (% total employment)	.65*
	Change in service sector employment (% total employment) 1960–85	.15
	Part-time employment (% total employment) (1973)	.61*
III.	*Supply-side characteristics and socio-demographic trends*:	
	Change in fertility rates 1961–81 (first differences)	–.47*
	Change in female-male ratio of enrolment in tertiary education 1960–81 (Castles and Marceau, 1989; UNESCO, 1990)	.36
	Change in share of female population 65 and over, 1960–85	.22
	Change in share of female youth population (0–14 years) 1960–85	–.13
IV.	*Effects of policy on supply of, and demand for, female labour*:	
	Employment in public sector (Cusack et al., 1989) 1960	.54*
	Growth of employment in public sector 1960–83	.48*
	Change in public spending on education 1960–85 (UNESCO, 1990)	.32
	Size of the tax state 1960 (revenues % GDP)	.44*
	Growth of child care facilities 1960–80 (Norris, 1987)	.44*
	Taxation incentives for female labour supply (OECD, 1990b, 166)	.55*
	Age of Equal Pay Policy (OECD, 1988a) (N=14)	.45
V.	*Political-institutional and political-cultural determinants*:	
	Non-socialist prime minister in post-war period, 1946–59	–.65*
	Centre party prime minister in post-war period, 1946–59	–.45*
	Centre party prime minister, 1946–59 and Catholicism/100	–.53*
	Left-wing party prime minister, 1960–85	–.25
	Centre party prime minister, 1960–85	–.05
	Left-wing prime minister, 1960–85 and Protestantism/100	.56*
	Organizational density of unions 1960s–70s (Cameron 1984)	.47*
	Age of female suffrage, 1960	.46*
	Change in women's share in parliament, 1960–85	.47*
	Protestants in % of total population, early 1980s	.66*
	Catholics in % of total population, early 1980s	–.51*

[1] Pearson's product-moment correlation coefficient. Change is measured by first differences (female participation rate in 1985 minus female participation rate in 1960). N = 18 unless otherwise stated. Level of significance p <.05 marked by "*" and p <0.01 marked by "**". All intercorrelations between independent variables <.70. Table 5.3 and the interpretation of the data in Table 5.3 report correlation coefficients only for those variables for which data on all or almost all nations of our sample have been available. Hence, there is no further discussion in this chapter concerning statistical relationships between change in participation rates and variables with data available only for smaller samples, such as egalitarian attitudes towards family roles (based on Norris, 1987, 135) (r =.60, N = 8) and the extent to which female-male hourly earnings ratios in manufacturing have been diminished (r = –.90 for 10 nations) (data source: OECD, 1988: 212). A detailed analysis of the impact of these variables and other potentially relevant factors on female participation rates must be deferred to a later study.

[2] Dependent variable: change in female participation rate 1973–85.

Sources: Labour force participation rates were taken from OECD, *Employment Outlook.* Data for GDP per capita from Summers and Heston 1988, all other economic and occupational data from OECD, *Economic Outlook – Historical Statistics* and for part-time employment from OECD 1983 and OECD 1988a. Data on supply-side characteristics were taken from OECD, *Employment Outlook 1988* and from Castles and Marceau, 1989, supplemented for data on Japan from *UNESCO Yearbook 1989*. Data on policy are from OECD *Economic Outlook – Historical Statistics*; OECD, 1988a; Norris, 1987, and for impact of taxation from OECD, 1990b, 166. Data on partisan composition of government was mainly taken from Schmidt, 1992. Data on union density are from Cameron, 1984, and religious data are from Barrett, 1982. All other political data were taken from Norris, 1987.

Discussion of the separate findings[3] constituting each of these sets of factors – historical participation rates of women, modernization and change in the occupational structure, changes in supply-side characteristics of female labour, the impact of policy and the role of political-institutional and political-cultural factors – take up the remainder of this section.

The Historical Participation Rate of Women

It can be shown that a catching-up process has been involved in the behaviour of the female participation rate from 1960 to 1985. A particularly pronounced increase in this period was reported from countries with a low female participation rate in the early 1960s, including most of the English-speaking nations, Belgium and the Netherlands. In contrast to this, a stagnating rate of economic activity of women, or only a modest increase, was characteristic of countries with a comparatively high female participation rate in the 1960s, such as Japan, Austria, West Germany, Switzerland and Finland.

Modernization and Change in Occupational Structure

The identification of the mechanisms which have generated the catching-up process requires a more detailed study of the factors that have influenced the supply of, and the demand for, female labour. Following the classical industrialism school of thought, it can be hypothesized that the change in the female participation rate is positively related to the level of economic development and to the long-run growth rate of GDP, measured by the annual average change in GDP at constant prices over the period studied. The first hypothesis passes the test reasonably well ($r = .55$), but it must be emphasized that the correlation masks divergent responses of female participation rates to a high level of economic development: the response in most of the Nordic states has generated rising female participation rates and, hence, has contributed to the process of 'the femininization of the labour force' (Jensen, Hagen and Reddy, 1988). In contrast, the change in female labour force participation relative to the level of economic affluence has been small in West Germany and Switzerland, and negative in Austria.

Even more pronounced is the difference in the response of the female participation rate to long-run economic growth rates. Economic growth has been associated with stagnating female participation rates in one group of countries (the German-speaking nations, Italy, Ireland and, to a truly dramatic extent, Japan) and with rising participation rates in another group (the Nordic and English-speaking nations). These differences are, of course, reflected in an insignificant relationship between long run growth rates and change in female economic activity rates, suggesting that the level-of-industrialization-view, defined in terms of changing levels of economic development and measured in terms of average annual rates of growth, is not compatible with the data for the period 1960 to 1985. Of course, this does not necessarily impair a theory in which the modernization process is defined much more broadly, focusing not only on levels of affluence and economic growth, but also on changes in the occupational structure and social organization. However, the data presented here are clearly incompatible with the more orthodox quantificationist modernization theory to be found in the studies of H. Wilensky (1968) and others.

Trajectory to economic modernity The interesting question that these findings suggest is the following: why has the response in the female participation rate to levels of economic wealth and economic growth varied so much? At least a partial answer to this can be derived from the impact that trajectories of economic modernization have on the occupational structure (see, for example, OECD, 1984; Bakker, 1988; Mallier and Rosser, 1987, ch. 8). We will examine this aspect of the modernization process before turning to the way in which supply-side, political and cultural factors also intervene in the process of determining female participation rates.

Table 5.3 demonstrates that the increase in female participation rates has varied with occupational structure and change in the occupational structure. These structural shifts included the decline in agricultural employment (a sector traditionally characterized by high shares of female workers), decline in the employment content of the industrial sector (in which male workers have prevailed), and a pronounced increase in the volume of employment in the service sector, in particular in the public sector in the period from 1960 to the mid-1980s (and, thus, the rise of a sector which has created a large number of new jobs for women; see, for example, Paukert, 1984; OECD, 1984, 50–51; Rein, 1985; del Boca, 1988, 127–8; Statistisches Bundesamt, 1987). The increase in the female participation rate therefore has been particularly pronounced in nations which were characterized by a small agricultural sector in the beginning of the period (r = –.46), modest decline in agricultural employment (r = .43), rapid decline in industrial employment (r = –.57) and rapid growth of employment in the public sector (r = .48), mainly in social services, education and health care (see also OECD, 1984; Bakker, 1988; Statistisches Bundesamt, 1987). In contrast to this, weak growth in the female participation rate, or stagnation, has been associated with a large employment share in the primary sector of the economy in 1960, rapid decline in agricultural employment, modest decline in industrial employment and a modest expansion of job opportunities in the public sector. An example which approximates the latter constellation of factors is Japan, and one approximating the former is Sweden.

However, there have been different trajectories to economic modernity. For example, the shift to a tertiary economy, as measured by the proportion of civilian employment in services, varies greatly from country to country. It is here that we again find ourselves confronted with a striking difference between the German-speaking family of nations and the Nordic family. Austria, Switzerland and West Germany are notorious for having large industrial sectors and comparatively small service sectors. Moreover, the decline in industrial employment in these countries has been rather modest, with Austria being amongst the countries with the smallest decrease throughout the period, just behind industrializing Japan. A consequence of this has been the maintenance of a large male-dominated employment sector, and, other things being equal, a lower level of job opportunities for women and weaker growth in the female labour force participation rate. The relatively high level of gender-differentiation in industrial employment is at least partly attributable to a complex interaction between female workers' job preferences, skills and levels of qualification, and the subcultural pattern (Erler, 1988).

Within the industrial sector of Germany, and also in Austria and Switzerland (Katzenstein, 1984), the dominant position is held by small and medium-sized, highly specialized companies. These companies are, as Piore and Sabel (1985) have pointed out, characterized by jobs, skills and subcultural patterns which are more likely to resist recruitment of female labour. Moreover, the interaction of a large industrial sector and the central role of apprenticeship in training young workers function as an obstacle to the extension of female labour force participation (Erler, 1988, 233). The reasons for this are largely attributable to the fact that apprenticeship mainly comprises training for highly-qualified and well-paid technical jobs and, hence, offers training for a field in which women are under-represented, partly due to their 'preference for office and interpersonal work' (Erler, 1988, 233), but also due to discrimination. Thus, the transition from school to vocational training is gendered and so is the transition from vocational training to work, not to mention access to the post-vocational *Meisterpruefung* certificate, which entitles holders to start up businesses and to train apprentices (see Kolinsky, 1989, 115–21).

Furthermore, compared with the Nordic nations, the share of employment in the public sector and the increase in that share have been modest in the German-speaking nations. Because a large proportion of state employment is concentrated in jobs in administration and in professional and semi-professional jobs in the social services, education and health care, a high share of public sector employment in total employment and the increase of this share are conducive to the employment of women, whereas a relatively small and weakly growing share of state employment works against improvement in women's labour force participation. Austria, Switzerland and West Germany exemplify a route to economic modernization in which a premium is placed on male economic activity and in which powerful barriers are imposed to extending and diversifying women's employment.

The opposite extreme is represented by the Nordic nations, and by Sweden and Denmark in particular. The economies of these countries are marked by a relatively small industrial employment share, considerable decline in industrial employment shares and exceptionally high increases in state employment, mainly at the local level and in the welfare state.

The change in the rate of female labour force participation has also been related to the rapid growth in part-time employment over the last two decades, itself a consequence of both demand and supply factors in the process of tertiarizing of the economy (see OECD, 1983, 46–9). Although part-time work has undoubtedly meant substantial deficits in income and social security entitlements – compared with full-time jobs on the part of most male workers – growth in part-time employment has improved labour market opportunities for women. This has been due to the fact that the female share in part-time employment has been high. In the countries covered by comparable data, the proportion of female part-time workers was at least 60 per cent in the mid-1980s, and in some countries between 80 and 90 per cent (OECD, 1988a, 149–50). Moreover, OECD-studies also point to significant contributions of part-time employment to the growth in female employment (OECD, 1988a, 149–50), and, hence, to significant effects of the supply of part-time jobs on the rise in female labour force participation, other things being equal. A similar picture emerges from the correlation of part-time employment, measured as the share of part-time employment in total employment in the early 1970s, with the change in female participation rates in the period from 1973 to 1985 (r = .61).

Here we are again confronted with a significant difference between the German-speaking nations and the Anglo-American and Nordic countries. The share of part-time employment in total employment has been high in the latter groups but low in the former. Precisely that difference has influenced the variation in the change of female participation rates in these countries.

Part-time employment and the role of the trade unions The analysis presented so far has pointed to the importance of changes in the demand for increasing levels of economic participation by women. However, what has not yet been explored is the extent to which the determinants of demand for female labour are influenced by policy, politics and cultural tradition. It is to this topic that we now turn.

Consider, for example, the case of part-time employment. Among the determinants of the share of part-time employment in total employment, the stance of firms and trade unions on working time policy deserves to receive first mention. Unions which have long preferred generalized working time reduction for all workers and have successfully bargained for wages and salary levels sufficient to support a one-income family have reasons to believe that part-time jobs will generate losses in income and social security entitlements are thus likely to oppose any significant increase in part-time employment.

This has precisely been the policy stance of unions of weak or moderate political strength, such as those in Italy (Del Boca, 1988) and in German-speaking nations (see, for example, Antal and Krebsbach-Gnath, 1985). The incentives to accept part-time work are significantly stronger when unions are more highly organized and when part-time employment is adequately compensated in terms of wages, taxation and social security benefits. In such cases, Sweden being a conspicuous instance, the unions will tend to accept a significant degree of part-time work (see, for example, Cook, Lorwin and Daniels, 1984). However, the response of unions, firms and job-seekers to part-time employment will also be contingent upon the nature of prevailing cultural traditions. When the dominant culture in a particular country places priority on women's work inside the family rather than outside the home, the response to part-time work will be much more muted. In contrast, that response will be much stronger in a Protestant environment and in a highly secularized society.[4]

Three routes to economic modernity The analysis presented in this section has demonstrated that the process of economic modernization must be counted as one of the major determinants of changes in female participation rates. It is, however, most important to identify the diverse ways in which policy, politics and cultural traditions impinge upon the relationship between modernization and changes in female workforce participation. Some clues to this diversity may be derived from an examination of the interaction between wage policy, tax load, and the type of welfare state.

In our sample of nations, one can distinguish, in an ideal-type fashion, three different routes to economic modernity in the period studied. The North American route is that of a nation which has early become modern and in which there has also been an early transition to the service sector economy. A large proportion of jobs in the tertiary sector are non-unionized, and for many of them the wage level is relatively low, in particular in social services, personal services and the retail trade. The relatively low level of wages, the weakness of trade unions and the relatively low tax load as a percentage of GDP have all contributed to the emergence of a large service sector labour market in the private economy and, hence, have been conducive to rising female participation rates.

A different route to economic modernity has been taken in the Nordic nations. The power of the unions blocked the low-wage policy along the lines of the North American service sector. However, the growth of the welfare state has generated a large employment share for women in the public sector and, hence, created a service sector mainly financed from tax revenues. To an even larger degree than North America, the Nordic route to modernity involved a dramatic increase in the female participation rate.

The path of economic development in the German-speaking nations is representative of a third route to economic modernity. The trade unions have been powerful enough to bargain for high wage levels in general and for a wage level sufficient for a one-income family in particular (Antal and Krebsbach-Gnath, 1985), thus effectively retarding the growth of employment in the service sector to a significant extent. But in contrast to the Nordic countries, the share of employment in the public sector remains relatively small and is not sufficient to compensate for the weaker level of employment content of the private market economy. This was partly due to a more restrictive stance in fiscal policy since the mid-1970s, and to strong political opposition from centre-right and liberal parties to further increases in the tax load, but it also mirrored the impact of the historical traditions of the welfare state in these countries. The welfare states in Austria, West Germany and Switzerland have been transfer-intense; hence, the share of public consumption expenditures in GDP and the share of public employment as a percentage of total employment are only of moderate strength. Thus, the interaction of wage policy, fiscal policy, taxation and the welfare state has generated an occupational structure which differs from that of most other rich Western nations: the share of service sector employment is moderate and it grows at a modest pace, and the share of industrial employment remains large. But that has enormous consequences for female labour force participation: the Germanic route to economic modernity has mainly been open to the male labour force, with little scope for increasing levels of female labour in the economy.

The Impact of Social and Political Factors on Female Labour Supply

So far we have explored the impact of demand factors on changes in female participation rates. However, God has given us two eyes, one to watch demand and one to watch supply. Samuelson's *bon mot* is, of course, also applicable to the study of labour force participation of women. Human capital theory, for example, has pointed to relationships between workforce participation and characteristics of the individual worker, such as work experience, and level of qualification, to mention but two of the major variables. Moreover, it is also uncontroversial that the 'fundamental supply-side characteristic' (Humphries and Rubery, 1988, 86) that distinguishes female workers – namely their primary responsibility for social reproduction – generates a distinctive pattern in their entry to and exit from the labour force. For example, labour force participation of women, and women with children in particular, depends to a large extent on their access to institutions which reconcile work inside the home and work in the paid labour force, such as child care and care for the elderly, maternity leave and parental leave arrangements. It is to the latter type of determinants and to standard variables from human capital theory (such as levels of educational attainment) and from demography (such as trends in fertility) that we now turn.

Fertility rates Among potential determinants of the supply of female labour, trends in fertility over the last few decades have been identified as of major importance (Sorrentino, 1990, 42–3). Indeed, evidence does exist to support the view that fertility trends matter. For example, the number of live births per women in the age groups from 15 to the mid-40s shows a marked downturn in the period from the early 1960s to the 1980s in most of the countries of our sample. Furthermore, in the 1980s fewer women in their teens and twenties became mothers than was the case in the 1960s; there were also fewer women in their thirties and forties with young children in large families. A consequence of this, it has been argued, has been better opportunities for women to participate in the labour force and rising levels of female labour force participation (see, for example, Paukert, 1984, 41; Killingsworth and Heckmann, 1986, 123; Blau and Ferber, 1986, 305; Sorrentino, 1983, 28).

The analysis of the data, indeed, supports the view that increasing participation rates of women are related to the decline in fertility rates over the last few decades (r = –.47). That association masks processes of reciprocal causality, but it is also indicative of the extent to which labour force participation for women is facilitated by declining fertility rates.

However, it must be emphasized that the extent to which trends in fertility rates are related to the labour force participation of women varies from one family of nations to another. Particularly instructive is the comparison of the Nordic nations with the German-speaking democracies. In both groups, the downturns in fertility rates were, broadly speaking, similar. However, the change in female participation in these countries has differed to a very large extent. The response of the female participation rate to declining fertility rates has been pronounced in the Nordic states, but has remained weak in Austria, Switzerland and West Germany.

Human capital Not all of the factors that supply side theory suggests are important in labour force participation pass the test of cross-national data analysis equally well. For example, according to a widely-held view, rising female participation rates over the last few decades can be accounted for by the improved educational attainment of women from generation to generation, and in particular by improved female-male ratios of educational enrolment (OECD, 1988a, 138, 1988b; Paukert, 1984, 41; Killingsworth and Heckman, 1986, 116, 120, 123). However, within the context of a cross-national research design, the relationship between change in the female participation rate and change in the female-male ratio of enrolment in tertiary education is insignificant (r = .36).[5] This is not to deny the importance that a higher level of qualification of women may have for the female labour force participation rate, but it suggests that the relationship between the two variables may be more complex in nature. A key to a better understanding of the weak relationship between the variables is to be found in the deviant case of the German-speaking family of nations, and hence in a political-cultural variable, missing in standard labour economics. Relative to the considerable improvement in female educational attainments in the period studied, the change in female participation in these countries has been small. In contrast to this, similar patterns of improved educational attainment have purchased a substantial increase in job opportunities for women in most Nordic and English-speaking nations. We are thus again confronted with the labour market anomaly of Austria, Switzerland and Germany relative to the high level of human capital that the female population of these countries has accumulated.

This anomaly has, of course, profound effects on the cross-national relationship between change in educational enrolment and change in the female participation rate. For example, the exclusion of Austria, Germany and Switzerland from the correlation between change in participation rates and improved female-male-ratios of enrolment in tertiary education generates a significant correlation (r = .58). An even stronger correlation could be obtained through excluding the remaining deviant cases – Italy and Ireland – from the sample (r = .67).

In the German-speaking countries, and also in Italy and Ireland, certain factors are suppressing the normal relationship between educational attainment and the labour force participation of women. It is tempting to argue that the central variable which accounts for the deviant cases is the important role that Catholicism (and the lower level of secularization which is associated with Catholicism) have played in the political culture of all these countries and, by inference, the presence of cultural obstacles to the recruitment of female labour. Furthermore, as earlier analysis has shown, the occupational structure of the economy has generated a lower level of demand for female labour in Austria, Switzerland, West Germany, and also in Italy and Ireland, which may contribute to the under-utilization of female human capital in these countries.

The Impact of Policy on Female Labour Supply

We have already established that public policy has direct and indirect effects on the demand for female labour, but it also affects its supply. Central to the latter is the impact of taxation and policies which free women from the duty of caring for children, elderly and other dependants, such as child care, public care for the elderly, and maternity and parental leave arrangements (Sorrentino, 1983, 28; Gustavsson, 1984; Norris, 1987; OECD, 1990a). Due to limited availability of comparable data, it is not possible to explore the impact of all these policies on female labour supply, although they do allow for a closer examination of the relationship between labour supply on the one hand and taxation and child care on the other.

Child care The extent to which the social infrastructure meets the needs of childbearing and childrearing varies across countries (see OECD, 1990a). The two extreme poles are marked by 'countries with social policy programmes directed towards an alternative and equal management of family and work roles', and 'those countries that have done virtually nothing in this area' (Bakker, 1988, 36), with Italy and Ireland, and to a lesser extent, the German-speaking nations exemplifying the latter type of response, and most of the Nordic nations the former (see, for example, Kamerman and Kahn, 1983). Furthermore, a line can be drawn between countries following a 'maximum private responsibility model' (OECD, 1990a, 139), according to which child care and familiy organization are regarded as private concerns, and those who have subscribed to the 'maximum public responsibility model' (OECD, 1990a, 139), according to which priority is placed on the educational value of child care outside the home. It can be arged that the type of response to the trade-off between family roles and work roles, together with the nature of the dominating responsibility model, are of the greatest possible relevance for female workforce participation. The model of alternative and equal management of work and family roles lessens the responsibility of women for work in the home and facilitates labour market entry on the part of women. In contrast to this, the traditional family policy model reinforces women's primary role in work inside the home and impedes the incorporation of female labour into the economy. More uncertain is the impact of the responsibility model, but the experience of the Nordic countries suggests that the maximum public responsibility model has been conducive to female work outside the home to a larger extent than the private responsibility model (see, for example Ruggie, 1984; OECD, 1990a). Comparative data on the growth of child-care facilities from the early 1960s to the early 1980s are compatible with this hypothesis, as well as with the family-and-work-role hypothesis: the pace of increase in female participation rates is associated with high growth rates in the provision of child care (r = .44).

Undoubtedly in some of the countries, there are processes of reciprocal causality at work. Swedish research, for example, has shown that the expansion in child care is at least partly attributable to the political demands of working women. However, it has also been the case that child care – and expanding child care in particular – complemented with generous parental leave arrangements have facilitated the entry of women to the labour market (Gustavsson, 1984), whereas a low level of child care provision and modest increases in care facilities, such as in the German-speaking nations, have strongly impeded female labour force participation (see, for example, Shaffer, 1981; Ruggie, 1984 and 1989; Sorrentino, 1990, 53–4; DIW 1990).

These data support the view that the stagnating female participation rate in Austria, Switzerland and West Germany can, at least partly, be attributed to the effects of a conservative stance in family policy and the muted response of governments to the needs of childbearing and childrearing. Moreover, there is also evidence in support of the hypothesis that the steep increase in female participation rates in the Nordic nations has been facilitated by a progressive stance in child care policy and in the underlying stance in family policy. The key to an understanding of child care policy is to be found in the impact of preferences of parties and cultural traditions. Public child care, for example, has been promoted by left-wing government, and by centre-left or left-wing governments in Protestant countries in particular,[6] whereas governments of a centre-right or rightish complexion, in particular in countries with a significant share of Catholics in the population, have regarded child care, and care for the elderly as a responsibility mainly of the family and hence, essentially, as a responsibility of women.

Taxation and female labour supply The supply of female labour, it has been argued, is to a significant extent influenced by incentives or disincentives created through the level of taxation as well as the structure of the tax system (see, for example, Gustavsson, 1984; Schmid, 1984b, 22–3; Schettkat, 1987a; OECD, 1990b). For example, a high level of taxation, such as in the Scandinavian countries and more recently also in the Benelux nations, may be argued to generate the economic necessity of increasing disposable household income through workforce participation of household members not already in paid work. However, it must be added that the evidence in support of this view tends to be based on case studies and country studies, and hence, can be argued to be relatively weak for the purpose of explaining of cross-national variations in sexual differences in labour force behaviour.

More firmly established is the inference that can be derived from the impact of the structure of taxation on female labour supply. For example, a powerful disincentive for female labour force participation is created in countries, such as the German-speaking nations, where joint income taxation and social security tax ceilings substantially lower the benefit that can be derived from earning additional income through work outside the home on the part of women. In contrast to this, a strong incentive for female workforce participation is generated through a taxation structure in which the incomes of couples are taxed separately and in which social security tax ceilings are absent (OECD, 1990b, 163–8).

Empirically, evidence exists in support of the view that changes in labour supply are related to the structure of taxation. For example, the change in labour force participation of women is significantly associated with incentives for female labour supply created in the structure of taxation, as measured by the 'Switch'-indicator developed by authors of the OECD *Employment Outlook* (see OECD, 1990b, 163–8) (r = .55). This indicator compares the change in net household income of a married couple that is caused by a standardized increase in gross earnings on the part of the wife with the change in net income caused by a standardized increase in gross earnings on the part of the husband.[7] The larger the difference in net income change, the higher the incentive for female labour supply. The regression of taxation incentives on change in female participation rates suggests that the difference between a powerful incentive for female labour supply, as in Sweden, and a disincentive for women's work outside the home, as in West Germany, Austria and Switzerland, generates a difference of 19 percentage points on the scale of change in female participation rates.

Thus, as far as taxation is concerned, a very powerful disincentive against female labour force participation is at work in the German-speaking countries. In contrast to this, the structure of taxation in most of the Nordic nations, and in Sweden in particular, creates a powerful incentive for entry to the labour force on the part of women. It is therefore not surprising that the increase in female participation rates has been pronounced in the Nordic nations and weak, if not absent, in the German-speaking nations.

It must be added that, at least in some of the countries, the underlying political logic in taxation policy is not difficult to disentangle. For example, a taxation policy which emphasizes disincentives for female workforce participation has mainly been a characteristic of countries in which organized labour has been weak or moderately strong, in which the government has generally chosen a conservative approach to the issue of female labour force participation, and in which governing parties, including the religious parties of Christian Democratic complexion, have incorporated the conservative stance of Catholicism in family policy into the structure of taxation, such as in West Germany in the early 1950s.[8]

The Politics of Female Labour Force Participation

In fact policy does matter in female labour force participation – as the analysis of the impact of the welfare state, taxation and child care on the demand for labour and on the supply side has shown. Moreover, the analysis presented here also suggests that the female participation rate is influenced by underlying political institutions and cultural traditions. For example, the three routes to economic modernity discussed previously are to a significant extent shaped by political factors; this may be regarded as offering further support for an approach which focuses in more detail on the 'politics of labour force participation', such as the one adopted in this section.

The pluralist-democratic theory of gender inequality Labour force participation of women and sex ratios of economic activity rates have, of course, been of major concern in feminist studies on gender inequality. In the debate on the extent to which 'politics constructs gender and gender constructs politics' (J.W. Scott, 1983, 156), the pluralist-democratic theory of gender inequality has been influential. According to this view, the level of gender inequality is inversely related to the degree to which women as an interest group, a social movement, or a distinctive category of voters or politicians has gained access to the political system; it is also inversely related to the impact of the female vote on parties and the degree to which women are represented in dominant political institutions, such as legislatures and political parties. According to this school of thought, both access to the political system and adequate levels of political representation significantly improve the chances for women 'to get things done' in a way which is beneficial to their interests (see, for example, Greven-Aschoff, 1981; Jensen, 1983; Norris, 1987; Bakker, 1988, 36–40; Crompton et al., 1990).

Hitherto, the evidence offered in support of the view that women's movements matter and that their strength varies with levels (and change in levels) of gender equality has been sketchy and, at best, inconclusive, as has been the evidence for the hypothesis that the political representation of women in legislatures varies with levels of gender inequality and changes in that level. The pluralist-democratic view of gender inequality does, however, receive support from tests comprising cross-national data. Change in political representation of women in legislatures, measured with data from the 1960–85 period, is significantly related to change in the female participation rate; furthermore, change in participation rates is correlated with a classical political-institutional variable, namely the length of time since the adoption of female suffrage (r = .46). This suggests that countries in which both men and women have enjoyed longer democratic experience are also somewhat more egalitarian in their labour force participation profiles.

Trade unions Also important to an understanding of the politics of female labour force participation is the role of power distribution, political institutions and cultural traditions. In contrast to the view that the labour movement is a male dominated institution and, therefore, pursues a 'male workers only' policy, the empirical analysis reveals a positive association between change in female participation rates and strength of trade unions in the 1960s and 1970s, as measured by union density data (Cameron, 1984). Studies on the response of unions to female labour force participation, such as the contributions by Cook, Lorwin and Daniels (1984), suggest that the critical variables are to be found in the degree to which unions are encompassing and in the unions' stance in employment policy. The 'male worker only' policy, for example, tends to be a valid formulae only for those unions which are politically weak at the national level and capable of mobilizing only segments of the workforce, such as in Japan (see, for example, Hanami, 1984, 223). In contrast to this, powerful and highly encompassing unions, committed to full employment, will prefer the incorporation of female labour into the economy (see also Ruggie, 1988).

The impact of political parties Furthermore, there is also evidence supporting the relevance of parties in the process of determining the supply of, and the demand for, female labour, partly through their role in shaping macroeconomic policy and social security arrangements, and partly through their impact on family policy, child care and taxation. Statistically, the partisan complexion of governments in the post-war period to 1959 is significantly related to change in female workforce participation in the 1960–73 period, as well as in the 1960–85 period as a whole. Particularly dampening has been the impact of governments of non-socialist, centre or centre-right complexion (r = –.65). Among these, centre party governments operating in a Catholic country (or in a country with a larger share of Catholics), such as in Ireland, Italy, Austria, and also in West Germany and Switzerland, deserve special mention (r = –.53). The reasons for this are straightforward: centre parties in Catholic countries transform the conservative stance of Catholicism in gender-related issues into public policy, such as in family policy, taxation, education, social security and care for children, the elderly and other dependants. These governments thus place priority on the maintenance of traditional patterns of gender differentiation (see, for example Eidgenoessische Kommission, 1984; Kolinsky, 1989; Moeller, 1989; Del Boca, 1988). That policy, of course, creates powerful disincentives and obstacles to the incorporation of female labour into the economy. This is at least partly mirrored in the stagnating female participation rate which has characterized these countries in the post-1960 period.

In contrast to this, an increase in female participation rates has been strong in countries governed in the period from 1946 to 1959 by parties of the left (r = .65) and has gained further momentum from a Protestant environment.[9] In contrast to the Catholic nations, left-wing party governments in general, and left-wing governments in Protestant countries in particular, have tended towards a more liberal stance in family policy, including areas of relevance for female labour force participation such as taxation (see also Wilensky, 1990 and 1992). For these reasons, few serious obstacles to rising female participation rates in the 1960s were erected or maintained in these countries in the period prior to the rapid expansion of female economic activity. In the post-war period until the early 1960s, left-wing government was mainly a characteristic of Protestant countries, such as the Nordic nations, the UK (1945–51) and Australia (1945–49). In contrast to this, in the 1970s and 1980s, left-wing parties participated in national government in Protestant countries and in nations with a substantial Catholic culture, such as in Austria, West Germany and Switzerland. As far as gender issues were concerned, the left-wing governments in Catholic environments faced more powerful constraints than their counterparts in Protestant countries. While a left-wing government in a Protestant country is relatively unconstrained in targeting policy towards increasing levels of gender equality, a left-wing government in a Catholic environment operates under powerful cultural constraints as soon as it seeks to redress the imbalance in the labour market between women and men. Unless the government is willing to accept major conflicts with both the Catholic church and religious parties, and dramatic losses in popularity, it will avoid policies of an overtly non-Catholic or anti-Catholic complexion and will shrink from attacking traditional patterns of division of labour between men and women. It will therefore also prefer not to promote a higher level of incorporation of female labour into the workforce.

It is at least partly for these reasons that female participation rates did not rise significantly in West Germany, Austria and Switzerland. But there have also been other political factors involved in maintaining female participation rates in Germany at the level of the early 1960s. Among these, the interaction between religious factors, partisanship of government, institutional inertia, and veto-positions on the part of the opposition deserve special mention.

Partisanship of government, religion, political institutions and the 'non-feminization of the labour force': West Germany and Switzerland The case of West Germany in the 1970s is indicative of the extent to which efforts to reduce gender inequality have been impeded by the interaction of conservative attitudes to gender egalitarianism, a gender gap in the female vote in favour of the Christian Democratic parties and institutional barriers to major policy changes, such as the consensus requirement inherent in the federal structure of the West German state. Any major effort on the part of the Social Democratic-Liberal coalition substantially to increase the level of female participation rates required the consent of the *Bundesrat*, the representative body of the West German state governments. What complicated policy-making was that the opposition party in this period, the Christian Democratic Union, commanded the majority of the seats in the *Bundesrat* and hence could veto all major legislation. The Christian Democratic party was thus co-governing and could block most of those policy changes which would significantly alter the path that the Christian Democratic governments of the 1950s and 1960s had created in policy areas of relevance to gender differentiation. Moreover, due to the fact that most of the social infrastructure required for the incorporation of women with children into the economy took place under the jurisdiction of the Länder government, and also due to the fact that the CDU/CSU held office in the majority of the Länder in the 1970s, the Christian Democratic party, although the opposition party at the national level, maintained full control over child-care policy. That control was used by the Christian Democratic party until the mid-1980s, and somewhat less so in the subsequent period, in favour of conservative goals in family policy.

The distribution of political power within this context and the preferences of the major actors did not impede all changes in gender related policy. In fact, legislation in the 1970s contributed to a reduction in the level of political and social inequality between women and men in a variety of ways. Examples include the extension of coverage of certain social security arrangements to women, the new marriage and divorce law of 1975, and the Labour Promotion Law of 1969, parts of which were designed to facilitate entry or re-entry of disadvantaged labour market groups, including women, into the economy mainly through training and further training measures for the unemployed and discouraged workers (Kolinsky, 1989, 56–60; see also Cook, 1984, 67).

However, a line was drawn at policies designed to promote 'feminization of the labour force' of the kind typically promoted in the Nordic states and in most of the Anglo-American countries. Moreover, the modest trend towards equal opportunity in the legislation of the early 1970s was halted as soon the German economy was hit by the recession of the 1970s and as soon as the opposition party, the Liberals, and the coalition government, adopted a restrictive stance in fiscal policy and in spending on social and labour market policy programmes (see Bruche and Reissert 1985; Kolinsky, 1989, 56–60). The West German case is indicative of the extent to which the interaction of Catholicism (and associated barriers to secularization), veto positions of the opposition party and federalism impeded the adoption of a more progressive stance in gender-related policy. A somewhat similar pattern emerged within the context of the Austrian political process, although the Austrian states command a less important position than the states in Germany and the cantons in Switzerland.

Switzerland is an example of a country with particularly powerful institutional barriers against policies which might reduce the level of gender inequality, such as public policy measures which could improve the compatibility of work within the home and paid work outside it. The extremely high consensus requirements that Switzerland's referendum democracy, federalism and consociational practices between the major parties impose on policy change place a premium on maintaining the status quo, and normally only allow for gradual change over a long period of time with a considerable time lag relative to pending problems (Kriesi, 1980; Neidhart, 1988a and 1988b). As in West Germany, Switzerland's political institutions safeguard the position and the preferences of the dominant actors in the conflict over the sexual division of labour. That means that conservative preferences on the part of the majority of the Swiss people, the majorities in the parliaments, and in the governments of the cantons, as well as at the local level, remain intact and continue to shape policy on gender issues. For these reasons, it is not surprising that Swiss female labour participation rates have not grown significantly between 1960 and 1985.

Religious traditions Recent comparative work on economic and social policy has shown how significantly policy choices are shaped by institutions (see, for example, Scharpf, 1987; Schmidt, 1988); the work reported here also points to the applicability of the institutionalist approach to the comparative study of gender inequality. However, a fully developed explanatory model requires the integration of cultural variables into the institutionalist frame of reference. Institutional differences clearly determine policy and policy outcomes, as do distributions of power between political parties (see, for example, Norris, 1987; Castles and Marceau, 1990). The specific comparison of labour force participation of female and male workers also shows that political-cultural variables influence the supply of and the demand for female labour to a surprisingly large extent. It can even be argued that a key variable of labour force participation of women resides among the political-cultural characteristics of the nations studied, namely Protestantism or, conversely, Catholicism.

One of the most striking results of the data analysis has been the correlation between Protestantism, measured as the Protestant proportion of the population, and the change in female participation rates (r = .66). The direction of the relationship is positive: the higher the share of the Protestant population, the larger the increase in numbers of women at work. Why does Protestantism matter in the explanation of labour force participation rates of women? It is conceivable that in recent decades Protestantism can be interpreted in terms of higher levels of secularization, and that higher levels of secularization facilitate labour force participation of women. Evidence exists to support this view (Barretta, 1982; Brettschneider, Ahlstich and Zuegel, 1991, 568–9), but fully comparable data on levels of secularization are not available. Better established is the understanding that Protestantism has constructed distinctive deep-seated belief systems on family roles and on work of women outside the home (see, for example, Weber, 1968). In particular, in contrast to Catholicism, Protestantism is more open to a non-traditional division of labour in the family and in the nation as a whole. While Catholicism (and other more traditionally oriented religions) tend to oppose the integration of women into the formal economy, mainly through its longstanding commitment to family policy, Protestantism has been more open to individual rights in the polity and in the economy and hence, other things being equal, has not been a serious obstacle to the incorporation of female labour into the economy.[10]

Moreover, rather early on, centre-left or left-wing governments presiding over Protestant countries adopted a universalistic full employment policy stance; that policy, by definition, comprising the integration of women into the economy. Furthermore, the governments of Protestant nations, and left-wing governments in particular, facilitated the entry of women into the labour force through a wide variety of policies that lessened the constraining effects of their responsibilities in the family so as to facilitate work outside the home.

Data on religion and changes in the female participation rate in the period studied point to striking differences between the countries of the sample. In contrast to the Nordic countries and the English-speaking nations, the Catholic share in the population of the German-speaking democracies is of considerable size and political importance, ranging in the early 1980s from 47 per cent in West Germany and 48 per cent in Switzerland to 81 per cent in Austria. Moreover, the level of secularization, as measured by proxy indicators of religious attachments of voters, seems to be lower in the

German-speaking nations than in the Nordic countries or in the family of larger Anglo-American democracies. The difference is at least partly attributable to differences in the interaction of cleavage structures and the party system.[11] In contrast to the English-speaking nations and the Nordic countries, the party systems of Austria, Germany and Switzerland are marked by a stable and powerful religious cleavage, most obviously manifested in the electoral support which the Christian Democratic parties in these countries receive from voters with higher levels of religious attachment. The German-speaking family of nations is thus marked by a religious tradition, a social structure and a party system which together impede the full integration of women into the economy.

It is thus in the direct and indirect effects of Protestantism, or conversely Catholicism, on labour force participation that we find one of the keys to an understanding of cross-national differences in gender inequality in general and in female labour force participation rates in particular. Here we also find a key to understanding why the German family of democracies has been characterized by relatively small increases in the level of gender equality.[12] That implies that the families of nations concept is an important factor. The German-speaking family has relatively high levels of gender inequality because of a common cultural pattern inherited from the past which, through politics and policy, impacts on labour market opportunities for women.

Determinants of Change in the Male Labour Force Participation Rate, 1960–85

The rising level of gender equality in labour force participation in most OECD countries over the last two or three decades has truly been dramatic. The analysis presented so far has focused attention on determinants of change in female rates of labour force participation, but in order fully to understand the total change in female-male ratios, the analysis must be complemented with a study of the process that has governed the male labour force participation rate in the 1960–85 period.

In contrast to female rates of economic activity, the male participation rate has declined everywhere in the OECD area. The pace of the decline, however, has been rather different across countries. For example, the Netherlands has experienced the largest drop in the male participation rate, followed by France, Italy, Germany and Sweden. In contrast to this, Japan, Norway, the US and Canada have reported relatively small decreases in workforce participation of male workers (see Table 5.2). Why has the male participation rate declined and how is the cross-country variation in this decline to be explained? It is to these questions that we now turn our attention. Here, just as in preceding sections of this chapter, the major focus will be on the impact of deep-seated political and social differences between countries on the supply of labour and the demand for workers.

The empirical analysis demonstrates that male and female participation rates are governed by different processes. For example, none of the predictors of change in male participation rates is significantly related to change in male rates. Change in the latter from 1960 to 1985 is mainly associated with – and, by inference, depends upon – the impact of social policy, labour market policy and the extent to which an economy has coordinated demand for labour and exit from the labour force. Although the decline in male rates of economic activity has been influenced by longer years of schooling and higher enrolment in tertiary education, no systematic statistical relationship has been established between these factors. Enrolment has grown slowly in the US since the 1960s and in some of the continental European countries more rapidly The fact that many youngsters in Canada and the US (in significant contrast to most other countries) combine school attendance with work and therefore do not decrease the male participation rate means that education does not significantly account for cross-country differences in the decline of male activity rates during the period. Change in the age structure of the population may also have some effect on participation rates, for the reason that 'the movement of a greater proportion of the male population into the retirement age group exerts a downward pressure on participation rates, even if ages at retirement do not change' (Sorrentino, 1983, 24 and 28–33; McMahon, 1986). In some of the countries, such as Italy, the substantial decline of male activity rates can be partly attributed to large increases in the share of men aged 65 and over in the population, while in others (e.g. the US and Canada), the proportion of older men in the population has remained largely constant – with the effect of only a relatively minor decline in male participation rates (Sorrentino, 1983, 24). However, in the context of our 18-nation study, change in the age structure of the population does not significantly account for differences in male participation rates from 1960 to 1985 (see Table 5.4). Moreover, it is also the case that another potentially relevant variable – the average rate of economic growth – is not systematically related to change in male participation rates either (see Table 5.4).

A full explanation of the cross-country differences in the decline of male activity rates must focus attention on the impact of the following institutional variables:

(1) The decline in male labour force participation tends to be particularly pronounced in countries in which the male participation rate was high

in the early 1960s (r = –.50); there has thus been a catching-up process involved in the behaviour of the male participation rate over time.

(2) The data also point to the existence of a significant relationship between the decline in the participation rate of male workers and the size of the public economy in 1960, as measured by total outlays of government as a percentage of GDP (r = –.51). Furthermore, a high share of social security and welfare state transfers to households as a percentage of GDP in the early 1960s, as measured by Varley's data (1986), is related to a decline in the male participation rate (r = –.57). This suggests that governments presiding over a large public economy and a developed welfare state in the early 1960s had a larger potential for the reduction of male participation rates in the next decades. From studies of the growth of welfare states in Western nations (see, for example, OECD, 1980; Flora, 1986–87) and from data on education, it can be inferred that this potential has mainly been used for the purpose of expanding levels of educational enrolment (see, for example, UNESCO, 1990) as well as levels of social income for temporary or permanent withdrawal from the labour force.

(3) The decline in male participation rates has also been inversely associated with the expansion in social spending efforts, measured as the change in the proportion of GDP spent on social security and welfare transfers to households in the period from 1960 to 1983 (r = –.64), and the increase in spending on old age, survivors' and disability transfers as a percentage of GDP (r = –.45, data from Varley, 1986). To a large extent, the intensification of social security efforts has generated higher levels of coverage in old-age pensions and higher levels of old-age pension benefits, which together have led to a greater attractiveness of income from the old-age pension relative to income from work than in the period before 1960.

(4) the existence of early retirement schemes (r = –.44),[13]

(5) a policy of pro-cyclical repatriation of foreign labour,[14] and

(6) the extent to which an economy has been coordinated. This is measured as the degree to which producer interest groups and the state have participated in tripartite arrangements across different policy areas, such as employment and wages, monetary policy, taxation, industrial policy and social policy (eta = –.57; see Table 5.4).

These relationships are strongest where conjoint. Thus, the decline in male participation rates was particularly pronounced where early retirement schemes, large-scale repatriation of foreign workers and coordinated economies were simultaneously present, as in the German-speaking nations. Moreover, the decline was that much stronger where the male participation rate circa 1960 was high, where the public economy and welfare state circa 1960 were relatively large, where social expenditure as a percentage of GDP had expanded markedly and where the share of old age, survivors' and disability pensions as a percentage of GDP was relatively high. As one might expect, these findings drawn from a general analysis of OECD nations, tend to mirror and largely confirm the conclusions of the earlier analysis by Gaby von Rhein-Kress of how the German-speaking countries used labour supply as a policy instrument in the somewhat more restricted period of economic crisis from 1973–1983 (see Chapter 4 above).

Table 5.4: Correlates of the decline in the male labour force participation rate, 1960–85[1]

Male participation rate in 1960	r = –.50*
Total outlays of general government 1960 (% GDP)	r = –.51*
Growth of the 'learning force' 1960–85	r = –.31
Change in size of the male 'learning force' (% population) 1960–85 (N=17)	r = –.31
Change in share of male old age population (65+), 1960–85	r = .23
Change in share of male youth population (0–24), 1960–85	r = –.26
Average annual rate of economic growth 1960–85	r = .39
Social security expenditure (% GDP), 1960	r = –.40*
Change in social security expenditure (% GDP), 1960–83	r = –.64*
Change in transfer to old age, survivors and disability pensions, 1960–84[1]	r = –.45*
Early retirement (= 1, else = 0)	r = –.44*
Coordination of economy[2]	eta = –.57*

1 First differences (male participation rate in 1985 minus male participation rate in 1960).
2 Recoded and slightly revised data from Czada, 1985: corporatist and sectoralist policy coordination between organized interests and state = 1, else = 0).

In contrast, male participation rates tended to remain at the 1960 level or declined at a much slower pace in the following instances: the lower the level of the male participation rate in the early 1960s; the smaller the relative size of the public economy and the welfare state in the early 1960s; the lower the rate of expansion in social expenditure and in old-age, survivors' and disability pensions; the lesser the emphasis of labour market and social policy on early retirement; the less the importance given to restrictive foreign labour policy measures, and the lower the level of coordination of the economy. While change in male rates of economic activity covary with social policy indicators and some other policy variables, the level of covariation with changes in the age structure, change in the size of the 'learning force' and economic growth have been insignificant (see Table 5.4).

Why have the welfare state, early retirement, foreign labour policy and the degree of coordination of an economy been important determinants of changes in male participation rates in the period from 1960 to the mid-1980s? The answer must largely be based on the effects of these institutions on the withdrawal of male workers from the labour market.

The most obvious case is that of the impact of a restrictive stance in foreign labour policy on the male participation rate. For example, pursuit of a policy of repatriating foreign workers and restrictive control of the inflow of migrant workers, such as in Austria, Switzerland and West Germany after the oil price shocks of 1973 and 1979–80, results in declining male participation rates, other things being equal (see, on this, OECD, 1985, 51; Schmidt, 1985, for Switzerland; Schmid, 1990, for Germany; Mißlbeck, 1983, for a similar though less pronounced trend in Austria).

More difficult to disentangle are the effects of the welfare state on male labour force participation rates. The expansion of the welfare state in the 1960s and 1970s may be regarded as a huge job creation machine. To a considerable extent the new jobs were designed for women, partly due to more flexible working arrangements, such as part-time work, and partly also due to the preference of many female workers for office and interpersonal work (Rein, 1985). The expansion of the welfare state thus facilitated a rise of the rate of labour force participation of women and, as the analysis of earlier sections has shown, generated a higher level of gender equality in workforce participation, other things being equal.

The effects of the welfare state on the male participation rate, however, are more diverse. The growth of the welfare state provided higher levels of social security for male workers and generated increasing demand for specific highly-qualified male workers, such as in administration, education and health care, but it was also conducive to voluntary and involuntary withdrawal of male workers from the labour market.

The pressure on male workers to withdraw from the labour force was particularly powerful in periods of economic crisis and/or in periods of large scale restructuring of economic sectors. Hence, it occurred mainly in countries in which larger segments of economically weak, non-competitive industries existed (such as in the steel and shipyards industries), and in which one or more of the following mechanisms was operating:

- a relatively high level of income was available from the old age pension, resulting in weaker incentives to work beyond the retirement age,
- a low statutory retirement age was in place or a significant drop occurred in the statutory retirement age,
- the encouragement of older workers to withdraw from the labour force through early retirement measures as well as relaxed earnings tests and easier access to disability pensions, provided that these measures involved sufficiently high levels of retirement income, and
- a guest-worker stance in foreign labour policy.

All these factors were conducive to a decline in the male participation rate, especially in the economic activity rates of male workers in the older age groups. However, the degree to which these factors affected the male labour force, varied from country to country.

Non-competitive economic sectors were a problem in most OECD nations, and it is difficult to come to firm conclusions on cross-country differences in the relative importance of sectoral economic decline and its impact on the male participation rate. However, evidence exists in support of the view that the labour markets in open economies were most vulnerable to the economic challenges of the 1970s and 1980s. The pressure on workers to withdraw from the labour force was therefore particularly pronounced in countries such as Italy and France, but also in countries with very high shares of imports and exports as a percentage of GDP, such as the Netherlands. However, the response of individual workers and of aggregate male participation rates to these challenges varied to a large extent according to the degree to which the welfare state provided sufficiently high levels of retirement income. In highly developed welfare states, such as in Sweden and Denmark, but also in Germany, France, and the Netherlands, relatively advanced levels of social income – including old-age pensions, reduced retirement age and sufficient income from early retirement – cushioned the shocks of the economic crisis of the 1970s and 1980s and facilitated the downward adjustment of male labour supply to decreasing labour demand. Moreover, in many of these countries, in particular in Italy, but also in the more advanced welfare states, the hidden economy may also have functioned as a safety-net for workers who retired from the labour force (Weck-Hannemann, 1984).

A fundamentally different response of the male participation rate to economic change was observable in countries in which the economy was less open, in which a weak welfare state had emerged and in which public policy on early retirement was absent, such as Japan and the US (see OECD 1988b, 68). In these countries the male participation rate declined only moderately. To some extent this mirrors the impact of stronger incentives for older workers and the sheer economic necessity to participate in the workforce. The incentive to participate in the labour market at a more advanced age springs from individual action as well as from collective action on the part of the unions. Given the constraints of a weak and highly selective welfare state in these countries, individual workers and unions must necessarily place more emphasis on maintaining labour force participation opportunities for male workers than unions in countries with more coordinated economies.

To a significant extent, therefore, the decline of male labour force participation rates can be regarded as a function of the welfare state and the stances adopted both in labour market policy and in foreign labour policy, but it is also influenced by the degree of coordination between the state, labour and business associations. In some of the countries of our sample, such as in West Germany (see, for example, Katzenstein, 1989), the downward adjustment of male labour supply to decreasing labour demand was politically facilitated by the longer tradition of social partnership between labour and capital, including works councils' participation in the management of labour market exit and entry. Details have varied from country to country, but the general tendency has been this: the presence of tripartite coordination between the state, organized labour and capital in general, and political representation of labour in works councils and other codetermination arrangements in particular (Dittrich, 1985), allowed both for deals between labour, business associations, single firms, and the state, and for packages of employment policy, labour market exit and social compensation for temporary or permanent withdrawal from the labour force. It has often been the case that these deals comprised practices of social closure at the enterprise level (Hohn, 1988) and intensified efforts to repatriate foreign workers and stop immigration. However, these deals also often generated attractive levels of social income for older retiring workers. Moreover, for the unionized core of the labour force – and for the unionized core of the male labour force in age groups up to the mid-50s – tripartite coordination of the economy typically involved employment guarantees and, hence, protection against economic and social uncertainty.

Rather different has been the trend in male labour force participation in countries notorious for their lack of a coordinated economy and for a more selective and weaker welfare state, such as the US and Japan. In these countries, the male labour force participation rate has decreased at a more modest pace. While the weaker decline in the male participation rate may be partly due to idiosyncratic factors (such as a high activity rate on the part of American youth or a full employment policy of the Japanese type), it can mainly be attributed to the weakness of the welfare state, the absence of tripartite coordination at the national level in these countries and the stance adopted in social and labour market policy.

It follows from this that the complex interaction between welfare state programmes, incentives and disincentives for labour market exit, degrees of coordination of the economy, and the stance in foreign labour policy must be regarded as some of the more deep-seated institutional circumstances which contribute to a better understanding of cross-country variations in the decline of male participation rates.

The Impact of Social and Political Push-and-Pull Factors on the Labour Force Participation of Men and Women

We have now arrived at a position in which the explanations of changes advanced so far in male and female participation rates in the period from 1960 to 1985 can be summarized by an index of social and political push-and-pull factors of rising female labour force participation and an index of push-and-pull factors of declining male participation rates. These indices are constructed from variables which are significantly related to change in female and male participation rates (see Table 5.3 and Appendices A and B).[15] For example, the index of social and political push-and-pull factors of female economic activity rates is an additive, unweighted index of the total number of factors which, according to the data analysis, have been conducive to rising female participation rates. Some of the most important variable include decline in agricultural and industrial employment, dynamic growth in employment in the public sector, high growth in child-care facilities, taxation incentives for female labour force participation, encompassing trade unions, party-political determinants of gender-related policy, early female suffrage and a secularized Protestant political culture (for details see Appendix A).[16]

The index of instititional push-and-pull factors suggests that the German-speaking nations' performance in female economic activity rates has been so weak in the period from 1960 to 1985 because of the large number of powerful obstacles to higher levels of sexual equality and the low number of factors promoting higher levels of gender equality. In West Germany, 11 factors of a total of 13 determinants of change in the female participation rate point to powerful obstacles to intensified incorporation of female labour into the economy, with only two of the central factors functioning as promoters of female economic activity (see Figure 5.1 and Appendix A). Thus, supply-side trends, changes in the demand-side, family policy, tax systems, cultural traditions and politics have been operating mainly as barriers to the 'feminization of the labour force' (Jenson, Hagen and Reddy,

1988). It is for this reason that the increase in female labour force participation rates from 1960 to 1985 has been so low in West Germany.

Similar results can be obtained for the two other German-speaking nations. Austria and Switzerland are countries in which the obstacles to higher levels of gender equality are almost as numerous and powerful as in West Germany (in each country, ten obstacles to and only three promoters of change), and it is precisely for this reason that the female participation rate has not significantly risen in these countries (see Appendix A).

In sharp contrast to this, the obstacles to gender equality in the Nordic nations are (by any conceivable standard) weak, while the push-and pull factors for higher levels of gender equality are numerous and powerful. The weakness of obstacles and the dominance of promoters of gender equality mirror the impact of a route to economic modernity in which employment of women in the service sector and in the welfare state was particularly important. The situation of this Nordic family of nations is also attributable to the impact of institutions, party politics and religious traditions, such as a Protestant culture. The scores of the Nordic countries on the index of gender equality promotion vary from 8 in Finland to 9 in Denmark, 11 in Sweden, and 12 out of a total of 13 in Norway.

The English-speaking countries (other than Ireland) have taken a position between the German-speaking nations and the major Nordic states. Why they have done so becomes apparent in the light of the relative weight of underlying obstacles to, or promoters of, higher levels of gender equality. The factors that have been conducive to the incorporation of women into the economy in the English family of nations (except for Ireland) are of substantial quantity and quality. Their total number varies from 7 in Canada and the US to 9 in Australia and in New Zealand. It is largely for this reason that the female participation rate increased in these countries to a significant extent.

Ireland is the deviant case in the English family of nations, but its weak performance in gender issues is also perfectly compatible with the explanatory model presented here. The obstacles to higher levels of sexual equality in Ireland are numerous and powerful; a very pronounced conservative climate in civil society and in government, which Irish Catholicism has supported, if not generated, is among the factors which deserve primary mention.

The index of promoters of female labour participation also helps to explain the situation of countries which do not fall within the families of nations focused on in this volume. Italy, as a Catholic country, dominated by a Catholic party and marked by a modernization process in which the male rather than the female workforce is dominant, has been among the major examples of countries with persistently high levels of gender inequalities in the social and economic order. Moreover, the explanation advanced here is also applicable to the Japanese case. Conservative cultural traditions, an underdeveloped welfare state, a dominant industrial sector, enterprise unions with preferences for social closure practices and the like have been among the determinants of stagnating rather than expanding female participation rates.

It can even be demonstrated that the analysis presented in this chapter shows an almost perfect fit to labour force participation rates of women in the East European socialist nations from the post-war period until the late 1980s. Consider, for example, the case of the former East German Democratic Republic. The socialist government of that country opted for a policy of full employment of men and of women, generating a female participation rate of more than 80 per cent in 1985. This high rate and the rapid increase of that rate since 1960 (18.5 percentage points, data from ILO *Yearbook of Labour Statistics* and from the *Statistisches Jahrbuch der Deutschen Demokratischen Republik*, various issues) can be explained by the model advanced in this chapter. The increase in the participation rate was mainly due to the interaction of the following factors:

- a state-led process of economic growth, in which the public economy emerged as the dominant labour market;
- a weakly declining share of agricultural employment;
- a rapid decline in fertility rates;
- support for women to work outside the home through public child care and youth organizations;
- powerful incentives for women to participate in the labour force, if not from sheer economic necessity, then from the impact of taxation, housing and social security policies;
- the presence of a state party and a trade union movement fully committed to a productivist ideology in general and to the full incorporation of women into the economy in particular; and
- the impact of cultural tradition, in which Protestantism and, to an increasing extent, 'state-led secularization' facilitated the full integration of women into the economy.[17]

The index of institutional promoters to gender equality in labour force participation is, of course, correlated with the change in the rate of labour force participation of women. That is not surprising, because the index was constructed with predictors of the female participation rate. However, relative to the fact that most of these predictors were not more than moderately significant, their cumulative impact, as shown in Figure 5.1, is rather impressive. The nature of the relationship is this: the larger the number – and,

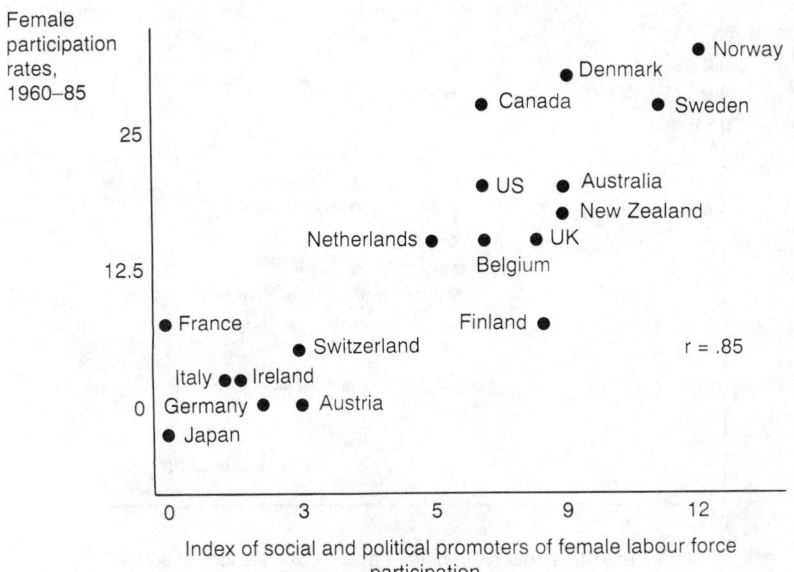

Figure 5.1: Change in female labour force participation rate 1960–85 and the index of social and political promoters of rising female participation rates

by inference, the greater the importance – of the equality-promoting factors, the larger the increase in female participation rates; the lower the number of push-and-pull factors (and, hence, the larger the weight of obstacles to higher levels of gender equality), the smaller the change in female participation rates (see Figure 5.1).

By analogy to the index of promoters of women's labour force participation, an additive index of institutional factors which have been conducive to the decline in male participation rates from age 14 to 64 has been constructed (see Appendix B). The index represents the total number of factors which, according to the empirical results reported in Table 5.4, have been significantly associated with change in male participation rates. High growth in pension transfers, early retirement schemes with attractive retirement income levels for older workers, and utilization of foreign labour as a reserve army mechanism for the domestic labour market are a few of the major variables.[18]

Most of the leading welfare states of Western Europe were high on the index of the institutional determinants of declining male participation rates, while the scores of the Anglo-American democracies and Japan were low.

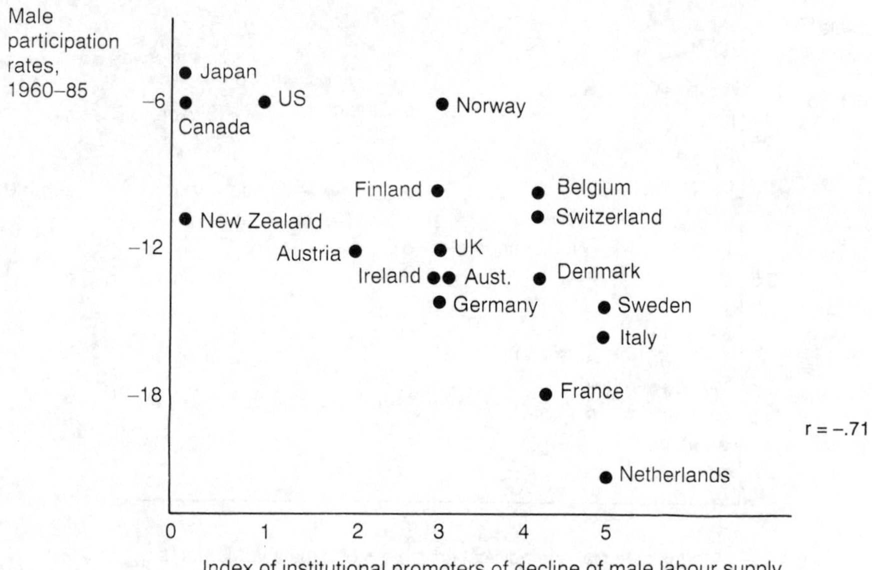

Figure 5.2: Change in the male labour force participation rate 1960–85 and the index of institutional promoters of declining male activity rates

The most dramatic drop in the male participation rate – that in the Netherlands – is compatible with the index, and so is the moderate downturn in male participation rates in Japan, the US and Canada. The steep decline in the male participation rate in the Netherlands, the analysis suggests, is mainly attributable to the impact of a high rate of male economic activity in the 1960s, major improvement in coverage and levels of benefits from old-age and disability pensions, early retirement arrangements, and concerted action between firms and unions on withdrawal of weaker labour market groups from the labour force. In contrast to this, the modest decline of the male participation rate in the US has been the outcome of a process in which a weak welfare state, the absence of major public retirement schemes and the absence of a guest-worker type of policy have played significant roles. It is also the case that the experience of most other countries is reasonably well accounted for by the index of social and political promoters of declining male participation rates. This may be regarded as offering further support to the hypotheses advanced in this study (see Figure 5.2).

Conclusion

There are several noteworthy conclusions to be derived from our study if female-male ratios of labour force participation in Western nations.

One concerns the institutional perspective which has guided the study presented here. Insofar as the political and social determinants of male and female participation rates analysed in this chapter mirror institutional characteristics of the nations studied, one can regard the evidence presented in this chapter and the explanation derived from the data as giving full support to the view that the large cross-country variations in labour force participation rates of men and women can, indeed, be properly appreciated only in the context of 'deep-seated institutional differences' (OECD 1988a, 129) between the countries studied. The key factors are routes to economic modernity, stances in family and taxation policy, political-institutional circumstances and religious tradition.[19]

Secondly, the dramatic increase in the level of sexual equality, as measured by the change in the female-male labour force participation ratio in the post-1960 period, was mainly generated by processes and institutions which began to operate before the post-war feminist movements emerged. Moreover, one-third of the total increase in female-male ratios of workforce participation has been due to unanticipated side-effects of the decline in the male labour force, and was thus driven by a process by no means targeted to the reduction of levels of gender inequality. For these reasons it is unlikely that the increase in the level of sexual inequality can be attributed to the strength of the new women's movement, as some writers have argued (see, for example, Greven-Aschoff, 1981, 329; Crompton et al., 1990, 346). In fact it seems that the opposite causal relationship pertains: since the 1970s, the new women's movements can largely be regarded as a political consequence of, and a response to, the transition from a highly inegalitarian society to one which is less inegalitarian in certain crucial aspects of gender differentiation.[20]

Thirdly, the increase in the female-male ratio of labour force participation has been the product of two separate processes unrelated to each other: the decline in male economic activity rates and rising (or stagnating) female participation rates. The decline in the male participation rate was mainly governed by the interaction of welfare state arrangements, labour market exit through early retirement and foreign labour policy, and state-interest group relationships. Thus, it was shaped by institutions and processes which are central to the paradigm of 'materialistic politics' and by social and political conflicts between classes and parties in advanced industrial states. In contrast to this, change in female participation rates was shaped by trajectories to economic modernity, but was also determined by attitudes, beliefs and norms concerning the appropriate division of labour between women and men, and the impact of social policy and family policy on the supply of female labour. The latter change must thus be regarded mainly as a function of deep-seated institutional and cultural differences in the social construction of responsibility for work inside and outside the home.

Fourthly, the increase in the level of gender equality can be conceived of as the outcome of a process to which targeted policy, unintended consequences of non-target ('tacit') policy, as well as social and economic processes have contributed. The countries studied differ in the extent to which increases in levels of gender equality are due to targeted and non-targeted policy and to socio-economic processes; they also differ in the degree to which that increase is attributable to rising female and declining male participation rates. The German-speaking family of nations, for example, is distinctively located: Austria, Switzerland and West Germany score low on the contribution of the female labour force to increasing levels of equality; in fact, most of the modest progress towards a higher level of gender equality in these countries was due to the downward adjustment of male labour supply to decreasing demand for labour. Moreover, most of that progress in Austria, West Germany and Switzerland cannot be attributed to policies which have been targeted to reduce of gender differentiation, but mainly mirrors unintended consequences of 'tacit' policy and anonymous socio-economic processes. When policy was targeted on gender-related patterns of labour force participation in the German-speaking countries, the emphasis was frequently on safeguarding the traditional division of labour between men and women, and on the stabilization of the family, rather than on providing better opportunities for women to work outside the home.[21]

In contrast to this, the increasing level of gender equality in the Nordic family of nations has been mainly due to the rise in female employment, and, to smaller extent, to declining male participation rates. Moreover, while the rapid increase in the level of sexual equality in Denmark, Norway and Sweden, and to a lesser extent in Finland, may have been partly due to unplanned effects of socio-economic development and non-targeted policy, it was mainly attributable to policies consciously focused on the reduction of levels of social inequality in general, and gender inequality in particular.

Important conclusions regarding the utility of the families of nations concept can be derived from the analysis presented here. Several points are noteworthy within this context. Statistically, there have indeed, been family-specific clusters of countries in female-male ratios of labour force participation, with the German-speaking nations as the most inegalitarian and the Nordic nations as the most egalitarian group of countries. Moreover, there have also been family-specific clusters of variables which contribute to an explanation of gender-related differences in labour force participation. Thus, the study presented in this chapter supports the view that the notion of families of nations is, at least in some policy areas, a heuristically useful instrument and an empirically significant concept. The families of nations concept seems to be particularly useful in policy areas which have been shaped by powerful cultural traditions, such as religious beliefs, norms and attitudes, and longstanding traditions in family law and social protection. Deep-seated beliefs about what is right or wrong in social and economic orders, including the degree of gender differentiation, and the institutionalization of these beliefs in law and policy routines, are powerful chains between nations with common cultural attributes and may indeed be regarded as a central aspect of a particular family of nations. For these reasons, it can be concluded that the families of nations concept does indeed contribute to a better understanding of certain types of public policy outcomes.

Above all, it is our conclusion that the families of nations concept and the political-institutional approach adopted in this study are highly relevant to an economic approach to the study of female labour supply. Within the context of standard economic theory, labour force participation of women is largely dependent on market wage rates and on reservation wage rates (see, for example, Blau and Ferber, 1986 and Weck-Hannemann and Frey, 1989). The higher the market wage rate, the more powerful will be the incentive for women to work outside the home, other things being equal. But it is also the case that labour force participation is dependent upon the reservation wage rate, which measures the economic value of time spent on work in the household and in the family. Central to labour force participation will be the difference between these two rates. A market wage rate above the level of the reservation wage rate generates a powerful incentive for women to work outside the home; in contrast to this, a powerful disincentive to work outside the home will be generated by situations in which the market wage rate is lower than the reservation wage rate.

Valuable as the distinction between market and reservation wage rates is, it must be emphasized that a full understanding of female labour supply in general, and of international differences in female participation rates in particular, requires the incorporation of institutional and cultural variables into the explanatory model of female labour supply. The reason for this is straightforward: the analysis presented in this chapter has shown that the core of the standard model of female labour supply – market wage rates, reservation wage rates and the comparison between these on the part of a potential female job-seeker – is to a very large extent shaped by institutional and cultural factors. For example, the level of market wage rates for female labour is strongly influenced by political factors, such as public policy on gender issues, the size and growth of the welfare state as a labour market, and trade union policy on male/female wage differentials. Moreover, the reservation wage rate is to a probably even larger extent dependent upon cultural and institutional factors, such as the availability and cost of public or private care for children and for older age groups, and cultural standards which guide the process of valuation of women's work inside the family. Last but not least, the process of comparing market wage rates with reservation wage rates is also profoundly shaped by cultural factors, such as religious denomination, degree of religious attachment and level of secularization.

In other words, the major factors of standard theory of female labour supply must be regarded not as constants, but rather as variables. Moreover, the variation of these factors is largely determined by institutional and cultural circumstances, which differ from one nation to another and from one family of nations to another. It is for these reasons that an approach to the study of rates of economic activity which from the beginning focuses attention on the institutional and cultural determinants of labour supply and on families of nations is essential to a fuller understanding of why gendered labour force participation rates vary between nations as much as they do.

Appendix A: Social and political promoters (= 1) and obstacles (= 0) to rising rates of female labour force participation

COUNTRY	EQF1960	FERT8161	AGRI8560	INDU8560	SB8360CU	CC6080
AS	1	1	1	1	0	0
AU	0	0	0	0	1	0
BE	1	0	1	1	0	0
CA	1	1	1	1	0	0
DM	0	0	0	1	1	0
FL	0	0	0	0	1	1
FR	0	0	0	0	0	0
GE	0	0	1	0	0	0
IR	1	0	0	0	0	0
IT	1	0	0	0	0	0
JA	0	0	0	0	0	0
NL	1	1	1	1	0	0
NZ	1	1	1	0	0	0
NW	1	1	0	1	1	1
SW	0	0	1	1	1	1
CH	0	0	1	1	0	0
UK	0	0	1	1	0	1
US	1	1	1	1	0	0

COUNTRY	PT1973	SWITCH	WLEG6085	FSUFFRAGE	RCNL4659	GEOGCAME	PROTEST	INDEX
AS	1	1	0	1	0	1	1	9
AU	0	0	0	1	0	1	0	3
BE	0	1	1	0	1	1	0	7
CA	1	1	0	1	0	0	0	7
DM	1	1	1	1	1	1	1	9
FL	0	1	1	1	1	1	1	8
FR	0	0	0	0	0	0	0	0
GE	0	0	0	1	0	0	0	2
IR	0	0	0	1	0	0	0	2
IT	0	0	0	0	0	1	0	2
JA	0	0	0	0	0	0	0	0
NL	0	0	0	1	1	0	0	6
NZ	1	1	0	1	1	1	1	9
NW	1	1	1	1	1	1	1	12
SW	1	1	1	1	1	1	1	11
CH	0	0	1	0	0	0	0	3
UK	1	1	0	0	1	1	1	8
US	1	0	0	1	0	0	1	7

Country Code:
AS = Australia, AU = Austria, BE = Belgium, CA = Canada,
DM = Denmark, FL = Finland, FR = France, GE = West Germany,
IR = Ireland, IT = Italy, JA = Japan, NL = Netherlands,
NZ = New Zealand, NW = Norway, SW = Sweden, CH = Switzerland,
UK = United Kingdom, US = United States

Variable names:
EQF1960 = Female labour force participation rate in 1960. *Source*: OECD *Employment Outlook*.
FERT8161 = Change in fertility rates 1961–81 (first differences). Source: OECD *Employment Outlook 1988*, 204.
AGRI8560 = Change in agricultural employment (% total employment) 1960–85 (first differences). Source: OECD *Economic Outlook Historical Statistics*.
INDU8560 = Change in share of industrial employment (% total employment) 1960–85 (first differences). Source: OECD *Economic Outlook Historical Statistics*.
SB8360CU = Change in employment share in public sector 1960–83 (first differences). Source: Cusack et al., 1989.
CC6080 = Growth in child-care facilities. Source: Norris, 1987, 101.
PT1973 = Share of part-time employment in total employment. Source: OECD, 1983.
SWITCH = Taxation incentive for female labour supply. Source: OECD, 1990b, 166–7.
WLEG6085 = Change in political representation of women in parliament (% total number of seats) 1960–85 (first differences).
FSUFFRAGE = Age of female suffrage (1960). Source: Schmidt, 1992.
RCNL4659 = Centre-party or right-party prime minister 1946–59 (% months). Source: Schmidt, 1992.
GEOGCAME = Organizational density of trade unions, 1960s and 1970s. Source: Cameron, 1984,165.
PROTEST = Protestant proportion of total population, early 1980s. Source: Barrett, 1982.
INDEX = Index of social and political promoters of rising female participation rates. For details of operationalization, see text and note 16.

Appendix B: Promoters (= 1) and obstacles (= 0) for declining male labour force participation rates, 1960–85

COUNTRY	EQM1960	SOCE6083	P8460	KORPCZAD	ER1987	FOREIGN	INDEX2
AS	1	0	0	1	0	0	2
AU	0	0	0	1	1	1	3
BE	0	1	1	1	1	0	4
CA	0	0	0	0	0	0	0
DM	1	1	0	1	1	0	4
FL	0	1	0	1	1	0	3
FR	0	1	1	1	1	0	4
GE	0	0	0	1	1	1	3
IR	1	1	0	1	0	0	3
IT	1	1	1	1	1	0	5
JA	0	0	0	0	0	0	0
NL	1	1	1	1	1	0	5
NZ	0	0	0	0	0	0	0
NW	0	1	1	1	0	0	3
SW	1	1	1	1	1	0	5
CH	1	0	1	1	0	1	4
UK	1	0	0	1	1	0	3
US	0	0	0	0	1	0	1

Country Code: See Appendix A.

Variable names:

EQM1960 = Labour force participation rate of men 1960. Source: OECD *Employment Outlook*.

SOCE6083 = Change in social security expenditure (% GDP) 1960–83 (first differences). Source: ILO.

P8460 = Change in transfers on old-age, survivors' and disability pensions as a percentage of GDP, 1960–84 (first differences). Source: Varley, 1986.

KORPCZAD = Degree of coordination of economy. Recoded and revised data from Czada's corporatism scale (1 = medium or high level of coordination, 0 = else). Source: Czada, 1986.

ER1987 = Early retirement dummy. Source: see note 13.

FOREIGN = Guest-worker approach to foreign labour policy(= 1), else = 0. Source: see note 14.

INDEX2 = Index of social and political promoters of declining male participation rates. For operationalization, see text and note 18.

Notes

1. See, for example, Sorrentino, 1983; Blau and Ferber, 1986, 305; the discussion in Schettkat, 1987a and 1987b and OECD, 1988a, ch. 2, especially pp. 56–7 and 80. Differences in statistical concepts and in methods of data collection, differences in the share of part-time work, variations in retirement age, and differences in working time and differences in labour force participation of youths in education are among the major problems of the comparability of data on labour force participation as published by the OECD. Despite inherent problems, it has been convincingly argued

that the conventional participation rate is a satisfactory measure of the extent to which the population has been socially integrated in paid work outside the home and, hence, particularly suitable for a study of the impact of social and political factors on labour force participation. Conversely, weighted participation rates can be regarded as the more appropriate indicator of the relative economic size of labour input to the economy and, hence, as particularly useful instruments for a study of genuinely economic aspects of labour force participation (Schettkat, 1987b).

2. See Table 5.1. It is almost unnecessary to add that the female component of the total change and the change in the female participation rate are, by definition, highly correlated (r = .99). The female labour force component is defined as the increase in the female labour force, holding constant the male labour force participation rate at its level at time point t. Conversely, the male labour force component of the total change in the sex ratio is a function of adjusted change in the male labour force, holding the female labour force constant at its (t+1) level. Hence, it is by definition associated with the change in male labour force participation from 1960 to 1985 (r = –.82). For these reasons the correlates of changing participation rates are similar to the correlates of changes in the sex ratio attributable to male and female labour force components. Since the sex ratio is a constructed measure derived from underlying real world changes in participation rates, the analysis itself must focus attention on the underlying real world processes and not on change in the constructed measure.
3. The level of significance has been set at $p < .05$, N = 18. For details of measurement of the variables and sources, see Appendix A and B.
4. Empirical support for this hypothesis can be derived from the association between the share of part-time employment in 1973, to mention just one point in time, and Protestantism, as measured by the Protestant share in the population (r = .70). Furthermore, the hypothesis concerning the trade union position on part-time jobs receives support from the correlation between part-time employment in 1973 and union density (Cameron, 1984) (r = .48).
5. Correlations of a similar magnitude were obtained with other comparative indicators of changes in educational enrolment of women, such as change in the share of female students in the total number of students in the period from 1960 to 1985 (data taken from UNESCO, 1990).
6. The growth of child-care facilities in the period for which data were available (1960–80) (Norris, 1987, 101) is significantly related to the extent to which left-wing parties have participated in government in general and in Protestant countries in particular (correlation with the left-wing participation measure, weighted by the Protestant share in the population: r = .78). Data from Norris, 1987, were recoded on a rank order from 0 to 9.
7. For details and data see OECD, 1990b, 165–6. Because data regarding taxation incentives for labour force participation have been available only for the late 1970s, we had to content ourselves with a correlation of change in female participation rates with the level of taxation incentives, as measured by 'Switch'. It is noteworthy that 'Switch' is largely a function of the presence or absence of joint income taxation and social security tax ceilings. A powerful incentive for female labour supply tends to be generated by separate income taxation and the absence of social security tax ceilings, whereas a powerful disincentive is generated by joint income taxation and the presence of social security tax ceilings (see OECD, 1990b, 163–8).
8. See, for a case study, Gustavsson, 1984. Correlation analysis supports this view. The data analysis reveals the existence of significant relationships between incentives for

female labour supply through taxation and trade union strength, as measured by data on organizational density in the 1960s and 1970s (r = .60), a centre party in office in the critical post-war period from 1946 to 1960 (r = –.43), a left-wing party prime minister in the post-war period from 1946 to 1960 (r = .50), with a correlation of similar strength existing for the following period, and Protestantism (r = .58), or, conversely, Catholicism (r = –.57), which emphasizes again the importance of cultural traditions for policy-making.

9. See, for example, results from a multiple regression: Change in female participation rate 1960–85: Y = 2.52 + .13 (left-wing government 1946–59) + .14 (Protestantism), R^2 adj. = .49, t-statistics: 1.93 and 2.04.
10. The statistical relationships between Protestantism on the one hand and indicators of policies which reconcile work of women inside and outside the home are significant: Protestantism is correlated with growth in child care 1960–80 (r = .60), share of part-time employment in 1973 (r = .78), change in the share of public sector employment from 1960 to 1983 (r = .32) and incentives for female workforce participation created by taxation (r = .67). Protestantism is also related to indicators of politics, such as a left-wing prime minister (or equivalent) in 1946–59 (r = .55), a left-wing prime minister (or equivalent) in 1960–85 (r = .49), age of female suffrage (r = .40), trade union density (r = .58) and change in political representation of women in legislatures in 1960–85 (r = .48). Protestantism is thus a major background variable in the determination of the supply of, and the demand for, female labour. It hardly needs mention that a broadly similar pattern emerges, though with inverted signs, in the correlation of Catholicism, measured as the percentage share of the Catholic population, with other predictors of female labour force participation.
11. On cleavage analysis, see Lane and Ersson, 1987; Lijphart, 1984; for country studies on party systems and religious cleavages, see Crewe and Denver, 1985.
12. It must also be pointed out that some of the attitudes to gender issues presented in Norris, 1987, are related to the change in the female labour force participation rate. However, the small number of cases and the absence of systematic comparative survey research on gender issues make it difficult, if not impossible, to draw firm conclusions from these data on the political culture of gender differentiation.
13. A dummy variable for extensive utilization of early retirement through labour market policy and social security policy has been constructed on the basis of OECD 1988b, 66, and 1988c and also using a number of single country studies, such as Schmid, 1990; Heinelt, 1991; Esping-Andersen, 1990.
14. On the basis of data provided by the OECD, a dummy variable for a pronounced 'guest-worker policy' stance in foreign labour policy was constructed, scoring '1' for nations in which the total number of foreign workers decreased in response to the oil price shocks of 1973 and 1979–80 (Switzerland, West Germany and Austria), and '0' for all other cases. See OECD, 1985, 51; see also Schmidt (1985) for Switzerland, and Schmid (1990) for West Germany. Austria's foreign labour policy has also been shaped by a guest-worker stance (Mißlbeck, 1983).
15. An exception rule must be mentioned: the indices include only those significant predictors which measure change in an independent variable, or a particular point in time within the period under investigation, but it excludes significant correlates which measure a given independent variable at time point 1960. The exclusion of these variables is based on the assumption that their impact has been captured by the labour force participation rate in 1960.
16. The cut-off point chosen for the country-by-country classification of a variable as an obstacle to, or a promoting factor for, gender equality is the arithmetic mean. For the

variables included, see Appendix A. I have deliberately chosen a basic, non-technical and quasi-multivariate strategy of interpreting the results of the sets of bivariate correlations reported in this chapter. That choice has been dictated by the effort to maximize the intelligibility of the presentation, but it is also due to the constraints that a small number of cases and a large number of determinants of the dependent variables generate. It needs to be added that all important intercorrelations between the explanatory variables have been reported in the text or in notes. All intercorrelations are substantially below a critical multicollinearity threshold (>.80). See also note 19.

17. The model advanced here is also perfectly compatible with differences in the change of the female participation rate across the socialist European countries in the 1960s, 1970s and 1980s. For example, Poland's lower level of female labour force participation (69.6 per cent in 1979 as compared to 78.1 in the German Democratic Republic in 1980), and the slower increase in the female participation rate in Poland (1960 to 1979: 4 percentage points, compared to 16.2 percentage points increase in East Germany (1960–80)) can at least partly be attributed to the differences in religious traditions. Poland is a Catholic country (95 per cent), whereas religious affiliation in East Germany has mainly been Protestant (46 per cent, compared to 7 per cent Catholics and 47 per cent non-affiliated respondents). Data were taken from ILO *Yearbooks of Labour Statistics* 1966, 1970, 1976, 1984, 1987 and 1988, and from Lovenduski and Woodall, 1987, Table 11.1.
18. The cut-off point chosen for the country-by-country classification of a variable as an obstacle or as a promoting factor to gender equality is defined by the arithmetic mean of that variable, with the exception of foreign labour policy (a guest worker policy stance was coded as 'promoter'), early retirement (public early retirement schemes coded as 'promoter') and coordination of the economy (measured with recoded corporatism scale from Czada); corporatism and sectoralism coded as 'promoter'; on the basis of Castles (1989), Australia's institutional set-up in macroeconomic policy was coded as 'sectoralist' and hence as 'promoter'. The selection of the variables is analogous to the procedure which was chosen in the construction of the index of promoters and obstacles of female labour supply (for details, see Appendix B). It should be added that the intercorrelations between the variables from which this index was constructed are low or moderately low, and are in general below the critical threshold of multicollinearity (>.80).
19. This is precisely the result of a factor analysis of the change in female participation rates using as variables the predictors arrayed in Appendix A. The first factor is a 'route to modernization factor', the second comprises politics and policy, and a third one ('cultural factor') refers mainly to religious traditions and trends in fertility.
20. There have been other dimensions of social inequality in which the level of gender equality was significantly increased in the post-war period. These include secondary and tertiary education (see, for example, Paukert, 1984; Schmidt, 1984; Castles and Marceau, 1989), female-male hourly earning differentials (see, for example, OECD, 1988a, 156–64), equal employment and equal pay legislation (OECD, 1988a, 166–70), extension of *de jure* rights of women and, more recently, significant increases in the level of political representation of women in political parties and national legislatures (see, for example, Kolinsky, 1989). Some of these trends have been related to the trend in female participation rates, such as the increase in hourly earnings. However, there have also been persistently high levels of occupational segregation (Roos, 1985; OECD, 1988a, 154–6), gendered social policy arrangements, significant female-male unemployment differentials (at least in some of the countries studied in this chapter, including France, Italy, Germany and the Benelux nations), and an over-

proportionately high load of housework for women who participate in the paid labour force, regardless of the extent to which the female participation rates have risen.

21. See, for example, the strong emphasis on a conservative stance in family policy in West Germany in the 1950s (Moeller, 1989). See also the view of the former West German Minister of Health, Family and Youth, Wuermeling, who defined the major objective of family policy as the protection of the family as a 'Freiheitsraum' (cited in Moeller, 1989, 168–9), i.e. an institution which guarantees and protects liberty on the part of the members of the family *vis à vis* the state and civil society at large. In the German case, and less so in the Austrian one, the restoration of a traditional stance in family policy must also be seen as a counter-move against the mobilization of men, women and children for the economic, political and military goals of the National-Socialist regime during World War II in particular. Conservative family policy along Catholic and Christian Democratic lines has, of course, also been interpreted as an alternative to what was regarded as the socialization, if not the destruction, of the family in Socialist East Germany. This is not to argue that the Christian Democratic party's stance on women's policy issues has remained constant over time. There were efforts in the 1980s to adopt in some respects a more liberal stance towards policy on women in general and on female labour force participation in particular. However, the general pattern is that processes of secularization and value change have operated in the Christian Democratic party and in the Christian Democratic electorate at a slower speed and with a considerable time lag compared to more secularized parties and milieus.

References

Antal, A.B. and Krebsbach-Gnath, C. (1985), *Working Women in West Germany*, Berlin: Wissenschaftszentrum Berlin für Sozialforschung.

Armstrong, P. and Armstrong, H. (1988), 'Taking Women into Account. Redefining and Intensifying Employment in Canada' in J. Jenson, E. Hagen and C. Reddy (eds), *Feminization of the Labour Force*, Cambridge: Polity Press, 65–84.

Ashenfelter, O. and Layard, R. (eds) (1986), *Handbook of Labor Economics*, 2 vols., Amsterdam/New York/Oxford/Tokyo: North-Holland.

Bakker, I. (1988), 'Women's Employment in Comparative Perspective' in J. Jenson, E. Hagen and C. Reddy (eds), *Feminization of the Labour Force*, Cambridge: Polity Press, 17–44.

Barrett, D.B. (ed.) (1982), *World Christian Encyclopedia: A Comparative Study of Churches and Religions in the Modern World AD 1900–2000*, Nairobi: Oxford University Press.

Blau, D. and Ferber, M.A. (1986), *The Economics of Women, Men and Work*, Englewood Cliffs, N.J.: Prentice-Hall.

Brettschneider, Frank, Ahlstich, Katja and Zügel, Bettina (1991), 'Materialien zu Gesellschaft, Wirtschaft und Politik in den Mitgliederstaaten der Europaischen gleich' in O.W. Gabriel (ed.), *Die EG-Staaten im Vergleich*, Opladen: Westdeutscher Verlag, 433–626.

Bruche, G. and Casey, B. (1982), *Arbeit oder Rente?*, Frankfurt a.M./New York: Campus.

Bruche, G. and Reissert, B. (1985), *Die Finanzierung der Arbeitsmarktpolitik. System, Effektivität, Reformansätze*, Frankfurt a.M./New York: Campus.

Bundesanstalt für Arbeit (ed.) (1989), 'Situation und Tendenz der Beschäftigung und des Erwerbsverhaltens von Frauen' in *Amtliche Nachrichten der Bundesanstalt fuer Arbeit* (ANBA), 938–51.

Cameron, D. R. (1984), 'Social Democracy, Corporatism, Labour Quiescence and the Representation of Economic Interest in Advanced Capitalist Society' in J.H. Goldthorpe (ed.), *Order and Conflict in Contemporary Capitalism*, Oxford: Oxford University Press, 143–78.

Cameron, D.R. (1985), 'Does Government Cause Inflation? Taxes, Spending, and Deficits' in L.N. Lindberg and C.S. Maier (eds), *The Politics of Inflation and Economic Stagnation*, Washington, D.C.: Brookings, 224–79.

Castles, F.G. (1989), 'Social Protection by Other Means' in F.G. Castles (ed.), *The Comparative History of Public Policy*, Cambridge: Polity Press, 16–55.

Castles, F.G. and Marceau, J. (1989), 'The Transformation in Gender Inequality in Tertiary Education', *Journal of Public Policy*, **9** (4), 493–507.

Collver, A. and Langlois, E. (1962), 'The Female Labor Force in Metropolitan Areas: An International Comparison', *Economic Development and Cultural Change*, **10**, 367–85.

Cook, A.H., Lorwin, V.R. and Daniels, A.K. (eds) (1984), *Women and Trade Unions in Eleven Industrialized Countries*, Philadelphia: Temple University Press.

Crewe, I. and Denver, D. (eds) (1985), *Electoral Change in Western Democracies. Patterns and Sources of Electoral Volatility*, London/Sydney: Croom Helm.

Crompton, R., Hantrais, L. and Walters, P. (1990), 'Gender Relations and Employment', *British Journal of Sociology*, **41**, 329–49.

Cusack, T.R. et al. (1989), 'Political-Economic Aspect of Public Employment', *European Journal of Political Research*, **17**, 471–500.

Czada, R. (1986), 'Zwischen Arbeitsplatzinteresse und Modernisierungszwang. Bestandsbedingungen und Auswirkungen gewerkschaftlicher Politikeinbindung im internationalen Vergleich', Konstanz: Dissertation.

Del Boca, D. (1988), 'Women in a Changing Workplace. The Case of Italy' in J. Jenson, E. Hagen and C. Reddy (eds), *Feminization of the Labour Force*, Cambridge: Polity Press, 120–36.

Dittrich, W. (1985), *Mitbestimmung – eine korporatistische Strategie? Eine international vergleichende Untersuchung zur Mitbestimmungspolitik in zehn europäischen Ländern*, Konstanz: Wisslit.

DIW (Deutsches Institut fuer Wirtschaftsforschung) (1990), 'Erwerbstätigkeit und Einkommen von Frauen in der DDR' in *DIW-Wochenbericht*, No. 19, 263–7.

Eidgenössische Kommission für Frauenfragen (1984), *Die Stellung der Frau in der Schweiz*, Bern.

Eidgenössische Kommission für Frauenfragen (1990), *Nehmen Sie Platz, Madame*, Bern.

Erler, G. (1988), 'The German Paradox. Non-Feminization of the Labor Force and

Post-Industrial Social Policies' in E. Hagen, J. Jenson and C. Reddy (eds), *Feminization of the Labour Force*, Cambridge: Polity Press, 231–44.

Esping-Andersen, G. (1990), *The Three Worlds of Welfare Capitalism*, Cambridge: Polity Press.

Farley, J. (ed.) (1985), *Women Workers in Fifteen Countries*, Cambridge: Cambridge University Press.

Flora, P. (ed.) (1986–87), *Growth to Limits*, Berlin/New York: de Gruyter, Vols 1, 2 and 4.

Giele, J.Z. (1977), 'Comparative Perspectives on Women' in J.Z. Giele and A.C. Smock (eds), *Women: Roles and Status in Eight Countries*, New York/London/Sydney: Wiley, 1–33.

Greven-Aschoff, B. (1981), 'Sozialer Wandel und Frauenbewegungen', *Geschichte und Gesellschaft*, **7**, 328–46.

Gustavsson, S. (1984), 'Equal Opportunity Policies in Sweden' in C. Schmid and R. Weitzel (eds), *Sex Discrimination and Equal Opportunity*, New York: St. Martin's, 132–54.

Hagen, E. and Jenson, J. (1988), 'Paradoxes and Promises. Work and Politics in the Postwar Years' in J. Jenson, E. Hagen and C. Reddy (eds), *Feminization of the Labour Force*, Cambridge: Polity Press, 3–16.

Hanami, T. (1984), 'Japan' in A.H. Cook, V.R. Lorwin and A.K. Daniels (eds), *Women and Trade Unions in Eleven Industrialized Countries*, Philadelphia: Temple University Press, 215–38.

Heinelt, H. (1991), *Frühverrentung als politischer Prozeß*, Wiesbaden: Deutscher Universitäts Verlag.

Hohn, H.-W. (1988), *Von der Einheitsgewerkschaft zum Betriebssyndikalismus. Soziale Schließung im dualen System der Interessenvertretung*, Berlin: Edition Sigma.

Humphries, J. and Rubery, J. (1988), 'Recession and Exploitation. British Women in a Changing Workplace, 1979–1985' in J. Jenson, E. Hagen and C. Reddy (eds), *Feminization of the Labour Force*, Cambridge: Polity Press, 85–105.

Inglehart, R. (1990), *Culture Shift in Advanced Industrial Society*, Princeton, N.J.: Princeton University Press.

International Labour Office (ILO), *Yearbook of Labour Statistics*, Geneva: ILO, various issues.

Jensen, U.S. (1983), 'Political and Economic Gender Inequalities in Capitalist Polyarchies', *European Journal of Political Research*, **11**, 265–82.

Jenson, J. (1988), 'The Limits of "and the" Discourse. French Women as Marginal Workers' in J. Jenson, E. Hagen and C. Reddy (eds), *Feminization of the Labour Force*, Cambridge: Polity Press, 155–72.

Jenson, J., Hagen, E. and Reddy, C. (eds) (1988), *Feminization of the Labour Force*, Cambridge: Polity Press.

Kamerman, S.B. and Kahn, Alfred J. (eds) (1983), *Family Policy*, New York: Columbia University Press.

Katzenstein, P. (1984), *Corporatism and Change. Austria, Switzerland, and the Politics of Industry*, Ithaca N.Y./London: Cornell University Press.

Katzenstein, P. (1985), *Small States in World Markets*, Ithaca, N.Y.: Cornell University Press.

Katzenstein, P. (ed.) (1989), *The Politics of Industry*, Ithaca, N.Y.: Cornell University Press.

Kaufmann, F.-X. (ed.) (1982), *Staatliche Sozialpolitik und Familie*, Munich: Oldenbourg.

Kaufmann, F.-X. (1989), 'Familie' in N. Blüm and H.F. Zacher (eds), *40 Jahre Sozialstaat Bundesrepublik Deutschland*, Baden-Baden: Nomos, 547–60.

Kerr, H.H. (1987), 'The Swiss Party System: Steadfast and Changing' in H. Daalder (ed.), *Party Systems in Denmark, Austria, Switzerland, the Netherlands, and Belgium*, London: St. Martin's, 107–92.

Kickbusch, I. (1981), 'Die Familiarisierung der weiblichen Arbeit', Konstanz (Dissertation).

Killingsworth, M.R. and Heckman, J.J. (1986), 'Female Labor Supply: A Survey' in O. Ashenfelter and R. Layard (eds), *Handbook of Labor Economics*, 2 vols, Amsterdam/New York/Oxford/Tokyo: North-Holland, Vol. I, 103–204.

Klein, V. (1963), 'Industrialization and the Changing Role of Women', *Current Sociology* **12**, 24–34.

Klingemann, H.-D. (1985), 'West Germany' in I. Crewe and D. Denver (eds), *Electoral Change in Western Democracies*, London/Sydney: 230–63.

Kolinsky, E. (1989), *Women in West Germany. Life, Works, and Politics*, Oxford/New York/Munich: Berg/St. Martin's.

Krebs, E. and Schwarz, M. (1978), 'Austria' in S.B. Kamerman and A.J. Kahn (eds), *Family Policy. Government and Families in Fourteen Countries*, New York: Columbia University Press, 185–216.

Kriesi, H. (1980), *Entscheidungsstrukturen und Entscheidungsprozesse in der Schweizer Politik*, Frankfurt a.M./New York: Campus.

Lane, J.-E. and Ersson, S.O. (1987), *Politics and Society in Western Europe*, London: Sage.

Lechner, W. (1990), 'Jeden Tag ein Kunststück' in *ZEITmagazin*, Nr. 25 v. 15 June, 8–11.

Lehr, U. (1988), 'Berufstätigkeit. Anteil der Frauen am Erwerbleben' in R. Wisniewski and H. Knust (eds), *Handbuch für Frauenfragen*, Stuttgart: Bonn Aktuell, 54–62.

Lenski, G. (1977), *Macht und Privileg. Eine Theorie der sozialen Schichtung*, Frankfurt a.M.: Suhrkamp.

Lijphart, A. (1984), *Democracies*, New Haven: Yale University Press.

Lovenduski, J. and Woodall, J. (1987), *Politics and Society in Eastern Europe*, London: Macmillan.

McMahon, P.J. (1986), 'An International Comparison of Labor Force Participation, 1977–84', *Monthly Labor Review*, **109** (5), 3–12.

Mallier, A.T. and Rosser, M.J. (1987), *Women and the Economy. A Comparative Study of Britain and the USA*, London: Macmillan.

Merz, J. (1990), 'Female Labor Supply: Labor Force Participation, Market Wage Rate and Working Hours of Married and Unmarried Women in the Federal

Republic of Germany', *Jahrbücher für Nationalökonomie und Stastitik*, **207** (3), 440–70.

Mincer, J. (1985), 'Intercountry Comparisons of Labour Force Trends and of Related Developments – An Overview', *Journal of Labour Economics*, **3**, Supplement, 1–32.

Mißlbeck, J. (1983), *Der Österreichische Gewerkschaftsbund. Analyse einer korporatistischen Gewerkschaft*, Frankfurt a.M.: Wisslit.

Moeller, R.G. (1989), 'Reconstructing the Family in Reconstruction Germany: Women and Social Policy in the Federal Republic, 1949–1955', *Feminist Studies*, **15**, 137–69.

Müller, W., Handl, J. and Willms, A. (1982), *Strukturwandel der Frauenarbeit 1880–1980*, Frankfurt a.M./New York: Campus.

Neidhart, F. (1978), 'The Federal Republic of Germany', in S.B. Kamerman and Alfred J. Kahn (eds), *Family Policy. Government and Families in Fourteen Countries*, New York: Columbia University Press, 217–38.

Neidhart, L. (1988a), 'Die Schweizer Konkordanzdemokratie' in H.-G. Wehling (ed.), *Die Schweiz*, Stuttgart: Kohlhammer, 44–52.

Neidhart, L. (1988b), 'Das Parteiensystem der Schweiz' in H.-G. Wehling (ed.), *Die Schweiz*, Stuttgart: Kohlhammer, 61–7.

Norris, P. (1987), *Politics and Sexual Equality. The Comparative Position of Women in Western Democracies*, Boulder/Colorado: Rienner.

OECD (1979), *Disadvantaged Groups on the Labour Market and Measures to Assist Them*, Paris: OECD.

OECD (1980a), *Women and Employment. Policies for Equal Opportunity*, Paris: OECD.

OECD (1980b), *The Tax-Benefit-Position of Certain Income Groups in the Member Countries of the OECD 1974–1978*, Paris: OECD.

OECD (1982), *Employment in the Public Sector*, Paris: OECD.

OECD (1983), 'Part-Time Employment in OECD Countries' in *OECD Employment Outlook 1983*, Paris: OECD, 43–52.

OECD (1984), 'The Contribution of Services to Employment' in *OECD Employment Outlook 1984*, Paris: OECD, 39–54.

OECD (1985a), *The Integration of Women into the Economy*, Paris: OECD.

OECD (1985b), 'The Labour Market Implications of International Migration in Selected OECD Countries' in *Employment Outlook 1985*, Paris: OECD, 47–63.

OECD (1986), *Employment Outlook 1986*, Paris: OECD.

OECD (1987a), *Employment Outlook 1987*, Paris: OECD.

OECD (1987b), *Economic Outlook Historical Statistics 1960–1985*, Paris: OECD.

OECD (1988a), 'Women's Economic Activity, Employment and Earnings. A Review of Recent Developments' in OECD, *Employment Outlook 1988*, Paris: OECD, 129–72.

OECD (1988b), 'Longer-Run Labour Market Issues' in OECD, *Employment Outlook 1988*, Paris: OECD, 53–83.

OECD (1989a), *Economic Survey – Switzerland*, Paris: OECD.

OECD (1989b), *Employment Outlook 1989*, Paris: OECD.

OECD (1990a), 'Child Care in OECD Countries' in OECD, *Employment Outlook 1990*, Paris: OECD, 123–51.

OECD (1990b), *Employment Outlook 1990*, June, Paris: OECD.

Paukert, L. (1984), *The Employment and Unemployment of Women in OECD Countries*, Paris: OECD.

Pencavel, J. (1986), 'Labour Supply of Men: A Survey' in O. Ashenfelter and R. Layard (eds), *Handbook of Labor Economics*, 2 vols, Amsterdam/New York/ Oxford/Tokyo: North-Holland, Vol. I, 3–102.

Pfarr, H. and Eitel, L. (1984), 'Equal Opportunity Policies for Women in the Federal Republic of Germany' in G. Schmid and R. Weitzel (eds), *Sex Discrimination and Equal Opportunity. The Labor Market and Employment Policy*, New York: St. Martin's, 155–90.

Piore, M.J. and Sabel, Ch.F. (1985), *Das Ende der Massenproduktion. Studie über die Requalifizierung der Arbeit und der Rückkehr der Ökonomie in die Gesellschaft*, Berlin: Wagenbach.

Pommerehne, W., Frey, B.S. and Weck, H. (1984), *Schattenwirtschaft*, München: Vahlen.

Przeworski, A. and Teune, H. (1970), *The Logic of Comparative Social Inquiry*, Melbourne: Krieger.

Rein, M. (1985), *Women in the Social Welfare Labour Market*, Berlin: Wissenschaftszentrum Berlin für Sozialforschung.

Ruggie, M. (1984), *The State and Working Women. A Comparative Study of Britain and Sweden*, Princeton, N.J.: Princeton University Press.

Ruggie, M. (1988), 'Gender, Work and Social Progress. Some consequences of interest aggregation in Sweden' in J. Jenson, E. Hagen and C. Reddy (eds), *Feminization of the Labour Force*, Cambridge: Polity Press, 173–88.

Schettkat, R. (1987a), *Erwerbsbeteiligung und Politik. Theoretische und empirische Analysen von Determinanten und Dynamik des Arbeitsangebotes in Schweden und der Bundesrepublik Deutschland*, Berlin: Edition Sigma.

Schettkat, R. (1987b), *Die Erwerbsquote, ein geeigneter Indikator zur Analyse der Erwerbsbeteiligung?* Berlin: Wissenschaftszentrum (IIMV).

Schettkat, R. (1987c), 'Dynamik der Erwerbsbeteiligung in Schweden und der Bundesrepublik Deutschland', *Internationale Chronik zur Arbeitsmarktpolitik*, Nr. 29, 1–4.

Schmid, G. (1984a), 'The Political Economy of Labor Market Discrimination: A Theoretical and Comparative Analysis of Sex Discrimination and Equal Opportunity Policy for Women' in G. Schmid and R. Weitzel (eds), *Sex Discrimination and Equal Opportunity*, New York: St. Martin's, 1–19.

Schmid, G. (1984b), 'Equal Opportunity Policy: A Comparative Perspective', *International Journal of Manpower*, **3**, 15–25.

Schmid, G. (1990), 'Arbeitsmarkt-und Beschäftigungspolitik', in K. von Beyme, and M.G. Schmidt (eds), *Politik in der Bundesrepublik Deutschland*, Opladen: Westdeutscher Verlag, 228–54.

Schmid, G. and Weitzel, R. (eds) (1984), *Sex Discrimination and Equal Opportunity*, New York: St. Martin's.

Schmidt, M.G. (1982), 'The Role of Political Parties in Shaping Public Policy', in F.G. Castles (ed.), *The Impact of Parties*, Beverly Hills/London: Sage, 97–176.

Schmidt, M.G. (1984), 'Zur sozialen, wirtschaftlichen und politischen Benachteiligung der Frauen im internationalen Vergleich' in B. Riedmüller and I. Kickbusch (eds), *Die armen Frauen*, Frankfurt a.M.: Suhrkamp, 73–102.

Schmidt, M.G. (1985), *Der Schweizerische Weg zur Vollbeschaeftigung*, Frankfurt a.M./New York: Campus.

Schmidt, M.G. (1987), 'The Politics of Labour Market Policy' in F.G. Castles, F. Lehner and M.G. Schmidt (eds.), *Managing Mixed Economies*, Berlin/New York: de Gruyter, 3–54.

Schmidt, M.G. (1988), *Sozialpolitik. Historische Entwicklung und internationaler Vergleich*, Opladen: Leske & Budrich.

Schmidt, M.G. (1989), 'The Political Management of Mixed Economies: Political Aspects of Macroeconomic Performance in OECD Nations (1960–1984)' in B. Struempel (ed.), *Industrial Societies after the Stagnation of the 1970s – Taking Stock from an Interdisciplinary Perspective*, Berlin/New York: de Gruyter, 101–30.

Schmidt, M.G. (1992), 'Regierungen – parteipolitische Zusammensetzung' in M.G. Schmidt (ed.), *Die Westlichen Länder*, Munich: Beck, 393–400.

Schultz, T.P. (1990), 'Women's Changing Participation in the Labour Force: A World View', *Economic Development and Cultural Change*, **38**, 457–88.

Scott, J.W. (1983), 'Women in History: the Modern Period', *Past and Present*, No. 101.

Semyonov, M. (1980), 'The Social Context of Women's Labor Force Participation: A Comparative Analysis', *American Journal of Sociology*, **86**, 534–50.

Shaffer, H.G. (1981), *Women in the Two Germanies*, New York: Pergamon Press.

Shonfield, A. (1965), *Modern Capitalism. The Changing Balance of Public and Private Power*, London/Oxford/New York: Oxford University Press.

Simona, I. (1985), 'Switzerland' in J. Farley (ed.), *Women Workers in Fifteen Countries*, Ithaca: ILR Press, 147–53.

Sorrentino, C. (1983), 'International Comparisons of Labor Force Participation, 1960–81', *Monthly Labor Review*, **106** (2), 23–36.

Sorrentino, C. (1990), 'The Changing Family in International Perspective', *Monthly Labor Review*, **113** (3), 41–58.

Statistisches Bundesamt (Hrsg.) (1987), *Frauen in Familie, Beruf und Gesellschaft*, Stuttgart/Berlin/Köln/Mainz: Kohlhammer.

Summers, R. and Heston, A. (1988), 'A New Set of International Comparisons of Real Product and Prices: Estimates for 130 Countries, 1950–1985', *The Review of Income and Wealth*, **34**, 1–25.

UNESCO (1990), *Statistical Yearbook*, Paris: UNESCO.

Varley, R. (1986), *The Government Household Transfer Data Base 1960–1984*, Paris: OECD Department of Economics and Statistics.

Weber, M. (1968), 'Asketischer Protestantismus und kapitalistischer Geist' in Johannes Winkelmann (ed.), *Max Weber: Soziologie – Weltgeschichtliche Analysen – Politik*, Stuttgart: Kröner, 357–81.

Weck-Hannemann, H. (1984), '"Weiche Modellierung" der Schattenwirtschaft – Ein internationaler Vergleich' in K. Gretschmann, R.G. Heinze, and B. Mettelsiefen (eds), *Schattenwirtschaft*, Göttingen: Vandenhoek & Ruprecht 167–86.

Weck-Hannemann, H. and Frey, B. (1989), 'Frauen und Arbeit. Eine ökonomische Betrachtung', *Wirtschaftswissenschaftliches Studium*, **18**, 562–68.

Wilensky, H.L. (1968), 'Women's Work: Economic Growth, Ideology, Structure' in *Industrial Relations*, **7**, 235–48.

Wilensky, H.L. (1990), 'Common Problems, Divergent Policies: An 18-Nation Study of Family Policy', *Public Affairs Report*, **31** (3), 1–3.

Wilensky, H.L. (1992), *Tax and Spend: The Political Economy and Performance of Rich Democracies*, Berkeley: University of California Press.

Wolchik, S.L. (1981), 'Ideology and Equality. The Status of Women in Eastern and Western Europe', *Comparative Political Studies*, **13**, 445–76.

Wright, E.O. (1989), 'Women in the Class Structure', *Politics and Society*, **17**, 35–66.

Youssef, N.H. (1972), 'Differential Labor Force Participation of Women in Latin America and Middle Eastern Countries: The Influence of Family Characteristics', *Social Forces*, **51**, 135–53.

PART III
FAMILIES AND FAMILIES OF NATIONS

6 The Politics of Childhood: The Rights of Children in Modern Times

Göran Therborn

Childhood shows the man, As morning shows the day. John Milton (1671), *Paradise Regained*, Book 1, Line 220.

The Century of the Child – Passed By?

'The only steady linear change [of the family] over the last four hundred years seems to have been a growing concern for children, although the actual treatment has oscillated cyclically between repression and permissiveness.' Thus Lawrence Stone (1977, 683) concluded his great history of *The Family, Sex and Marriage in England.* According to Lloyd DeMause's decidedly more linear conception of history (1988/1974, 52), a new mode of parent-child relations, the sixth since the beginning of Antiquity, opens up in mid-20th century – the 'helping mode'. It 'involves the proposition that the child knows better than the parent what it needs at each stage of life. …' That is meant by its author as an emergent ideal type, rather than an accomplished reality. But in the aftermath of the UN Convention of the Rights of the Child of 1989, and of the World Summit for Children in September 1990,[1] it seems that the hopes of the Swedish feminist and educationalist Ellen Key (1900)[2] of the 20th century becoming 'the century of the child' have turned out at least as much on target as the more well-known vision of this century (of the Western world) as the 'century of Social Democracy'.

The difference of scholarly attention paid to the two 'centuries' is amazing, however, in particular as far as comparative research (comparative in time as well as place) is concerned. In fact, systematic comparative childhood research hardly exists. A major problem with even the greatest historians is that their coverage ends too soon. Stone's (1977) fascinating account ends in 1800, albeit with a postscript chapter pointing to 19th-century developments and commenting on some aspects of the current situation. Philippe Ariès (1962) concludes his magnificent story before the French Revolution. Shorter (1976) finds the modern family somewhat later than the century of Louis XIV, but only brings us into the 19th century. Linda Pollock's (1983) grand defence of a continuist conception of parent-child relations also stops in the 19th century. Pinchbeck and Hewitt (1973) do take us to England in the mid-1940s, but their main emphasis lies before 1908. The anthology edited by Lloyd DeMause (1988/1974) makes a few forays into the 19th century and a proposition about the 20th, but its main contributions refer to earlier periods. The 19th century still remains, by and large, the last to produce historians of childhood (e.g. Donzelot, 1977; Flandrin, 1979; Heywood, 1988; Jordan, 1987; Walvin, 1982; Grossberg, 1985; Sommerville, 1990; cf. Johnson, 1990). The inevitable exceptions seem to be primarily American, in particular Hawes and Hiner (1985), Hawes (1991), Stearns and Haggerty (1991), and more family-focused works such as Mintz and Kellogg (1988).

Historians may have a legitimate excuse for their lack of interest in the current century. The modest contribution of the social sciences is more remarkable. Reasons are plentiful. One is that the recently booming welfare state research industry primarily focuses on income maintenance or income redistribution – their amount, their composition, their causes, and their effects. Little room remains for children, although they may enter through the Anglo-Saxon interest in poverty in the form of child poverty, or as the background to the payment of family or child allowance. Of course, the welfare state may also be considered in terms of human reproduction rather than political economy. That is, as a set of state institutions and state arrangements in order directly to influence the simple and expanded reproduction of a given state population, whereby 'reproduction' means both maintaining alive already existing human beings and sustaining a population over time, and 'expanded' refers not only to numbers but also to conditions of existence. A human reproduction perspective on the welfare state would include the patterning of social services and social relations, as well as expenditure patterns and relationships to the market. In this way 'the child's century' would not be lost. So far, however, that is clearly a dissident position (see further, Therborn 1987), relating to more explicitly feminist perspectives on the welfare state (Baldock and Cass, 1988; Freeman, 1984; Jacobsson, 1988; Wilson, 1977; Zaretsky, 1976).

In the general comparative public policy literature, one searches in vain for policy on children or childhood. That may very well be an accurate reflection of the language and the experience of national policy-makers. 'Nowhere are the inconsistencies and fragmentation in public policies more evident than in programs and policies directed towards children', writes Rosalie Genovese (1984, 31) about US experiences. There are some studies dealing explicitly with a broad range of contemporary child policies, but they tend to be more or less exclusively national in scope (e.g. Steiner, 1976; Hayes, 1982; van Krieken, 1992). Exception have the medically oriented but broad-ranging studies assembled by Cooter (1992). More often policies with regard to children are grouped under the rubric of family policy. That subject is also kept on the sidelines of comparative policy research, so that the policy relationships between family and children have not been much clarified. The major contribution to comparative family policy, edited by Kamerman and Kahn (1978), for all its richness, illustrates that problem too. Some more recent contributions (e.g. Boh et al., 1989 and Zimmerman, 1988) are even less helpful to the child-interested reader. Research on comparative education appears to focus on the institutions of systems of education, rather than on the conditions of pupils (Heidenheimer et al., 1990, ch. 2)

European cooperation has brought fresh and important inputs into childhood studies, however. Since 1986 there has been a European Commission Childcare Network, coordinated by Peter Moss, continuously monitoring the situation of and the policies towards children (see Moss, 1988). The Spanish Ministry of Social Affairs appears to have taken special pains to study European social policy experiences and reflections, including those on child policy. In 1989 it organized and published the proceedings of the First International Congress on Childhood and Society (Ministerio de Asuntos Sociales, 1991). From the Vienna-based European Centre, Jens Qvortrup and others have started and brought to realization a series of contemporary national reports on *Childhood as a Social Phenomenon* (Bardy et al., 1990–91). Qvortrup has also edited a special issue of the *International Journal of Sociology* devoted to the sociology of childhood (**17** (3), 1987). With regard to Central and Eastern Europe, UNICEF has compiled a very timely collection of studies on the position of children in countries on the threshold of the reconstruction of capitalism (Cornia and Sipos, 1991).

Law, as we shall elaborate below, is a major determinant of childhood. Lawyers and legal scholars have been diligent in exploring the legal position and rights of children (e.g. Eekelaar, 1986; Freeman, 1983a). But like the situation regarding child policy, child law studies seem to be mainly national, perhaps also incorporating comparisons of a few other countries with similar legal systems, for instance among the Anglo-Saxon Common Law family of nations. The monumental German reference work on *International Marriage and Childhood Law*, launched by Alexander Bergmann in the late 1920s and continued in current times by Murad Ferid, constitutes the major exception, supplemented by some encyclopaedic articles and international symposia (see e.g. Krause, 1976; Stoljar, 1980; Bates, 1976;

Council of Europe, 1974; Kirk et al., 1975). Of the large number of reports gathered for the UN Year of the Child in 1979, only a scattered selection was published, for instance by Pappas (1983). On the other hand, again as a parallel to policy studies, there do exist a few very important contributions to comparative family law, pertinent to our concerns here. Among them are Rheinstein (1972), Glendon (1977 and 1989) and the recurrent international surveys of *The Journal of Family Law.*

The rights and the conditions of children and their pattern of change in the 20th century do not, then, offer themselves as a 'dependent variable' to be picked up and submitted to statistical software packages and/or to other explanatory treatment. As a first step, a basic analytical framework has to be constructed.

A Brief Discourse on Method

Basically, we shall pursue two lines of investigation, of law and of public policy. There are three reasons for this state-childhood perspective being common to both. First of all, laws, in their moments of decision and practice, just like public policies, may be taken as indicators of ruling conceptions, values and norms in a society – though not necessarily majoritarian ones. In this case, child law and child policy can be taken as manifestations of adult perspectives, values and norms with regard to children, notions otherwise difficult to grasp. Another rationale pertains to the more enclosed field of policy studies. The very meaning of childhood is largely defined by public intervention, whose parameters have changed enormously in the course of the 20th century. Childhood has rarely been explicitly studied at all, and hardly ever comparatively across nations. Finally, there is the special argument of the comparativist. The picture of childhood to be offered here (with the help of legal and policy indicators) will certainly lack a great number of features of concern to the family/child sociologist or historian, as well as the colours and the smells of the narrative. However, it may have one redeeming feature – a systematic comparative approach, which so far has been largely absent from the field. Insofar as it succeeds, this kind of analysis will be able to show with some precision when and where important changes in adult-child relations have taken place. Having done that, it will also to be able to raise, and to some extent to answer, the question: what accounts for this pattern of development?

Comparative law and comparative public policy belong to different disciplines of academia and are seldom studied together, although law may be regarded as an outcome of public policy-making by legislators, by judges, or both. In the case here, law is of particular significance, because the social position of the policy-takers (i.e. the position of children in adult society) is an especially interesting variable, one defined and/or expressed by law. For reasons of space, this study of the politics of childhood is divided into two physically separate parts, this first one focusing on law.

Legal developments concerning childhood over the past two centuries may be summarized in two words – constitution and emancipation. The *Darstellung* (presentation) here of a complicated research process will focus on these two processes. The process of constitution is particularly important because it has defined our topic. The constitution of modern childhood has defined what childhood is and what children are. Therefore the proper object of investigation and explanation is what has happened to the legal situation of children in the course of the 20th century. On the whole, that development has been an expansion of children's rights *vis à vis* parental and general adult controls and constraints.

However, the analytical perspective adopted here will not emphasize the general trend, but its different national temporalities and forms. That nations have differed widely, and still differ, is clearly evident from the process of investigation. The methodological problem is to turn the national texts of legal codes and court verdicts into a few international variables.

In what follows, the legal emancipation of children has been compressed into three such variables, embodying (1) conceptions of a child-centred family, (2) equality among children regardless of parental interrelations, and (3) the autonomous integrity of children. Since this research topic is far from established, these variables have nothing self-evident about them and have been constructed by the present author. Their rationale is given below.

Once the pattern of cross-national variation has been grasped, the task is to explain it. Here, the searchlight will be on the processes and forces of decision-making, rather than on factors of covariation.

The area covered by this study is made up of the Western nations in the conventional post-World War II sense. That is, Western Europe from Norway to Greece, America north of the Rio Grande, Australia and New Zealand.[3] The number of units is much larger than in conventional cross-national analyses, however. Family legislation is a state competence in the US, currently comprising 50 jurisdictions; it is also mainly a state or provincial competence in Australia and Canada, adding at least 16 more jurisdictions (excluding those of 'territories'). For the purposes of child law, the UK is divided into the three major contemporary jurisdictions of England and Wales, Scotland, and Northern Ireland. Although there is a Swiss Civil Code, cantonal legislation and custom also pertain to family matters (Zweigert and Kötz, 1987, 182). Nor is Spanish family law fully unified nationally (Bergmann and Ferid, 1955, Vol. VIII, 96). Faced with this complexity, the pragmatic solution has been to focus on selected key units, when national legislation or Supreme Court verdicts have not been available, and in the US case to search for a pattern encompassing a majority of states. The key units chosen in other countries with complex jurisdictions have been New South Wales and Victoria in Australia, Ontario and Québec in Canada, and England-Wales and Scotland in the UK. Swiss cantonal and Spanish regional variations have been excluded.

With respect to their legal systems these nations form families – legal families – of nations. The Continental European Civil Law and the Anglo-American Common Law countries constitute the two major lineages. Legal scholars usually further distinguish two or three families among the former: the Romanistic, the Germanic and, increasingly, the Nordic. Zweigert and Kötz (1987, 69) point to five distinctive features of a legal family: '(1) its historical background and development, (2) its predominant and characteristic mode of thought in legal matters, (3) especially distinctive institutions, (4) the kind of legal sources it acknowledges and the way it handles them, and (5) its ideology'.

The sociological history and functioning of these juristic affinities vary. The Common Law family derives from outright imperial diffusion and is kept together – in spite of important internal variation, above all between British unwritten parliamentarism and US judicial constitutional evolution – by continuous attention by lawyers to legal cases in other members of the family, particularly to cases in England and USA.

The Romanistic family is also based on modern diffusion, primarily by the victorious armies of the Chairman of the French Civil Law commission, Napoléon Bonaparte, and later by French intellectual attraction. The centrality of statutory rules in all the Continental European legal systems means that this socially functioning legal family needs some form of law-making cooperation – and not just judicial case attention. Currently, there is little evidence of any such cooperation within the Romanistic family which historically comprises France, Belgium, Luxembourg, Netherlands, Spain, Portugal and Italy and, in North America, Québec and (to a considerable extent) Louisiana.

The Germanic legal family, of Germany (with Prussia and Northern Germany as its core), Austria and Switzerland, came together in the 19th–early 20th century in much the same way as the Romanistic family seems to operate today. That is, in autonomous national processes against the background of a (partly) common legal heritage.

The Nordic family is the tightest one, set up and maintained for more than a century by law-drafting collaboration and regular, institutionalized cross-national juristic exchange. Nordic cooperation began in 1872, before even the decision to bring about a legal unification of Switzerland (in 1874) and before the inter-state legal conferences in the US (which started in 1892). Originally it comprised Denmark, Sweden and Norway – which was in a dynastic union with Sweden but which had her own legislation. After World War I independent Finland – which had kept her Swedish legal tradition under Russian rule after 1809 – and autonomous (from 1944 independent) Iceland also joined.

The families of jurisprudence provide even the legal layman with a useful map of orientation and also furnish the heuristic comparative public policy notion of 'families of nations' with some significant institutional underpinning. The distinctive style of a legal family does not necessarily and permanently correlate one-to-one with the basic contents of child and family law, however. For instance, Greece adopted a, by and large, Germanic legal system in the 19th century, but until very recently her family law derived mainly from Orthodox ecclesiastical law (Zweigert and Kötz, 1987, 162). In general, the varying relationships between secular and church law bear very heavily upon the form of all family norms. While the Dutch Burgelijk Wetboek of 1838 clearly stemmed from the Code Napoléon, by the early 20th century certain crucial stipulations of parental relations had moved closer to those of the Germanic world (see further below).

The Constitution of Modern Childhood

Philippe Ariès (1962), the great French historian, taught us, that childhood is an historical social product, not simply a fact of human biology. However, from a late 20th century vantage-point, Ariès' contrast between the Middle Ages and the 17th century – according to him, the crucial formative period of modern childhood, *le grand siècle* in a broad French historical tradition – is more an inspiring background than a real starting-point. Furthermore, aside from the colour and vividness conveyed by the social historian, there is also a need for the dry systematicity of the social scientist or the comparative lawyer.

The current everyday meaning of 'childhood' refers to a particular period of the human life-cycle. The point to be emphasized is that this period, and what it entails of possibilities and constraints, of rights and duties, is something delimited, constructed and sanctioned in the course of an historical era that had hardly begun before the time of the French Revolution. The epochal importance of this process has largely been ignored, neglected, submerged or lost by histories of *mentalité*, by Foucaldian infatuation with policing or simply by the unbridged ravines between academic disciplines and specialities.

Law and administrative forms of state intervention have played a crucial part in the constitution of modern childhood. The two most important definers of childhood have been legislation concerning compulsory education and labour. A child has become someone who is too young to work and someone who has not finished his/her elementary education. But other legal regulations have also been important. Criminal and penal law define children as persons too young to be (fully) responsible or liable for their acts and who therefore should be sanctioned differently from adults. The regulation of sexuality and marriage singles out children as too young to be able to consent to sexual intercourse and as too young to marry. Laws on majority indicate entrance into full adulthood, but childhood has often been considered to have ended well before that.[4]

To write a history of the constitution of modern childhood is beyond the scope of this Chapter. But the neglected importance of the background to such a proper analysis calls for some brief illustrative elaboration.

Legal Definitions

Literacy was fairly widespread in Protestant Europe by the end of the ancien régime, pushed by the Bible-oriented Protestant churches (Johansson, 1981) but often learnt in non-institutionalized forms (Maynes, 1985, 84). General literacy and public schooling legislation goes back to the 17th (Swedish Church Law of 1686) and 18th (Prussian General County School Regulation of 1763 and the Austrian Edict of 1774) centuries. However, modern schooling, which started only in the course of the 19th century, added three new aspects of relevance to the construction of childhood.

Firstly, it covers virtually all children. Secondly, it starts at the same age (with insignificant exceptions) for all. By contrast, 'the idea of an age limit [for entering school] was entirely unknown in the seventeenth and eighteenth centuries', writes Ariès (1962, 225). He also gives data regarding the age composition of some French schools from the early 17th to the early 19th centuries. In the same school class the age of pupils could range from 9 to 18 (219ff). Thirdly, modern schooling also involves a certain number of years at school for all children. (For wide variations in these respects pre-19th century, see Maynes, 1985, 84ff.) Together, these three aspects of educational legislation create two uniform groups, set off from the rest of the population – pre-school children and school children.

Modern school-based childhood took a long time to develop fully. In Western Europe – north of the Pyrenées (in parts of southern Europe it is a recent, post-World War II phenomenon) it was only completed after World War I, when Belgium began implementing her 1914 decision to make schooling obligatory.[5] About a century earlier the Protestant and Enlightenment principles of universal education had gradually begun to be enforced in Prussia, in other German states and in Denmark (Maynes, 1985, 50;

Flora, 1983, ch. 10; Frijhoff, 1983). The most concentrated period of primary school legislation was the 1870s, broadly speaking. Uniform systems of primary education were then legislated in Australia (Victoria and New South Wales, 1872 and 1880), Austria (1869), England and Wales (1880), France (1882), Germany (1871), Italy (1877), Scotland (1872), Sweden (1878, 1882) and Switzerland (1874). By 1870 illiteracy in the US had gone below 20 per cent, two decades later than in Germany and one decade ahead of the UK (Heidenheimer, 1981, 295ff).

Countries still differ somewhat with regard to school age definitions. British, Dutch, Greek, Luxembourgian and New Zealand children normally start school at five; other continental Western European (and in some Swiss cantons) at seven; Irish, American, Japanese and Australian at six; Nordic at seven (EC 1990, 10; OECD 1990, 120). In some countries, such as France and New Zealand, and some states/provinces of Australia, Canada and US, entry and exit to/from compulsory education tends to follow the birthday of the individual child, in others the dates of the school year. [6]

> ... One of the most striking changes in attitude towards children as the [19th] century advanced was the emergent view that it was immoral to employ children, a view that was often furthered by the declining economic viability of child labour. ... Yet in 1914 there were still millions of children employed on a full or [more often] part-time basis in Britain.

So writes an historian of 19th-century English childhood (Walvin, 1982, 61). The phenomenon was universal, but Britain was a forerunner both of industrial child labour and of child labour legislation, beginning in 1802. Legislation, not to speak of its enforcement, took a long time to mature. Only in 1873, in the Agricultural Children's Act, did it became illegal to employ children under eight in agricultural work (Walvin, 1982,75).

Minimally effective child labour legislation – that provided with at least some institutions of inspection and enforcement – began with the British Factory Act of 1833 (forbidding the use of children under nine in the textile industry, except silk, and limiting the working week of children for nine to twelve years to 48 hours). In 1867 industry as a whole was covered and, in 1874, the minimum industrial age was set at ten years. France enacted Child Labour law in 1841, whereby the industrial use of under-eight year olds was forbidden, with hour limits prescribed for persons aged eight to twelve, but there was no enforcement provided. Only in 1874 did France adopt German-inspired inspected child labour legislation, with 12 years as the normal age limit for industrial labour. Prussia had enacted a prohibition of industrial child labour, again with 12 as the age limit, in 1853. Twelve years had also been the non-enforced limit of the Swedish Economic Freedom Edict of 1846. This was adopted in the Swedish Factory Act of 1881, in the Dutch acts of 1874 and 1889, and in the Belgian act of 1889. Such legislation usually provided for special limitations on the possible industrial deployment of persons under 14 or 16. The Swiss factory legislation of 1877 and the Austrian of 1885 set the minimum age at14 years. Denmark in 1873 set it at only 10 years.

New England legislation in the 1840s posited no minimum age but did stipulate maximum hours for children under 12. Pennsylvania was the first American state to stipulate a 12-year limit in 1848, but without any enforcement. A breakthrough in the US came only in the last two decades of the 19th century, and only in 1903-6 did the Southern textile states – Alabama, the Carolinas and Georgia – adopt minimum age laws, again at 12 years.

In most cases 19th-century legislation did not cover the use of children on farms, in retail trades or in other small businesses.[7] But in this respect the new vigorated regulation of compulsory schooling soon became relevant.[8] By the 1890s education to age 13 or 14 had been installed everywhere in northwestern Europe, except Holland (1900), Italy (to 12 years from 1904), and Belgium (1914).

The late 19th–early 20th century also saw the consolidation of childhood in another important sense – in penal law. The 104 very young people (children as we would say today) who were sentenced to death at the Old Bailey in London between 1801 and 1836 were apparently not hanged in the end, and in the course of the 19th century an increasing leniency *vis à vis* young offenders tended to develop. Although it did happen, the rule was that children under the age of seven should not be sent to prison (Walvin, 1982, 160).

From the 1870s onwards there developed an international movement of penal reformers and philanthropists aiming to raise the age of criminal responsibility and to establish special juvenile courts and special correction institutions for young offenders. From the beginning the Scandinavian countries played a prominent part in this movement, the Norwegian Child Welfare Act of 1896 establishing the world's first system of juvenile courts, just before the state of Illinois did likewise (Dahl, 1985). A Swedish Child Welfare Act was passed in 1902. In Britain the Children's Act of 1908, by its age delimitation of criminal responsibility, 'confirmed the growing practice of regarding a person as a child until the age of fourteen' (Walvin, 1982, 167).

The age of sexual consent was also raised in the second half of last century, from 11 to 13 in France in 1863 (Levasseur, 1975, 67) and to 15 in 1945; from 12 to 13 in England in 1871, and to 16 in 1885 (Walvin, 1982, 144–5). The legal eligibility for marrying was lower in the latter country, though; in line with canon law, it was 14 for the bridegroom and 12 for the bride till 1929 (Glendon, 1977, 34).[9]

Childhood has never been regarded as ending with full majority, there usually being a period of adolescence in between. In contrast to childhood age limits, the age of majority was not raised in the same period, but had occurred earlier. Since the late Middle Ages it had been at 21 in England and Normandy, an age also selected by the French Revolution from where it spread over the rest of Europe, lowering the majority age in Prussia, for example, from 24 to 21 in 1875. Twenty-one had been the age at which a mounted knight could be expected to be strong enough to wear his armour. But earlier, and for adult males other than knights, 12 to 15 year olds were often considered mature and full-bodied men in Western Europe (Stoljar, 1980, 34–5).

In 1972 a resolution of the Council of Europe set in international motion a lowering of the age of majority to 18 years.

Protection

A further historically recent aspect of current conceptions of children is the notion that they can be abused and maltreated by the people closest to them, by parents and other guardians, and that public authority should intervene against child abuse. Until the late 19th century the protection of children basically comprised only a legal sanctioning of murder, maiming, and incest.

The protection of children against adult cruelty and neglect was to follow only after, and indeed to be modelled upon, interventions against cruelty to animals. In New York in 1873 an eight-year-old girl kept in chains was able to be legally rescued from the persons she had been indentured to only because it could be claimed that, as a human being, she was an animal and thereby protected by the law against cruelty to animals (Stoljar, 1980, 61; Freeman, 1983a, 105). Thereupon a New York Society for the Prevention of Cruelty to Children was formed, mirrored after the already existing organization for animals.[10] From the US the idea spread to England in the 1880s, which, of course also had its own existing animal protection societies (Pinchbeck and Hewitt, 1973, 622).

In 1889 more significant developments began. Britain adopted the Prevention of Cruelty to, and Better Protection of, Children Act, making ill-treatment, neglect, abandonment, and dangerous exposure of a child by its custodian a punishable offence. The initiator expressed his anxiousness in Parliament that children should be given 'the same protection that we give under the Cruelty to Animals Act and the Contagious Diseases Act for Domestic Animals', which went back to 1823 (Pinchbeck and Hewitt,

1973, 625). Legislation protecting children was broadened and consolidated in the Children Act of 1908. In the same year as the first British act, French law opened the possibility of a forfeiture of parental rights over children, basically for otherwise criminal acts against them. But the courts also received a discretionary option to intervene in other cases of ill-treatment. Somewhat earlier, in 1874, partly inspired by the British Infant Life Protection Act, French legislators instituted major regulation and control of the wet-nursing business, which involved about a fourth of all French infants prior to World War I (Sussman, 1976).

The French example of putting some limits to paternal power over children guided similar legislation somewhat later in Germany and Switzerland (Stoljar, 1980, 60ff) and in the Netherlands (Rood-de Boer, 1984, 124ff; Sevenhuijsen, 1987, 145). The Scandinavian child welfare legislation of the 1890s and early 1900s was part of the international 'child saving' and penal reform movements, but seems to have had autonomous legal roots (cf. Dahl, 1985 and Malmström, 1957). In Scandinavia and the US state legal interventions with regard to children in late 19th–early 20th century were bound up with discrepancies between penal reform and juvenile courts (cf. Stoljar, 1980, 61). In other words, the problems of ill-treated children and of delinquent or deviant children were entangled in the minds of both reformers and reform institutions around the turn of the century (cf. Cohen, 1985). Indeed they have remained controversially intertwined in the practices of welfare agencies, courts, corrective institutions and foster parents ever since.

As in factory legislation, Britain was a forerunner of legal child protection, in the latter case together with some American states like New York and Illinois. Both countries experienced strong currents of upper- and middle-class reform, but their problems were also probably more acute and/or visible as a result of gigantic industrial urbanization in Britain and mass immigration in America. Horror stories about children, which are abundant in British social history and in 19th-century reportage and social fiction – mastered by Dickens – are more rare and less distressing in Scandinavia, for instance.

If we think that school learning and freedom from labour are two major elements of modern childhood, childhood became a normal feature of young people's lives only towards the end of the 19th century. At about the same time other significant aspects of the modern status of childhood came into place: general exemption from normal sanctions against crime, protection from illegitimate sexual advances, and from physical violence and maltreatment even from family members.

This constitution of modern childhood is the baseline for the core of this study. Why it happened when it did is outside our scope. However, speculation is permissible about the direction in which the answer might be found. Modern childhood is clearly intimately related to the development of the state (in a non-definitional sense) and of the market. Related to the development of the state in the following ways: becoming more dependent upon the population as a resource for inter-state power, acquiring financial and administrative capacity for ensuring universal education and labour inspection, and opening up to popular forces, using the state as a resource of social change. Related to the development of the market in the following ways: making industry increasingly independent of ultra-cheap, unskilled labour, demanding more educated labour, generating fiscal revenue and separating household income from household production. The constitution of modern childhood should also be seen as part of a broad cultural movement – the rise of modernity – with its novel relationships between individuals and extra-familial and extra-local collectivities.[11]

Children Last: The Rise of Children's Rights

Protective legislation around the turn of the last century created certain paternal and guardianship obligations *vis à vis* children. Universal public education also put children as individuals in a direct relationship with the state. Even with those qualifications, children were still defined as the subordinate members of an hierarchical collective, to the head of which they owed obedience and deference: to the father of the family, to the master of the school, and possibly of other institutions, in *loco parentis* (cf. Stoljar, 1980).

An extension of *egalitarian individualism* is, in broad strokes, what the historical process has been about. It began with adult males gaining rights as equal individuals before the law and in society, with choice of occupation, trade and marriage partner. It continued with women, from the second half of the 19th century, slowly gaining rights as equal individuals instead of only unequal duties as wives, daughters and females. It is in this context of uneven and multilinear development of egalitarian individualism, that the emancipation of children should be seen. That is, the recognition that children too have rights, not only to life, but also to liberty and to the pursuit of happiness.

The emancipation of adult males was a liberation from gerontocracy and from feudalism, slavery and other socioeconomic despotisms. That of women and children has in both cases above all been a process of liberation from patriarchy. The two processes have therefore been closely linked, but they are certainly not identical and may very well be in competition or in conflict with each other.[12] And children came last; freeing a legitimate space for children beneath the weight of paternal power began to occur about half a century after the first significant advances of women.

It is one thing to hint at the contours of a vast and complex process, but quite another to dissect it analytically in a comprehensible way. The different wordings of statutes and law-making court decisions have to be translated into a common, simple language. Without any claim to exhaustiveness, it seems that a substantial proportion of the variations in parent-child relations and children's rights can be formulated by three categories.

One involves the substitution of a child-centred, legitimate and consensual union of parents and children in place of a transcendental paternal hierarchy. The schismatic convulsions of Christianity in the 16th and 17th centuries tightened the screws around the institution of marriage and family which the subsequent secularization of matrimonial jurisdiction did not loosen (cf. Glendon, 1977, 313ff; Malmström, 1957, 126f). Institutional change involves two steps, both of which have to be accomplished for this part of the historical process to be completed. The principles of equal parenthood and of the paramountcy of the best interest of the child in cases of family litigation both have to be embraced, by statute and/or by explicit court practice.[13] Together, the two principles express the establishment of the *child-centred family* as a ruling norm, against both patriarchal superiority and adjudication on the basis of guilt/innocence in broken parental interrelations.

However, not all children are born into two-parent families. Indeed, a good insight into a country's attitude to the rights of children may be gained from the rights, or lack of rights, of children born outside marriage. While historically in a clear minority, in many countries a small minority, the rights of illegitimate children are clearly distinguishable from, and have often been seen as in conflict with, the rights of adults, including adult society at large and, in particular, with adult society's conception of the 'family'. Historically, no other children's right has been perceived as such a threat to adult concerns – be it the authority of the family father, the sanctity of marriage, or the stability of the social order – as that of the 'illegitimate' child (cf. Cornu, 1975; Grossberg, 1985, ch. 6)

Many Western legal systems have condemned these children from the moment they were born. At common law – the Anglo-Saxon legal tradition of both the Old and the New World – an illegitimate child was *filius nullius*, that is 'nobody's child'. The French Code Napoléon of 1804, which also provided the model for the civil law of Belgium, Italy, Luxembourg, Portugal, Spain, the American state of Louisiana and the Canadian province of Québec, had an infamous clause (Article 340) concerning 'illegitimate' children: 'The search for paternity is forbidden.' A recent treatise on comparative law has discussed the legal position of illegitimate children as a defining feature of the Romanistic legal family.[14] By the beginning of the 20th century, all Western countries made a sharp distinction between 'legitimate' and 'illegitimate' children. Perhaps the latest major Western European codification of civil law emphasizing this principle was the Swiss Civil Code of 1907 (Hegenauer, 1976). Shortly before that, it had also been underlined by the German Civil Code of 1896.

Whether or not some children are treated as 'bastards' provides us with a sensitive indicator of the position of children in a society's normative system. As a second aspect of the position of children, then, we shall look at the recognition of equal rights for children born outside of marriage. Two rights are of particular importance in this respect: the right to a father and the right to inheritance equal to that of other children. If and when both paternity and inheritance rights are recognized, we reach a situation of child *equality*, meaning equality between children regardless of their parents' marital status.

A third set of rights refers to and legitimizes the autonomy and the personal *integrity* of the child, both inside and outside the family context. Insofar as it exists at all, this is everywhere a recent phenomenon. In the final analysis this right might be approached in two ways, one minimalist, the other maximalist. The minimalist option would focus on any legal and/or judicial recognition of child autonomy – be it the right to contraceptives or abortion without parental involvement, freedom of expression at school, the legal admonition to parents to pay attention to the wishes of the child or some other matter. If differentiating between countries, it would single out a rearguard – more neutrally put, a set of outliers – still emphasizing patriarchal or parental authority. The maximalist option, on the other hand, would look for the providers of the most extensive children's rights and would then point to a vanguard. That is the option chosen here.

Two rights thus seem to provide decisively differentiating criteria. One is the explicit freedom from corporal punishment, always a deliberately degrading form of sanction. The maximalist option would look at countries in which not only school teachers, but also parents, are legally prohibited from smacking/spanking their children. The other right gives children a legal possibility to divorce their parents or guardians.

The large number of dates of relevant enactments and verdicts can be assembled to form a clear temporal pattern. After the 19th and early 20th century of elementary constitutional protection, there have been two major periods of child legislation, both advancing children's rights. The first started in the mid-1910s and ebbed out by the end of the 1930s. The second spurt of legislation has come from the end of the 1960s to the end of the 1980s peaking, as far as can be seen at present, in the UN Convention of

Table 6.1: The development of children's rights in Western nations[1]

	Rights[2]		
	Child-centred family	Equality	Integrity
By end of World War I	Norway, Sweden	Norway (Sweden)[3]	
By World War II	Denmark, Finland, England, N. Zealand, Scotland (US)[4]	Denmark (Finland)[3]	
By 1970	Australia, Ireland, Germany	Sweden, England, N. Zealand (US),[5] (Germany)[6]	
By 1980	Canada,[7] Austria, France, Italy, Netherlands, Portugal, Spain	Finland, Australia, Canada,[7] (Austria),[6] (Switzerland),[6] (France),[6] Italy, Portugal, Spain	(Norway)[8] (Sweden)[8]
By 1990	Greece	Ireland, Scotland, Austria, Belgium, Netherlands, Greece	(Denmark)[8] (Finland)[8] Norway (Austria)[8]

[1] The nations covered are Australia, Austria, Belgium, Canada, Denmark, England, Finland, France, (West) Germany, Greece, Ireland, Italy, Netherlands, New Zealand, Norway, Portugal, Scotland, Spain, Sweden, Switzerland, US. Within an appropriate cell the countries appear in the order of legal families and of the alphabet.

[2] Child-centered family: explicit legal formulation of equal parental obligations and of the best interest of the child as a paramount principle, e.g. in custody litigation. Equality: equality between children of married and non-married parents with regard to both paternity and inheritance; parentheses refer to significant limitations of equality. Integrity: legal prohibition of corporal punishment by parents and other custodians plus children´s right to divorce their parents/guardians; parentheses refer to limitations.

[3] Paternity rights but not equal inheritance rights.

[4] Great variation of state legislation, but in the 1930s at least a majority of states had adopted equal parental obligations and best interest of the child statutes.

[5] US Supreme Court decisions of 1968 endorsing the principle of equality, but not upholding it in inheritance. Enduring large inter-state variation, both with regard to paternity and inheritance.

[6] Endorsement of principle of equal paternity rights and of paternal inheritance rights, though not quite equally. Formal restrictions on the possibility of paternity proceedings remain.

[7] Both Québec and Anglo-Canada.

[8] Ban of corporal punishment by parents but no recognition of children's right to divorce their parents.

Sources: See Appendix.

the Rights of the Child of 1989 and in the World Summit on Children in 1990.

Both periods may be significantly subdivided, the first between moves made before or after the general anti-authoritarian upheavals in the aftermath of the First World War. (As it turned out, no major change in our three variables was made in the heat of the upheaval itself.) The second may be trichotomized with regard to the two first variables into new vanguard changes made by 1970 (after those accomplished before 1939), international bandwagon advances in the 1970s and rearguard actions of the 1980s.

On the basis of the above distinctions, the development of children's rights may be summed up in Table 6.1 above.

Patterns

The table exhibits two immediately striking kinds of patterns, one temporal, the other spatial. There is, first, a wide time span of more than two generations in the development of children's rights between countries not generally regarded as divergent, like Norway and Sweden on one hand, and Belgium, Netherlands and Switzerland on the other. Among the first 90 years of this century, the decade 1970–80 exhibited particular legislative activity. Children's rights follow a three-stage sequence, from the principle of a child-centred family to child equality to child integrity.

The only exceptions are Belgium and Switzerland, whose civil codes still contain no clear principle of the paramountcy of the interests of the child. (The supremacy of the husband, on the other hand, disappeared from the legal system even there in the course of the 1980s.) Article 156 of the Swiss Code gives the court no concrete guidelines on how to adjudicate custody cases, although the interests of the child do have a tradition in Swiss law, going back at least to the Zürich civil code of 1853 (Huber, 1886, Vol. 1,219). It is true, though, that the practice of the courts in the last two decades has been moving to emphasize parental abilities rather than the guilt of either spouse (Grossen and Guillod, 1989, 284). Article 302 of the Belgian Code invokes the guilt principle in divorce custody cases, stating that any child should go to the innocent party, but continues that the court 'can' also decide according to the best interests of the child.

Secondly, there also clearly emerges a spatial configuration, along the boundaries of the legal style families of nations. In terms of each of the three variables, the Nordic family of nations is on top, witnessing its status as the pioneer. The concentrated location of the Nordic countries in the top left of the table is the most visible family gathering of all. It would be further confirmed, if Iceland were included, having initiated child-oriented and egalitarian legislation as early as 1921–23 (Blom and Tranberg, 1985,

124ff). The Common Law countries tend to cluster second on two of the three variables, where a full family pattern is still discernible. The Germanic family comes next, in spite of long-lived Swiss patriarchy. While Orthodox Greece is clearly part of the rearguard, the Romanistic is the last of the families, concentrated in the lower right part of the table. (Luxembourg would be situated between Belgium and France; see further below.)

The Vanguard

The first breakthrough towards an egalitarian child-centred family and towards equal status for children outside marriage came in the second half of the 1910s in Scandinavia, first formulated in the Norwegian Children's Acts of April 1915 and in the Swedish Marriage Act of 1915 and Marriage Code of 1920. Similar pieces of legislation were passed in Iceland in 1921–23, in Denmark in 1925, and in Finland in 1929. The main thrust of Scandinavian family law was enthronement of affective and egalitarian individualism, the former nicely captured in the official marriage formula of the Swedish Marriage Act of 1915: 'The end of marriage is the welfare of the individuals who desire to enter matrimony' (cf. Rheinstein, 1972, 127n).[15] The new marriage legislation declared an explicit basic equality between husband and wife, father and mother, provided for no-fault divorce (after a procedure of separation), and established the principle of the best interests of the child as the main criterion for deciding issues of custody. For its time, conceived well before World War I and enacted in the late 1910s–early 1920s, this was a unique contribution. The rights of children outside marriage were part of this broader family regulation.

Also in 1915, Norway pioneered the most advanced legislation of child equality, adopted in Iceland in 1921 and somewhat later in Denmark (with regard to equal rights of inheritance, in 1937) (Arnholm, 1959; Krause, 1971, 175ff; Schmidt, 1971, 211). At that time, a Norwegian child born outside of marriage gained the right both to a father and to his name and his inheritance. The latter has more important consequences in civil law countries of the European continent where children with inheritance rights cannot be disinherited by parental will, in contrast to the case of the Anglo-Saxon common law countries (Krause, 1976, 62). Should it not be possible to ascertain the paternity of the child, Norwegian and Icelandic law provided for a special category of male support. If it could be shown, in court, that a man, or two or more men, could possibly have fathered the child, he/they would be obliged to provide support for it. In those cases the child did not obtain rights of name and inheritance, however.

The Swedish law of 1917 was more restrictive (Malmström, 1957) although it did away with the concept of illegitimacy and established the right to paternity. This right was allowed generously, requiring only the possibility that the man in question had been the father. An official committee of jurists proposed in 1954 that all Swedish children should have the same inheritance rights (Malmström, 1957, 134), but this was carried into political effect only in 1970 (Schmidt, 1971, 211). In 1976, the Swedish Parents and Children's Code removed all distinctions between children born 'in wedlock' and 'out of wedlock' (Agell, 1980, 33). The Finnish Illegitimate Children Act of 1922 was the most restrictive of the Nordic acts of the time. It was replaced by the Paternity Act in 1975 (Savolainen, 1986). More recently, the Scandinavian view of a child's right to a father is backed up by a centralized, uniquely elaborate and sophisticated blood-testing system (Krause, 1976, 50ff).

Common Law Variations

After Scandinavia, England (followed by New Zealand) has tended to be relatively child-oriented. In 1925 the Guardianship of Infants Act, which was enacted both for Scotland (Clive, 1982, 551) and England, declared that the child's welfare should be the 'first and paramount' consideration in custody disputes (Eekelaar, 1986, 174). Before that, in 1923, the remaining most blatant legal inequality between husband and wife had been abolished in a new divorce rule. New Zealand was the first common law country to follow suit, with her Welfare of the Child Act of 1926.

Australian courts took notice of the English legislation, but statute-wise the paramountcy of children's interests was not fully established until 1959 (Finlay, 1979, 172).[16] Canada (Shipley, 1986; Stone, 1982) did not take this course till the wave of reform legislation in the late 1970s, and then about the same time in Québec and Ontario. That was after the Irish Guardianship of Infants Act of 1964 (Shatter, 1977, 193–4).

Equality between children came later and only after greater struggle. At common law, a child outside marriage was 'nobody's child', and had only the most elementary right to life. The Poor Law authorities had an interest in acquiring paternal support and paternity proceedings were not prohibited. The Bastardy Laws Amendment Act of 1872 set the British stage for almost a century. The Poor Law Guardians could initiate paternity proceedings, but if no corroborative witness could be found, the case had to be dropped: there was no question of the child's rights. Attempts after World War I to give children out of wedlock a right to inherit were stopped at a parliamentary committee stage (Pinchbeck and Hewitt, ch. XIX). Only in 1969 did the English Family Law Reform Act provide for simplified paternity searches and for equal inheritance rights which, however, can be undone by a will. New Zealand's Status of Children Act, which also gave basic child equality, was of the same year.[17] Scottish legislation, having a family law jurisdiction of her own, although derived from the UK Parliament, remained unchanged. In Scotland, the last declaration of 'bastardy' took place in 1986, before the new Parent and Child (Scotland) Act took effect in December (Sutherland, 1987, 181).

The states of Australia introduced equality between children outside and inside marriage in the mid-1970s (Chisholm, 1983, 17n). As the first province of Canada, Ontario legislated child equality by its 1977 Children's Law Reform Act (Shipley, 1986, 154n), followed soon by Québec, whose new Civil Code of 1980 adhered to both a child-centred family norm and to child equality (section 594 of the Civil Code).

Every formulation of US child law has to be qualified by the complexity inherent in a country with 50 state legislatures plus judge-made law. A large number of states added explicitly patriarchal formulations to their statutes, emphasizing the superiority of the father/husband; these disappeared in a majority of the states only in the course of the 1920s (*Fordham Law Review*, 1936). But a few states, such as Ohio (Glendon, 1977, 183n) retained the concept of husband superiority even in the 1970s' statutes; others made disobedience to parents a delinquency at least in the early 1980s (Brenner, 1983). Although the doctrine of the best interests of the child had emerged in divorce court proceedings in the course of the 19th century, it took a long time to become institutionalized as paramount – hardly before the interwar period. By 1900 equal rights of guardianship between father and mother had been put on the statutes books in nine states only (Grossberg, 1985, 247).

With regard to 'illegitimacy' the American states exhibit an even broader range of variation of application and amendment of Common Law. Arizona and North Dakota followed the Norwegian example of equality, but they were alone, while other pieces of legislation restricted the possibility of ascertaining paternity even in North Dakota (Grossberg, 1985, 232). In 1917 Minnesota adopted a Scandinavian system for settling paternity rights and protecting children of non-married parents. However, according to historian Michael Grossberg (1985, 232), 'This tough statutory language had little immediate impact.' In general, paternity proceedings in the US have been allowed only for obtaining material support from the father to the child's mother. Texas maintained the *filius nullius* doctrine till 1975, which then had to be scrapped upon a Federal Supreme Court decision. In some states, such as in Pennsylvania and in Missouri till it was forced off the books in the mid-1970s, paternity proceedings were heard only under criminal law jurisdiction (Krause, 1976, 35n, 58).

It was in 1968 that the US Supreme Court – in two rulings against Louisiana legislation[18] as a violation of the equal protection clause of the

14th amendment of the US constitution – asserted the principle of equality between children with parents of different marital status (Krause, 1971, 65ff). Most states maintained throughout the 1970s that children outside marriage could inherit only by will,[19] the US Supreme Court upholding such statutes (Krause, 1976, 62–3; Soler et al., 1983, 689n). In 1973 the National Conference of Commissioners of Uniform State Laws promulgated a Uniform Parentage Act, embodying children's legal equality. But by 1983 only ten states had adopted the Act (Krause, 1985, 836).

Germanic Trajectories

In the countries of Germanic law before the reform legislation of the late 1960s and onward, paternity rights were located somewhere between the regulations of the Romanistic and the Scandinavian countries (as in the common law world), albeit in different forms and with a somewhat different rationale. (Krause, 1976; Zweigert and Kötz, 1977, 123ff). The West German legislation of paternity in 1969 is similar to that of Scandinavia (Krause, 1976, 59), but inheritance rights remain somewhat unequal in Germany. By the mid-1970s that inequality was even more pronounced in Austria – where the existence of 'legitimate' children excludes 'illegitimate' ones from inheritance altogether – and in Switzerland, where the latter may inherit only half of the former's right (Krause, 1976, 65–6). In the course of the 1970s, however, elementary egalitarian conceptions were introduced into Austrian family law, and on 1 January 1990 full legal equality between children regardless of parents' marital status went into force. Changes were also made in the Swiss civil law reform bill of 1974: parental rights of 'correction' were no longer mentioned, and respect for children's opinions was advised (Hegenauer, 1976, 345). But full legal recognition of an egalitarian family came only later (see further below).

West Germany started to move somewhat earlier than the other countries of central western Europe, just before the international wave of family reform legislation in the 1970s. In spite of the general provision of equality in the 1949 Constitution, equal rights between father and mother were apparent not very attractive to the political majority of the West German legislature in the 1950s. Four years were allowed to change family law in accordance with the new Constitution. That deadline passed, in 1953, without any legislative action. Only after a clear verdict by the Constitutional Court did the Equality Act ensue in 1957 (Moeller 1989; Glendon, 1977, 119). The 'decisive vote' (Stichentscheid) of the father was replaced by father-mother, husband-wife equality. Further, in the new 1958 formulation, the German Civil Code (section 1671) introduced 'the welfare of the child' (Wohl des Kindes) into German family law (Fthenakis, 1987, 184,

211n). In 1959 the German Constitutional Court declared that 'the welfare of the child' (Kindeswohl) should be the supreme state consideration in family matters.[20] A restricted duty of silence from school counsellors *vis à vis* parents has even been upheld on the basis of that principle (Derleder, 1987, 164ff).

West Germany established elementary equality between children in 1969 and revamped her child-parent legislation very significantly in 1979. The old notion of 'parental power' (elterliche Gewalt) was replaced by 'parental care' (elterliche Sorge). The law admonished parents to let children participate in decisions about their education and upbringing, and against parental use of 'humiliating treatment' of their children (Glendon, 1989, 99).

The Rearguard

The opposite of the Scandinavian model is provided by the countries of Code Napoléon (of 1804), basically in force in France, Italy, Belgium, Luxembourg, Spain and (conservatively reformulated in 1967) in Portugal well into the 1970s.[21] The two most notorious clauses of the Code were section 213, 'The wife owes obedience to her husband', and section 340, 'The search for paternity [of extra-marital children] is forbidden.' Some modifications were later added, first by the courts and then by the legislature, but these were very limited and for the most part did not have the interests of the child in mind. For instance paternity searches came to be allowed in France after 1912, for instance, in cases of rape. In 1938 section 213 was changed, but hardly in any very profound way. For the obedience stipulation was substituted 'the husband is the head of the family [le chef de la famille]' (Dhavenas, 1978, 90–91).

Only in 1970 was the principle of conjugal and parental equality recognized by French law, after a government proposal to modify the head of the family paragraph (by the old and by then discarded German notion of the father's final say) had been rejected by Parliament (Dhavenas, 1978, 107ff). Fathers kept control over children's property till 1985 (Glendon, 1989, 98). The other Romanistic countries followed this lead in the course of the 1970s.

The French remain cautious concerning children's rights. The 1970 change of 'paternal power', into 'parental authority' (from puissance paternelle to autorité parentale) retained some old notions of authority. Though parental duties of care and protection were added, article 371 of the new Civil Code suprisingly retained the Napoleonic formulation that 'A child of any age owes honour and respect to its father and mother' (Glendon, 1989, 98; Terré 1975). A comment on parental admonition was also to be found in the Swiss Civil Code (§ 273) of the mid-1970s (Nowotny, 1975, 586), as well as in the Portuguese Civil Code of 1977 (section 1878) and in the Spanish one of 1981 (section 155), which explicitly advises parents to 'castigate their children in a reasonable and moderate way' (§154) (Bergmann and Ferid, 1955-, Vol. VIII).

Before 1972, even if 'adulterous' children were recognized, they had no inheritance rights in France (Krause, 1976, 63). Thereafter, only paternal violence or admission (implicit or explicit) made paternity proceedings possible (Krause, 1976, 38ff). Very strong restrictions on possible paternity proceedings were also still in force in Belgium, Italy, Netherlands, Portugal and Spain until the mid-1970s (Krause, 1976, 48n; Van der Kaa, 1975, 488; Zweigert and Kötz, 1977, 128ff). The 1975 Italian Family Law Reform, however, did introduce the principle of equal rights between children of parents with different marital status (Kirk, 1975, 696, appendix). So did the Portuguese in 1977 and the Spanish 1978 and 1981, in their new post-dictatorial flurry of legislation. Just before 1980 Luxembourg also gave equal inheritance rights to extra-marital children (Ferid-Filsching, 1969-90, Vol. IV:14). Belgium was condemned in 1979 by the European Court on Human Rights for its discrimination against non-marital children. After that, the relevant paragraphs of inequality ceased to be applicable. However, a new legal formulation was passed only in 1987 (Meulders-Klein, 1990, 409–10).

A further step towards child equality in France was taken in the Malhuret Act of 1987, written mainly with unmarried cohabiting couples and their children in mind. But French courts are still reluctant to process paternity proceedings, and a paragraph (342-4 of the Civil Code) still forbids the child of a mother who has lived 'a life of debauchery' to seek out his/her father! (Rubellin-Devichi, 1988, 148). The old Napoleonic principle of legally protecting males from the consequences of their sexuality at the expense of the rights of children is still echoing in the France of the late 1980s.[22]

Convergence and Integrity

Since the late 1960s and accelerating in the 1980s there has been considerable international development regarding children's rights. The UN has devoted considerable energy to the issue, resulting in the family-oriented Declarations of the Rights of the Child of 1959; a 1967 statement by a UN Human Rights Sub-Commission, that 'every person [born out of wedlock] ... shall have the same legal status as a person born in wedlock' (Krause, 1971, 175); the International Year of the Child in 1979; the work on a Convention on the Rights of the Child, adopted for national ratification by the General Assembly in 1989 (Bailey, 1990, 344ff). In 1975 the European

Convention of Human Rights established the principle of equality between children born outside or inside marriage.The European Court in Strasbourg has defended this against recalcitrant states.

Characteristic of recent developments – apart from a converging tendency to equalize the rights of children inside and outside marriage – have been an increasing attention to and recognition of *children's autonomy and integrity* – in classical human rights language, of their right to liberty and the pursuit of happiness. Put otherwise, one may say that the history of children's rights has been the opposite of T.H. Marshall's (1964) idea of the history of citizenship rights. With regard to children, elementary social rights – of survival, care and education – have come first, and political rights of expression and civil rights of personal autonomy later. The latter developed strongly in school situations, but have also and increasingly been asserted as rights against parents and other custodians.

Leaving aside movements of school pupils in the wake of the students' movements, there appears to have been much more explicit concern with and public debate about children's rights, more active (albeit sporadic) 'children's rights movements' or 'children's liberation movements' (Freeman, 1983a, ch. 1; Wringe, 1981, ch. 1) in the Anglo-Saxon countries – with Britain and in some cases the US in the lead (Bailey, 1990, 350ff) – than on the European continent (cf. Freeman, 1983b and Wringe, 1981 with, e.g., Büchner et al., 1990; Moeller, 1989; Derleder, 1987; Fthenakis, 1987; Michel, 1975; Glendon, 1989, 97ff). In line with the common law tradition, the courts (ultimately the House of Lords and the US Supreme Court) have been very important in establishing children's rights. Due process in custodial proceedings (re Gault), freedom of political expression in schools (Tinker), access to contraceptives (Carey) or advice on contraceptives (Gilick) have been supported against governmental and school authorities and against parents by the US Supreme Court and the British House of Lords in the above-mentioned famous and model-setting cases (Houlgate, 1980, 34ff; Bailey, 1990, 348ff; Hoggett and Pearl, 1987, 388ff). Enlightened legal opinion was expressed by the British Law Commission in its 1982 Report on Illegitimacy as follows: '... the concept of parental rights, in the sense of conferring on a parent control over the person, education, and conduct of his children throughout their minority, reflects an outdated view of family life which has no part to play in a modern system of law' (Glendon, 1989, 100). The sexual rights of young teenagers and the expressive rights of school pupils are the most clear gains of children's rights here.

In the early 1980s there were, however, four American states which still regarded children's disobedience of their parents as delinquent behaviour: Indiana, Minnesota, Missisippi, and West Virginia. In Pennsylvania disobeying one's parents constituted delinquency untill 1972. Almost all other states, Maine being the only complete exception, allow a child to be declared 'dependent' (i.e. put under state supervision) for disobedience. There are also court cases from about 1980 in which such statutes have been upheld (Brenner, 1983). Recent legislative tightening of parental abortion controls at state level has been upheld in 1990, in divided verdicts, by the US Supreme Court, while referring to the possibility of judicial complaint by children (*Time*, 9 July 91).

The last Western countries to institute elementary legal equality in their child law were Belgium (1987), Greece (1983), Ireland (1987), the Netherlands (1986), Scotland (1986), Spain (1978, 1981) and Swtizerland (1977, 1988). The year denotes the coming into force of legislation – or in the Dutch case of Supreme Court jurisdiction[23] – of basic equality of children of married and non-married parents. Belgium, Ireland and the Netherlands had all been indicted by the European Court (Meulders-Klein, 1990, 409; Rood-de Boer, 1987, 144). In Greece and Spain, child equality was part of a revision of the family code, which also at last scrapped legal stipulations of husband superiority, whereas in 1985 Belgium had put into operation the UN Convention against sex discrimination (Meulders-Klein, 1986, 23). In Switzerland, equality between spouses was the object of an 1984 law which, after a narrow referendum victory, became valid law from 1988 (Grossen, 1986, 255; on children's rights from 1977 Guillod, 1989, 312).[24]

The gap between countries, which opened up in the 1910s by the Norwegian-Swedish egalitarian and individualist thrust, has narrowed enormously, but the Nordic countries have remained in the forefront of children's rights. After Swedish children in 1970, Finnish children also gained fully equal inheritance rights, regardless of parental status, in 1975, the last of the Nordic countries in this respect. Divorce legislation has devoted increasing attention to children's rights in the 1970s and 1980s, favouring joint custody by divorced parents, even in the case of previous non-marriage.

Corporal punishment has for long been banned from the schools,[25] and in 1972 Norway abolished the right of parents to spank their children (Lorange Backer, 1982, 192). Sweden followed suit in 1980, Finland in 1983, Denmark in 1985 (Gravesen, 1986a, 85), though without attaching any sanction against parents who did so. A very extensive educational campaign accompanied the Swedish 1980 act, however (Glendon, 1989, 99n), and in Finland spanking parents are deemed to be liable under the Criminal Code (Savolainen, 1986, 118). In Sweden the latter has been decided by an Appellate Court.[26] As the only non-Nordic country to date, Austria adopted a no-spanking law in 1989.[27] In the Anglo-Saxon countries, by contrast, the right of schools to mete out corporal punishment against children was done away with in English state schools and community homes only in 1987, remaining legal in private schools, while that right of parents is hardly even contested (Chisholm, 1983, 45; Freemana, 1983, 653; Soler et al., 1983, 719; Bailey, 1989, 346–7).[28]

Norwegian children have the right to divorce their parents – but parents have no right to leave their children – according to the 1981 Children Act (Bratholm and Matheson, 1983, 559). A Swedish official Commission proposed a similar right in 1987, but it did not materialize (then). Outside the Nordic countries, versions of children's divorce or separation rights exist in the American states of Iowa and Utah (Mintz, 1989, 401) and in the Australian state of Victoria, according to its Children and Young Persons Act of 1989.

Patriarchy, Religion and Law

An explanation of the pattern of uneven development of children's rights among Western nations in the 20th century will here be explored along two lines. One is the cultural context of legal norms concerning children. The assumption is that the latter may be grasped as deriving from a broader, more general set of *Weltanschauungen*, values and norms. The other is the structure of the legal decision-making process. The actors in that process are, of course, the immediate movers of changes in childhood norms. Our explanatory hypothesis is that the variable location of these actors with regard to political resources and constraints has borne upon their legislative and judicial outcomes. Together, the cultural context and the structural location of the actors are expected to furnish us with a plausible account of why children's rights have differed. (For further discussion of this sociological type of explanation, see Therborn, 1991.)

The development of children's rights may be seen as part of a vast cultural process of modernization, whereby certain principles of egalitarian individualism or, alternatively, individualist egalitarianism are asserted. As such, it is parallel to the rise of male civil society and to women's emancipation. The routes to and through modernity still constitute a largely unexplored area from any systematic point of view, in spite of the first maps drawn by Karl Marx's theory of the modes of production and by Max Weber's analyses of comparative religion.[29] While here refraining from investigating the difficult questions of the dynamics of modernity expressed in the long-term trend towards children's emancipation, we shall focus on cultural traditions resisting that process.

This brings us most directly to patriarchy, the rule of the father and the husband. Other things being equal we should expect that the greater children's rights, the less patriarchal the society.[30] This for two reasons: firstly, there should be less concern with the legitimacy-illegitimacy distinction and less protection of fathers from the consequences of sexual forays; secondly, fatherly power over children in the family should be less exempt from public scrutiny and public intervention.

Were there any significant differences in the degree or the extension of patriarchy among Western nations at the beginning of the constitution of modern childhood, on the eve of children's emancipation process? If so, does that cultural legacy covary with the pattern of the emancipation process? And if so, how can we account for the variation of early modern patriarchy? We have seen already that there is a covariation between legal families of nations and children's rights. How can we make sense of that, or is it only a spurious relationship?

From an overview of western family law just before the onset of the emancipation process in the early 20th century, we can distinguish four varieties of patriarchy: Church law and secular traditional variants and moderate and extreme modern variants. In the secular traditional variant, a number of parental and marital rights are invested in the father/husband only. In the moderate modern variant, there is in addition to this certain explicit formulations about who, in the ultimate instance, holds legitimate power in the household, i.e. the father/husband. The extreme modern type adds to the other two an elaboration of patriarchy and husband power, with no explicit concessions to joint parenthood. 'Modern' patriarchy means that all legal stipulations were formulated after 1789 and derive, most immediately, from the cultural contexts of Enlightenment, bourgeois revolution and post-feudal civil society.

If we compare Table 6.2 with Table 6.1, we find that the degree of patriarchy around 1900 is a good predictor of what was to happen in 'the century of the child'. The secular traditional patriarchies equalized first, and the extreme modern patriarchies last. However, legal patriarchy does not single out the Nordic from the Anglo-Saxon countries, as did the later developmental trajectory; moreover Australia and Canada changed more slowly than one would have expected. Austria and Germany did slightly better, and the Netherlands and Switzerland worse. There are obvious reasons to suspect that the degree of initial patriarchy should weigh upon the development of children's rights. But given the convulsively discontinuous modern history of about half of the countries represented,[31] finding a strong link to early 20th-century patriarchy is far from easy.

A second look at Table 6.2, the categorizations of which are made exclusively on the basis of legal texts, reveals another pattern, also far from self-evident. The countries in the secular traditional (least patriarchal) column are all totally or overwhelmingly Protestant; the countries in the far right column are all totally or overwhelmingly Catholic, while those in the middle, of modern moderate partiarchy, are all Protestant with significant

Table 6.2: Forms of legal patriarchy in the early 20th century (before 1914)

Traditional		Modern (Secular)	
Church Law	Secular Law	Moderate	Extreme
Greece	Denmark	(US)[1]	Austria
	Finland	Germany	Belgium
	Iceland	Netherlands	France
	Norway	Switzerland	Italy
	Sweden		Luxembourg
	Australia		Portugal
	Anglo Canada		Québec
	New Zealand		Spain
	UK[2]		

Definitions Traditional: major parental and marital rights invested in the father/husband, but without any explicit post-1789 formulations of the superordination of the husband/father. Modern moderate: major rights plus explicitly formulated powers in the last instance in the husband/father; also explicit recognition of parental authority. Modern extreme: the above without recognition of joint parental authority, plus explicit formulations of the husband/father leading the family.

Notes: [1]A large number of states, but not all, had varieties of patriarchal statutes; Louisiana had Napoleonic patriarchy. [2]Including the whole of Ireland at this time, as well as England, Wales and Scotland.

Sources: General legal overview: Zweigert and Kötz (1987); Scandinavia: Schmidt (1971), Blom and Tranberg (1985); Common Law and UK: Bromley (1974a); Australia: Finlay (1979); Canada: Mendes da Costa (1972), Bala and Clarke (1981); New Zealand: Inglis (1968); US: *Fordham Law Review* (1936–50), Glendon (1977); Germanic countries except the Netherlands: Bromley (1974b), Rheinstein and Glendon 1980); Netherlands: Rood-de Boer (1987), Sevenhuijsen (1987); Romanistic countries: Bromley (1974b), Rheinstein and Glendon (1980); Greece: Moschos (1983).

Catholic minorities. That looks like a perfect fit between patriarchy and religion. Is it?

There are two sets of reason for a certain amount of scepticism in face of this perfect statistical fit. One pertains to the history of Protestantism. There seems to be nothing in the theology nor in the formative historical practice of Protestant societies in the 16th, 17th and 18th centuries which indicates that Lutheranism, Calvinism and Anglicanism (and their main subvariants) should have been significantly less patriarchal than contemporary Catholicism or Orthodoxy.

Secondly, there is the legal history. The bulk of the extremely patriarchal countries were under the Code Napoléon. That Code derived, not from canon law, but from the Enlightenment and the French Revolution, although it did represent a post-Thermidor reversal of the egalitarian family legislation of the revolutionary Convention (cf. Burguière 1991). Indeed, some of its family clauses were in direct contradiction to canon law, for instance by providing for divorce by mutual consent. It spread with the Napoleonic sword and with the general power – intellectual as well as political – of France, but its adopters and admirers were the most secularized intellectual and political forces, more often than not in open conflict with the Church (cf. Zweigert and Kötz, 1987, chs. 6–7). The extremely patriarchal sentences of the Code were inserted at the insistence of Bonaparte personally (Zweigert and Kötz, 1987, 85–6; Glendon, 1977, 182n; 1989, 89n).[32]

There appears to be no evidence of any significant Catholic input into the making of the German and the Swiss Civil Codes of 1896 and 1907 respectively, which would also have been surprising after the *Kulturkampf* and the defeat of the *Sonderbund*. The authors and the legislators of the German Civil Code resisted religious, mainly Catholic, demands for confessional marriage regulations and insisted upon a uniform code. The only significant concession was a formulation in section 1588 that the 'ecclesiastical [kirchliche] obligations with respect to marriage are not touched upon' by the legal stipulations.

The Swiss Civil Code was written by one man, the liberal Basle law professor and journalist, Eugen Huber. He started his work with a systematic history of cantonal law, whereupon he found (Huber 1886, Vol. 1: 50ff) that the German Catholic *Urkantone*[33] had no codified private law; that the centre of Catholic Switzerland, Luzern (as well as Bern) had the Austrian Code as its model; that liberal, Protestant Zürich had a code of its own from 1853 which had also inspired some other cantons; and that the French-speaking cantons and Ticino were under the influence of Code Napoléon. The ensuing Swiss family law turned out quite similar to the earlier Zürcher code in many aspects of key relevance to the present work (cf. Huber 1886, 1: 219ff, 424ff, 488ff; 2: 112ff), including the criteria noted above concerning modern moderate patriarchy (Huber 1886, 1: 434).

The Austrian Civil Code had been written by lawyers of the Enlightenment (Zweigert and Kötz, 1987,147ff, 164ff, 175ff). From a perspective of individual natural law, it accorded children certain rights, of alimony and education, *vis à vis* their parents. Upon church pressure, canonical marriage law was introduced for Catholics in 1855, but in 1868 the Civil Code again became valid for all citizens of Austria. Generally speaking, both before and after the 1866 war, late Habsburg legislation was constructed with a keen eye to Prussian-German developments.

Only in respect of the complicated issues concerning Dutch child legislation about 1900 was there a clear religious – strongly patriarchal – contribution, but the terms of the whole debate were also markedly patriarchal (Sevenhuijsen, 1987, ch. 5).

On the other hand, it may legitimately be contended that to personalize a vast and persistent social phenomenon is not a very satisfactory explanation either. If, in spite of strong prima facie evidence, the Protestant-Catholic/Orthodox divide is rejected as an explanation of the Western pattern of patriarchy, then something else has to be offered.

Temporalities of Cultural Traditions and their Intertwining

The cultural context of the unfolding of children's emancipation should, in my opinion, be seen as an intertwining of at least three different cultural traditions, each having its own particular temporality. One of these traditions is, clearly, religion. The major world religions have always allocated a great deal of attention and concern to family and sexual matters. All of them, even in their younger main subdivisions, like Christian Protestantism, seem to be strongly patriarchal in their orthodox expressions. This may relate to their common pre-modern origin in societies where kinship was central.

In any event, with regard to their effect on patriarchy – and thereby on children – the most important difference of religions, I would posit, is not, as Weber argued with regard to capitalism, the (unintended) consequences of their ethics and their worldview, but their capacity for maintaining an original orthodoxy of doctrine, their grip on their adherents, and their relationship with political power. In all these respects Lutheranism is clearly weaker than the other Christian religions.

As a national church and, in its Germanic and Nordic heartlands a state church, Lutheranism was more exposed to fissiparous and eroding national influences than Catholicism, and more vulnerable to them than the more heavily liturgical Orthodoxy. To the extent that Calvinism became the official church, like the Hervormde Kerk in the Netherlands, it became exposed to the same pressure. Similarly, in the 19th century, the Zwinglian reformation in Zürich become subject to powerful cantonal liberal support for modern, text-critical theology.[34] When massive social change got under way in late 19th century, with the take-off of European industrial capitalism, Lutheranism was put at the losing end of both its characteristic links to political power. As a state church it functioned like a state bureaucracy; also, with the collapse of traditional social controls, it could not (unlike Catholicism and radical Calvinism) reach out and organize the masses of industrial society (see further Therborn, 1989b). This meant a decisive weakening of the popular hold of the Lutheran Church.

On the other hand, contrary to the other main Christian churches, Lutheranism had recognized the legislative power of the state in family matters. By contrast, the supranational Catholic church was rather successfully fighting back, both against the liberal state and against the secularization of the masses. It is noteworthy, that in the major Catholic programme of modern mass organization, the *Rerum novarum* encyclica of 1891, there is (in sections 9 and 10) also a spirited defence of *patria potestas*, of the power of the father. 'Children are something of the father'[35] (Rodriguez, 1964, 258ff). In 1983, though, Catholic Canon Law recognized the equality of wife and husband (Bergmann and Ferid, 1955-, Religiöse Eherechte).

The Nordic countries are all totally Lutheran, and Germany mainly Lutheran. This was favourable for women and children, not because orthodox Lutheranism is less patriarchal but because, by the early 20th century, Lutheranism had become less orthodox and less powerful in its hold over its own adherents.

Legal corpora and legal styles have their own specific internal logic of reasoning and their own specific inertia. Therefore moments of legislation may have very long-term effects. The Code Napoléon was, in fact, not a monster of patriarchy and misogyny, but the earliest of the modern codes. Even with the Napoleonic amendments it was an important step into modernity, into individualist egalitarianism, in particular in family matters with its clauses on female maturity, equal inheritance rights and divorce. As such it was also a model to the most advanced Swedish legal thinkers in early 19th century, to Johan Gabriel Richert above all, the leading male proponent of women's rights. Richert, the guiding spirit of the official Law Commission, proposed a Swedish Civil Code in 1826. Although too radical to be adopted, its marriage part, for instanced include a clear stipulation that the husband was the representative and guardian (målsman) of the wife (Förslag … 1826 Giftermålsbalk, ch. 9).[36]

Once in force and with its special historical aura, the patriarchy of the Code Napoléon acquired a patina of its own. Without its influence, it is difficult to see how, in 1900, a leading enlightened Liberal jurist and politician could have expressed himself like the Dutchman Cort van der Linden did in a parliamentary debate: 'The character of marriage is … in my opinion incompatible with a principled equality between man and woman …' (Sevenhuijsen, 1987, 235). Without this legal tradition it is almost impossible to understand why, in 1938, a left-wing parliament – the 1936 Popular Front majority – should have accepted the argument, 'The French family tradition is [based on] respect for the head of the family', and have put into the Civil Code (instead of the old obedience clause), 'the husband is the head of the family' (Dhavernas, 1978, 90–91). Or why that article was removed only in 1970, after the May 1968 uprising.

The patriarchal Austrian Civil Code, which also sounds extremely patriarchal, was early modern (1811), while Greek family law derived from Orthodox church law, modernized by 19th century German lawyers. It is, of course, also relevant, that these markedly patriarchal legal formulations survive easily in an atmosphere, in which patriarchy, in one form or another, is perceived as the natural order.

Finally, we should keep in mind that certain legal styles are more amenable to normative preaching and to detailed prescription than others. By and large, the civil law traditions are much more prone to this than common law, and than British legal tradition in particular. The terse language of the Nordic legal inheritance, since the Viking age, for instance, in no way lends itself to French or German kinds of admonitions.

The conclusion from this legal interpretation is that the Nordic and the Common Law countries should be expected to have had weaker patriarchal norms by the early 20th century, because their legal framework was older than early modernity (in Sweden, the Code of 1734) and because their inherited legal style did not easily lend itself to general normative prescriptions. On the other hand, the civil law tradition meant that once a work of legal revision had begun it was likely to become far-ranging, much more so than in the Common Law countries.

There is also an irreducible third cultural tradition – patriarchy itself. We can spot it in the different social views of the authors of the German and the Swiss Civil Codes and of the pioneering Nordic family lawyers. Between the former and the latter there was only one or two decades, all in the same Belle Epoque. At least one reason for the difference was probably the different temporality of Nordic modernization.

Patriarchy was very much part of the Nordic cultural tradition, like in other countries. In the first half of the 19th century Scandinavia was in several respects rather more patriarchal than other parts of Western Europe. Men and women got equal inheritance rights in Sweden only in 1845, in Denmark in 1857. Before 1857 in Denmark, and 1858 in Sweden, women, except widows, were neither mature nor in full legal capacity. Only then did unmarried women acquire the status of legal maturity. Towards the end of the 19th century married women got legal rights of their own, but the Swedish 'målsmans' (guardian-representative) institution, going back to Viking times and re-codified in 1734, invested property rights with the husband. This remained till the new marriage code in 1920, in Finland till 1929 (Blom-Tranberg, 1985; Hafström, 1978). This patriarchal background expressed the conditions of a relatively undeveloped cultural periphery, little affected by the Enlightenment and by the French Revolution, still largely touched by commodification, industrialization, and urbanization.[37]

However, common to all the Nordic countries (with the partial exception of Finland) right after the civil war and in the 1930s, there seems to have been an absence of any strong and militant post-traditional conservatism or post-traditional patriarchy.[38] We have already taken notice of the erosion of traditional Lutheran patriarchy.The Lutheran state churches never succeeded in capturing the new popular classes, while the revivalist movements competed between themselves, and tended to align with the Liberals politically against the High church establishment. Such militant family conservatism as there was in Scandinavia came to focus on 'concubinage', on non-marital cohabitation, which was outlawed in Norway in 1902 and only saved from being outlawed in Finland in the late 1930s by the Russo-Finnish Winter War.[39]

The late, rapid (economically), relatively egalitarian, and peaceful route to high modernity in the core countries of Scandinavia – which also had an important moderating influence on Finland, through various forms of Nordic exchange and cooperation – provides an historical reason for this absence. Women and children were the first beneficiaries, because issues of economic and political power were not directly involved. Enlightened male opinion could agree that the former should have rights too, and not-so-enlightened male opinion did not bother (very much).

The cultural traditions of religion, law, and patriarchy, and their interlinked, specific temporalities, all contributed to shaping the cultural context of the development of children's rights as well as to forming the cultural identities of the decisive actors. The legal traditions of the Nordic and of the Common Law countries can account for the absence of elaborate norms of explicit patriarchy. The weakening of official Lutheranism and Anglicanism in industrial mass societies meant that a crucial pillar of patriarchy was undercut. The late but then very rapid and successful socio-economic modernization of Scandinavia reduced opportunities for the consolidation of early modern conservatism in general, and patriarchy in particular. The little known Scandinavian high jurists who made a unique contribution to the global history of children's rights may be seen as sitting on the shoulders of Georg Brandes, Henrik Ibsen, and August Strindberg. The civil law character of Nordic legal practice made it likely, that a change in traditional law would take the form of comprehensive revisions and new codes.

The Nordic configuration of religion, law, and patriarchy provided a favourable cultural context for the modern world's first advance towards children's rights in the 1910s–1920s, most immediately because an enlightened minority was less encumbered by early modernity and met less resistance than elsewhere.

However, a context of a thing should not be confounded with that thing itself. In order to capture the developments of the century of the child, we shall also have to look to some extent into the actual process of decision-making.

Legal Politics

The temporal pattern of developments in children's rights (as in Table 6.1) indicates a special kind of politics. The crucial dates tend not to coincide with other major changes, except for the 1970s–early 1980s, the high plateau of working-class and left-wing politics in the West (cf. Therborn, 1984). Children's rights appear little affected by the waves of democratization after the two World Wars,[40] or by the coming of otherwise very important progressive political regimes, like Scandinavian Social Democracy, the American New Deal, and Australian and New Zealand Labour in the 1930s and 1940s.

The Swedish Marriage Act of 1915 and the 1917 Children Outside Marriage Act – both very early and advanced steps towards individualist egalitarianism in family and child matters – highlight starkly the peculiarity of the kind of legal politics involved here. They were put before the Diet by what the Liberals and the Social Democrats of the time often called 'the Royal Courtyard Coup Government', a clearly conservative (if not reactionary) cabinet with its main parliamentary support in the upper-class First Chamber. It had originally emerged from an extraparliamentary crisis in early 1914 which brought down the Liberal cabinet. Outside Norway, whose pioneering child legislation took place under a Liberal government and was passed by a Liberal-cum-Labour majority, the major Nordic family codes occurred from 1920 to 1929, a decade of stalemate between conservative and progressive forces, not known for major reforms in other areas.

The forces responsible for establishing and changing children's rights have tended to differ considerably from ordinary policy-makers. Jurists have played a decisive part, both as official investigators-cum-law drafters and as judges. And here I am not thinking about legal formulations and legal applications, both trivially invested in the legal profession. The point is rather the *initiative* in legal changes, which to an overwhelming extent has been in the hands of jurists, either preparing statute law or in courts establishing judge-made law. This holds, then, not only for the Common law world,[41] but also for the civil law countries.

On the other hand, with few exceptions – the Norwegian crusader in the 1910s for the rights of 'illegitimate' children, the left-wing liberal Johan Castberg, being one, but he was also a lawyer, a legal civil servant and a judge – politicians have rather dragged their feet.[42] Perhaps the most clearcut case of instigating judicial concern with family equality and the welfare of the child in the face of (majoritarian) political indifference or hostility is West Germany in the 1950s (the reader will remember from above). A similar contrast also emerged above with regard to the relationship between the state legislatures and the US Supreme Court.[43] The rights of children have hardly ever been a popular political slogan, certainly no means to win an election.

Why has this been the case, an issue near to everyday experience and intimately bound up with the core of cultures, as indicated by the fact that in multicultural and multi-religious societies the regulation of family matters is often left to culture-specific laws or customs? The very cultural centrality of parental-child relations should lead us to expect a strong element of cultural conservatism among the carriers of that culture, in particular from its beneficiaries. The main beneficiaries of traditional family cultures are clearly adult males, fathers and husbands. Except for a few recent exceptions, adult males have dominated all modern political systems. Children, on the other hand, have no political clout, and women have had little most of the time. A strong conservative tendency is what we should expect from most politicians with regard to children's rights, and family law more generally.

But why should lawyers have been more child-oriented than politicians? Enlightened minorities of egalitarians have developed in all walks of society. But at least in the northern and central continental European countries, it is not likely that they grow particularly vigorously in the legal profession, because in these countries, the profession of law is dominated by civil servants, by judges and state university academics. Rather, a good bet is that jurists of those countries are even more conservative than other professionals.[44] Probably a better reason why judges have tended to be more respectful of children (and women) than politicians is the formers' professional concern with the logic and consistency of social rules. In modern times, constitutional and other fundamental rules normally express some form or other of legal equality. Politicians however, like most male mortals, have had little trouble harbouring at the same time, individualist, egalitarian, democratic, and/or participatory ideas in society at large, and practising and enjoying patriarchal collectivism, hierarchy, and discipline at home. Then there is, of course, the further reason that among egalitarian individualist minorities, lawyers are the most important for the making and interpreting of laws.

The Structuration of Childhood Politics

From the above-mentioned experiences we may try to put together what seems to be key determinants of the structure of the politics of children's rights. Key actors, though by no means the only ones, are lawyers, in the sense of writers and interpreters of law, and legislators generally. Two sets of resources of and constraints on these actors appear to be crucial. One concerns inputs into legal thinking, the other the location of the legal decision-making process.

Given the characteristic importance of precedence and logic in legal thought, the less a legal system contains of early modern patriarchy, and/or the more it enjoys explicitly egalitarian ground rules, the more room there is for child-friendly legal thought. Nordic children in the early 20th century could clearly benefit from the former; post-war West German children from the latter. Latin children suffered from the Napoleonic outcome of the French Revolution and also, perhaps, from the more immediate tradition of Roman law in the Latin world. If there should be a difference between England and Scotland with regard to children's rights (which in fact we did find above) legal history would lead us to expect Scottish law to be less advanced because more influenced by Roman law, from whose *patria potestas* the early modern paternal power legally derives (Bromley, 1974a, b). Similarly the French South, le Midi, has historically been the bulwark of patriarchy, and the part of France most affected by Roman law.

If the state competence of legislating a certain matter is non-controversial in a religious sense, the better are the opportunities for legislative change. This singles out Lutheran countries favourably over Anglican, Calvinist and Catholic ones with regard to matters of marriage and family. Further, other things being equal, the less the conservative forces of a nation are bound up with religion, the more room there should be for legal recognition of children as equal individuals. This has favoured Nordic and Anglo-Saxon children and has disadvantaged Irish and most continental European children.

Given the fact, that the extension of children's and women's rights so far, has been part of a cultural trend, the more open a legal system is to international debate, the higher the probability of child-friendly inputs. Nordic, and in particular Swedish and Finnish children – born into the most conservative countries in the pioneering period – should have benefited from the intensive and unique inter-Nordic legal cooperation which began in the last quarter of the 19th century. Anglo-Saxon children, particularly in the more peripheral regions of Australia, Canada and New Zealand, should also have benefited from the diffusion of cases and lawyers within the Common Law world. In recent decades the Council of Europe and the

Court of the EC have similarly widened the horizons of Irish and continental European legal systems in favour of children.

With regard to decision-making, we should expect that, other things being equal, the more centrally located the law-drafting body is in the structure of legitimate power, and the more centralized the procedure of legal decision-making, the higher the probability for the legislation of children's rights. This should favour British and New Zealand children over the federal Common Law countries, where child law is a state/province competence. Among the civil law nations, it should clearly disadvantage Swiss children, considering that country's powerful and conservative referendum procedure, and Dutch children, with the Netherlands' cumbersome dualism of Cabinet-Parliament legislating methods. The formal government instability of the French Third and Fourth Republics and of postwar Italy should be expected to have had a conservative effect.

The Nordic countries and Austria-Germany share a long tradition of a state-centred legal profession and of well-established political-legal cooperation at the pinnacle of the state apparatus. By itself, this should have positive effects on children's rights.

The existence of a Constitutional Court or of judicial constitutional reviews of legislation should, *ceteris paribus* and given a democratic constitution, be favourable to children's rights. West German and US children have gained from this. Although Austria was the first European country to establish a Constitutional Court after World War I, it has left no positive imprint on children's rights. This seems to be related to the lower profile of the Austrian court generally in comparison with its West German and US counterparts.

Finally, other things being equal – which, as has been pointed out above, should be taken as a strong qualification – we should expect legislatures with left Liberal, Social Democratic, and (at least non-ruling) Communist majorities to be more favourable to children's rights than those with right-of-centre dominance. Such rights are logically part of the left traditions of Enlightenment, modernity, individualism, and egalitarianism. In the early 20th century this should have favoured children in Denmark, Finland, Norway, Australia, and New Zealand. It should also have benefited children in most countries immediately after World War II and most children in the 1970s-early 1980s.

The Scandinavian Vanguard

It was not only the general cultural context that was strongly favourable to children in Scandinavia. The legal system there was uniquely open to novel, egalitarian and individualist conceptions, without being dominated by them. The politico-legal decision-making system was very favourable to legal change, without being totally geared to reform. Two of the countries, Norway and Denmark, had a highly favourable domestic political situation, though Sweden was still politically conservative, and Finland was an autonomous Russian Grand-Duchy.

Denmark was economically and culturally the most developed Nordic country and, after the fall of the landowners' regime in 1901, had a left-liberal political orientation. By 1915 she had become a full political democracy, with female suffrage and no upper-class political privileges. Norway, till 1905 in a dynastic union with Sweden but with internal autonomy before that, had never had an aristocracy and was the first Nordic country to establish parliamentary government (in 1884) and full male suffrage (in 1898). Like Denmark, Norway had also developed a fully domestic democracy with universal suffrage in 1913. The left Liberals (Venstre, 'Left') were the dominant party in the 1910s, the party of national independence.

The contemporary emergence of a Nordic family of nations gave a strong impetus to comprehensive legal change, and made it possible for Sweden to play an active part in this process, in spite of her First Chamber redoubt of upper-class privilege and her Conservative governments. Legal cooperation for the purposes of unifying Scandinavian law started in 1872 (v. Eyben 1962). This was 20 years before such cooperation began between the states of the US in their areas of legislative competence (Rheinstein, 1972, 42),[45] and two years before the new Swiss constitution gave the federal legislature competence for Swiss legal unification (Zweigert and Kötz, 1987, 175–6). Legal cooperation in Norden has had Denmark, Norway and Sweden as its core. It has usually started on a Swedish initiative, been pushed most enthusiastically by the Danes, and been limited by the Norwegians (v. Eyben, 1962; Schmidt, 1971).

The fields first entered into were aspects of commercial law. Family law came next, with Scandinavian commissions of jurists working from 1909 to 1918 on a major law revision. Among the Nordic lawyers, it was the Danes who most strongly and eloquently argued for women's rights. From the first meetings in the 1870s, Professor Goos set the tone in calling for an egalitarian marriage law (Gravesen, 1986b, 331). The Danish jurists later denounced the recent Danish act of 1899, which provided for the possibility of legal maturity for married women, because it 'did not at all give the wife the independence and equality to which she was entitled' (Schmidt, 1971, 200).

The Norwegians constituted the children's vanguard, and here a political initiative was crucial; this was taken by the radical Liberal politician Johan Castberg (Arnholm, 1959, 15). The Swedes distinguished themselves only by being the first to codify the common recommendations. Their 1915

Marriage Act largely involved catching up with Danish and Norwegian statutes and practice. But it also expressed, as we saw above, some beautiful formulations of a principled affective individualist view of marriage.

Legal power was still all male, whether it was used for or against egalitarian individualist reform. However, the Scandinavian vanguard also involved women fighters. On the eve of World War I, women's organizations were regarded, as legitimate bodies to be consulted on the drafts of family law reform (Bentson, 1924). A driving force behind Castberg and the Norwegian children's laws was a woman, Katti Anker Møller, and an active, though divided, women's movement (Rosenberg, 1981).

Norwegian left-wing Liberalism and the lawyers' interactions in the Nordic cultural and legal family of nations thus opened the Century of the Child. Neither has left any strong and enduring memories, but it has taken the rest of Western Europe 70 to 75 years to catch up with their achievement.

Notes

1. Although clearly a sideshow of world politics, the meeting in New York on 29–30 September 1990 was attended by 70 heads of state, including those of the superpowers. Little concrete came out of it except an endorsement of UNICEF's goals for international child health, bearing primarily upon conditions in the Third World, and a call for ratification of the UN Convention of the Rights of the Child, adopted by the General Assembly on 20 November 1989. By the time of the summit 48 countries had ratified the Convention. *Keesing's Contemporary Archives* 1990, 37732; 1989, 37054.
2. For an international location of Key and her book, see Romein, 1978, ch. XLI.
3. I have to plead guilty to some big state bias. Luxembourg and Iceland will be touched upon only occasionally. There is hardly any other excuse than laziness; it is, of course, easy to be lazy in the company of most other comparativists.
4. The UN Convention of the Rights of the Child defines a child as a person under 18, unless the country's age of majority is lower.
5. The Catholic conservatives were against the idea of compulsory schooling, but its introduction was also delayed by entanglement in clerical-anticlerical politics. By 1900, a fifth of the Belgian population was still illiterate (Kossman, 1978, 507).
6. Iceland originally had a uniquely high age of obligatory school entry, 10 years according to the 1901 Act (Blom and Tranberg, 1985, 121).
7. Child labour legislation has been little studied on a systematic cross-national basis, nor is it covered by the handbook literature. An accessible overview used above is Nardinelli (1990, chs. V–VI) who covers elements concerning Britain, France, Germany, Japan and the US. Other sources used here have been Tálos (1981, 16ff, 52ff; Austria), Walvin (1982; Britain), Harmsen and Reinalda (1975, 46ff; Netherlands), Olsson (1980; Sweden), Stadler (1991, 140; Switzerland).
8. At the outset there was not necessarily coordination between industrial and education legislation, however. In France, for example, the 1874 child labour law was in

several respects contradicted by the Ferry laws of education of 1879–86, giving rise to inter-ministerial conflict (Weissbach, 1989, 214–15) until the working-age limit was set equal to the end of compulsory education (Heywood, 1988, ch. II).

9. It was raised to 16 in order to avoid any 'stones and glasshouse' effect so that the empire could take part in good faith in a League of Nations effort against child marriages in India and other countries. In Greece, even in the early 1970s, a woman at the age of ten could enter into a valid marriage with her parents' consent (Siampos, 1975, 377).
10. The New York SPCC soon became a very powerful organisation, taking abusive parents to court and putting children into institutional care. The latter was of course controversial, then as now (Ferguson Clement, 1985, 262–3).
11. To me, this vast historical process seems to provide a more promising cultural context than the disembodied '"sacralisation" of children's lives', which Viviana Zelizer (1985) invokes in her empirically very interesting book on the changing social value of children occurring around the turn of the last century.
12. A telling example includes the English Guardianship of Infants Act of 1925 and the Alberta (Canada) Domestic Relations Act of 1927. The English act equalized parental rights and subordinated them to the paramount interests of the child. This was an epochal step, but it had the limitation of coming into operation only when a case was in court proceedings and of not abrogating the common law assumption of parental rights as synonymous with paternal rights. For that, the Act was criticized by women. The Alberta legislature, for its part, strengthened the stipulations of parental equality, but omitted the paramountcy of children's interest (Stone, 1982, 47n).
13. As used here, 'the best interests of the child' does not exclude the possibility of a judicial presumption in favour of one of the parents (eg. the mother with regard to small children) as being the best guardian. Jon Elster (1989, 130ff) discusses a more specific interpretation of the rule, while giving the impression that the principle itself dates back only to the 1970s.
14. Zweigert and Kötz, 1987, 134: 'The Legal Position of Illegitimate Children: A Distinctive Feature of the Style of the Romanistic Legal Family'; spelled out in Zweigert and Kötz, 1977, 123 ff.
15. This may be compared with the pronunciation, only a few years earlier, by the Austrian Supreme Court on section 44 of the Austrian Civil Code: the sole purpose of marriage is procreation (Ornauer, 1975, 113).
16. That is, by the Commonwealth Matrimonial Causes Act. Victoria had a similar piece of legislation passed in 1958; New South Wales in 1934 (Joske, 1969, 644n).
17. Earlier than other members of the British Empire/Commonwealth, New Zealand had provided for the possibility of granting children legitimacy (Inglis, 1968, 9).
18. Alone among the states of US, Louisiana has a legal system derived from Code Napoléon. A combination of that tradition with a native blend of common law made Louisiana law and courts the most extremely inegalitarian of the Union. The two cases in which the US Supreme Court intervened concerned claims against tortfeasors by a mother for the wrongful death of her 'illegitimate' child, and by a child for the wrongful death of his non-married mother (see further Krause, 1971, 65ff, incl. notes 44 and 52).
19. Alaska, North Dakota and Oregon did, however, abolish the concept of (il)legitimacy in the 1960s (Krause, 1976, 36n).
20. The formulation could, of course, have an ambiguous meaning. In Germany it was first used by the Nazi marriage law of 1938. There may have been state and natalistic interests behind that formulation, but in comparison with the 1896 Civil Code, the

1938 marriage law may also be considered progressive, allowing couples over 18 to marry without parental consent and introducing no-fault divorce. See further Glendon (1977, 31ff, 215ff) and Rheinstein and Glendon (1980, 24).

21. Also Dutch civil law, the Burgerlijk Wetboek of 1838, derived largely from the Code Napoléon (Zweigert and Kötz, 1987, 104).
22. Contrast this with the explicit provision, mentioned above, by the Norwegian legislature of 1915 and by the Icelandic in 1921 for the male to support the children of polygamous women.
23. The verdict basically did away with the old Dutch distinction between children of two married parents having parents, and all other children having a guardian (Rood-de Boer, 1987, 144–5).
24. Husband-wife equality won a 55–45 all-Swiss majority, largely due to massive support in the francophone cantons. In most of German-speaking Switzerland, there was a majority for legal husband superiority (Grossen, 1986, 255).
25. In Norway physical punishment in schools is forbidden by the 1969 Elementary Education Act (Bratholm and Matheson, 1983, 576). In Sweden it was prohibited in the late 1940s as an outcome of the preparatory work on a comprehensive school system proposal. It took the form of a change in the Elementary Schools Statute (Folkskolestadgan).
26. The Swedish Children in Marriage Act, which was in force until the Parental Code of 1949, included a castigation clause, which had its equivalent in the Criminal Code's restrictive formulations about damage by physical violence, if the latter had been inflicted by a parent or guardian. Only in 1957 was that legal leniency abolished.
27. Bundesombudsfrau Dr. Naber (Familieministerium) oral communication.
28. In Australia some states have also abolished physical punishment in state schools (John Seymour of the ANU Law School personal communication 1991), as have two American states, Massachusetts and New Jersey (Soler et al., 1983, 719).
29. For a modest contribution with regard to the development of the right to vote, see Therborn (1992).
30. That is, at least from the beginning of modernity and the decline of kinship, clientage and community, and the rise of the nuclear family. The pre-modern 'open lineage family' was much more callous to children (Stone, 1977, part II).
31. Very different regimes in Finland, Germany, Austria, France, Italy, Portugal, Spain and Greece; foreign occupation and liberation from it in Denmark, Norway, Netherlands and Belgium.
32. Bonaparte took a very active part in the final wording of the Code, both as First Consul and as chairman of the Conseil d'État which went over the first draft. He attended 57 of the latter's 102 meetings and directed the legislative decision-making process.
33. Uri, Schwyz, Unterwalden. The situation was similar in Appenzell, Thurgau, St. Gallen and Basle.
34. The Zürich liberal politicans invited the German philosopher-theologian David Friedrich Strauss, the author of a famous text-critical work on the Evangelists, *The Life of Jesus*, to their town as professor of the Theology of the New Testament, an affair which led to a miniature civil war. This was a setback but finally led to a victorious comeback of Liberalism (Craig, 1988, 65ff).
35. *Filii sunt aliguid patris*, emphasis in the original.
36. A brief account in English of how the Code Napoléon was once the ideal of radical Swedes is given by Zweigert and Kötz (1987, 290).

37. In one respect at least, Scandinavian law was less patriarchal than the Code of Napoléon even apart from general rules. The former had, in contrast to the latter, a symmetrical view of male and female adultery.
38. Telling manifestations of the latter are post-revolutionary, pre-Restoration clauses of the Code Napoléon legally requiring of a son under 30 and a daughter under 25 a ceremonial request of parental consent to marry, a system finally abolished only in 1933; also the stipulation of the 1896 Civil Code of the German Reich requiring parental consent to marry for sons and daughters under 25, a rule abolished only by the Nazis (Glendon, 1977, 29ff).
39. The Norwegian statute remained in effect till 1972 (Bull, 1986, 45). In the 1930s, when authoritarianism was ascendant in Finland, the Finnish government, upon instigation by the Lutheran church (much more powerful in post-Civil War Finland than anywhere else in Norden), prepared a bill outlawing non-marital cohabitation with the punishment of imprisonment. The Finnish-Russian Winter War of 1939–40 and the subsequent mood of national reconciliation put an end to that plan (Mahkonen, 1988, 127ff).
40. Democratization in Portugal and Spain, but not in Greece, did have fairly direct effects though.
41. Cf. an overview of the key actors in the family law reform process in the 1980s in the Canadian jurisdictions of Alberta, British Columbia, Ontario and the Yukon, who were all lawyers except for one senior civil servant in BC (Barnhorst, 1986, 281).
42. We have noticed above that this held also for Swedish politicians in the 1950s and 1960s, deciding not to implement a Law Commission proposal of equal rights for children inside and outside of wedlock. Even in Norway in 1913–15, law-making gathered a momentum of its own. The 'Castbergske children laws' were actually passed a year after Castberg had left the Cabinet after a tariff conflict with the Prime Minister.
43. A relationship of conflict and 'compromise' between a conservative legislature and its statutes on the one hand and liberal courts on the other seems to a common feature of the American politico-legal system (Rheinstein, 1972, 257–8).
44. Late 19th century Norway is a telling example. Between 1880 and 1900, 12 persons held chairs of law at the country's single university. Each one was a conservative, and five served as Conservative cabinet ministers (Dahl, 1985, 148).
45. The background was the tendency of New Yorkers to seek divorce in more permissive states. The first session of the National Conference of Commissioners on Uniform State Laws was held in 1892, exactly 20 years after the first Nordic meeting.

Appendix: Sources of Table 6.1

A. Cross-national legal sourcebooks: Bergmann and Ferid (1955-); Ferid and Filsching (1969–90)

B. Cross-national legal overviews of inter-parental and parent-child legislation and jurisdiction: Bromley (1974b); Glendon (1977, 1989); Zweigert and Kötz (1977, 1987); Krause (1976); Rheinstein and Glendon (1980); Stoljar (1980)

C. Nordic legal overview: Blom and Tranberg (1985)

D. National sources:
Denmark: Koch-Nielsen (1975); Graversen (1986a, 1986b); Schmidt (1971)
Finland: Lindgren (1975); Mahkonen (1988); Savolainen (1986)
Norway: Arnholm (1959); Bratholm and Matheson (1983); Lorange Backer (1982)
Sweden: Beckman and Höglund (1983–90); Hafström (1978); Malmström (1957); Saldeen (1988); Schmidt (1971)
Australia: Chisholm (1983); Finlay (1979); Mr. P. Bailey (1991, ANU interview); Mr. J. Seymour (1991, ANU interview); Joske (1969)
Canada: Bala and Clarke (1983); Bala and Bissett-Johnson (1988); Barnhorst (1986); Brierley (1972); Shipley (1986); Statutes of Quebec; Stone (1982)
England: Bromley (1974a); Freeman (1983b, 1988),
Ireland: Bromley (1974a); Duncan (1986, 1988); Kirk (1975); Shatter (1977)
New Zealand: New Zealand Statutes 1926, 1969; Casey (1979); Ms. Helen Clark, MP (1991, oral communication); Inglis (1968)
Scotland: Bromley (1974a); Sutherland (1987, 1990); Clive (1982)
US: *Fordham Law Review* (1936); Krause (1971, 1977, 1985); Mintz (1989); Soler et al. (1983)
Austria: Krebs and Schwartz (1978); Bundesombudfrau Dr. Naber (oral communication, 1991); Ornauer (1975)
Germany: Derleder (1987); Frank (1990); Fthenakis (1987)
Netherlands: Rood-de Boer (1987); Van der Kaa (1975)
Switzerland: Grossen (1986); Guillod (1989); Hegenauer (1976); Nowotny (1975)
Belgium: Lohlé-Tart (1975); Meulders-Klein (1986, 1990)
France: Cornu (1975); Rubellin-Devichi (1986, 1988); Terré (1975)
Italy: Ferrari (1975); Kirk (1975: appendix); Moro (1991)
Portugal: Varela (1987)
Spain: Garcia Cantero (1989); Castan Tobeñas (1985)
Greece: Koumantos (1986); Moschos (1983); Siampos (1975)

References

Agell, A. (1980), 'Swedish Legislation on Marriage and Cohabitation', *Scandinavian Studies in Law*, **24**, 9–48

Archer, M. (1977), *Social Origins of Educational Systems*, London: Sage.

Ariès, P (1962), *Centuries of Childhood*, London: Jonathan Cape.

Armitage, A. (1978), 'Canada' in S. Kamerman and A. Kahn (eds), *Family Policy*, New York: Columbia University Press, 367–99.

Arnholm,C.J. (1959), 'The New Norwegian Legislation Relating to Parents and Children', *Scandinavian Studies in Law*, **3**,9–20.

Bailey, P. (1990), *Human Rights: Australia in an International Context*, Sydney: Butterworths.

Bala, N. and Clarke, K.L. (1981), *The Child and the Law*, Toronto: McGraw Hill Ayersen Ltd.

Bala, N. and Bissett-Johnson, A. (1988),'Canada: Supreme Court Thunder – Abortion, Finality of Separation Agreements, Custody, and Aceess', *Journal of Family Law*, **27**.

Bala, N. and Clarke, K. (1980), *The Child and the Law*, Toronto: McGraw Hill-Ryerson.

Baldock, C. and Cass, B. (eds) (1988), *Women, Social Welfare and the State*, 2nd ed., North Sydney: Allen and Unwin.

Bardy, M. et al. (1990–91), *Childhood as a Social Phenomenon*, Vienna: European Center, Eurosocial, Vol. 36.

Barnhorst, R. (1986), 'Child Protection Legislation: Recent Canadian Reform' in B. Landau (ed.), *Children's Rights in the Practice of Family Law*, Toronto: Carswell.

Bates, F. (ed.) (1976), *The Child and the Law* I–II, Dobbs Ferry, N.Y.: Oceana.

Bentson, V. (1924), *Familieretten I*, Copenhagen: G.E.C. Gobi.

Bergmann, A. and Ferid, M. (eds) (1955), *Internationales Ehe- und Kindschaftsrecht*, Frankfurt: Verlag für Standeswesen.

Blom, I. and Tranberg, A. (1985), *Nordisk lovoversikt*, Oslo: Nordisk Ministerråd.

Boh, K. et al.(eds), (1989), *Changing Patterns of European Family Life*, London: Routledge.

Bratholm, A. and Matheson, W. (1983), 'The Rights of the Child in Norway' in A.M. Pappas (ed.), *Law and the State of the Child*, New York: UNITAR, Vol. 2, 537–600.

Brenner, S. Wolf (1983), 'Disobedience and Juvenile Justice: Constitutional Ramifications of Childhood as a "Moral" Concept', *Journal of Family Law*, **21**, 457–96.

Brierley, J.E.C (1972), 'Husband and Wife in the Law of Québec: A 1970 Conspectus' in D. Mendes da Costa (ed.), *Studies in Canadian Family Law*, Toronto: Butterworth, Vol. 2.

Bromley, P.M. (1974a), 'The Law of the United Kingdom and the Republic of Ireland', in Council of Europe, *Legal Representation of Minors*, Strasbourg: Council of Europe.

Bromley, P.M. (1974b), 'Meaning of "Legal Representation" and "Custody"' in Council of Europe', *op. cit.*

Büchner, P. et al. (eds.) (1990), *Kindheit und Jugend im interkulturellen Vergleich*, Opladen: Leske & Budrich.

Bull, K. Strøm (1986), 'Non-Marital Cohabitation in Norway', *Scandinavian Studies in Law*, **30**, 29–48.

Casey, M.E. (1979), 'Custody of Children', *New Zealand Universities Law Review*, **8**, 345–58.

Castan Tobeñas, J. (1985), *Derecho Civil Español, Común y Foral*, Madrid: Reus.

Chisholm, R. (1983), 'Children and the Law in Australia' in A.M. Pappas (ed.), *Law and the State of the Child*, New York: UNITAR, Vol. 1, 1–69.

Clive, E. (1982), *The Law of Husband and Wife in Scotland*, Edinburgh: W. Green & Son.

Cohen, R. (1985), 'Child Saving and Progressivism, 1885–1915' in J. Hawes and R. Hiner (eds), *American Childhood*, Westport, Conn.: Greenwood Press, 273–310.

Cooter, R. (ed.) (1992), *In the Name of the Child*, London: Routledge.
Cornia, G.A. and Sipos, S. (eds) (1991), *Children and the Transition to Market Economy*, Aldershot: Avebury.
Cornu, G. (1975), 'La filiation', *Archives de la philosophie du droit*, **20**, 29–44.
Council of Europe (1974), *Legal Presentation and Custody of Minors*, Strasbourg.
Craig, G. (1988), *Geld und Geist. Zürich im zeitalter des Liberalismus 1830–1869*, Munich: C.H. Beck.
Dahl, T. Stang (1985), *Child Welfare and Social Defence*, Oslo: Norwegian University Press.
DeMause, L. (1974), *The History of Childhood*, New York: Harper & Row.
Derleder, F. (1987), 'Verfassungsaentwicklung und Familienwandel', *Jahrbuch für Rechtssoziologie und Rechtstheorie*, **12**, 162–81.
Dhavenas, O. (1978), *Droit des femmes, pouvoir des hommes*, Paris: Seuil.
Donzelot, J. (1977), *La police des familles*, Paris: Ed. de Minuit.
Duncan, W. (1986), 'Ireland: Waiting for Divorce', *Journal of Family Law*, **25**, 155–66.
Duncan, W. (1988), 'Ireland: The Status of Children and the Protection of Marriage', *Journal of Family Law*, **27**.
Edgar, D. et al. (eds) (1989), *Child Poverty*, Sydney: Allen & Unwin.
Eekelaar, J. (1986), 'The Emergence of Children's Rights', *Oxford Journal of Legal Studies*, **6** (2),161–82.
Elster, J. (1989), *Solomonic Judgments*, Cambridge: Cambridge University Press.
Eyben, W.E.V. (1962), 'Inter-Nordic Legislative Co-operation', *Scandinavian Studies in Law*, **6**, 65–93.
Ferguson Clement, P. (1985), 'The City and the Child, 1860–1885' in J. Hawes and R. Hiner (eds), *American Childhood*, Westport, Conn.: Greenwood Press, 235–74.
Ferid, M. and Filsching, K. (eds) (1969–90) *Internationales Erbrecht*, München: C.H. Beck, 7 vols.
Ferrari, G.(1975), 'Law and Fertility in Italy' in M. Kirk et al.(eds), *Law and Fertility in Europe*, Dolhain: Ordina, Vol.2, 426–61.
Finlay, H.A. (1979), *Family Law in Australia*, Sydney: Butterworth.
Flandrin, J.-L. (1979), *Families in Former Times*, Cambridge: Cambridge University Press.
Flora, P. (ed.) (1983, 1987), *State, Economy and Society in Europe 1815–1975*, Frankfurt and New York: Campus, 2 vols.
Fordham Law Review (1936–50), 'Comments', reprinted in *Selected Essays on Family Law*, compiled and edited by a committee of the Association of American Law Schools, Brooklyn: The Foundation Press, 607–14.
Förslag till allmän civillag, Stockholm: 1826.
Frank, R. (1990), 'Germany, Federal Republic of: Changes and Continuity in Family Law', *Journal of Family Law*, **28**, 508–71.
Freeman, M. (1983a), *The Rights and Wrongs of Children*, London: Frances Pinter.
Freeman, M. (ed.) (1983b), 'The Rights of Children in England' in A.M. Pappas, *Law and the State of the Child*, New York: UNITAR, Vol 2, 601–74.

Freeman, M. (ed), (1984), *The State, the Law, and the Family*, London: Tavistock.

Freeman, M. (1988), 'England's Moral Quagmire', *Journal of Family Law* , **27**, 101–25.

Frijhoff, W. (1983), *L'offre d'école. The Supply of Schooling*, Paris: Publications de la Sorbonne.

Fthenakis, W. (1987), 'Psychologische Beiträge zur Bestimmung von Kindeswohl und elterlicher Verantwortung', *Jahrbuch für Rechtssoziologie und Rechtstheorie*, **12**,182–224.

Garcia Cantero, G. (1989), 'Spain: Family in the Eighties', *Journal of Family Law*, **27**, 281–93.

Genovese, R. (ed.) (1984), *Families and Change*, New York, Praeger.

Glendon, M. (1977), *State, Law and Family*, Amsterdam, North-Holland.

Glendon, M. (1989), *The Transformation of Family Law*, Chicago: Chicago University Press.

Gravesen, J. (1986a), 'Denmark: Custody Reform', *Journal of Family Law*, **25**.

Gravesen, J. et al. (1986b), *Familieret*, Copenhagen: Juristforbundets Forlag.

Grinde, T.V. (1979), *Barn og barnevern i Norden*, Oslo: Tano.

Grossberg, M. (1985), *Governing the Hearth*, Chapel Hill: University of North Carolina Press.

Grossen, J.M. (1986), 'Switzerland: Further Steps Towards Equality', *Journal of Family Law*, **25**, 255–9.

Grossen, J.M. and Guillod, O. (1989), 'Le concubinage en droit suisse' in J. Rubellin-Devichi (ed.), *Les concubinages en Europe*, Paris: CNRS.

Guillod, O. (1989),'Switzerland: Hints of Things To Come', *Journal of Family Law*, **27**, 305–13.

Hafström, G. (1978), *Den svenska familjerättens historia*, 9th ed., Lund: Studentlitteratur.

Harmsen, G. and Reinalda, B. (1975), *Voor de bevrijding van de arbeid*, Nijmegen: SUN.

Hawes, J. (1991), *The Children's Rights Movement*, Boston: Twayne.

Hawes, J. and Hiner, R. (eds) (1985), *American Childhood*. Westport, Conn.: Greenwood Press.

Hayes, C. (ed.) (1982), *Making Policies for Children*, Washington D.C.: National Academy Press.

Hegenauer, C. (1976), 'Civil Law Reform in Switzerland' in F. Bates (ed.),*The Child and the Law*, Vol. II, Dobbs Ferry, N.Y.: Oceana.

Heidenheimer, A. (1981), 'Education and Social Security Entitlements in Europe and America' in P. Flora and A. Heidenheimer (eds), *The Development of Welfare States in Europe and America*, New Brunswick: Transaction Books.

Heidenheimer, A. et al. (1990), *Comparative Public Policy*, 3rd ed., New York: St. Martin's Press.

Hess, B. (1984), 'Protecting the American Family: Public Policy, Family and the New Right' in R. Genovese (ed.), *Families and Change*, New York: Praeger, 11-21.

Heywood, C. (1988), *Childhood in Nineteenth Century France*, Cambridge: Cambridge University Press.

Hoggett, B. and Pearl, D. (1987), *The Family, Law and Society*, London: Butterworth.

Howe, B. (1989), 'Statement' in D. Edgar et al. (eds), *Child Poverty*, Sydney: Allen & Unwin.

Houlgate, L.D. (1980), *The Child and the State: A Normative Theory of Juvenile Rights*, Baltimore: John Hopkins University Press.

Inglis, B.D. (1968), *Family Law*, Vol. 1, 2nd ed., Wellington: Sweet & Maxwell.

Jacobsson, G. (1988), *Familjen i välfärdsstaten*, Åbo: Åbo Akademis Förlag.

Johanson, R. (1987), 'Centuries of Childhood/Centuries of Parenting: Philippe Ariès and the Modernization of Privileged Infancy', *Journal of Family History*, **12**, 343–65.

Johansson, E. (1981), 'The History of Literacy in Sweden' in H. Graff (ed.), *Literacy and Social Development in the West*, Cambridge: Cambridge University Press.

Johnson, D. (1990), 'A Multidimensional History of Early Modern Western Childhood', *Journal of Comparative Family Studies*, **XXI**, 1–11.

Jordan, T. (1987), *Victorian Childhood*, Albany: State University of New York Press.

Joske, P.E. (1969), *Matrimonial Causes and Marriage Law and Practice*, Sydney: Butterworths.

Kamerman, S., and Kahn, A. (eds), (1978), *Family Policy*, New York: Columbia University Press, 1978.

Key, E. (1900), *Barnets århundrade*, Stockholm: Albert Bonniers.

Kirk, M. (1975), 'Ireland' in M. Kirk et al. (eds), *Law and Fertility in Europe*, Dolhain: Ordina, Vol. 2.

Kirk, M. et al. (eds) (1975), *Law and Fertility in Europe*, Dolhain: Ordina, 2 vols.

Koch-Nielsen, I. et al. (1975), 'Law and Fertility in Denmark' in M. Kirk et al. (eds), *Law and Fertility in Europe*, Dolhain: Ordina, Vol. 1.

Kossman, E.H. (1978), *The Low Countries 1780–1940*, Oxford: Clarendon Press.

Koumantos, G. (1986), 'Greece: Towards Freedom from Discrimination', *Journal of Family Law*, **25**, 137–49.

Krause, H. (1971), *Illegitimacy: Law and Social Policy*, Indianapolis: Bobbs-Merrill.

Krause, H. (1976), 'Creation of Relationships of Kinship', *International Encyclopedia of Comparative Law*, Tübingen: J.C.B. Mohr.

Krause, H. (1977), *Family Law in a Nutshell*, St. Paul Minn.: West.

Krause, H. (1985), *Family Law*, 2nd ed., St. Paul Minn.: West.

Krebs, E. and Schwartz, M. (1978), 'Austria' in S. Kamerman and A. Kahn (eds), *Government and Families in Fourteen Countries*, New York: Columbia University Press, 185–216.

Krieken, R. van (1992), *Children and the State. Social Control and the Formation of Australian Child Welfare*, Sydney: Allen & Unwin.

Levasseur, G. (1975), 'Les transformations du droit pénal concernant la vie familiale', *Archives de philosophie du droit*, **20**, 57–70.

Lindgren, J. (1975), 'Finland' in M. Kirk *et al.* (eds), *Law and Fertility in Europe*, Dolhain: Ordina, 1975, Vol. 1.

Lødrup, P. (1987), 'Norway: Reforming the Law of Matrimonial Property and Maintenance and Artificial Insemination', *Journal of Family Law*, **27**, 253–60.

Lohlé-Tart, L. (1975), 'Belgium' in M. Kirk et al. (eds), *Law and Fertility in Europe*, Dolhain: Ordina, Vol. 1.

Lorang Backer, I. (1982), *Barneloven*, Oslo: Universitetsforlaget.

Mahkonen, S. (1988), 'From Control of the Family to its Autonomy', *Scandinavian Studies in Law*, **32**, 117–34.

Malmström, Å. (1957), 'Children's Welfare in Family Law', *Scandinavian Studies in Law*, Vol. l, 123–36.

Marshall, T.H. (1964), *Sociology at the Crossroads*, New York: Doubleday.

Maynes, M.J. (1985), *Schooling in Western Europe*, Albany, NY: State University of New York Press.

Mendes da Costa, D. (ed.) (1972), *Studies in Canadian Family Law*, Toronto: Butterworth, 2 vols.

Meulders-Klein, M.-T. (1986), 'Belgium: Reforming Paternity', *Journal of Family Law*, **25**.

Meulders-Klein, M.-T. (1990), 'Belgium: The Year of the Child', *Journal of Family Law*, **28**.

Michel, A. (1975), 'Modèles sociologiques de la famille dans les sociétés contemporaines', *Archives de la philosophie du droit*, **20**, 127–36.

Ministerio de Asuntos Sociales (1991), *I Congreso Internacional Infancia y Sociedad*, 3 vols, Madrid: Min. de Asuntos Soc.

Mintz, S. (1989), 'Regulating the American Family', *Journal of Family History*, **14**, 387–408.

Mintz, S. and Kellogg, S. (1988), *Domestic Revolutions*, New York: The Free Press.

Moeller, R. (1989), 'Reconstructing the Family in Reconstruction Germany: Women and Social Policy in the Federal Republic, 1949–1955', *Feminist Studies*, **15**, 137–67.

Moro, A.C. (1991), *Il bambino è un cittadino*, Milano: Mursia.

Moschos, S. (1983), 'The Rights of the Child in Greece' in A.M. Pappas (ed.), *Law and the Status of the Child*, New York: UNITAR, Vol.2.

Moss, P. (1988), *Childcare and Equality of Opportunity*, Brussels: European Commission.

Nardinelli, C. (1990), *Child Labor and the Industrial Revolution*, Bloomington: Indiana University Press.

Neidhardt, F. (1978), 'The Federal Republic of Germany' in S. Kamerman and A. Kahn (eds), *Government and Families in Fourteen Countries*, New York: Columbia University Press, 217–38.

Nowotny, H-J. (1975), 'Law and Fertility in Switzerland' in M. Kirk et al. (eds), *Law and Fertility in Europe*. Dolhain: Ordina, Vol. 2, 566–98.

OECD (1990), *Education in OECD Countries 1987–88*, Paris.

Olsson, L. (1980), *Då barn var lönsamma*, Stockholm: Tiden.

Ornauer, H. (1975), Law and Fertility in Austria' in M. Kirk et al. (eds), *Law and Fertility in Europe*, Dolhain: Ordina, Vol.l, 109–29.

Pappas, A.M. (ed.) (1983), *Law and the Status of the Child*, 2 vols, New York: UNITAR.

Pinchbeck, I. and Hewitt, M. (1973), *Children in English Society I–II*, London: Routledge & Kegan Paul.

Pollock, L. (1983), *Forgotten Children: Parent-Child Relations from 1500 to 1900*, Cambridge: Cambridge University Press.
Rheinstein, M.(1972), *Marriage Stability, Divorce, and the Law*, Chicago: University of Chicago Press.
Rheinstein, M. and Glendon, M.A. (1980), 'Interspousal Relations', *International Encyclopedia of Comparative Law*, Vol. IV, ch. 4, Tübingen: J.C.B. Mohr.
Rodríguez, F. (ed.) (1964), *Doctrina Pontificia*, Vol. III, Documentos sociales, Madrid: La Editorial Católica.
Romein, J. (1978), *The Watershed of Two Eras. Europe in 1900*, Middletown Conn.: Wesleyan University Press.
Rood-de Boer, M. (1984), 'State Intervention in the Family in the Netherlands' in M. Freeman (ed.), *The State, the Law, and the Family*, London: Tavistock, 124–38.
Rood-de Boer, M. (1987), 'The Netherlands: How to Tackle New Social Problems', *Journal of Family Law,* **26**, 141–7.
Rosenberg, L. (1981), 'Hagar og Ismael i Saras Telt?', Bergen: Dept. of History at Bergen University, Hovedfagsoopgave.
Rubellin-Devichi, J. (1986), 'France: The Reform Wagon Rolls Again', *Journal of Family Law,* **25**.
Rubellin-Devichi, J. (1988), 'France: More Equality, More Solidarity in Family Relationships', *Journal of Family Law*, **27**.
Saldeen, Å. (1988), 'Sweden: More Rights for Children and Homosexuals', *Journal of Family Law,* **27**.
Savolainen, M. (1986), 'Finland: More Rights for Children', *Journal of Family Law,* **25**, 113–26.
Schmidt, F. (1971), 'The Prospective Law of Marriage', *Scandinavian Studies in Law,* **15**, 193–218.
Sevenhuijsen, S. (1987), *De orde van het vaderschap*, Amsterdam: IISG.
Shatter, A.J. (1977), *Family Law in the Republic of Ireland,* Dublin: Wolfhound Press.
Shipley, A. (1986), 'Custody Law Reform in Ontario: The Children's Law Reform Act' in B. Landau (ed.), *Children's Rights in the Practice of Family Law,* Toronto: Carswell.
Shorter, E. (1976), *The Making of the Modern Family,* London: Collins.
Siampos, G. (1975), 'Greece' in M. Kirk et al. (eds), *Law and Fertility in Europe,* Dolhain: Ordina, Vol.2.
Soler, M. et al. (1983), 'Legal Rights of Children in the United States of America' in A.M. Pappas (ed.), *Law and the Status of the Child,* New York: UNITAR, 1983, Vol. 2, 675–743.
Sommerville, J. (1990), *The Rise and Fall of Childhood,* New York: Vintage Books.
Sorrentino, C. (1990), 'The Changing Family in International Perspective', *Monthly Labor Review,* March, 41–56.
Stadler, P. (1991), 'Die Schweiz von der Verfassungsrevision 1874 bis zum Ersten Weltkrieg (1874–1991)' in H.V. Greyerz et al., *Geschichte der Schweiz,* München: Klett-Cotta/dtv.

Stearns, P. and Haggerty, T. (1991), 'The Role of Fear: Transitions in American Emotional Standards for Children, 1850–1950', *American Historical Review*, **96**, 63–94.

Steiner, G.(1976), *The Children's Cause*, Washington D.C., The Brookings Institution.

Stoljar, S.J. (1980), 'Children, Parents and Guardians', *International Encyclopedia of Comparative Law*, Vol. IV, ch. 7, Tübingen: J.C.B. Mohr.

Stone, L. (1977), *The Family, Sex and Marriage in England 500–1800*, London: Weidenfeld and Nicolson.

Stone, O. (1982), *The Child's Voice in the Court of Law*, Toronto: Butterworth.

Sussman, G. (1976), 'The End of the Wet-Nursing Business in France, 1874–1914', *Journal of Family History*, **1–2**, 237–58.

Sutherland, E. (1987), 'Scotland: The Reform Process Continues', *Journal of Family Law*, **26**, 175–86.

Sutherland, E. (1990), 'Scotland: Financial Provision, the Status of Children and Child Protection', *Journal of Family Law*, **28**, 588–99.

Sutch, W.B. (1966), *The Quest for Security in New Zealand 1840 to 1966*, London: Oxford University Press.

Tálos, E. (1981), *Staatliche Sozialpolitik in Österreich. Rekonstruktion und Analyse*, Wien: Verlag für Gesellschaftsakritik.

Terré, F. (1975), 'A propos de l'autorité parentale', *Archives de la philosophie du droit*, **20**, 45–56.

Therborn, G. (1984), 'The Prospects of Labour and the Transformation of Advanced Capitalism', *New Left Review*, **145**.

Therborn, G. (1987), 'Welfare States and Capitalist Markets', *Acta Sociologica*, **30**, 237–54.

Therborn, G. (1989a), 'States, Populations and Productivity: Towards a Political Theory of Welfare States' in P. Lassman (ed.), *Politics and Social Theory*, London: Routledge.

Therborn, G. (1989b), '"Pillarization" and "Popular Movements". The Variants of Welfare of State Capitalism: the Netherlands and Sweden', in F. Castles (ed.), *The Comparative History of Public Policy*, Cambridge: Polity Press.

Therborn, G. (1991a), 'Cultural Belonging and Structural Location', *Acta Sociologica*, **34**, 177–91.

Therborn, G. (1992), 'The Right to Vote and the Four Routes to Political Modernity' in R. Torstendahl (ed.), *The State in Theory and History*, London: Sage.

Van der Kaa, D. (1975), 'Law and Fertility in the Netherlands' in M. Kirk et al.(eds), *Law and Fertility in Europe*, Dolhain: Ordina, Vol. 2, 462–94.

Varela, A. (1987), *Direito da Familia*, Lisboa: Livraría Petrony.

Walvin, J.(1982), *A Child's World*, Harmondsworth: Penguin.

Weiisbach, L.S. (1989), *Child Labor Reform in Nineteenth Century France*, Baton Rouge: Louisiana State University Press.

Wilson, E. (1977), *Women and the Welfare State*, London, Tavistock.

Wringe, C.A. (1981), *Children's Rights: A Philosophical Study*, London: Routledge and Kegan Paul.

Zaretsky, E.(1976), *Capitalism, The Family and Personal Life*, New York:
Zelizer, V. (1985), *Pricing the Priceless Child*, New York: Basic Books.
Zweigert, K. and Kötz, H. (1977), *Introduction to Comparative Law*, Vol. 1, 1st edition, Amsterdam: North-Holland.
Zweigert and Kötz (1987), *Introduction to Comparative Law,* 2nd edition, Oxford: Clarendon Press.
Zimmerman, S. (1988), *Understanding Family Policy*, London: Sage.

7 Why Divorce Rates Differ: Law, Religious Belief and Modernity

Francis G. Castles and Michael Flood

Introduction

The decision to divorce is an action in the domestic sphere based largely on private considerations and yet very much constrained by public policy enunciated through legal enactments. Indeed marriage and the conditions under which it may be terminated are one of the oldest arenas in which the law has been used to regulate relations amongst citizens. Even under Roman law, where marriage was essentially a private contract to be dissolved at the behest of either party, certain formalities had to be observed, such as the delivery by one party to another before witnesses of a document expressing the intention to terminate marriage; in cases where the future of children or the division of property were in dispute, issues were settled by the courts (Kitchin, 1912, 6–7).

Irrespective of the extent to which it is considered a private matter, divorce is also necessarily a public concern for at least three reasons. First, the dissolution of marriage raises important issues of social protection, including, first and foremost, the duty of the collectivity to protect children and (in some times past, including under Roman law, and a major consideration in most contemporary divorce legislation) the duty to ensure the protection of the weaker party from exploitation by the stronger. Second, the termination of marriage involves issues both of public morals and political economy. Governments have always seen it as their role to reinforce religious or community standards concerning the proper observance of marriage and have often been concerned with the possible demographic consequences of increased marital instability. Today, they are extremely aware of the economic burdens imposed on the state by the disruption of matrimonial ties: the effectiveness of family law and family services are frequently evaluated with an eye to cost-benefit analysis (see, for instance, Wolcott and Glezer, 1989, 5–6). Third, divorce is an issue of public policy because changing social and economic circumstances may outmode existing laws and motivate strenuous demands on the part of concerned groups for reform. As later sections make clear, the post-war era has witnessed a massive movement for divorce law reform in the countries of advanced capitalism and, with it, a very substantial increase in the divorce rate in most of these countries.

Not only is divorce law a matter of public concern, but it is also an area of extreme cross-national variation. Indeed, as a major authority points out, it is arguably the field of private law in which national diversity is most glaring (Rheinstein, 1972, 8). This chapter, therefore, proceeds from the perspective that the divorce rate and the changes that take place in it over time are public policy outcomes susceptible to comparative analysis in a manner similar to others examined in this book. The volume of divorce occurring at any time may be seen as the consequence of the complex interplay of social and economic forces influencing individual behaviour, and of legal enactments, simultaneously shaped by citizen demands and collective views as to the moral and economic repercussions of change. There are, however, *a priori* reasons why we might expect public policy outcomes in the arena of family law to be responsive to a somewhat different balance of forces from those with which we are familiar in the spheres of economic and social policy. Because the decision to seek a legal dissolution of marriage is personal, the aggregation of such decisions in the divorce rate does not involve the direct intervention of government. Rather the intervention is an indirect one which conditions the probability of applications for legal dissolution being actualized. This means that the law enjoins what shall not be permissible rather than stipulating what actions the government will undertake. Whereas public policy analysis is most usually concerned with the positive interventions of governments or the consequences of laws in terms of 'who gets what, when and how',[1] here we shall be concerned with the character of laws as policy outputs *sui generis*, empowering individuals to adopt certain courses of action and blocking others.

Moreover, the moral dimension of marriage implies that cultural and attitudinal dimensions of social behaviour are inherently likely to have a greater impact on outcomes than in many other public policy arenas. Religious beliefs and social customs stipulating the proper conception of marriage will clearly influence law-makers; the same factors will help to shape individuals' decisions to stay within or seek relief from the marital state.

The transmission of such beliefs and customs occurs through processes of socialization within the family and community and are, in general, subject only to gradual change. That, in turn, implies a degree of historical continuity within nations over time and within groups of nations sharing a common culture and some common historical experience; it implies the likelihood that laws regulating marriage, as well as attitudes as to circumstances justifying the dissolution of marriage and the rates of divorce that are their joint consequence, will be in some measure similar. In the context of this research endeavour, which seeks to establish the extent to which public policy outcomes in contemporary states manifest patterns of similarity within 'families of nations' defined by their historical and cultural affinity, the domestic arena of marriage and the family constitutes a critical case, for if such patterns are not apparent here, they are scarcely likely to be evident to any greater degree in economic or social policy arenas, which are so much more obviously responsive to the changing character of structural constraints.

Families of Nations and the Law of Divorce

In order to comprehend the nature of the relationship between families of nations and divorce rates, it is necessary first to define the boundaries of groupings of nations in terms of the historical development of the law relating to the dissolution of marriage. Since the rules regulating divorce, no less than the rights accorded children, are first and foremost legal matters, the groupings which emerge in this context quite strongly resemble the legal families of nations located in Göran Therborn's analysis of the previous chapter.

The development of the law of divorce in Europe and the nations of European settlement is, as we might expect, quite inseparable from religion and the major historical watersheds in the process of secularization – the Reformation and the French Revolution. Prior to the Reformation, the law regulating marriage in Europe was the canon law of the Roman Catholic church, essentially based on the indissolubility of nuptial bonds. The only significant relief from the marital state was the possibility of annulment or judicial separation without the right of remarriage, the latter under a variety of circumstances rendering the sharing of 'bed and board' intolerable, but usually intolerable only to men. In England and Ireland, alone of the countries of Europe, the canon law remained almost entirely intact until well into the 19th century although, in England, divorce by Private Act of Parliament alleviated its stringent application for the very rich (see Stone, 1990).

The great change brought about by the Reformation for a large part of the rest of Western Europe was not so much any immediate alteration in the stipulations of canon law, but a transfer from ecclesiastical to civil jurisdiction and the rejection of the principle of indissolubility, which over a period of centuries permitted some extension of the grounds for divorce, but only where such grounds might be deduced from scriptural text. Adultery was the ground that obviously had such Biblical provenance although, of the Protestant divines, only Calvin saw men's adultery as justifying the same opprobrium as that of women (Rheinstein, 1972, 22). Moreover, in virtually all the countries of Western Europe excluding England and Ireland, but including the Catholic areas untouched by the Reformation, the French Revolution and the subsequent transferal of its principles into the Civil Code of Napoleon Bonarparte marked some reversion to the gentler notions of Roman law in its later Christian development, departing still further from the concept of the indissolubility of marriage and in principle permitting divorce by mutual consent and allowing judicial separation to be converted into divorce.

The influence of the Code Napoleon was relatively short-lived in several of the more Catholic countries, leaving a reasonably clear division between European families of nations by the early 19th century: (1) the countries where the canon law was essentially unchanged (England, Ireland, the Italian principalities and France, these latter reverting to Catholic ecclesiastical practice with the Restoration), (2) the countries where Protestantism was conjoint with the influence of certain of the ideas stemming from the French Revolution (essentially Scandinavia and the German-speaking nations), and (3) the countries in which the mutual consent notion was more than somewhat trammelled by restrictions imposed by Catholic influence (Belgium and the Netherlands). In addition, outside Europe, the varied laws of the US were dominated by the Reformation ethos unalloyed by the reformist spirit of the revolution in France, but strongly affected by canon law influences inherited from the common law of England.

Further developments over the course of a century led to a further differentiation of types of divorce law so that, in the pre-war decades of this century it is possible to distinguish five reasonably distinct families of nations.[2] First, there was an English-speaking family, excluding Ireland, and with the US as a partial exception. These nations essentially imported the law of England, prohibiting divorce except on the grounds of adultery (permitted under English law only from 1857), which was still interpreted more permissively for men than for women. As Kitchin (1912, 231–33) notes:

> The colonies and dominions of British origin which enjoy responsible government commenced, like America and the Crown colonies, with the English law and all its ecclesiastical anomalies. In Canada the law has been allowed to remain for the most part as it was ... In Australia and New Zealand the English Divorce Act was put into force between 1860 and 1873, and has in those dominions always operated against all attempts to introduce a more liberal and equitable law.

Moreover, this standardization of divorce laws in the colonies was an outcome of conscious policy design, with the British government 'anxious that [laws] continue to conform to English law and practice', since otherwise there might have been 'problems of recognition of divorce decrees from one jurisdiction to another' (Phillips, 1988, 436). In the Australian and New Zealand colonies, some changes were introduced in the late 19th century, including the equal standing of women and some extension of the grounds of divorce. However, prior to 1919, when New Zealand introduced separation as a ground, divorce in all the English-speaking dominions was based firmly on the concept of fault, with adultery the fault *par excellence*.

Until this time, perhaps the easiest way to characterize the development of divorce law in England and its dominions would be to say that it had entered into its Reformation phase two centuries or more after the same development had occurred in north-western Europe. In the US, the far earlier Reformation impulse had led to a vast proliferation of grounds for complaint, but fault remained firmly entrenched as the guiding principle of the system, with adultery the one ground common to all states circa 1931. Only around a third of the states had any provision for separation as a ground and then, usually, separation only for a very lengthy period (see Vernier, 1932, 3–4, 61, 70–71).

In the countries where the Reformation spirit was combined with the secularizing tendency of the French Revolution, a degree of divergence developed between the Scandinavian countries of homogeneous Lutheran faith and the German-speaking countries. In the former, Lutheranism and liberalism combined to make divorce progressively a private matter, with the burden of proof that marriage had failed resting on the fact that the parties had been separated for several years. In the case of the Scandinavian nations, just as much as the English-speaking ones, an historical diffusion of ideas can readily be identified, culminating in high-level intra-Nordic meetings between leading jurists which led to very similar liberal laws being promulgated in the second and third decades of the 20th century in Denmark, Finland, Iceland, Norway and Sweden.

In Austria and Germany, over a long period of evolution and with reversions to fault-only provisions, separation also became an important ground, but lack of consent by the respondent was an absolute bar, whereas the normal practice of the Scandinavian countries was 'to accept the fact that one party petitioned for judicial separation as sufficient proof of the marriage being as profoundly and permanently disrupted as required' by the law (Rheinstein, 1972, 144). Switzerland was unlike the other German-speaking nations in that non-specific grounds amounting to mutual consent and a restricted right of unilateral petition[3] were allowed by the courts, practices owing something to the Napoleonic code, but more still to an exceptionalism in marriage law persisting throughout the period of canon law and, perhaps, also reflecting Calvin's views on the equality of the sexes before God and the law.

What distinguishes the rather more loosely articulated German-speaking family was an uneasy combination of indigenous trends towards divorce by mutual consent, exhibited in the Prussian Civil Code of the late 18th century as well as in Switzerland, and a bifurcation of Protestant and Catholic laws of marriage. The former permitted some relief from marriage on grounds of misconduct, whilst the latter remained firmly grounded in the notion of indissolubility. For instance, the law in force in Austria for much of the 19th century and through to the 1930s distinguished between Catholics, who were legally barred from the divorce remedy, and the adherents of other religious beliefs, to whom it was available on various grounds including 'irremediable aversion' after a period of separation (Phillips, 1988, 432). The eventual combination in all the German-speaking countries of statutory grounds based on mutual consent or separation by consent – and an effective bar in the absence of such consent – expresses a compromise between these several contrasting traditions. In Austria and Germany, it also reflected another, more directly, family of nations influence in that the 1938 law of divorce applied to all of Greater Germany and encouraged separation by consent on eugenic grounds. Stripped of other more blatant racist and eugenic elements, the 1938 legislation persisted in both countries until reforms in the 1970s.

A few other nations retained elements of the Code Napoleon. Belgium and the Netherlands each had a much trammelled right of mutual consent. France reintroduced some aspects of the Code in 1884, although without the mutual consent provisions. These three countries constitute a separate legal tradition and for us a separate family of nations, as do the two most Catholic countries under examination here – Ireland and Italy – where canon law continued to reign supreme, with no provision for the dissolution of marriage save for judicial separation.

In Table 7.1, we present a tabulation of divorce law provisions in 1960 and ensuing reform in the period 1960–76. In the table, we code the liberality of the law on the following basis:[4]

3 = No-fault grounds permitting uncontested proceedings after three years or less, with contestation delaying the process for no more than two further years.
2 = Mutual consent with no substantial restrictions or three years separation as ground for uncontested divorce.
1 = Other more restrictive legislation.
0 = Most restrictive (ie. no national divorce legislation).

The rationale for this coding includes the following factors: that liberal access requires only a relatively short period to establish incompatibility or marital breakdown, that proceedings should not require the necessity of demonstrating the marital failings of either party, and that divorce should be available irrespective of the consent of both parties. Reasonably unrestricted mutual consent (as in Switzerland) and separation on the basis of agreement (as in Germany and Austria) constitute halfway houses, allowing a guilt-free dissolution of marriage for those who can accommodate their differences, although no remedy for those who cannot. Other more restrictive arrangements and those resting exclusively on fault do permit divorce under some circumstances, but invariably with great anguish and often at considerable financial cost.

In 1960, the correspondence between the liberality of the law and its historical evolution in distinct families of nations is extraordinarily clear. The Scandinavian group of nations is wholly consistent in its liberalism and the German-speaking group in its halfway status. Only New Zealand, in the English-speaking group, sufficiently departed from fault principles to allow a designation of partial liberalization. Both the Code Napoleon and canon law families are wholly consistent in the degree of access to the divorce remedy permitted in their statutes.

By 1976, however, there had been a very substantial degree of divorce law liberalization throughout much of the Western world, to some degree eroding the distinctiveness of these legal families of nations. The English-speaking nations experienced the greatest shift from essentially fault-based systems to ones in which the no-fault element was either paramount or the only ground available. This process is again, at least in some part, attributable to a diffusion in legal practice, the stimulus to which were the recommendations of a Church of England report under the title *Putting Asunder: A Divorce Law for Contemporary Society.* Departing from the long history of the Church in England, its views were based not on how the 'doctrine of Christ should be interpreted and applied within the Christian Church … but on what the Church ought to say and do about secular laws of marriage and divorce' (Mortimer Commission, 1966). The report's main recommendation was that 'the doctrine of breakdown of marriage should be comprehen-

Table 7.1: Legal barriers to divorce and divorce law reform, 1960 and 1960–76

	1960 Law	Score	1976 Law and subsequent reform	Score	Change score
English-speaking:					
Australia	Fault or 5 years separation	1	Irretrievable breakdown of marriage (1975)	3	2
Canada	In most provinces, only adultery	1	3 years separation (5 years where petitioner deserted respondent) (1968). Irretrievable breakdown (1985)	3	2
New Zealand	Fault or 3 years separation, but only with consent	2	Legal separation for 2 years/de facto for 4 (1963). Irretrievable breakdown (1981)	3	1
England and Wales	Fault	1	Fault or 2 years separation with consent/ 5 without (1969)	3	2
US	Varied laws in different states/ various stipulations of fault, with long separation a ground in a minority of states	1	Liberalization in New York (1966), California (1970). By 1985, 18 states had pure no-fault divorce with incompatibility as sole ground/22 combine fault with marital breakdown	3	2
Scandinavian:					
Denmark	Fault or 3 years separation	3	Some further liberalization (1969)	3	0
Finland	Fault or 2 years separation	3	Some further liberalization (1969)	3	0
Norway	Fault or 1 year legal separation with consent/ 2 without	3	Some further liberalization (1969)	3	0
Sweden	Fault or 1 year legal separation/3 years de facto	3	Wish of one or both partners to end marriage/ 6 months delay where objection or small children (1973)	3	0

German-speaking:					
Austria	Fault or 3 years separation, but only with consent	2	Unchanged, but later reform in 1978	2	0
Germany	Fault or 3 years separation, but only with consent	2	1 year separation/3 without consent (1976)	3	1
Switzerland	Fault or non-specific grounds amounting to mutual consent	2	No change	2	0
Code Napoleon:					
Belgium	Fault or mutual consent (much restricted by eligibility and cost)	1	Fault or unrestricted mutual consent (1969) or separation of 10 years (1974)	2	1
France	Fault	1	Misconduct or unrestricted mutual consent or separation for 6 years (1975)	2	1
Netherlands	Fault or mutual consent after 5 years legal separation	1	Lasting dislocation – immediate on joint petition /3 years on unilateral petition (1971)	3	2
Canon Law:					
Ireland	No divorce	0	No change	0	0
Italy	No divorce	0	Legal separation for at least 5 years/6 if without agreement (1970). Some further minor changes (1975)	1	1

Sources: On European nations (except Denmark): Chester, 1977. On Australia, Canada, Denmark and New Zealand: Law Reform Commission of Canada, 1975. On the US: Weitzman, 1985. Some further information on dates of later reforms from Phillips, 1988, 562.

sively substituted for the doctrine of matrimonial offence as the basis for all divorce'. This dramatic change in religious doctrine, issued with the imprimatur of the Archbishop of Canterbury, was a spur to and a platform for reform throughout the English-speaking world (except Ireland) and beyond. In England and Wales, Australia, Canada and New Zealand, as well as in a number of the American states, starting with New York, relatively liberal grounds for dissolution of marriage by separation were instituted by the late 1960s. In 1970, the world's first divorce law based solely on irreconcilable breakdown of marriage was introduced in California, and by the 1980s, exclusively no-fault provisions had been adopted in Australia, Canada, the Netherlands, New Zealand, Sweden and some 40 per cent of the American states.[5]

This dramatic reform process in the English-speaking family of nations meant that the distinctive liberal character of the Scandinavian family had disappeared by 1976, with both groupings now being essentially similar in basing marital dissolution substantially on no-fault grounds. Outside the English-speaking countries, the only liberalization of comparable magnitude occurred in the Netherlands. This change made it an atypical member of the Code Napoleon legal family, since change in Belgium and France was more muted, combining fault provisions with a more unrestricted criterion of divorce by mutual consent. The German-speaking nations also ceased to be characterized by common provisions, since Germany adopted liberal separation laws, whilst Austrian and Swiss law remained essentially unaltered. Finally, change also occurred in one of the two remaining canon law nations when Italy adopted somewhat restricted legislation permitting divorce in 1970 which was subsequently reaffirmed by a hotly contested popular referendum in 1974. Of the countries under survey here, only Ireland had no law of divorce in 1976.[6] Indeed, the 1937 constitution forbade the making of laws for the dissolution of marriage and a 1986 referendum to reverse that position was soundly defeated.

This necessarily summary presentation can only be interpreted as confirming the existence of quite distinct families of nations in respect of the historical and cultural continuity and development of the law of divorce in European nations and nations of European settlement at least until the 1960s. But the historically conditioned similarity of the law as an output of government is no guarantee of a comparable similarity of outcomes in terms of aggregate divorce rates and divorce rate change. That depends both on the way in which the law is interpreted and the influence of social and economic factors on the individual propensity to seek dissolution of the marital bond. In the next section, we seek to locate the degree of correspondence between legal outputs and divorce outcomes.

On Divorce Rates and Divorce Rate Change

Table 7.2 presents data on average divorce rates for 17 nations for the periods 1961–68 and 1976–83 and the change in the divorce rate occurring between these periods. Of the countries normally featuring in comparative public policy studies, only Japan is omitted on the ground of the inappropriateness of including a nation with a wholly incommensurable cultural development in an analysis where a crucial focus of causation is presumed to be variation in religious belief systems. The periods selected are deliberately chosen with a view to providing a test of the impact of the provisions of the law in 1960 and 1976 as set out in Table 7.1.

Rheinstein argues that in countries that have proceeded far along the path of economic modernity, but where the contemporary intellectual climate is either conservative or pluralistic, the divorce law of the statute books will be strict, but will simultaneously tend 'to become a dead letter' (Rheinstein, 1970, 128). This helps to explain, for the 1960s at least, the most obvious anomaly we encounter in contrasting the provisions of divorce laws with divorce rates in the countries under survey: the fact that the US, with legislation based very largely on various definitions of matrimonial offence, had a divorce rate almost twice as high as any other Western nation throughout the period under review. For much of this century, the US has constituted the most dramatic instance of a country in which legal interpretation is at variance with statute law.[7] Collusion, the withholding of information from the courts or the presentation of false information by both parties became a standard practice, and although in itself a bar to divorce, the evidence presented by the parties was scarcely ever contested or investigated by the courts.

This amounted to a practice of divorce by mutual consent in many states and was compounded by the practice of 'migratory divorce', allowing divorces conducted under the liberal interpretations of other states and nations to be recognized in most circumstances, even in states where the grounds for divorce were much stricter. The possibility of migratory divorce rested on the unique maintenance of state sovereignty over family law, itself reflecting the unusual degree of decentralized authority of the US. More sociologically, it reflected the existence of frontier mores, behind which more conservative legal enactments only slowly consolidated. Always to the west and south-west, there were one or more states where divorce laws were more permissive and where those in search of marital relief might find a solution to their difficulties. In effect, then, by 1960 and indeed from the latter part of the 19th century onwards, from the perspective of the citizen confronting the supra-state system of marriage laws, the practice of the law in the US – in contradistinction to its letter – was as

Table 7.2: Divorce rates and ranks, 1961–68 and 1976–83, and divorce rate change, 1961–68 to 1976–83 in diverse families of nations

Family of Nations	1961–68			1976–83			Change		
	Country	Rate	Rank	Country	Rate	Rank	Country	Rate	Rank
English-speaking	US	2.5	1	US	5.1	1	US	2.6	1
	Australia	0.7	8	UK	2.9	2	UK	2.2	2
	NZ	0.7	8	Australia	2.8	3	Australia	2.1	3
	UK	0.7	8	Canada	2.6	6	Canada	2.1	3
	Canada	0.5	14	NZ	2.4	8	NZ	1.7	6
Scandinavian	Denmark	1.4	2	Denmark	2.7	5	Denmark	1.3	8
	Sweden	1.3	3	Sweden	2.5	7	Sweden	1.2	9
	Finland	1.0	5	Finland	2.1	9	Finland	1.1	10
	Norway	0.7	8	Norway	1.7	12	Norway	1.0	11
German-speaking	Austria	1.2	4	Germany	2.8	3	Germany	1.8	5
	Germany	1.0	5	Austria	1.8	11	Switz	0.8	14
	Switz	0.9	7	Switz	1.7	12	Austria	0.6	15
Code Napoleon	France	0.7	8	Neth	1.9	10	Neth	1.4	7
	Belgium	0.6	13	France	1.7	12	France	1.0	11
	Neth	0.5	14	Belgium	1.5	15	Belgium	0.9	13
Canon Law	Italy	0.0	16	Italy	0.2	16	Italy	0.2	16
	Ireland	0.0	16	Ireland	0.0	17	Ireland	0.0	17
Correlations with scores for liberalism of legal provision and change in liberalism:		r	rho		r	rho		r	rho
including US		0.45	0.70**		0.77**	0.83**		0.71**	0.72**
excluding US		0.85**	0.85**		0.91**	0.83**		0.66**	0.67**

Definitions: Divorce rate = divorces per thousand of the population averaged for the periods 1961–68 and 1976–83. Change = the difference between the divorce rate 1961–68 and the divorce rate 1976–83.

Source and notes: United Nations, *Demographic Yearbook*, various dates. ** = significant at .01 level.

liberal as (and for much of the period more liberal than) that of any other country in the Western world. In general, however, the law forced those seeking legal dissolution to dissemble or to travel in order to obtain the relief it formally prohibited.

The effect of the American discrepancy can readily be ascertained from the correlations between divorce law liberalism and divorce rates in 1961–68 appearing at the bottom of Table 7.2. Including the US, the relationship is only marginally significant; excluding that country, it is extraordinarily strong, accounting for some 70 per cent of divorce rate variation. Excluding the US, the coherence of our five families of nations is very strong indeed; the highest and the lowest in the remaining English-speaking group differing by only 0.2, in the German-speaking group by 0.3, and in the Code Napoleon group by 0.2. Only in the Scandinavian group is there any significant variation, with Norway registering a divorce rate half that of Denmark.

Almost exactly the same story can be told of the period 1976–83, although the discrepancy between the correlations including and excluding the US is less, at least partly because of that country's intervening process of legal reform. The absolute gaps within the families of nations have increased somewhat in line with the more than twofold increase in the average divorce rate as between 1961–68 and 1976–83, but only two countries are out of synchronization with the others in their grouping: once again Norway, now joined by Germany, the only member of the German-speaking family to have substantially changed its statutes by 1976. Change over time, again, follows the same pattern. The US is, by this criterion of evaluation, a typical member of the English-speaking family, with New Zealand being furthest from the group norm, as one might expect of the nation that had effected the least legal change during the period. The charge of 'English-speaking awfulness' noted elsewhere in this volume with regard to low rates of economic growth and low social security can also be levelled here, with five English-speaking nations featuring amongst the six nations to experience the greatest increase in divorce rate in this period. In contrast, change in the Scandinavian group was much more moderate, although the pattern of change was equally coherent. In the other families, only Germany within the German-speaking group and the Netherlands within the Code Napoleon family diverged substantially from the rank ordering of other members. Both were nations in which legal change had been more rapid than in the rest of the relevant grouping.

With the exception of the American case, the evidence presented here supports the notion that statute law is an important determinant of the frequency of the legal dissolution of marriage, although it would be mistaken to deduce from that fact that liberal laws destroy marriage, since there is well-grounded empirical literature showing the inverse relation between divorce and judicial and *de facto* separation (see Rheinstein, 1972, 277–316). What can be deduced from the evidence is a strong *prima facie* case for the influence of long-term cultural factors transmitted through the historical continuities of distinct legal families of nations in this arena of domestic policy.

The case is only *prima facie* for at least two major reasons. First, the lesson of our earlier investigations of apparent family resemblances amongst nations tells us that similarity is frequently dissolved when we come to examine the impact of social and economic structures on policy outputs and outcomes. Such a possibility is highly consonant with the view of many of those who study comparative law, like Rheinstein, who suggest that the law is ultimately a reflection of its social context; where it remains too long incongruent with that context, it is either reinterpreted or swept away. Second, our account so far has concentrated on legal outputs and has not considered the social and economic variables that may be associated with the individual decision to seek legal remedies. Even the relatively high correlations recorded at the bottom of Table 7.2 leave sufficient scope for explanations of divorce rates and especially divorce rate change in terms of the impact of structural variables on individual behaviour. Perhaps, more crucially, we have some reason to believe that what, in terms of simple bivariate relationships, appears as the shaping influence of legal families of nations may merely involve a masking of other kinds of relationships manifesting themselves at the individual level. Of the cultural factors shaping the law, that which has featured most prominently in our historical account has been the evolving impact of doctrinal differences between religious faiths, but religious beliefs in the population are not separate or necessarily different from those which shape the decisions of the legislators of statute law. It could well be that, in investigating the direct effect of religious belief on behaviour, we may discover that divorce rates would be little different irrespective of the effect of laws. To cite but one possible example, the divorce rate in Ireland might well be negligible because of the dominance of the Catholic faith, even if there were no legal prohibition on the dissolution of marriage in that country. This might speak for a variant of the families of nations view resting on the importance of cultural factors, but would be destructive of a still stronger variant pointing to the significance of long-term historical continuities. It is to issues of this kind that we now turn our attention.

On the Correlates of Divorce

There is a substantial empirically based sociological literature on the contextual factors associated with divorce in particular nations, a literature which has gained much of its impetus in recent decades from a growing awareness of the need to distinguish the macrostructural from the microsociological dimensions of the process of divorce. It is generally acknowledged that mono-causal explanations of recent divorce trends are insufficient and inaccurate, and that we must seek multi-causal explanations, both because the factors influencing marital stability are many and because macrostructural and microsociological factors simultaneously impinge on individual decisions to seek a legal dissolution of marriage (see Hart, 1976).

However, the increasing sophistication of the sociological literature has not generated an equally sophisticated empirically based corpus of cross-national research. The reasons are not difficult to discern. Differences and changes in legal systems have been seen as central variables in explaining national differences in divorce rates and divorce rate change, but the very fact that different nations have different laws has equally been seen as a major barrier to systematic comparison using the methods of applied social research. In consequence, what cross-national research there has been has tended to adopt an historical and legal approach rather than the more quantitative methods of sociology and comparative public policy analysis. Moreover, the predominant focus of most research in the field has been on the post-war growth of the divorce rate that has been a phenomenon of virtually all Western societies. This has encouraged those with an interest in international comparisons to stress factors common to many nations – for instance, general attitudinal and ideological shifts associated with secularization and modernization (see Ambert, 1980, 54–57; Goode, 1963, 81; Price and McKenry, 1988, 7) – rather than factors pertinent to the substantial differences between nations as revealed in Table 7.2. Finally, the awareness of the desirability of an approach combining macrostructural and microsociological factors has in itself been a discouragement to cross-national research, which necessarily relies very heavily on routinely collected aggregate data that by its very nature obscures the subtle interaction between these classes of causation, whilst being inherently biased towards macrostructural explanation. For instance, feelings of marginality within a social network (Hart, 1976, 171) may be an important contributory factor to discontent within a marriage at the microsociological level, but no comparable cross-national data on such attitudes exist. Nevertheless, the impact of marginality is likely to be picked up by a host of more macrostructural factors, such as the process of urbanization which disrupts such networks, or the trend towards lessened fertility which may disturb traditional patterns of interaction within communities, allowing only a very broad-gauge interpretation of the causal mechanisms involved.

We acknowledge the very real limitations imposed by this latter difficulty, but nevertheless seek to devise a model for the cross-national analysis of divorce rates and divorce rate change by combining key social context variables with our earlier categorization of the legal impediments to divorce in different nations as presented in Table 7.1. It is our view that, by providing a quantitative index of the liberality of national divorce laws and their liberalization over time, this categorization permits us to overcome the problem of the barrier to systematic cross-national research constituted by the existence of diverse legal hurdles to the dissolution of marriage in different nations. The resulting model should make it possible to establish, at least within the broad-gauge terms dictated by the available data, whether a legally defined families of nations approach retains its heuristic value when the law is contextualized by its social setting. The first stage in the process of model-building is to test some of the hypotheses which feature most conspicuously in national studies against cross-national data. These hypotheses may be broadly grouped under the headings of modernization, secularization, demographic factors and policy constraints. In light of the difficulty of distinguishing the impact of macrostructural from microsociological factors on the basis of the available data, we pay more than the usual lip service to the standard caveat of applied social research: that, in examining the correlates of divorce, what we are establishing are associations between variables and not definitive causal explanations.

In accounting for divorce trends over the last two centuries, long-term economic or materialist factors have been widely identified as fundamental in creating the conditions for an increasing tendency to divorce. The three most crucial trends are the shift in the economic base of households, a growth in married women's formal and practical economic independence, and a growth in women's employment opportunities and labour-force participation (Phillips, 1988; Price and McKenry, 1988; Halem, 1980). This last factor has been particularly influential in some interpretations of post-war divorce rate change and is an instance where the same variable has been used to generate both macrostructural and microsociological interpretations. Thus, quite apart from the effect of labour force participation in facilitating female economic independence, North American studies have established that a husband's sporadic employment and low wages, relative to his wife's employment and wages, are key determinants of marital instability (Cherlin, 1979; Ambert, 1980).

The three major economic trends identified in the literature are all part of an overall process of modernization, which Goode (1963), focusing on the joint impact of the processes of industrialization and urbanization, has shown to be highly influential as a force transforming the structure and stability of the family. Socio-economic modernization variables are the standard fare of sociological and comparative public policy analysis. In what follows, therefore, we examine the degree of association between divorce rates and GDP per capita (an indicator of the shift in the economic base of households towards greater affluence), the size of the service sector (an indicator of the expansion of an economic sector particularly associated with female employment), the size of the non-agricultural labour force (a broad indicator of the modernization of the social structure and disruption of traditional patterns) and urbanization (indicating the shift away from traditional ways of living). It should be noted that the model we develop here, which rests on the analysis of successive national cross-sections and the change taking place between them, does not allow an investigation of the impact of short-term economic fluctuations on the propensity to divorce (see Cahen,1968; Rowe and Krishnan, 1980). Because of the hypothesized special importance of female opportunities for independence, we utilize female labour force participation (the most direct indicator of women's potential to maintain their economic independence) as a variable theoretically able to capture a separate dimension of the modernization process.

Religious belief, or rather its decline through the process of secularization, is of course another factor strongly associated with the process of modernity and may be seen as the attitudinal component of that process. The most common shift discussed is the erosion of religious sanctions upholding marriage or negatively sanctioning divorce. We have already noted the formative influence of religious belief in shaping the law of divorce, and it is not surprising to find that the major variable singled out as expressing this trend is the relative strength of different Christian denominations, with the strongest emphasis on the basic divide between Protestantism and Catholicism (Chester, 1977; Halem, 1980). Unfortunately, we do not have access to a religiosity variable capable of measuring the degree of secularization on a cross-national basis. As a substitute, we use Catholic adherence, hypothesized to be a negative predictor of divorce rates and divorce rate change, as the key test variable for the influence of religious belief on divorce rates. Whilst this choice may be criticized on the ground that it measures only the impact of a particular brand of the Christian faith, we plead in extenuation that the long post-Reformation shift away from the tenets of the Catholic faith represents a progressive weakening of ecclesiastical power in human affairs, and is thus part of the broad shift towards secularization. Unfortunately, speculation as to the positive impact on divorce rates of further normative shifts of a secularizing kind – including individualism, liberalism and hedonism (Ambert, 1980; Price and McKenry, 1988) – cannot be tested here for lack of suitable cross-national data.

Demographic factors may be related to divorce, either quasi-automatically as factors influencing the proportion of the population eligible to divorce or as factors with a more substantive bearing on marital instability. In the first category, we include the crude marriage rate (i.e. per 1000 of the population) as a means of controlling for the fact that the crude divorce rate (the only cross-nationally available measure of our dependent variable) may well be strongly influenced by the proportion of the population that is married. More substantively, fertility has been hypothesized to be linked to divorce by virtue of a propensity for those with few or no children to find it easier to escape from the bonds of matrimony. It has also been argued (Hart, 1976, 77; Fergussson et al., 1984, 539, 542; Norton and Glick, 1979) that this propensity is likely to increase if the age at marriage is relatively young. Below we examine the degrees of association between both fertility rates and early marriage (percentage of brides below the age of 20) and divorce rates.

A final factor much discussed has been the impact of *policy constraints*, in particular the availability of welfare payments to single mothers and the welfare state payments available to mothers and children more generally. Hart (1976, 71) hypothesizes 'that access to this meagre income is an important element in the increasing availability of divorce, particularly for couples at low income levels'. However, in a later assessment, Moles reviews both census data studies and longitudinal analyses of this possible welfare-dissolution link and finds the evidence to be either inconsistent or inadequate (although there is stronger evidence for an inverse relationship between welfare and remarriage) (Moles, 1979, 172–8). Albrecht et al. (1983, 54–5) describe similar disagreements concerning the findings of Cutright and Scanzoni, Bahr and Hannan. We would like to test this hypothesis by cross-national comparison because wide differences in national welfare systems suggest that any effects are likely to be more pronounced in such a context. There are, however, insuperable difficulties in obtaining data on the generosity of expenditure to single parents for a sample of nations anything like as extensive as the 17 under examination here.[8] The best proxy we can use is family transfers as a percentage of GDP (available for all our nations except Belgium), but we note that, since some part of such transfer expenditure is in varying degrees intended to preserve the integrity of complete families, any interpretation of the resulting correlates has to be speculative in the extreme.

Table 7.3 presents the bivariate correlations between these 10 contextual variables and divorce rates and divorce rate change. With the exception of Catholic religious affiliation, where data are only available for 1970 and

Table 7.3: Bivariate correlations between divorce rates, divorce rate change and contextual factors

	GDP	Services	Non-agricultural labour force	Urbanization	Female labour force	Catholic	Marriage rate	Fertility	Early marriage	Family transfers
1960 variables with 1961–68 divorce rate										
including US	.67**	.34	.37	.08	.38	–.47*	.46	.01	.54*	–.40
excluding US	.49*	–.02	.29	.05	.56*	–.56*	.41	–.44	.29	–.29
1976 variables with 1976–83 divorce rate										
including US	.69**	.66**	.70**	.39	.49*	–.55*	.58**	–.40	.30	–.17
excluding US	.60**	.58**	.73**	.56*	.57*	–.67**	.24	–.57*	.15	.10
change in variable with change in divorce rate										
including US	.17	–.29	–.71**	–.21	.50*	.57**	.39	–.73**	–.48*	.34
excluding US	.10	–.19	–.70**	–.15	.50	.44	.23	–.67**	–.38	.36
1960 variables with change in divorce rate										
including US	.73**	.76**	.75**	.53*	–.12	–.55*	.45	.37	.78**	–.36
excluding US	.64**	.70**	.74**	.57*	–.14	–.56*	.38	.25	.71**	–.27

Sources: GDP: Summers and Heston, 1988. Civilian employment in services, civilian employment in the non-agricultural sector and female labour force as a percentage of female employment: OECD, and notes, 1988. Percentage in Catholic religious affiliation: Barrett, 1982 (only 1970 and 1980 data available). Fertility rates and urbanization: United Nations, 1989. Marriage and divorce rates per 1000 of the population and early marriage (percentage of brides below the age of 20): from UN *Demographic Yearbook*. Family transfers as a percentage of GDP calculation: Varley, 1986 (data from Belgium missing).
Notes: *= significant at .05 level; **=significant at .01 level.

1980, the independent variables are lagged, 1960 and 1976 data being correlated with average divorce rates for the periods 1961–68 and 1976–83 respectively. This is necessary since at least some of these variables – most conspicuously female labour force participation and family transfers – might, in part, be inferred to be as much caused by, as causes of, divorce. Given that the US divorce rate is of a distinctly higher order of magnitude than that of the other nations included in the comparison, and that its status as a statistical 'outlier' might be expected to bias some of the relationships to a marked degree, correlations are reported both including and excluding that country. This expectation is strongly confirmed in respect of the size of the service sector and fertility in the earlier period and the marriage rate in the later period.

The data in Table 7.3 strongly affirm a link between a range of contextual factors and both the level of and the change in the divorce rate. With the single exception of family transfers, every variable is in some respect significantly related statistically to features of the post-war divorce phenomenon in this range of advanced capitalist societies. Moreover, the direction of the reported associations with the average level of divorce in both 1961–68 and 1976–83 is generally as might be expected from the hypotheses derived from the literature. The modernization variables are, with only one very minor exception (service sector size in 1960 excluding the US), positively associated with the divorce rate. Catholic affiliation is uniformly a significant negative predictor of divorce rates, and female labour force participation is only slightly less uniformly a positive predictor. With the exception of the sample including the US for the earlier period, fertility is always negatively associated with the level of divorce. Both marriage rate and early marriage correlate positively with divorce rates, although the former relationship is more consistently statistically significant. Although not quite significant, we note that the association for family transfers in 1960 is negative, possibly to be counted as evidence against the welfare availability hypothesis or, equally likely, a reflection of the problematical way in which that hypothesis is operationalized here. Finally, it is extremely noticeable that the overall impact of social context variables is far greater in the later than in the former period. For the 1960 variables, only one relationship is significant at the .01 level in the sample including the US, and none achieves that level in the sample excluding that country. For the 1977 variables, however, four achieve that level in both samples and two more are significant at the .05 level. This increasing influence of social context variables is a point to which we shall return later in our analysis.

When we come to change, we discover rather more departures from the relationships hypothesized in the literature. Two relatively minor anomalies are encountered in respect of the demographic variables: the fact that a decline in the rate of early marriage was marginally associated with an increase in the divorce rate, and that it was the countries which in 1960 had the highest levels of fertility that had the highest subsequent increase in divorce rates. Both findings somewhat contradict our expectations concerning predicted patterns of change, but only in the case of early marriage in the sample including the US to a degree which is statistically significant. A further anomaly is the positive association between change in Catholic affiliation and divorce rate change. Most probably, this is a consequence of a spurious relationship thrown up by the very minor changes in religious affiliation over the course of a decade which left the cross-national variation in strength of Catholicism wholly untouched, with the correlation between the 1970 and 1980 values of the variable being no less than .99.[9]

A much more interesting set of anomalies seems, on the surface at least, to characterize the associations between change in the degree of economic modernity and change in the divorce rate. With the exception of GDP and female labour force participation, change in modernity is negatively associated with a change in the divorce rate and, in the case of non-agricultural labour force change, very significantly so. On this basis, it would seem that the more rapidly countries were modernizing their economic and social structures, the *less* their divorce rates increased. A clue to understanding this counter-intuitive finding is to be discovered in the final part of the table, showing the very high correlation between all the 1960 economic modernization variables and divorce rate change in the ensuing period. In other words, it was in the nations that were already modern in 1960 that the divorce rate grew most rapidly, the apparent paradox of the change relationships being accounted for by the fact that it was these early modernizers that experienced least change in their social and economic structures thereafter. The seeming paradox here is one of convergence, shown at its most dramatic in a correlation (for all 17 countries) between the 1960 non-agricultural labour force and 1960–76 change in the same variable of no less than –.96.

A similar phenomenon would also be apparent in the case of GDP if that variable were measured as an economic growth rate rather than, as here, by the change in the size of GDP (see Castles and Dowrick, 1990). That might suggest to some that a negative association between economic growth and divorce rate change should be interpreted in terms of marital dissatisfaction caused by declining economic expectations. However, we reject such an interpretation. If we were to interpret the non-agricultural labour force association in the manner suggested as appropriate for economic growth, it would imply that the increasing disruption of the social structure caused by the shift out of agriculture was conducive to increased marital stability. The latter interpretation is clearly nonsensical and we prefer the clear evidence of the final lines of Table 7.3 that all these relationships demonstrate the lagged impact of economic modernity on marital behaviour. Although the demonstration of such a lagged effect goes beyond what is stated in the literature, it certainly does not contradict it; nor is it surprising, to the degree that we might reasonably expect changes in the economic base of society to take time to filter down to a level where they would impact on fundamental norms influencing marital behaviour.

On Paths to Divorce

Given the relatively small number of cases on which our comparative analysis is based, it is not possible to include all ten contextual variables in the final elaborations of our model which follow the advice of Kitson and Raschke (1981, 30) that multivariate designs are the best way forward for understanding 'the simultaneous and relative impact of a number of variables'. Our criteria for inclusion are based on theory and the character of the families of nations concept we are seeking to explore. We wish to include at least one economic modernization variable, since hypotheses linking modernization to changing social behaviour are at the very core of the sociological enterprise. We choose the size of the non-agricultural labour force as our key variable in this respect because an examination of correlation matrices for both periods shows that this variable alone is consistently strongly associated (in excess of .70) with all the other economic modernization variables in both periods. In that sense, it seems appropriate to regard the size of the non-agricultural labour force as the pivotal variable best expressing the multi-faceted aspects of the modernization process. It is also important to include female labour force participation as an indicator of what is also, almost certainly, a separate dimension of the modernization process. In support of the view that female labour force participation is unlike other components of modernization, we note a negative relationship (–.40) between that variable and the size of the non-agricultural labour force in the earlier period superseded by a small positive one (.27) in the later period. In fact, the relationship between economic modernization and female independence is almost certainly not a linear one. Phillips is convincing in suggesting a three-stage process, whereby the traditional family economy, in which women's work on the land created a complementarity of tasks and mutual dependence, was replaced in the early modernization phase by women's dependence based on the performance of home tasks, with greater female independence only resulting from the later shift of married women into manufacturing and service employment (Phillips, 1988,

590–92). Hence, in order to capture the impact of the major trends presumed by the literature to have shaped the trajectory of the divorce rate, it is necessary for our model to focus on the special factors influencing women's economic independence as well as on broader correlates of economic modernization.

At least two additional variables have to be included in our model in order to be able to confront a legal families of nations explanation with one based on social context. On the one hand, we have to include our operationalization of the extent of the liberality of the law in order to assess the separate impact of legal provisions; on the other, we need to include a test for the impact of religious belief, the variable that we might most readily assume could explain the character of the law without some reference to a continuity of legal procedures inherited from the past. As pointed out previously, if our negative indicator of secularization – the strength of Catholic affiliation – were capable of accounting for the vast proportion of the cross-national variance in divorce laws, it would at best argue for a cultural variant of the families of nations concept. However, it would simultaneously argue against a stronger variant of the families of nations concept: that these outputs, and the divorce outcomes to which they contribute, can be understood only in terms of historical continuity and distinctiveness of legal forms in different groupings of nations.

These four factors – economic modernization, female independence, religious belief and the liberality of the law – exhaust the number of variables it is possible to include in a reasonably coherent statistically based model of divorce rates and divorce rate change. Fortunately, they are simultaneously the variables which our calculations in Table 7.2 and 7.3 show to be most strongly and consistently associated with divorce outcomes. Welfare availability, whether because of the way we have measured it or because of the weakness of the basic hypothesis, did not manifest any degree of significant association with the divorce phenomenon. The demographic variables are, at best, inconsistent in their relationships with the level of and change in divorce rates, being only rarely (if at all) strongly associated with both level and change and frequently manifesting quite divergent associations depending on the inclusion or exclusion of the US. A few of the associations between demographic variables and change are, however, quite strong. In particular, declining fertility and high levels of early marriage in 1960 are both strongly associated with an increase in the divorce rate; in consequence, there may well be some misspecification of our model insofar as it pertains to change.

However, this is rather less probable in respect of divorce levels, with early marriage and the marriage rate being significantly positive predictors only for the samples including the US. We surmise that the exceptionally high marriage and early marriage rates throughout the period in the US may well have contributed to that country's exceptional divorce rates to some degree, but note that these factors contribute little to understanding variance in the remainder of the sample. Fertility in the later period in the sample excluding the US is significantly associated with the divorce rate, but over time this variable has become markedly more strongly associated with our measure of economic modernization – the size of the non-agricultural labour force (in 1960 only .05, by 1976, .66). In other words, fertility only becomes a predictor of the divorce rate once it also becomes a part of the syndrome of socio-economic modernization. In this necessarily broad-gauge model of the impact of social context, it may be that any independent effects of fertility are to some extent picked up by other modernization variables included in the model.

Figures 7.1 to 7.4 present versions of our preferred model of divorce outcomes for the periods 1961–68 and 1976–83 and for change over the period as a whole. The figures consist of path diagrams showing, by means of standardized regression coefficients, the strength of the associations between variables in a theoretically derived ordering of probable causal influences. In Figures 7.1 and 7.2, given the status of the US as an outlier, we estimate separate equations for the samples including and excluding the US. In respect of change, where the US ceases to be an outlier, this is no longer necessary and Figures 7.3 and 7.4 are derived from data for the entire sample.

The theoretical argument implicit in these path diagrams is that economic modernization and religious belief are prior influences impacting on the size of the female labour force and that all three impact on the law of divorce which, in turn, regulates the possibility of the legal dissolution of marriage. Such a causal ordering has very important implications for the families of nations concept. To the extent that we are able to account for variance in the divorce rate by the direct influence of the three social context variables alone, it is possible to discount explanations resting on the impact of distinctive legal families of nations. A similar conclusion would also be justified if we could fully account for the distinctiveness of variance in the law, even if the law were shown to be closely associated with variance in divorce rates. In the first instance, we could argue that the law was irrelevant and, in the second, that it was merely a reflection of social forces.

In order to establish a *prima facie* case for the importance of families of nations as a determinant of policy outcomes, we would need to demonstrate first that laws (the variance of which we have already shown to be closely associated with a long-term historical development in distinct families of nations) are at once a crucial factor in accounting for observed variation in divorce rates and, at the same time, are themselves only in part accounted for by social context. In the 1961–68 path diagram presented in Figure 7.1, this does appear to be the situation we confront. There are three significant predictors of divorce rates in the generally successful model for the smaller sample, which accounts for some 84 per cent of the variance observed. Two are contextual factors – the size of female labour force participation and of the non-agricultural labour force – with the latter rather more important. However, even when we control for both these contextual variables, much the strongest predictor is the degree of liberality of the law. The law itself is less than adequately accounted for by the model variables, with only around 60 per cent of the variance explained. The only statistically significant predictor of liberality is the negative impact of Catholic affiliation. One simple indicator of how important the influence of the law was at this date is the decline in explained variation of the model from 84 to 57 per cent when its impact is removed. Thus for 1961–68, the story is as follows: that the law is the single most important influence on variance in divorce, that the law itself only to a very minor degree reflects the extent of economic modernization, and that only changing religious belief (a vital cultural dimension of modernization) produces a strong and statistically significant path to divorce via variance in divorce law. We note with little surprise that whilst paths to the 1960 liberal law are almost identical in the samples including and excluding the US, the model including the US is wholly unsatisfactory in accounting for the 1961–68 divorce rate.

If it is possible to make separate cases for both cultural and historical families of nations approaches in the 1960s, the latter case is much diminished for the later period. In the period 1976–83, as shown in Figure 7.2, it is the law alone which is a significant predictor of divorce rates in the model excluding the US (the full model is again unsatisfactory, although not to quite the same degree), and variance in the law of divorce is now itself adequately accounted for by the effects of economic modernization and religious belief. The big changes in the structure of the relationships between the earlier and the later period are the replacement of the direct association between economic modernization and divorce rates by an indirect relationship mediated by the nature of legal provision and the disappearance of the somewhat more tenuous links between female labour force participation and both divorce rates and legal provision. The latter set of changes is interesting in casting some doubts on the hypothesis of a link between women's independence provided by labour market position and the propensity to seek dissolution of marriage. It is possible that the tendency might be more pronounced if the model were not lagged, which would suggest that divorce itself contributes to enhanced female labour force participation; as it stands, however, it would appear that much of the quite strong bivariate association between the two variables is accounted for by the increasingly strong negative relationship between Catholicism and women's labour force participation. Although within the structure of the model, the law is now the only direct influence on outcomes, it is an influence mediating these other effects; removing the law from the model now only reduces the degree of explained variance from 83 to 71 per cent.

A more direct insight into the processes that took place over the period as a whole can be gained from Figures 7.3 and 7.4. Figure 7.3 shows how transformations in social context and the law impacted on change in the divorce rate. Only one significant path to divorce rate change emerges, with change in the non-agricultural labour force highly negatively associated with the liberalization of the law – the only substantial predictor of change in the divorce rate.[10] As explained previously, the counter-intuitive effect of the shift out of agriculture is to be accounted for by the dramatic

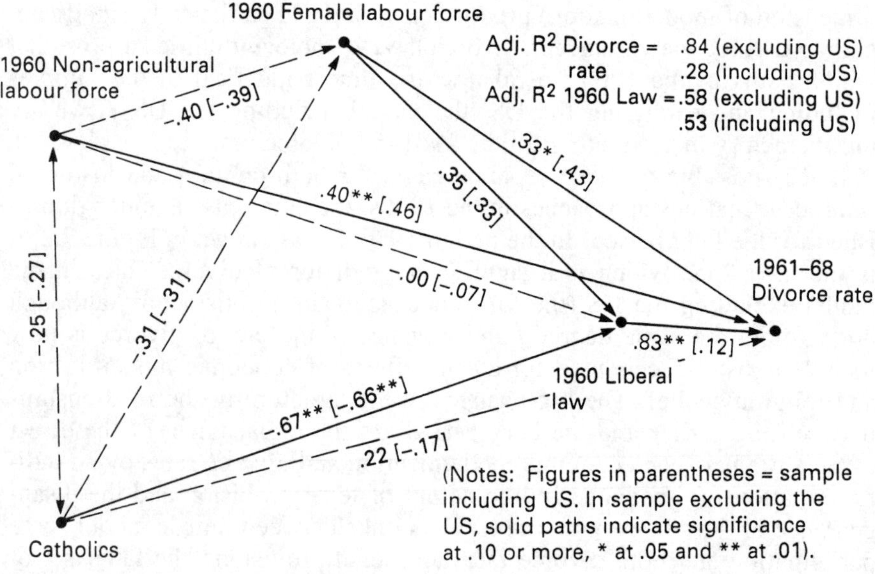

Figure 7.1: Paths to divorce, 1961–68

convergence of this indicator of economic modernization. This is clearly demonstrated in Figure 7.4 which illustrates the antecedents of liberalization of the law and subsequent divorce law change. Here it is shown that liberalization occurred precisely in those nations which were the most economically modernized in 1960 and in which the influence of Catholicism was least, leading to a dramatic shift away from prior legal forms; thus the liberality of the law in 1960 was a strong negative predictor of the change that took place thereafter.

In other words, with the exception of the cultural continuity by which Catholicism negatively conditioned legal barriers to the dissolution of marriage, the trajectory of legal transformation was shaped by a reaction to the contradiction of outdated laws persisting under conditions of economic modernity. That contradiction, assessed in terms of the discrepancy of the size of the non-agricultural labour force in 1960 and the liberality of the

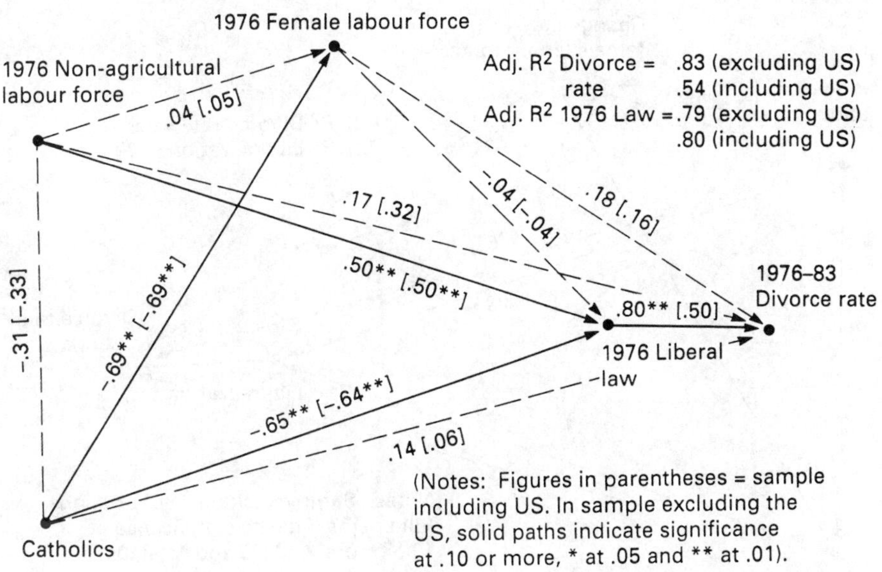

Figure 7.2: Paths to divorce, 1976–83

law at the same date, was at its greatest in the UK, the US, Belgium, the Netherlands, Australia and Canada in descending order of economic modernization. Only Belgium of these six countries failed to make the transition from fault-based divorce laws to ones based largely on separation or irretrievable breakdown of marriage in the period 1960–76: Belgium is also the only one of these countries in which Catholicism is the predominant Christian denomination. Moreover, given that the liberalization of the law is the only significant predictor of change in divorce rates over the period, this concrete identification of the countries in which the contradiction was most apparent explains why the phenomenon of 'English awfulness' is so strongly associated with divorce rate change in the period. Pre-eminently, it was in the English-speaking world that this contradiction between divorce law and modernity existed. This finding makes a fascinating counter-point to the analysis of the earlier chapters on policy dynamics in the 1980s and

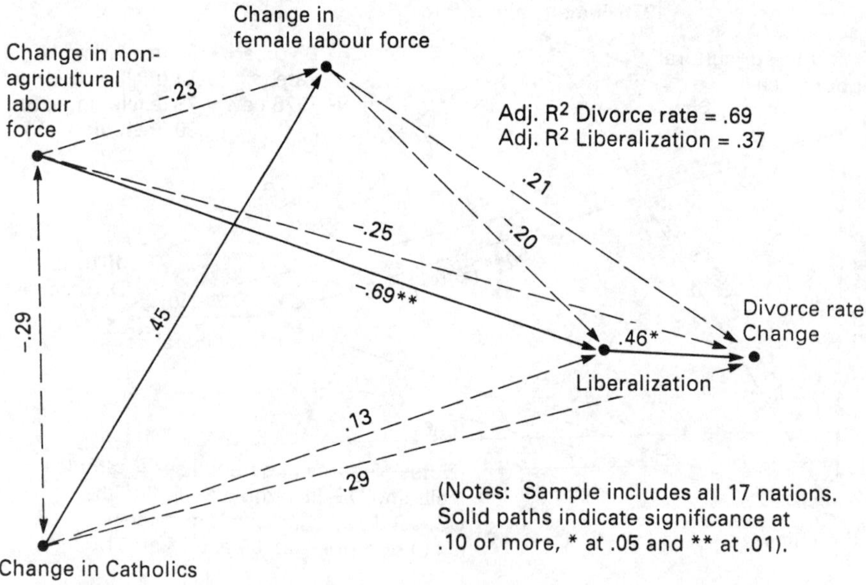

Figure 7.3: Paths to divorce rate change

on the relationship between welfare transfers and equality, in which it was demonstrated that many of the singularities of the English-speaking family of nations stemmed from their early modernity.

The major deficiency of the explanation offered here is, of course, its failure to account for divorce rates in the US, the country in which divorce was much the most prevalent in both periods. On the other hand, the same model which fails to explain the level of the American divorce rate is wholly adequate as an account of changes over the period in the sample as a whole. That suggests that the model itself may not be inadequate, but rather that the exceptionalism of the US may relate either to additional factors specific to the American experience or some misspecification of the character of that experience in terms of the model variables. In respect of the former, demographic factors may well be of some relevance insofar as that country manifests much the highest marriage and early marriage rates

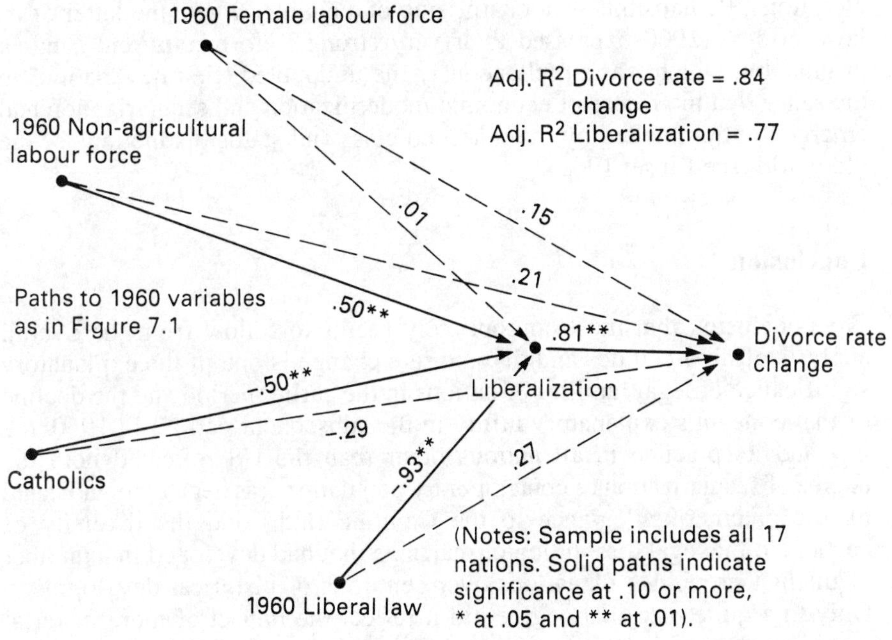

Figure 7.4: Antecedents of liberalization and divorce rate change

of any country in this study. Further factors, unfortunately impossible to analyse in a comparative study of this kind, are the suggestion that the US is characterized by a particularly individualistic ethos, conducive to a search for greater self-fulfilment in marriage (see Weiss, 1975) and the undoubted fact of the country's decentralized power structure, allowing a unique divergence of family law along a moving frontier.

With regard to possible misspecification of the model, we may hark back to the exceptional disparity between the practice and the letter of the American law of divorce. Although we do not wish to build it into a major point, we note with some interest that, were we to classify the US in terms of the practical permissiveness of its laws in 1960 and 1976, scoring it as being as liberal as the Scandinavian nations at the former date and one step more so than any nation except Sweden in 1976 (for a justification of the latter, see note 5), the path diagrams for the sample including the USA become far more like those which exclude that country. The obvious implication is that, in terms other than the strict stipulations of the law, the US is incorrectly classified as a typical member of the English-speaking family of nations. Perhaps this is not surprising of a country where the letter of its laws prior to 1960 expressed their very strong Reformation and English origins, but which was simultaneously the undoubted 'first new nation' in the sense that the forces of economic modernization and secularization had emerged untrammelled by the inherited class and status distinctions of the old world (see Lipset,1963).

Conclusion

The conclusion that most appropriately seems to follow from the overall analysis of divorce rates and divorce rate change is one of the explanatory significance of legal families of nations in the earlier period and the decline of that concept's explanatory utility in the subsequent period. In 1960, the law and its practice in all nations other than the US reflected both the degree of secularization of contemporary populations (as negatively indicated by the extent of allegiance to the Catholic faith) and the diversity of barriers to the legal dissolution of marriage that had developed in a number of distinct groupings of nations over centuries of historical development. Only to a quite marginal degree did it reflect the impact of more material manifestations of modernization, and then it was women's capacity to exert their independence through employment that counted rather than the general modernization of the socio-economic structure.

What appears to have occurred in the 1960s and 1970s was a dramatic breakthrough of the impact of economic modernization on the law, although this was still somewhat constrained in the countries where Catholicism was strongest. The mechanisms of that breakthrough are not stipulated in the model presented here and could only be located with any precision by a comparative study of the ways in which various facets of economic modernization shaped a normative re-evaluation that encouraged diverse groups within the non-Catholic churches and the population at large to press for legal reform. It was these reforms which finally undermined the continuity and persistence of the legal families of nations that had hitherto exercised so potent an influence on public policy in the domestic arena of marriage. A full account of the sources of national diversity in divorce outcomes prior to those reforms and of the starting point for the trajectory of the reform movement itself is not possible unless we start from an understanding of the divorce phenomenon which allows for the notion of the historical continuity of distinct families of nations.

Notes

1. This also applies to many aspects of the increasingly explicit adoption of integrated packages of 'family' policy, where the state intervenes to provide a whole series of services to the family with the dual objectives of providing social protection and maintaining family stability (see Kamerman and Kahn, 1978). Clearly, some aspects of family policy in this sense may be relevant to the incidence of divorce, a point discussed somewhat more fully in a later section.
2. A simpler distinction, common to earlier work in comparative law, would be between Anglo-American, Nordic and Romano-Germanic legal systems. This typology, regarded by Glendon as illuminating the character of national differences in both the contemporary law of abortion and divorce, is another illustration that the families of nations concept is neither new nor alien to the analysis of legal systems (Glendon, 1987). The Romano-Germanic system apart (which our typology of five families of nations further subdivides), the two other systems identified in the comparative law tradition are identical with the families of nations used throughout this study.
3. From 1907, the courts had the discretionary right to disallow a petition where the non-consenting partner was not guilty of a fault.
4. For an alternative categorization of post-1960 divorce laws only, see Glendon, 1987, 68.
5. If one were to offer a more fine-grained typology respecting the liberality of contemporary divorce laws, Sweden and these more liberal American states might feature as a separate category. Glendon suggests that by the mid-1980s, the US taken as a whole was second only to Sweden, where most divorces are granted on application, in respect of making marriage freely terminable (Glendon, 1987, 64).
6. Divorce *a mensa et thoro* ('from bed and board') or judicial separation, inherited directly from the jurisdiction of the ecclesiastical courts, is permitted on grounds of adultery and cruelty (see Shatter, 1981).
7. Others were Sweden and Denmark, before the liberalization of family law in the first decades of the century, and France, where the law of 1884 was progressively inter-

preted in such a way as to permit *de facto* mutual consent. In Italy, the recognition in 1902 of divorces made abroad offered a channel for legal dissolution, amounting by the 1920s to 10 per cent of the annual number of judicial separations (see Sgritta and Tufari, 1977, 258).

8. We do have data for ten countries on the percentage of lone families defined as poor post-transfers (see Mitchell, 1991), but this hardly supports the welfare availability hypothesis. On the contrary, three of the four most divorce-prone countries of Table 7.2 – the US, Canada and Australia – qualify as providing the worst deal for lone parents, with poverty rates ranging from 45.7 to 38.7 per cent.
9. However, it is just possible that it is indirectly indicative of a positive relationship between large-scale migration and an increase in divorce, insofar as the only countries to experience any appreciable increase in Catholic affiliation (1 per cent or more) were the Anglo-Saxon countries of mass migration (the US, Australia and New Zealand), which in the immediate post-war decades attracted a somewhat disproportionate number of Catholics to their shores.
10. The only other paths in Figure 7.3 of any importance are the positive associations between change in Catholic affiliation and both change in the divorce rate and change in female labour force participation. As argued earlier, the relationship with divorce rate change (see exposition in the section *On the Correlates of Divorce*) may well be spurious, although it could be that the spuriousness arises (see note 9) because change in Catholic affiliation stands as an indirect proxy for the impact of migration on divorce rate change.

References

Albrecht, S.L., Bahr, H.M. and Goodman, K.L. (1983), *Divorce and Remarriage: Problems, Adaptations and Adjustments*, Westport, Conn.: Greenwood Press.

Ambert, A-M.(1980), *Divorce in Canada*, Ontario: Academic Press Canada.

Barrett, D.B. (ed.), (1982), *World Christian Encyclopedia: A Comparative Study of Churches and Religions in the Modern World AD 1900–2000*, Nairobi: Oxford University Press.

Cahen, A. (1968), *A Statistical Analysis of American Divorce*, New York: AMS Press.

Castles, F.G. and Dowrick, S. (1990), 'The Impact of Government Spending Levels on Medium-Term Economic Growth in the OECD, 1960–85', *Journal of Theoretical Politics*, **2** (2), 173–204.

Cherlin, A. (1979), 'Work Life and Marital Dissolution' in G. Levinger, and O.C. Moles (eds), *Divorce and Separation: Context, Causes, and Consequences* , New York: Basic Books.

Chester, R. (ed.) (1977), *Divorce in Europe*, Belgium: Netherlands Interuniversity Demographic Institute.

Fergusson, D.M., Horwood, L.J. and Shannon, F.T. (1984), 'A Proportional Hazards Model of Family Breakdown', *Journal of Marriage and the Family*, **46** (3), August.

Glendon, M.A. (1987), *Abortion and Divorce in Western Law*, Cambridge, Mass.: Harvard University Press.

Goode, W.J. (1963), *World Revolution and Family Patterns*, New York: The Free Press.

Halem, L.C. (1980), *Divorce Reform: Changing Legal and Social Perspectives*, New York: The Free Press.

Hart, N. (1976), *When Marriage Ends: A Study in Status Passage*, Great Britain: Tavistock

Kamerman, S.B. and Kahn, A.J. (eds), (1978), *Family Policy: Government and Families in Fourteen Countries*, New York: Columbia University Press.

Kitchin, S.B. (1912), *A History of Divorce*, London: Chapman and Hall.

Kitson, G.C. and Raschke, H.J. (1981), 'Divorce Research: What We Know; What We Need to Know', *Journal of Divorce*, **4** (3), 1–37.

Law Reform Commission of Canada (1975), *Studies on Divorce,* Ottawa: Information Canada.

Lipset, S.M. (1963), *The First New Nation: The United States in Historical and Comparative Perspective*, New York: Basic Books.

Mitchell, D. (1991), 'Comparing Income Transfer Systems: Is Australia the Poor Relation?' in F.G. Castles (ed.), *Australia Compared*, Sydney: Allen and Unwin.

Moles, O.C. (1979), 'Public Welfare Payments and Marital Dissolution: A Review of Recent Studies' in G. Levinger and O.C. Moles (eds), *Divorce and Separation: Context, Causes, and Consequences*, New York: Basic Books.

Mortimer Commission (1966), *Putting Asunder: A Divorce Law for Contemporary Society*, London: SPCK.

Norton, A.J. and Glick, P.C. (1979), 'Marital Instability in America: Past, Present and Future' in G. Levinger and O.C. Moles (eds), *Divorce and Separation: Context, Causes, and Consequences*, New York: Basic Books.

OECD (1988), *OECD Historical Statistics*, 1960–86, Paris.

Phillips, R. (1988), *Putting Asunder: A History of Divorce in Western Society*, New York: Cambridge University Press.

Price, S.J. and McKenry, P.C. (1988), *Divorce*, Berkeley: Sage Publications.

Rheinstein, M. (1968), 'Divorce Law in Sweden' in P. Bohannen (ed.), *Divorce and After*, New York: Doubleday and Co.

Rheinstein, M. (1972), *Marriage Stability, Divorce and the Law*, Chicago: Chicago University Press.

Rowe, G. and Krishnan, P. (1980), 'A Comparative Analysis of Divorce Rates in Canada and the United States, 1921–1967', *Journal of Divorce*, **4** (1), 61–72.

Sgritta, G.B. and Tufari, P. (1977), 'Italy' in R. Chester (ed.), *Divorce in Europe*, Belgium: Netherlands Interuniversity Demographic Institute.

Shatter, A.J. 1981), *Family Law in the Republic of Ireland*, Dublin: Wolfhound Press, 2nd edition.

Stone, L. (1990), *Road to Divorce: England 1530–1987*, London: Oxford University Press.

Summers, R. and Heston, A. (1988), 'A New Set of International Comparisons of Real Product and Price Levels: Estimates for 130 Countries, 1950–85', *Review of Income and Wealth*, **34** (1), 1–25.

United Nations (various dates), *UN Demographic Yearbook*, New York.

United Nations (1989), *World Population Prospects*, New York.
Varley, R. (1986), *The Government Household Transfer Base 1960–84*, Paris: OECD.
Vernier C.G. (1932), *American Family Laws*, Stanford: Stanford University Press.
Weiss, R.S. (1975), *Marital Separation*, New York: Basic Books.
Weitzman, L.J. (1985), *The Divorce Revolution*, New York: The Free Press.
Wolcott, I. and Glezer, H. (1989), *Marriage Counselling in Australia*, Melbourne: Australian Institute of Family Studies.

CONCLUSION

8 Beyond the Lonely Nation-State

Göran Therborn

Ideas and Concepts

The idea of families of nations derives from the observation that nation-states are not always or usually a set of unattached singles looking at, comparing and occasionally pairing up with each other in now this, then that, temporary combination. It implies that analysts should not assume that nation-states always constitute separate 'cases' of variable constellations, and that the larger the number of the former, the more reliable the latter. Instead, nation-states may be part of patterned interrelationships, of families of nations. Relationships between the independent and the dependent variables of comparative researchers do not necessarily occur within each country separately, but may be part of complex inter-state, inter-national linkages – and not only of the world system.

We may distinguish between four types of families or groupings of nations. First, there is the *lineage* type, held together by descent from a common origin of some sort. Secondly, there are the *separated siblings*, kindred nations kept apart by state boundaries or, more concretely, non-state-bound social units with significant similarities between them, irreducible to common ancestry. Then, we have what might be called (elective) *affinity groups*, the *Wahlverwandtschaft*, connected by processes of diffusion, of imitation or avoidance (negative affinity), freely elected or established by pressure. Finally, there are the *partnerships*, the unions of deliberate coordination. The kinship of nations is multilinear, overlayered and subject-centred. Any given member may count his or her kinship affiliation in terms of different overlapping lineages, affinities and partnerships. So should the observer.

'Nation' and 'country' are used here in the pre-modern, pre-nationalist sense, in the same sense in which we would say that old universities have students from different nations or in the way that a wine-seller would refer to a wine of the country. In other words, the terms are used to denote meaningful localities of variable size and with fuzzy, not always guarded, boundaries. Thus, the families of nations idea has nothing in common with any kind of pan-nationalism nor with any equation of state and nation. 'Nations' are conceived as having only contingent relationships with states and state boundaries. For most practical purposes of comparative research, 'nations' will no doubt refer to states and state-bounded societies. But it should be emphasized that involved in the families of nations perspective is a post-modernist transcendence of the individualist state nationalism characteristic of the modern era.

Meanderings of Descent

In the commoner world of social science, descent is the more important the less direct it is and the less visible its current expressions. The reason is that if ancestry is straight-lined and conspicuous, it is rather likely to be discerned even by conventional variable searchers. Religion, for instance, constitutes old lineages of nations, the existence of which is fairly obvious. But unless there is a direct effect of religious affiliation upon current behaviour or current institutions in non-genealogical research, patterns of covariation will either stop at the black-box level of correlation or be dismissed as meaningless. Lineages of nations acquire their special importance as explanatory variables to the extent that they refer to effects of common ancestry which are not immediately or directly present, but which operate primarily by bending or shaping posterior variables and relationships.

A brilliant piece of genealogical political analysis, making use of what we here call lineages, is the late Stein Rokkan's (1970) accounting for modern European political cleavages and party systems. Religion plays a key role, but in a complex way which explains both the importance and the non-importance of religious political affiliation. Religious ancestry, according to Rokkan, shaped 20th-century European party politics in two generational waves. The first was the Reformation, which brought about two families of nations, one in which the state controlled the national Protestant church, another in which the state was allied to the international or inter-state Catholic church.

The second determinant generation was that of the French Revolution and its continental repercussions of mass popular mobilization. Rokkan here points to the conflicts over the control of mass education as a key instance. The result was a further division of the Christian inheritance. Among the state-controlled churches, another divide acquired new importance: between overwhelming national Protestantism and nations with strong Catholic minorities. From the Catholic anciens régimes came a new divide between the states of secularizing revolution (France, Italy, Spain) and those still allied to the Church (as in Austria and Belgium).[1] These religious cleavages have variously affected the character of modern party systems, social policy development (see discussion of the Conservative welfare state in Chapter 3; cf. Therborn, 1989a) and labour market outcomes (see Chapter 5, pp. 207–9).

In comparative law, the family concept is well established in the notion of *legal families*. This is primarily a lineage concept, although legal comparativists may define the characteristic 'style' of a legal family in a compound manner: '(1) its historical background and development, (2) its predominant and characteristic mode of thought in legal matters, (3) especially distinctive institutions, (4) the kind of legal sources it acknowledges and the way it handles them, and (5) its ideology' (Zweigert and Kötz 1987, 69). Zweigert and Kötz distinguish eight legal families: the Romanistic, the Germanic, the Nordic, the Common Law, the socialist (currently largely emptied of members), the Far Eastern, the Islamic, and the Hindu families of law.

A modern state like Canada belongs to two legal families: Anglo-Canada to that of Common Law, Québec to the Romanistic family. The latter is also important in the hybrid legal system of Louisiana in otherwise Common Law United States.

When taking legal output as a policy outcome, conventional policy studies may easily miss the reason for certain features of a piece of legislation or jurisdiction or of a process of (attempted) legislation, if the legal family of the state or states in question is not taken into account. Certainly, wherever law has been to the forefront in the analysis of policy outcomes in this volume – laws delineating the citizen status of 'guest workers' in Chapter 4, laws adumbrating the rights of children in Chapter 6 and laws regulating the dissolution of marriage in Chapter 7 – the families of nations approach has appeared as a vital key to understanding otherwise incomprehensible policy similarities between nations.

The advent of religion and law was, of course, originally an event which constituted a crucial experience, a founding moment of an institutionalized culture of a group of nations. But we may also distinguish decisive moments of historical experience which have weighed heavily upon subsequent generations without crystallizing in a single cultural form.

One example is the kind of entry into political modernity and its ensuing effects upon political cleavages and cultures. In a literally global comparative study of political rise of the suffrage (Therborn, in press a), I have distinguished four basic routes to modernity, defined in terms of the rights to vote and to political participation. In these terms, we may identify four major global lineages of nations: the pioneering endogenous European one, developing through civil wars and ideological battles between native tradition and native modernity on the basis of ancient electoral traditions; the ethno-conflict-centred, socially and ideologically underdetermined New Worlds (of both Americas and Oceania) ensuing from early modern mass migration; the traumatized colonial zone, to which modernity arrived out of the barrels of guns and had to be learnt and appropriated by the colonized before being turned against them; and finally the countries of externally-induced modernization, threatened but never conquered by European and American imperialism, countries in which modern political rights were granted from above as means to cultural and political survival in face of foreign threats.

Formative historical experiences might also, from another angle, be divided into those of achievement, with ensuing cultures of pride, trust and hope, and into experiences of history as defeat, betrayal, frustration. The Swiss anthropologist Christian Giordano (1992) has looked into the lineage of defeats or, as he has put it, into the 'subjection mentality' (*Überlagerungsmentalität*) of those 'betrayed by history' (*Betrogenen der Geschichte*). Giordano has studied Mediterranean societies, Sicily in particular, as an instance. This phenomenon may be occurring, in variants, in other societies with long and deep experiences of foreign conquest and heteronomy. The subjection mentality harbours an 'hierarchical ontology', a personalistic and particularistic conception of social relations, a mistrust of people outside the circle of family and friends, a deep alienation from the state, a worldview that socio-economic improvement depends on violence, connections or luck, rather than on achievement and foresight.

Both types of cultural lineage tend to be self-perpetuating, and both should weigh heavily upon the implementation and the results of public policies.

Lineages of nations need not necessarily manifest themselves in cultural forms. They may also derive from formative structurations of resources and constraints on action. Rokkan dealt with both. Whereas the European state-culture dimension runs north-south, there is also a state-economy axis going east-west. To agrarian and early modern political historians, the east-west divide of Europe along the Elbe and its extensions has been a crucial partition between two lineages of European social formations.

Rokkan also brought into focus an area in between, the 'city belt' of urban networks along the trans-Alpine medieval trade route (for a final formulation see Rokkan and Urwin, 1983, ch. 2). This is, in our era, Italy, Switzerland, Benelux and the Rhineland, to this day characteristically urban, mercantile, polycephalic and central, but neither becoming strong national state centres nor being well-integrated into nation-state centres located elsewhere. Instead, save for the Swiss, this city belt became in the post-World War II period the heartland of the strivings towards an economic union of Western Europe, providing its leading politicians, the bulk of its mass support, and the most reliable loyalty to it (see further Therborn, in press b).

Institutional structures may be common to descendants of a common power, e.g. a former imperial power, or to the children of decisive moments of power. On the whole, there has been rather limited comparative political research into lineages of institutional structure. One example refers to structures of local government and of local-central government relations. Concluding a major overview of European local government, Hesse and Sharpe (1990–91) distinguish three families of local government in Western Europe: the 'Franco' group deriving from the Napoleonic organization, the 'Anglo' one and a 'North and Middle European' family.[2]

In Different State Homes

This case is not concerned with 'the German question' prior to 1990. The nationalist unification conception of one nation, but two, three or many states[3] falls analytically under the lineage of common descent. Instead, attention should be paid to the fact that, instances of irredenta aside, there are significant cultural, and perhaps also structural, affinities cutting through state boundaries. Here we have a mixture of kinship mechanisms. Elements of ancestry and elective affinity are involved, as well as moments of coordinated partnership. It is the combination of state and non-state traditions and environments which is characteristic of this type of family of nations.

The most typical cultural example in the Western world is the commonality of Wallonia, 'romande' Switzerland, Québec and France. Or, turning the picture around, looking at the same kind of relations from the geography of the meeting-point, there is the convergence of German, French and Italian cultures in Switzerland. How important these bonds across state boundaries actually are, or have been, to presumably sensitive policy areas like education, family, culture, mass communication, or to administrative and judicial procedure, seems to be little known.[4] While the ignorance of this writer is without doubt significant here, it might be suggested nevertheless that the separated siblings aspect of comparative policy research is not very strongly developed.

The separated siblings notion is, however, clearly taken very seriously by French policy-makers, with their special ministry of international francophony, although in the spring of 1992 the Socialist majority rejected a constitutional amendment which would have put France's adherence to the international francophone movement constitutionally on a par with its belonging to the European Union.[5]

Another set of issues may be raised about the effects of structural similarities cutting through state territories. An example of their potential importance in current Europe, underlined by the slogan of a 'Europe of regions', arises from an analytical economic re-division of the Western part of the continent. The OECD-defined regions of the EC and of the six major EFTA countries[6] (Austria, Finland, Iceland, Norway, Sweden and Switzerland) were submitted to a cluster analysis with a view to finding a new Western European Twelve, this time the most homogenous units in terms of GDP per capita. Of the 16 countries comprising more than one region in the OECD sense, none had all regions in the same cluster. Only Greece, with three regions, had its regions in two adjacent clusters. For the rest, the spread was quite wide. West German regions fanned out between clusters 1 and 7, French between 2 and 9, British between 5 and 9, Swiss between 3 and 6, etc. The EC (population-weighted) inter-country variation is smaller than the regional variation of France and Italy, and equal to the regional variation of West Germany or of Spain [7] (Therborn, in press b). The possible effects of this divergence of economic structuration from state borders still has to be assessed.

Poles of Affinity and the Deviousness of Attraction

Quiz for policy analysts (and others): what do the State of New York, Lord Beveridge, the Politburo of the ex-CPSU and the Bundesbank have in common? Answer, they have all been important poles of reference for trans-border policy affinities. True, their areas of radiation have differed, from states of the American Union to Eastern Europe plus parts of Africa, Asia and a piece of the Caribbean, while the kinship with Beveridge or the Bundesbank has been recognized primarily in (parts of) Western Europe. The processes of diffusion have certainly also varied.

However, there are families of nations (or 'states') bonded by elective affinity, an affinity which as an empirical rule, although not with any logical necessity, has a central node or a pole pulling or attracting the other members. It should be noticed that families of this kind are also defined in terms other than a proximity of variable values. It is the extrovert orientation of the key policy actors and the diffusion of policy measures and stances which concern us here. The rationale is, again, that to the extent that borrowing, imitation, creative selection or other processes of diffusion are involved, explanations relying on domestic variables alone will be misplaced.

The behavioural effects of attraction are rarely instant, simple, and non-variable. That is, in my view, what makes this kind of connection interesting. In practice, however, it seems that assumptions to the contrary have stood in the way of any great use of such a perspective in comparative analysis. To my knowledge, it has not (as it might well have done) guided research on the once Communist countries; moreover, in welfare state research, the use of a diffusionist approach has sometimes been dismissed with little ado, as being unable to explain the whole historical process of the founding of modern social security legislation (Flora and Alber, 1981, 60ff).

But undoubtedly, Bismarck and Beveridge have constituted two major poles of affinity to people concerned with social issues in a number of countries. Stein Kuhnle (1978) has submitted to subtle analysis the very selective process of Scandinavia's Bismarckian orientation. The variable results of attempts at following Beveridge in post-war Western Europe have been studied by Berben et al. (1986). How American states form affinities of policy-making was the object of a pioneering study by Jack Walker (1969). It was Walker who found that New York, together with Massachusetts and California, had been the leading policy innovators in the US from 1870–1965.

The links of affinity appear, in the main, to be of three kinds. One consists of political attraction or, put more generally, of common or similar cultural *values*. The affinity with Beveridge or with the Soviet Politburo was clearly of this type. The intercontinental attractiveness of privatization is a noteworthy current example, quite apart from its lineage aspects discussed in Chapter 1. But explanations in terms of value affinity tend, in turn, to raise questions regarding the causes of vanguards and of their attractiveness. Thereby we tend, sooner or later, to get at the two other major bonds of affinity.

Another link is more governed by *cognitive familiarity* and a sense of *cultural identity*. It is here that language comes in as a significant aspect of families of nations, probably as a medium of cognition more than as a point of identity. Unless state borders run along lines of current political conflict, proximity should also favour cognitive familiarity. However, cognitive familiarity should not be seen as a cultural given, but as something *de facto* actively constructed – as something easily accessible culturally. You can spot it as an analyst by looking at what sources of information public investigation committees, policy-makers and policy commentators avail themselves of.

The attraction of Bismarck's social policy was probably more related to cognitive familiarity with Germany in northern Europe than with any strong attraction his values held. The Nordic policy family of nations operates as an affinity primarily through linguistically and geographically favoured knowledge and through a vague sense of common cultural identity. Within the Nordic context, a special bond exists between Finland and Sweden, deriving from descent, proximity and language connection (Swedish is Finland's second official language, although very much minority one), as well as structural relations of relative prosperity, most immediately manifested in active Finnish familiarity with Swedish policies and experiences. That relation has been the occasion for one of the most beautiful studies of this type of affinity of national family relations by Lauri Karvonen (1981).

The reason why Danish constitutes the ninth world language as a source of translations, well ahead of Arabic, Japanese and Chinese, for example, stems from the Nordic affinity of cognition and identity, manifested in translations into the other Nordic languages (Therborn, in press b).

A third basis of affinity is primarily *structural*, deriving from a distribution of power and constraints and from an actor's centrality in it. In Eastern Europe, attention to the policies of the Soviet Politburo was certainly determined not only by ideological attraction but also by considerations of power. The most clear-cut recent example of structural affinity, though, is arguably the pull of the Bundesbank and of West German monetary policy. It is little inspired by fear, which certainly was strongly instilled in the Eastern European watchers of the Politburo of the CPSU, but neither does it seem to be characterized by any strong amount of value attraction.

Contemporary Western European monetary policy is largely governed, not (only) by domestic policy-making variables but (also) by consideration of what the Bundesbank is doing. The Austrians pioneered it, in 1973.[8] The Dutch and the Belgians, in particular, followed suit. On 15 June 1990, the Belgian government officially pegged the franc to the D-Mark (*Economie Europénne* 1990, 39, 71ff). However, the weight of German influence is not only felt and acknowledged by the smaller states of Western Europe. In July 1992, for instance, there was a discussion in Britain about how short or how long were the reins of the Mark and the Bundesbank to British policy-makers (*Financial Times*, 18–19 July 1992, 5–7). In October, those reins were stretched too far and the link was broken (see also the discussion of Chapter 3).

To what extent the Bundesbank, the European Monetary System (dominated by Germany), the IMF and other forces of external constraint are directly determinant or only re-weighting a variety of national options which are still open is an important issue of current economic policy discussion. Perhaps the strongest case for the latter view has been argued by Richard Cooper (1987).

The Marriage Boom

Current public policy-making is increasingly influenced by a boom of cross-national deliberations and agreements. There are world summits on the environment (in 1992) and on children (in 1990). Since 1975 there have been regular meetings of the seven wealthiest countries of the world, now familiar as the G7. Benelux economic cooperation goes back to the immediate post-World War II period. The finance ministers of Germany, Austria and Switzerland meet regularly once a year. Recently, a tradition of Iberian summits has been created.

The EC was conducive to the latter, and has also spawned a set of regional cross-state deliberative bodies. One example is the 'Arge Alp', formed by the Swiss cantons of Graubünden, Sankt Gallen and Ticino, the Austrian Länder Salzburg and Vorarlberg; the German Länder Baden-Württemberg and Bayren, and the Italian provinces of Alto Adige/South Tirol, Lombardy and Trento.

The most important of these marriages is, of course, the EC, which is also having repercussions in the Americas and in Asia. The treaties of Rome to Maastricht, together with the adjudication of the European Court of Justice create a very significant family of nations bonded by contracts freely entered into.

The modern trailblazers of contractual bonding among states were those of the German Bund after the Napoleonic Wars. In retrospect, though, that may be seen as a preparatory step to German unification. The oldest surviving marriage of joint deliberation and coordination between sovereign states is that of the Nordic countries, going back to legal cooperation between Denmark, Norway and Sweden in the early 1870s; this was before the legal unification of Switzerland had begun and two decades before the start of legal coordination among the states of the US (Chapter 6 above).

Europe is currently overlaid by a whole set of partly overlapping cross-national organizations of deliberation and cooperation. There is the widest European Conference on Security and Cooperation, followed by the North Atlantic Council of Cooperation (grouping Nato and the ex-Warsaw Pact), the Council of Europe, the EC-EFTA European Economic Area, the EC and EFTA, the Confederation of Independent States, the Common Market of the Black Sea, the Western European Union, the Nordic Council and the Benelux Group, down to more *ad hoc* inter-state deliberations and inter-regional organs, of which the potentially most significant is the link-up of the 'four engines' of prosperity – Baden-Württemberg, Catalunya, Lombardia, and Rhône-Alpes.

The Present Contribution and Our Bet on the Future

The present book did not originate in any elaborate reflection on families of nations, but rather in some observations of transnational commonalities, and in putting onto the same level very different family baselines of analysis. With reference to what we have called 'the English-speaking nations', the commonalities directly promised to open up novel areas of analysis and investigation. With regard to the Nordic countries, their family character looked familiar to the point of triviality, calling for some thought about how to avoid repeating existing studies and modelling. In 'the German-speaking' case, there was a smack of an historicist cultural *Sonderweg*, which had to be overcome before the notion would appeal to current empirical social scientists.

The main emphasis of our families of nations conception has been on lineages or descent, and therein on culture, although in Chapter 1 Castles did emphasize the structural aspects of the early prosperity of the English-speaking family and their later policy effects. The macroeconomic/labour market policy focus of the 'German-speaking' chapters did not involve issues concerning the encounters of French and Italian cultures and institutions with the predominant German one in Switzerland, leaving the 'separated siblings' case untreated. Nor have we paid much systematic attention to processes of elective affinity. Deliberate cooperation – 'marriage' in the conceptualization of this chapter – was referred to in Therborn's chapter on childhood with reference to Nordic law and also figured in Busch's speculative conclusions on the emergence of European monetary institutions.

From the privileged perspective of hindsight, it is clear then that, with the exception of the very varied delineation of the policy implications of lineage and descent in the chapters contained here, what we are offering our colleagues are sketchmaps of new areas of exploration rather than a developed cartography of all the varied forms of family resemblance to be encountered in the field of public policy outcomes. Hopefully, however, what we have shown also is that the families of nations approach, both in the lineage sense investigated extensively throughout and in other senses identified in this chapter, simultaneously constitutes a way of adding new dimensions to our understanding of cross-national differences in policy outcomes and a basis for comprehending the dynamic of emergent policy trends in the post-modern dialectic of states and nations.

In this latter, we are making a bet on the future. Ethnic particularisms and ethnic conflict are not likely to fade away in the foreseeable future. Rather, their importance seems to be increasing. However, nation state particularism is going to make less sense. The 'marriage boom' of deliberations and agreements across state boundaries is chipping away at the edge of the separatness of nation-states. So are structural and cultural processes of elective affinity, of trans-state orientation. Lineages of descent may be of diminishing weight, and the trend of separated siblings is uncertain. But our best bet is that families of nations (in the broad sense of nations referred to above) will increase in importance. If that is correct, it should be reflected in the future practice of social scientists.

Notes

1. *Pace* Rokkan, one should perhaps say that the intra-Catholic divide ran within Belgium, between early secularized Wallonia and strongly Catholic Flanders.
2. Neither their definitions nor their criteria of attribution are crystal clear, however, and this writer would range the Dutch system, with its centrally appointed mayors and lack of any significant local fiscal autonomy, to the Napoleonic system rather than (as do Hesse and Sharpe) to the German-Scandinavian one. It is true that the mid-19th century liberal statesman, Thorbecke, who instituted modern Dutch local government, saw it as a decentralist reaction against the French legacy, but by international standards that self-conception does not look very strongly founded in institutional reality.
3. The 'many states' issue was the cause of 19th century German nationalism. The 'two states' problem was the co-presence of the FRG and the GDR, and previously, in the interwar period, of Germany and Austria. The 'three states' issue was in existence for a few years in the early 1950s and then only *sotto voce*. Apart from the FRG and the GDR, there was also Austria where, as late as 1956 (i.e. after the successful end of ex-Allied occupation in 1955), only half of the population held Austria to be a nation, the other half denying it. The implication must have been that, to roughly half the population, Austrians belonged to the same nations as the people of the FRG and the GDR. After that, Austrian patriotism increased rapidly (Katzenstein, 1976, 185).
4. A very interesting legal overview of Switzerland prior to its Civil Code unification in 1907 is given by the author of the code, Eugen Huber (1886): in the French and Italian-speaking cantons Code Napoléon reigned, with some local subvariants; in the *Urkantonen* there was no codified private law; Zürich had developed its own code, which had become the model for some other cantons; finally, the codes of Bern, Luzern and a couple of other cantons were derived from the Austrian Civil Code.
5. *Le Monde*, 15 July 1992, p. 5.
6. 'Major' is here, as always, relative. Liechtenstein was left out.
7. Domestic transfer payments are, of course, much larger inside national states than within the EC, which means that regional income differences are smaller than those of regional product. But the correlation between the two is rather strong. For a middle-sized welfare state like Finland, for which exact figures are available for calculation, the correlation between regional income and regional product was 0.86 for the mid-1980s.
8. Adding a diplomatic reverence to the Dutch guilder, bowing to Soviet German sensitivity (Scharpf, 1987, 87).

References

Berben, T., Roebroek, J. and Therborn, G. (1986), 'Stelsels van sociale zekerheid: Na-oorlogse regelingen in West-Europa', *Res Publica* (Brussels), **XXVIII** (1), 111–37.

Cooper, R. (1987), 'External Constraints on European Growth' in R. Lawrence and C. Schultze (eds), *Barriers to European Growth*, Washington D.C.: The Brookings Institution.

Economie Européenne (1990), no. 46.

Flora, P. and Alber, J. (1981), 'Modernization, Democratization, and the Development of Welfare States in Western Europe' in P. Flora and A. Heidenheimer (eds), *The Development of Welfare States in Europe and America*, New Brunswick: Transaction Books.

Giordano, C. (1992), *Die Betrogenen der Geschichte*, Frankfurt: Campus.

Hesse, J.J. and Sharpe, L.J. (1990–91), 'Local Government in International Perspective: Some Comparative Observations' in J.J. Hesse (ed.), *Local Government and Urban Affairs in International Perspective,* Baden-Baden: Nomos, 603-21.

Huber, E. (1886), *System und Geschichte des Schweizerischen Privatrechts*, Vol. 1, Basel: Detloffs Buchhandlung.

Karvonen, L. (1981), *'Med vårt västra grannland som förebild'*, Åbo: Meddelanden från Stiftelsen för Åbo Akademi Forskningsinstitut.

Katzenstein, P. (1976), *Disjointed Partners*, Berkeley: University of California Press.

Kuhnle, S. (1978), 'The Beginnings of the Nordic Welfare States: Similarities and Differences', *Acta Sociologica*, **21**, Supplement, 9–35.

Rokkan, S. (1970), 'Nation-Building, Cleavage Formation and the Structuring of Politics' in S. Rokkan, A. Campbell, U. Torsvik and H. Valen (eds), *Citizens, Elections, Parties*, Oslo: Universitetsforlaget.

Rokkan, S. and Urwin, D. (1983), *Economy, Territory, Identity*, London: Sage.

Scharpf, F. (1987), *Sozialdemokratische Krisenpolitik in Europa*, Frankfurt: Campus.

Therborn, G. (1989a), '"Pillarization" and "Popular Movements". Two Variants of Welfare State Capitalism: the Netherlands and Sweden' in F. Castles (ed.), *The Comparative History of Public Policy*, Cambridge: Polity Press, 192–241.

Therborn, G. (1989b), *Borgarklass och byråkrati i Sverige*, Lund: Arkiv.

Therborn, G. (in press a), 'The Right to Vote and the Four World Routes to/through Modernity' in R. Torstendahl (ed.), *State Theory and State History*, London: Sage.

Therborn, G. (in press b), 'Social Modernity in Europe 1950–1992' in W. Barberis et al. (eds), *Storia d'Europa*, Vol. 1, Torino: Einaudi.

Walker, J. (1969), 'The Diffusion of Innovations Among the American States', *American Political Science Review*, **3**

Zweigert, K. and Kötz, H. (1987), *Introduction to Comparative Law,* Vol. 1, Oxford: Clarendon Press.

Index